Honor Thy Fathers & Mothers

Niagara Frontier's Legacy of Patriotism and Survival

Suzanne Simon Dietz

Library of Congress Control Number: 2008909376

ISBN: 978-0-615-25804-1

Layout, cover design and printing by: BeauDesigns
Youngstown, NY
www.beaudesigns.biz

Every reasonable effort has been made to trace present copyright holders of the materials used in this book. Any omission is unintentional, and the author will be pleased to correct errors in future editions.

This book was printed in the United States of America.

Cover photos:

Above, in Berchtesgaden. Left to right, Joe Marnien, Eddie ?, and John Simon. (Courtesy Simon family)

Right, Frances Serchia chauffeured soldiers in a Motor Transport Corps vehicle parked near the Red Coach Inn, Niagara Falls, New York. (Courtesy of Frances Serchia Esser)

Left, nurses wore pants to treat soldiers in their bunks on the hospital trains. The military did not want the soldiers looking up the nurses' skirts. (Courtesy Marge Slattery Dyer)

Dedicated to the memory of my father and mother
John Victor Simon and Salome Authier Simon
1923-1998 1925-2007

CONTENTS

Note: The names in this manuscript were from available primary source materials. The author will be glad to receive information leading to corrections and additions for subsequent printings and apologizes for any errors or omissions.

FOREWORD

"Everyone has a story!" Unquestionably, this maxim is true especially for those men and women of the generation we now refer to as the greatest generation. Tom Brokaw raised our awareness of the sacrifices of so many brave Americans, yet have we noticed our own neighbors who served so gallantly?

The winners of conflict generally record history from the view of generals and admirals, and presidents and prime ministers. Textbooks and maps, journals and websites, libraries and archives record their perspective. However, when we take a moment to listen to our own friends and neighbors, parents and grandparents, aunts and uncles, and cousins who served, the cataclysmic events of World War II allow us a glimpse into their STORIES. The stories are wrapped in the dreams of young men and women; dreams composed of falling in love, of travel to distant lands, of learning skills and completing educational studies, until our world slipped into the abyss of dictatorial evil on a scale never imagined.

The stories and sacrifices as related to Suzanne over the last two years provided an extraordinary opportunity. Soldiers and pilots, POWs in Europe and Japan, farm families who worked with German POWs from Fort Niagara, aircraft design engineers and mechanics at Bell Aircraft, staff serving General Eisenhower and Operation Overlord, concentration camp survivors, and displaced children unfolded and are now recorded in the following several hundred plus pages.

We are blessed to have been present as several veterans for the very first time in their lives unburdened their souls by telling their stories of loss, of faith, of miracles, of suffering, of fear, and of triumph. Their stories leap from their memories to the following pages. By knowing their stories we are participating in the history of individuals who are family and neighbors we know and love. Their courage as youths and their courage now to share themselves is a priceless heritage we treasure.

May their stories in the following pages be a testament to their strength of faith and patriotism!

~ Raymond Jon Dietz

INTRODUCTION

Ian Sherman is a student at Lewiston-Porter Primary School in Youngstown, New York. He competed in a contest sponsored by the Lewiston-Porter United Teachers in May of 2006 to write a paragraph about his community hero and how, "knowing this person makes my community a better place to be." Ian wrote, "Knowing my grandpa John Jircitano makes my community a better place to be! The town historian is writing a book about him. He was a volunteer fireman for over ten years. He knows a lot about science. He showed a lot of bravery and courage being a pilot in WWII. I hope I can be like him."[1]

My father also made the community and the world a better place. I found occasion to differ with him about life's issues as a young woman. At the moment I was about to embark on a course he did not approve, dad in an attempt to change my mind responded, "Remember the fourth commandment, honor thy father and mother." I respected my father and his death brought a great void to my life. He did not want to talk about the war, like many of his generation who served, but I do because my father and my mother, and all the men and women of that time period who served on the battlefront and at home are "the greatest generation!"

We live in a quiet little town nestled in the northwest corner of Western New York. The Town of Porter and its Village of Youngstown evolved around the walls of Old Fort Niagara bounded by the Niagara River on the west and Lake Ontario on the north. Many chapters of the history of our nation's conflicts are wrapped around this picturesque spot and WWII was no exception. New Fort Niagara was an Induction Center and later housed a major camp for German Prisoners of War. River Road, connecting Lewiston and Youngstown, was trafficked with soldiers on their way to Fort Niagara.[2] After a brief induction period they were trucked to the railroad station in Niagara Falls bound for other forts and more training, and eventually duty overseas. As the war progressed, the trucks returned with the enemy.

The birth and heart of this story evolved from a life-long desire to learn about my father's military service during the war and to honor him. Almost eight years after his death, a series of events turned back the pages of time and brought the past to life. While writing a book about the neighboring Town of Lewiston I was given a photograph by Dorothy Boyce of prisoners of war (POWs) who worked on her grandfather J. Warren Morgan's farm in the Town of Lewiston, south of Porter.[3]

The POWs in the photo stood in an orchard, their work pants with a "P" on one pant-leg and "W" on the other. But these men were Asian in appearance, not German. It stimulated my desire to research and verify these soldiers were from Fort Niagara and that they worked on the Morgan farm.[4] "There were only German prisoners of war at Fort Niagara," I was told by an authority. Yes, the prisoners of war were soldiers from German regiments, but they were not all German!

Coincidentally, our family lived in the Percy Morgan house at 4684 Lower River Road, Lewiston, next door to his brother, Warren, in the late 1950s and 1960s. Percy Morgan was the Town of Lewiston Supervisor during the war. His daughter, Elizabeth, and her husband, Dr. Charles Hobbie, owned a home across the road and also a residence in Sodus, New York. Dr. Hobbie performed physicals at one of Fort Niagara's sub-camps in Sodus and brought supplies to the infirmary.[5] At that time I was unaware of Dr. Hobbie's connection to the POWs.

It was as if a magnet pulled our family and my life closer to the history of the war and Fort Niagara. In 1967 we moved further north to 3719 Lower River Road in Porter. The following year I transferred from Loretto Academy, Niagara Falls, Ontario, to Lewiston-Porter High School for my senior year. A local boy, the love of my life, with deep roots in the town, took me to the senior prom at the Officers' Club of Fort Niagara in June 1969. The mural on the east wall in the ballroom and its history, at that moment, were insignificant to me, a minute part of the ambiance of an exciting evening. That event is wrapped tightly to the evolution of this journey and unanswered questions about my father's military service and my high school history teacher at Loretto, Miss Mary Grotowska, who served in the Polish Underground.

Also unknown to me, my twelfth grade homeroom teacher, William Murphy, was an ex-POW. Bill served with the Army's 101st Airborne Division at the Normandy Invasion in the European Theatre. He was wounded in combat, captured, and treated by German doctors at Rennes Military Hospital Camp. Bill taught United States History at Lewiston-Porter High School for several decades.

William Murphy passed away August 10, 2005.

On April 20, 2004, I stood again in the Officer's Club as David L. Dickinson, the Niagara County Historian, received the *Knight's Cross of the Order of Merit* from the German government for his work to preserve and bring attention to the mural painted by Ernst Wille, a German POW. Dickinson worked with a coalition to preserve the building and its murals. He told us at the ceremony that Wille was ordered to paint a picture of war by Col. William R. Bolton. In 1998 *Der Volksfreund* covered Wille's return to Fort Niagara and how he refused to paint a war mural because of his "horror over the bloodshed he'd seen."[6] Instead, he painted a picture of peace.[7] Wille was born in Germany in 1916 and attended the Cologne Art School when he was drafted into the German Army in 1940. He was an artillery spotter at a beach in Normandy on June 6, 1944, and captured that day by the Canadian Regiment de la Chaudiere. Wille was held at Fort Niagara from 1944 until the autumn of 1945.[8]

When Wille returned to Fort Niagara in 1998 he lodged at Dave and Kathleen Eames McMurray's home in the village. Their house was the St. John's Episcopal Guild Hall used for the area Red Cross activities during the war. Kathleen recalled Sunday rides as a girl to Youngstown with her parents. "We could see the prisoners on the grounds beyond the barbed wire and my mother waved to them. My father said 'don't wave, they are our enemies.' My mother replied they are just young boys."[9] How we treated those we called our enemies was a testament to the ideas and values of a democratic society, and to the humanity of the people in this story.

My research into the POW photograph and desire to learn the details of my father's war experiences led me on this journey to connect people and their personal experiences to one of the most destructive global moments in time. Carl Jung called it synchronicity or meaningful coincidence, but I believe that to those that have faith there is no such thing as coincidence, only God. I am indebted to each person for sharing their life's chapter of the war. My quest wove together moments in history at Fort Niagara, Bell Aircraft, POW camps in Germany, Russian labor camps, concentration camps in Poland, and more, in a time when the world stood on the precipice of evil.

Honor Thy Fathers and Mothers is a collection of memories of the mammoth effort of our nation at home and abroad to bring an end to the war. It evolved from people in my life, neighbors in the Town of Porter, and the experiences of many. Some of these personal narratives are snapshot images and others landscapes, but all are important pieces of the history we call WWII. It is recollections and impressions of a time of personal sacrifice that should not be forgotten, and how a minority political party in Germany came to power, attempted to destroy the Jewish people, and dominate the world. There are lessons for those who served, those who live here, and those we considered the enemy. As Santayana said, "Those who do not learn from history are doomed to repeat it."

My mother said, "The war was a noble cause." May this work give the memories of all those who served at home and abroad in WWII peace and honor. May we never forget the sacrifice of the men and women who served our country and the world!

NOTES

[1] Richard "Dick" Tower, the author's neighbor, served in the 42nd Infantry Rainbow Division. He was the link to John Jircitano and the beginning of this manuscript.

[2] Fort Niagara was referenced in this work as "New Fort Niagara" mid-nineteenth century brick barracks, officers' quarters, rifle range etc. constructed south of the colonial era buildings and fortifications known as "Old Fort Niagara."

[3] Suzanne Simon Dietz, *Lewiston*, (South Carolina: Arcadia Publishing Co., 2006) 99.

[4] J. Warren Morgan, and his brother, Percy, farmed *Red Bank Farm* during the war. William Morgan, Warren and Percy's father, was the Comptroller of New York State under Governor Theodore Roosevelt in 1900. The farm and its orchards on the east side of Lower River Road were eventually replaced by a housing development known as *Morgan Farms Subdivision.*

[5] Annette T. Harris, *WWII Prisoner of War Camps in Wayne County, New York and Their Prisoners*, (New York, 2004), 12.

[6] "Noted German Artist, Former POW, Returns to Camp Where He Was Held, Progress Noted in Fight Over Murals," *Der Volksfreund/People's Friend*, July/August 1998.

[7] Wille's mural was entitled *American History.*

[8] Joseph Roetter, "Consul General Awards Medal to Area Historian," *Der Volksfreund/People's Friend*, May/June 2004.

[9] Kathleen Eames McMurray, telephone interview by author, March 15, 2007.

LIST OF TABLES

Honor Thy Fathers & Mothers

CHAPTER 1

WAR REMEMBERED

"WE KNEW IT WAS COMING," he said, but it didn't soften the blow. Nine-year-old Tony Clark lived on Third Street in the Village of Youngstown as the war was coming to a close. The announcement came over the radio during the early evening of April 12, 1945, that President Franklin Roosevelt died while at Warm Springs, Georgia. "I was listening to my Sears Silverstone Radio. The country went into mourning. There was a somber mood even at school," Tony remembered.[10]

As he turned back the pages of his memories, Tony talked about the severe rationing. His father was making money from his job in Niagara Falls, but couldn't spend it. They were lucky and had a friend who worked at the Coast Guard and bought some sugar at the station for the family.

There was some animosity in the community about how well the POWs were being treated. People in the town were very self-sufficient. Many were farmers. But, "those prisoners were pretty damned well off. They were tall, blue eyed, blond Aryans, and looked in good shape," Tony said.

It was a vivid irony from those days that the American inductees from Fort Niagara marched down Third Street while the guys in the trucks brought the German soldiers in their POW dress to the farms to work.

Tony shared his impressions of the POW days in the town. "I remember the camp was very clean and neat and reflected the German traits. My father told me 'that they (the German soldiers) were very good at making things and cobbling scraps together.' They were industrious." Tony didn't remember any hatred of the German prisoners and noted that many people in the area were of German ancestry.

"One particular event that struck me was a fire at the Carter farm." The farm, across from the prison camp, was on the east side of Lake Road with orchards on both sides of the road. The tenant house in the back of the farm was on fire. Tony joined his dad, a Youngstown fireman, to help at the scene. There was no hydrant near the Carter place. The prisoners came out and marched in a line. They formed a bucket brigade from a well or cistern. Tony couldn't recollect any guards in the line.

"No one was intimidated by them. The fire burned the house to the ground. The prisoners returned in a line to the camp," Tony said.

Tony's family had strong military roots. His father, Herman Clark, had six sisters. Five of the sisters married Army men and one sister, a Navy sailor. Herman worked at the DuPont chemical plant in the City of Niagara Falls. In 1945 he was injured from sulfur gas and received doctor's orders to find outdoor work. Herman began a forty-year career in January 1946 working at Fort Niagara.

"Youngstown was politically very Democratic at that time," and he smiled since today the Republican Party has a strong foothold in the area.

In less than a month VE (Victory in Europe) day arrived. It was May 8, 1945. The Allies formally celebrated the defeat of Nazi Germany and the end of Hitler's Third Reich. Youngstown joined in the massive celebrations of the Allied nations. The fort was full of soldiers and people came out in the streets to celebrate. Tony played the drums as a member of the Youngstown High School's Band.

The band marched around the village while the town's people celebrated on the streets and filled the bars and taverns. However, people knew the war was not over in the Pacific; nor were there any signs that the end was in sight. But on August 6, 1945, the United States dropped an atomic bomb on Hiroshima, Japan, and then on August 9 on Nagasaki, Japan. Emperor Hirohito announced to the Japanese people on August 15, 1945, the acceptance of the terms of the Potsdam Declaration, which defined the terms of surrender.

VJ Day on August 15, 1945, marked the victory over Japan and Youngstown celebrated again. "It was almost a replication of VE day, but it was bigger and longer. Canadians came across the river to join in the celebration," Tony recalled. The high school band stood in front of Jeffords' Gas Station on Lockport Street and posed for a photograph as Dick Ulrich, the druggist, captured the historic moment.

SECRETARY TO CAPT. FREDRICK A. De WILDE ~ Nine German armored divisions with more than a million troops tore into neighboring Poland without warning on September 1, 1939.[11] "I was listening to the Polish radio station from Buffalo about the news and took the radio into the bar. My father was very upset because his father, mother, and a sister were still in Poland," Rennie said.[12] There was no communication from the family during the war.

Renata "Rennie" Holody Sikoski's mother, Caroline Sciera, came to Niagara

Falls, New York, in 1909 from Bochnia, Poland. Rennie's father Martin came later in the 1920s. The family operated the Ontario House known to the locals as the Stone Jug.[13] The radio again brought the world news into the main crossroads of the Youngstown village at Main and Lockport Streets on December 7, 1941. Rennie exclaimed, "Oh my God it sounds like war. It just came over the radio that Pearl Harbor was bombed."

The Niagara Falls area quickly became an armed camp to protect the power and chemical plants, the railroad yards, the Niagara Falls airport, and the Canadian border. The first detachment from the garrison at Fort Niagara moved into the city on December 8, 1941, in the afternoon. Other soldiers from Fort Niagara were sent to the City of Buffalo. A squad of twenty-five soldiers went on duty at the international bridges in Niagara County: the Rainbow, the Whirlpool Rapids, and the Lewiston-Queenston. Col. Clayton J. Herman was the acting commandant at Fort Niagara. He established headquarters at the State Armory and ordered the gates at Fort Niagara closed.[14]

Nine months later in September 1942 the principal of the Youngstown High School, Edith Ripson, encouraged the administration of Fort Niagara to hire some of her students. "Mrs. Ripson believed our Regents education made us very capable of doing secretarial work," Rennie said. She received twenty-five dollars a week in wages and gave the entire paycheck to her mother. Rennie was unaware that her mother saved it and when Rennie married John Sikoski, her mother returned all the money.

The reality of the war became visible as the soldiers left the area after their induction at Fort Niagara. People stood on the porch of the Stone Jug and on the streets in the village. They waved to the soldiers leaving Fort Niagara to prepare for duty overseas, as the trucks rolled down Main Street.

Rennie became secretary to Capt. Fredrick A. De Wilde, the head of the Signal Office. "His son was the famous movie star, Brandon De Wilde. He was in *Blue Denim*, *Shane*, and *Member of a Wedding*. He was very famous and then was killed in an automobile accident," Rennie said.

"We couldn't smoke in the offices. We had the best little lunches at the Post Exchange. It cost twenty-five cents for a sandwich. Those were the good old days," she said with a smile. "When the POWs came, the Quartermaster's Mess Hall was opened. Lunches cooked by the prisoners were available at a reasonable price."

The prisoners washed the windows in the offices where Rennie worked. She recognized some were not of German ancestry. "They had round faces and smiled. De Wilde said that those POWs were captured when Germany invaded Russia. They were conscripted to fight with the German Army. They were Mongolians."

Life at Fort Niagara for the prisoners was very different from their American counterparts in German POW camps. Rennie reflected about those days. "Most of the German soldiers were young and good looking. On Sunday you could see the prisoners sitting around their campgrounds. They played musical instruments and sang. Their American relatives would come for a visit. Some came from as far as Chicago."

"Rationing was terrible. Gas, especially, and soap were rationed. There were a lot of things rationed. But my father always seemed to get what we needed," and Rennie smiled.

YOUNGSTOWN COLD STORAGE ~ We drove into Fort Niagara State Park via the south-entrance as Frank Gilson identified the boundaries of the POW camp and the position of the guard towers. The road north into Fort Niagara was one-way at that time and called Porter Avenue. We walked by the closed theatre building on the northwest corner of the large parking lot near Shelter D; perpendicular to the parking area is a long rectangular brick building whose front faces the river. The communication tower and its wires, that provided local and overseas communication, were still connected to the second floor of Barracks Building #88, also known as the Naval Reserve building. These buildings are vacant now and some of the last vestiges from Fort Niagara's WWII era that remain in the park.

Frank Gilson, son of James and Clara, grew up in a home with an outhouse and a cistern, during the depression years, in Wilson, New York. His father worked for the New York Central Railroad and was laid off in 1935. "I stood in the Wilson School gymnasium and listened to President Roosevelt describe the attack on Pearl Harbor. Wilson was a war town and we had blackouts. Spotters identified the passing aircraft from posted charts. Japanese American inspectors checked the chickens for gender at the local Hamlin Hatchery," Frank said remembering the uneasy feelings and concerns about Japanese working in the area after the Pearl attack.[15]

Frank, his little brother Jim, and their parents moved to the Village of Youngstown in the fall of 1943. His seventh grade teacher that September was Ida Martin. The Gilson's home at 718 Second Street and their neighbor's, the VanKill family, were moved from Model City as part of the Lake Ontario Ordnance Works project[16] to construct a munitions factory and clear the surrounding area for the war effort. "Near the end of the war we played in Model

City near a junkyard like pile of all kinds of aircraft parts including P-40s and P-38s." After the war, one of Frank's science teachers, E. K. Stevens, told his students that he had worked on the Manhattan Project.

Frank's father was already working as a refrigeration engineer on the Frick machines that ran the Youngstown Cold Storage and the Ice House that was in the Gilson backyard. His experience on the railroad was an asset at the storage for switching diesel locomotives. The switch engine handled half a dozen cars. "I went to Lewiston with my father to get mutton that came from Canada. It was stored for a short time in the Cold Storage and iced to keep it from spoiling and then shipped to England. Fruit was packed in bushel baskets with a paper pad and wooden cover."

"I spent a lot of time at Fort Niagara. Some of my classmates from school lived there so the guards got to know me. Fred Kirby's father was the commander of the Coast Guard Station. Fred eventually entered the Naval Academy and was killed on a cross-country flight during a flameout on a jet. He bailed out and his chute failed to open. Another friend, Lee Massett, lived around the corner from us on Campbell Street. I helped Lee with his paper route that included Fort Niagara and the POW camp. Paper was in short supply during the war so the Boy Scouts held paper drives around Youngstown to assist with the recycling effort."[17]

After Frank spent some time at Fort Niagara and knew his way around, he ventured to the movie theatre. Soldiers lined up on the walkway for the 7:00 p.m. film. Frank approached soldiers with some money in hand and the request: "Would you mind taking me in as your son? I did it several times and they (the soldiers) always said, yes!"

"My father had a Class C ration permit sticker on our car which made it easier to get gas, but sugar was very hard to come by and there was that funny yellow-colored oleomargarine. I was interested in photography, but you couldn't buy the photochemicals during the war. My grandparents lived near Sherkston in Canada, and I bought photo supplies while we visited that were made in the states! It was ironic that they were not available at home."

In the fall of 1944 the POWs did a lot of the work at the Cold Storage. "There were eight to ten POWs with a guard. Usually there were two guards with rifles. They did not want us to speak with the POWs as they unloaded fruit and sorted it. There was a lot of machinery at the storage and many of the POWs who worked there understood some English. I think it was probably a safety issue unlike at the farms where you didn't need to know English to pick fruit."

Frank worked at the PX at Fort Niagara as a teenager. "One of the POWs

Canadian soldiers embarked by steamer at Niagara-on-the-Lake to go to war in this 1940 image. Village of Youngstown shore in the background. (Courtesy of Niagara Falls Ontario Public Library Francis J. Petrie Collection).

broke a leg at the bowling alley at the base. He was down in the hole setting the pins. A soldier didn't see him and sent a ball down the alley." At the south end of the camp Frank and his friends enjoyed watching the POWs play soccer. The reality and heartbreak of war broke into these playful moments. "Mrs. Serba, a neighbor on the corner of Elliot Street, came over to see my mother while I was with her in the kitchen. Mrs. Serba was crying and holding a tattered box with a fruitcake that she made and sent for Christmas to her son serving overseas. The stamps on the box were from different places and it was marked 'not deliverable.' Her son, Pfc. Frank M. Serba, was killed more than a year earlier." Private First Class Serba was wounded in action in Germany on November 7, 1943, and evacuated to a British hospital where he died on December 24, 1943.

Frank's picture of Youngstown during the war was that it was a "G.I. town. There were sporadic planes flying over Fort Niagara and the soldiers frequented the local watering holes like the Stone Jug, the Fort Inn owned by Jack Beatty's father, and Comerford's run by brothers Ken and Stu. After some fights the military made Comerford's off-limits for awhile. Each morning at 6:00 a.m. we heard the Canadians marching along the riverbank adjacent to Fort George and playing bagpipes. It was noisy!" Fort George is due west across the river from the village.

After the first atomic bomb was dropped in Japan, Frank's memories included the nuclear protest demonstrations in Niagara Falls and Buffalo, but not in Youngstown. Frank was drafted during the Korean War and worked in military intelligence. He taught mathematics at LaSalle Senior High School for forty-two years before retiring in 1995.

PLAN TO ESCAPE ~ "I have a lot of stories," and he smiled as he began to speak.[18] Ronald Quiett lived with his family on Chestnut Street in the Village of Youngstown from 1936 until November 1953. It is a short walk from Chestnut to Fort Niagara. Ron's father Lewis was part of the Corps of Engineers at Fort Niagara. Bill Russell was the foreman. A number of civilians worked at Fort Niagara while it was an Induction Center, Ron said.

The prisoners worked with Lewis doing plumbing work at Fort Niagara and also at the TNT plant. One day, Viola Freidrichs Quiett, Ron's mother, was preparing lunch in her kitchen. Two of the prisoners sat at the kitchen table planning an escape, unaware that Viola spoke German. She tapped her husband on the shoulder and motioned for him to go into the next room.

Viola told her husband of the prisoners' plan. Lewis was the village constable at the time. He took out his pistol and handcuffs and returned to the kitchen to cuff one prisoner, then used his belt and bound the hands of the other man. The authorities at Fort Niagara were called. Maxy Fox, the Sergeant of the MPs, came and took the prisoners. "They weren't let out again," Ron said.

Ron reflected, "A lot of the prisoners were excellent fellows. They didn't want to be in the war anymore than we did. At the end of the war some didn't want to go back. They were afraid of how things were going to be."

In the spring of 1949 Ron became part of an unusual piece of Fort Niagara's history. Alfred Johnston was the superintendent of Riverdale Cemetery at 5605 Lewiston Road in the Town of Lewiston just south of the access road to Interstate 190. He was also the superintendent at Oakland Rural Cemetery[19] on Lake Road in the Town of Porter. "Everyone called Johnston *Riverdale*," Ron said. Johnston enlisted Ron as a teenager to help with some work at Fort Niagara.

The Modern Post Cemetery was in the woods south of the present north entrance to Fort Niagara State Park. Soldiers from WWI, civilians, and German prisoners of war were buried at this cemetery. Attempts were made to contact the families before the digging began and a few of the remains were shipped back to the families. Ron said that there were caskets of wood and others of metal. The markers were of stone and some engraved with crosses.

In 1949 the remains of German soldiers from the Modern Post Cemetery were re-interred at Woodlawn National Cemetery, 1825 Davis Street, Elmira,

Chemung County, New York. David Dickinson, the Niagara County Historian, wrote in an article in 1996 that it was one of the little ironies of WWII that the dead German POWs were re-buried among thousands of graves of American GIs. The government issued marker was identical to those of the other soldiers with one added word "German."[20]

The seventy-five graves from Fort Niagara are in Section E at Woodlawn. (See Appendix E) Among these remains are four German Prisoners of War. Erhard Gerdes died July 18, 1945, and was re-interred in Site E 3792. Karl Freudenstein, Site E 3795, died on the Hurtgam farm on August 23, 1945. Hugo Schreier, Site E 3794, suffered a heart attack on August 29, 1945. Gerdes and Schreier are listed as German civilians on their burial permits at Woodlawn. Johannes Maron, Site E 3793, was burned from steam at the Haxton Canning plant in Oakfield.[21] He suffered cardiac arrest and passed away on September 6, 1945.[22]

POWs IN DUNKIRK ~ Douglas Tower walked from home to Rural School No. 3 on Blairville Road near Creek Road. Blairville was identified as a hamlet in early Youngstown area maps. Doug skipped a couple of elementary grades then went on to graduate from Youngstown High School at the age of fifteen in 1931. He began to retrace the map from his memory of the area around the Tower family farm off Blairville.[23] The Frank Lutts farm was south on the west side of Calkins Road and the Kolloff family on the east side of Creek Road at the intersection of Calkins. The Balmer farm was on the east side of Creek Road and Leonard Henry, father of Mort, lived on the west side of Creek.

They were idyllic days before the war and while Doug attended college. He played hockey and baseball, and went to the Youngstown Cold Storage to get ice for refrigeration. On Labor Day the Tower family drove a stake body truck with peaches to storage. The fruit was loaded on top of ice on the railroad cars and shipped to Cincinnati and other places. "We worked one of the nicest producing farms in the area. We grew sweet cherries and muskmelons. There were prunes, apples, and peaches, and five or six dairy cows too," Doug said.

From 1931 to 1935 during vacation and on weekends Doug worked as a guide at historic Old Fort Niagara with his friend, Malcolm Wilson. Wilson attended Fordham University and lived with an aunt in Youngstown while working at the Old Fort. He served as lieutenant governor of New York State for almost four terms from 1959 to 1973 under Gov. Nelson Rockefeller. Wilson was the governor himself from 1973 to 1975.[24]

Doug drove his Model T Ford to Niagara University, graduated from Niagara with a B.A. degree in Mathematics, and received his Master's Degree in 1936 at the age of twenty! "It was difficult finding a job in those days," Doug commented. His first job was teaching at Springville High School. He married June Henry on October 17, 1940. (June graduated from the University of Buffalo. She taught Social Studies and English at Wilson High School.) Women could not teach once they married in those days. Doug taught Mathematics in Springville for five years and held various administrative positions in Monroe and Erie Counties. The last seventeen of his thirty-eight years in education were as Superintendent in North Collins.

Doug reflected on the drive back home to the farm in those early years. "It took a long time to get to my parent's farm. I remember when Niagara Falls Boulevard was a cow pasture. We would get fruit and vegetables from home. There weren't any freezers. A butchered pig would be in a crock filled with fat in a barrel in the basement."

"There wasn't much talk about the war before Pearl Harbor, but I remember when the announcement came. While in Macedon,[25] they (the military) were trying to get Math people for navigation work, but I flunked the physical. When the draft started there was a chartered bus from Churchville to Buffalo, but I flunked the physical again," he said. Doug was working as a principal in the Macedon School District. "There was an announcement of a Navy program to recruit math people for navigation work. I went to Rochester to apply, but again failed the physical. Later on, while in North Collins, I went through the draft, but got a 4F classification."[26]

"My wife manned a station to observe the approach and identification of aircraft during the war. She was part of the Civilian Air Patrol. She was a volunteer. There was a regular schedule of rotation." Doug said. The piercing sound of the sirens was the signal to go into the basement until they stopped.

In some ways the war seemed remote in this rural area. Rationing had little impact on Doug and his wife because of foodstuffs from the family farm. But the war and the prisoners of Fort Niagara entered Doug's workspace at the Gro-Pack canning factory. Doug remarked about the co-operatives which processed small fruit and tomatoes: Pro-Can and Gro-Pack. "There was a big encampment at Dunkirk. The prisoners worked in the canning factories. I worked with the POWs at Gro-Pack. They never caused a problem." Dunkirk was a side-camp for POWs from Fort Niagara.

"The casualties of war became apparent later when people returned for their class reunions in the 1970s. There were many missing who lost their lives in the war." Doug paused and repeated, "I tried to enlist twice."

THE GERMAN CATECHISM ~ The box of history treasures next to the couch was covered with her crochet work and full of newspaper clippings of the history of Youngstown and Fort Niagara. Olga Strassburg Wermuth sat next to the window with a gateway view of Fort Niagara State Park and in the 1940s a view of the POW camp.

Olga was born in Sanborn, New York. "I went to the German school in Bergholz, St. John's Lutheran. We studied the German language for one hour everyday at school. My father spoke low German," she said.[27] In 1940 Olga married Fredrick Wermuth and moved to 121 Jackson Street in the Village of Youngstown where Olga continues to reside.

Fred was a finishing carpenter with the maintenance department at Fort Niagara. He walked to work everyday saving his gas ration coupons so he could visit his mother and two sisters in Chili, near Rochester, New York. "Fred helped truck the POWs out to the farm. Shirley Lester, a neighbor, drove the truck too. I asked Shirley, 'Aren't you afraid driving with the prisoners.' Shirley responded, 'No, they are all good.' Fred rode in the front with Shirley. The truck was filled with POWs. Some sat on the running boards. Some of the trips with prisoners were to Akron, New York," Olga said.

When the German prisoners first arrived, the POWs told Fred they were afraid. They thought they were going to be killed. Olga continued, "My husband told them, 'then why are the barracks being built for you?' One did try to run away. He got as far as the abandoned apple orchard (at the south end of the camp) and climbed up in an old apple tree. He was found quickly."

Sometimes Fred brought the prisoners to the Wermuth house. Olga sat on the stoop in front of the house and taught them English from her German Catechism. One of the prisoners asked if the Wermuths would help him write to Germany to his folks, but he didn't have postage stamps. The prisoners sat in the yard and played with Olga and Fred's children. Some prisoners had three or four of their own children.

"The prisoners asked for shoes for their kids. Their kids had no shoes. I gave them some of my own children's shoes that they didn't wear anymore. I didn't do enough. I had four kids myself," Olga said. The image of children without shoes pained Olga.

Olga talked about her vegetable garden and stand by her house and Fred bringing home delicious bread made at the Fort's commissary. It cost two cents a loaf! Olga smiled describing the parade in front of their house. The soldiers marched. Large decorated floats and all the school children paraded from Fort Niagara to the Youngstown school and back. They were good memories in the middle of the war.

BOMBING OF COVENTRY ~ It was the spirit of adventure that drew the young man to Labrador, Canada, in 1965. He married, raised six children, and was widowed. In 1973 John Rolfe married Rita Bongiourno, an American, and in 1981 moved to Youngstown. He studied American history, beginning with the founding fathers, to reconcile his impressions and memories of life in England during WWII.[28]

John was sheltered in the womb of his mother the night of November 14, 1940, but the bombing of Coventry became an integral part of his impressions of British history. Coventry was a major manufacturing city. The German Luftwaffe dropped about 400 tons of bombs on the city causing significant damage to life and property. Several days earlier in November the RAF (Royal Air Force) bombed Munich. Near the end of the war in February of 1945 the controversial bombing of Dresden was justified as retaliation for Coventry.

John Rolfe was born in Birmingham, a large industrial city in the Midlands, northwest of London, England. He saw the sky full of airplanes and barrage balloons. Barrage balloons were an air defense system composed of a balloon attached to a steel cable that was anchored to the ground. The objective was to deny low-altitude flight to the enemy. The balloons were an integral part of the air defense system.[29]

John's impressions of the war included tales of Lord Haw Haw, the nickname of a radio announcer of German propaganda. It was illegal to listen to him, but people listened anyway. The broadcasts played on people's fears and some were afraid to go to work. Others, tired of the seemingly endless air raid sirens, stayed in bed, and waited for the inevitable. The workhouses for the poor, epitomized in the works of Charles Dickens, were converted into hospital sites. But the traditions of singing, patronizing the pubs, and dancing to bands continued during the war.[30]

John's family was part of the military and civilian story of the war from England. His father was in the army in Burma and India and became ill. John, like many other children, began to grow up while his father was off at war. His mother and other family members sought refuge in the air raid shelters during the bombings. His aunt died of a heart attack from fright during a raid. An uncle was killed three days after the war ended. After the bombings stopped, the Rolfe family moved into a house that was rebuilt from the rubble.

The celebration of VE day was ingrained in John's childhood memories. "There was a big celebration in the city. I remember the American soldiers and Italian prisoners of war celebrating. Near the air raid shelter a large papermaché image of Hitler was thrown on a bonfire during the festivities and there was singing from the Hydraulic Pub," he said.

With the eyes of a child John saw the bombed buildings as normal and great places to play. But the reality of the aftermath of war eventually impacted even the children. "There were shortages of everything. Occasionally, when we went to school our shoes were checked. We lifted up our feet. If we had holes we might get a voucher for new shoes. How nice to have dry feet," he wished. "We went to the *Birmingham Mail* newspaper offices to select the shoes." To a child one of the more serious rations was candy. This lasted until about 1948.

John was brought up to hate Germans. Family and fellow countrymen did not like the French either. John said that the British stereotype of Germans was that they believed they were superior. The British knew this was ridiculous, because they were superior.

During the 1950s British students were never taught that America had an important role in the war. The teaching was that America came into the war after the worst part of it. "I believed that at the Normandy Invasion the British had three times the number of American troops and twice the number of Canadian forces," John said.

John grew up in a working class district of Birmingham. One day in school the teacher talked about the heroes of Britain in "times of need." When Winston Churchill's name was read everyone in the class booed. The working class never forgave Churchill for his role in using the troops during the labor strike of 1926. But, there was an appreciation for Churchill's wisdom in opposing the Munich Agreement giving concessions to Hitler in 1938.

The students' real hero was Field Marshal Sir Bernard Law Montgomery. He commanded the Allied forces at the Battle of El Alamein in the desert of North Africa. This battle was a major turning point in the war. In 2006 John looked back at the war. His study of American history supported his belief that the British were very brave. John was born during the Battle of Britain. He said that, "If Britain had fallen, the Americans couldn't have defeated the Germans."

Shortly after the war, conflict arose in Palestine as Jews began to establish their own country. The British sent in troops to keep order in a region that had been carved up after the fall of the Ottoman Empire and the end of WWI. "Uncle Albert enlisted in the Red Beret Parachute Regiment at the end of the war. He wanted to fight during the war, but was kept in England because he had a critical skill to make armaments. All men were required to give two years of military service. Most went in at the age of eighteen." John's uncle returned home in the late 1940s to a grand celebration with a welcome home sign hung over the street. "I was very proud to see my uncle in his red beret and uniform carrying his kit (bag) over his shoulder."

Severe shortages of coal existed after the war and into the early fifties. "During the winter holidays from school, my younger sister and I weren't allowed to light the fire until mom came home from work; otherwise, we ran out of coal before the next delivery." John told of the many canals in the Birmingham area. "Occasionally, news spread that a barge arrived on the canal with coal. People lined up with homemade wheelbarrows or old baby carriages trying to get some coal." In the early days of recovery from the war, students used slate and chalk at school because there was no paper.

Conservation of electricity was important during the winter. "We put shillings in the meter to get gas for cooking and in the electric meter for lights and electrical outlets. When the shillings ran out so did the lights. Sometime you had no change or no money, so you sat in the dark," John said. During the winter the lights were turned off to conserve electricity in favor of keeping power for the radio. The evenings in the dark were spent telling in great detail a recently seen movie or repeating a ghost story. "I remember my mother describing *How Green Was My Valley*[31] to a group of neighbors and kids."

In 1951 John passed what he called the "dreaded 11 plus exam" and then joined the cadets. The students were given second-hand official military uniforms. John was given a WWI uniform. His mother went to school and insisted he wear a uniform from WWII. The cadets were taught to march and use Sten and Bren Guns, and .303 and .220 rifles with blank ammunition in mock military battles and camouflage dress with cocoa on their faces. The rifle bodies and bolts were stored in separate areas of the school to make it difficult for the IRA to steal the weapons. Once a year the cadet forces used live ammunition at a nearby military barracks. A few teachers were ex-officers and ran the cadet force. To young boys it must have appeared that another war was close at hand and they needed to be prepared.

During the 1950's many houses that were hit during the bombings were rebuilt. The resonance of war and of a young boy's play around bombed buildings was in the background now. It was overshadowed by the delight of a young man walking to the pub and enjoying cricket, soccer, rugby, and other sports, which became part of the rebuilding of life after the war.

SHINEY ROW is about eight miles from the Town of Sunderland on the northeast coast of England. More than twenty-five percent of England's total tonnage of merchant and naval ships for the war effort were built at Sunderland.[32] It was one of the most heavily bombed towns during the war.[33]

Ellen Graves Truesdell, the daughter of a coal miner, was born in Shiney

Row in 1933. Her mother was a baker at her grandparents' bakery. "We were on holiday at a seaside resort when my father read about the Anschluss in the newspaper. He was so worried. 'We are going to be at war,' he said."[34] Ellen's older sister, Elizabeth, enlisted in the Air Force and was stationed in England and served as a cook on the base. Her older brother Timothy was drafted and assigned to medical supplies, and served in Ceylon and Burma. "I was six years old when the war broke out. We carried a gas mask with us everywhere. You never went anywhere without it. There was a hefty fine if you didn't carry your gas mask. Sometimes tear gas was deliberately forced into the school air raid shelters to check that your mask worked. If you didn't have it on properly, the gas burned."

It seemed like everything was rationed during the war, "'Two ounces of butter per person and six ounces of meat per person per week, and one or two eggs if they were available or powdered eggs. Sweets and candy were at a premium. Sometimes we used our coupons to buy marshmallows, because you could get more. There were also coupons for bread and clothes. Our feet were measured at school. If you had big feet, you were given more coupons," Ellen remarked, shaking her head and commenting that everyone needed shoes, big feet or not.

There was a soccer field behind the Graves home. When troop convoys came through the town "People ran out and took tea or cookies out to the men, even if they might not have something for themselves to eat that day. One time my father brought about a dozen American soldiers into our home. They cooked some sausage for breakfast that was full of fat and grease, which sprayed all over the fireplace. My mother didn't say anything, but just cleaned up the mess after they left." There was no running water inside, but a fireplace in every room and a coalhouse across the street.

Draperies covered the windows and the doorways because of the blackouts. Air raid wardens checked the homes to make sure the rules were followed. Cars and buses couldn't use headlights at night either. "They were painted black with a little slit. Many nights were spent in our air raid shelter during the bombings until the all clear sounded. Sometimes we went to the neighbor's shelter and sang and told stories. We sang *Ten Green Bottles Sitting on the Wall, White Cliffs of Dover, It's a Long Way to Tipperary, Lovely Bunch of Coconuts*, and rhymes we made up about Hitler. Sometimes we just went to sleep. The shipyards were near us, along the coast." Ellen's bedroom window faced the coast. "I looked up in the sky one day and saw a plane drop a bomb in a mineshaft. It is something I will never forget. I was about seven or eight years old."

"My family were staunch Methodists and mother belonged to a Women's Institute. We took a bus trip to a special service at the Durham Cathedral.[35] People came from all over the country. My mother bought me a new hat, which wasn't easy without coupons. During the service the Durham Light Infantry marched into the cathedral just before they left for Germany. It was an impressive sight as the troops marched down the aisle. I wondered how many men made it home."

The cathedral was the source of a number of amazing stories. Ellen told of a lady who looked out of her upstairs bedroom window at the cathedral during an air raid. A mist came over the cathedral and lingered during the bombing. When the all clear sounded and the mist faded the church was untouched by the devastation that surrounded it. This happened a number of times and in other churches that suffered damage the altars stood unscathed.

A nearby POW camp housed the German pilots who parachuted from their aircraft that were hit. "Sometimes we saw the German planes coming down and the pilot parachuting out. The prisoners worked on the farms. After the war, the POWs could walk into town, but would have to step off the sidewalk into the road if someone else was walking by. My mother said that they are just young men like ours doing what they were told."

Through Winston Churchill's radio messages, German propaganda, and air raid shelters Ellen celebrated birthdays and Christmas. "We played games at my party. My mother held a paper bag with chocolate bars in it. Each child pulled out one of the bars and I was to be the last, but couldn't wait. The last child got the largest chocolate bar that was meant for me. I learned an important lesson. My mother must have got the chocolates on the black market. At Christmas we hung our stockings. There was always a piece of coal in it and sometimes an orange or nuts."

After the war some goods were rationed until about 1952. The war memorial at the end of the street was a reminder of the girlhood crush on a young man who served in the North African campaign. He was home on leave and gave Ellen an Egyptian bracelet, but when he returned to duty he was killed in battle. In some ways it was the worst of times and the best of times. "Neighbors took care of neighbors," Ellen said.

In 1952 after almost daily correspondence with a Ransomville boy, Ellen married Duane Truesdell in England at her home on Shiney Row. Duane was the son of Archie and Florence Truesdell.[36] Archie was the first school bus driver for the Schultz Bus lines in Ransomville that began with one bus in 1934. Today, in 2007, Ellen contributes to the lives of the Ransomville children as a foster grandmother at W. H. Stevenson Elementary School.

CHICKEN POX QUARANTINE ~ Fort Niagara was home to Mary Hodge Wieland. Her father, Private Orsino V. Hodge, was a drummer in the Band of the Twenty-eighth Infantry. "He lied about his age to join in 1928. He told me that he had to have three names so he picked 'V' for his middle name. It did not stand for anything. The other men called him 'OV' and later 'Sarge.' He was a Master Sergeant when he retired. My mother's name was Margaret Amsdill, but everyone called her Midge," Mary said.[37]

TABLE 1.1
Contributors to the Red Cross from Fort Niagara in 1938

Alderman, Lt. H. R.
Andrews, Lt. R. W.
Anthony, Pfc. A. H.
Band
Bolduc, Capt. Lucien. E.
Bonney, Lt. Col. Frank E..
Carswell, Maj. Stuart. R.
Co. E
Co. F
Co. G
Co. H
Cohen, Lt. A. A.
Cooper, Col. Hiram. M.
Dahnke, Capt. H.
Drees, Sgt. H. S.
Ducat, Lt. Col. R. W.
Duncan, Lt. J. W.
Evans, Capt. Jos. R.
Fairbrother, Capt. H. W.
Goldstein, Lt. Walter
Gouvneau, MSgt.
Hahan, Lt. George R.
Hq. Co.
Hutton, Lt. Carlt
Jeffcott, Lt. George F..
Jesperson, Capt. Hans
Leeper, Lt. Earle. B.
Mallory, Capt. Frank
Mc Keever, Capt. B.
Meekins, Lt. Raymond
Q. M. Dept.
Reidy, Lt. R. F.
Ser. Co.
Tillipough, Lt. H. J.
Tuttle, Maj. William. B.
Van Valin, Capt. James
Waters, Lt. E. O.
Wilders, Capt. Pearre
Wooley, Maj. Harold. D.

Source: 1938 Red Cross Contributors from Fort Niagara 28th Infantry, *Red Cross Day Book*, Porter Town Hall, Youngstown, NY.

Mary started school when her father left Fort Niagara. Orsino was transferred to Fort Benjamin Harrison in Indianapolis, Indiana, near the end of the war and then he was shipped overseas. He was in France and Germany. "My mother sent

Twenty-eighth Infantry Band at Fort Niagara in 1938. (Courtesy Mary Wieland)

packages to my father. Booze was hard to come by. I can remember her putting round pineapple slices in a jar and filling it with rum. She packed the jar very well and also sent him homemade cookies. You listed the contents on the outside of the box. Mother wrote 'pineapple slices' on the package," and Mary smiled.

Mary developed chicken pox during the war. Their home was quarantined with big signs on the house so that everyone knew to stay away. The mailbox was her connection to the outside world. Her mother put money in the mailbox to pay for the groceries left on the porch. Homework arrived from the teachers via the mailbox too.

VJ Day was a vivid image for Mary. "Bells were ringing and fire sirens were going off. My mother said, 'Thank God I don't have to have any ration books any more.'" After returning from the war, Orsino was stationed at Fort Lee in Virginia then Fort Oglethorpe in Georgia. The Hodge family moved back to the area in 1952 and built a prefab house on Third Street in the Village of Youngstown when Orsino retired from military service. "My father never talked too much about the war. He didn't like France, but I don't know why. He thought Germany was beautiful, the parts that weren't bombed," she said.

When Mary was sixteen years old "it was hard to find a job and so I took several different business courses at Lewiston-Porter," she said. Her father found work at the Niagara Falls Airbase in a civil service position. Mary became a volunteer for the Civil Air Patrol in 1952 for a couple of years. It was part of the last vestige of the war that remained in the town.

A little guardhouse station was located on Lake Street in the village in the 1950's. "We had a telephone and a pair of binoculars. There were a couple of posters on the wall so you could identify what kind of airplane was flying by the shape of its wings. The posters were mostly of Japanese and German planes, but we thought the planes most likely would be the Russians," Mary exclaimed.

LAKE ONTARIO ORDNANCE WORKS (LOOW) ~ The Order for immediate possession of a new government arsenal site was filed in the United States Western District Court on February 9, 1942. It was the result of a Petition filed by the United States of America against "Certain tracts of land in Town of Porter and Lewiston, Niagara County, New York, and Reuben A. B. Widmer, Elmer G. Clark, Mary A. Walsh, Harriet Wagner, Mary Diez Lloyd, Albert L. Baker, Duane Moss, Della Robertson, William Marsh, et al. Defendants."[38]

The government argued that an Order was necessary to take immediate possession of lands in the Towns of Lewiston and Porter in the interest of national defense for the construction of the Lake Ontario Ordnance Plant. The legal description of the property defined 7,500 acres, excepting the land and property of the Lutheran Church and Parsonage at the corner of Balmer and Blairville Creek Roads.[39] One hundred sixty-seven parcels were covered under the Order that also demanded dates for each parcel's possession to be delivered to the United States, from February 10 through March 10, 1942.[40] The government was already in possession of some properties prior to the Court Order.

The initial government plan for this enormous federal munitions project was to utilize about 10,000 acres of the farmlands in the two towns and employment of 1,200 men on the job within three weeks and 10,000 within three months.

Col. Paul Parker of the Army Corps of Engineers took possession of space for the construction headquarters of the project in the Tugwell and Wiseman canning factory in Model City. Rumors swept through the village exciting local merchants and Mayor Lewis Falkner at the prospect of increased business, but farmers held mixed opinions.[41]

The location of the site was controversial and Town of Porter Supervisor, Frank Lutts, expressed anger at the government officials' action in ordering 150 families from their homes with only a few days' notice in some cases. His farm was part of the initial project, but eventually the west side of Creek Road was excluded. The government quickly scheduled a hearing on January 6, 1942, at the Lewiston Presbyterian Church to record objections. It was followed by a series of meetings at the Model City Presbyterian Church, Lutts Road School, Youngstown High School, and Blairsville School to inform the affected families of general details. Area residents did not want to obstruct the war effort, but believed better sites existed in Wheatfield, Pendleton, and Cambria with less agricultural impact. Niagara County organizations and officials expressed their concerns at a hearing in Washington, DC, on January 7, 1942.[42]

J. Boardman Scovell, a Lewiston Attorney, represented thirty-four property owners impacted by the court Order.[43] The owners questioned the government statements relative to amounts paid and the lack of assurance of future payments. They also protested their obligation for the 1942 property taxes and mortgage lien interest without the use of the land.[44]

The government believed the site was ideal because of its proximity to the chemical manufacturing plants in the City of Niagara Falls, for security by the military at Fort Niagara, ample supplies of electrical power and water, and the location of the New York Central Railroad[45] and existing highways. The new arsenal plant was to produce Trinitrotoluene, TNT. The tract of land was eventually reduced from the original proposal, which included Creek Road.[46]

A few local leaders such as Percy Morgan, Lewiston Town Supervisor, appealed to the community about the importance of the production from the plant and emphasized that the nation was at war.[47] The government's representative, Colonel Parker, appealed to the patriotism of the community to assist in this project as part of the response to Pearl Harbor.[48]

TABLE 1.2
Landowners in the Towns of Porter and Lewiston Ordered to Turn over their Property for the LOOW

Name of Landowner	Acreage	Date for possession to be delivered to the government
Amsdell, Frank H.	60.0	3/10/42
Baker, Emily J.	159.5	2/24/42
Baker, Emily J.	100.36	2/24/42
Belden, Norman and Mable	10.0	3/10/42
Blacklock, John Est.	12.7	3/24/42
Blacklock, John Est.	29.8	3/24/42
Bowman, John E.	1.20	2/24/42
Broeker, Arthur C.	100.0	3/10/42

Brocker, C. C.	60.00	3/10/42
Brocker, C. C.	blank	3/10/42
Brocker, C. C.	blank	3/10/42
Bullock, Carrie	100.0	3/10/42
Buttery, Frank	150.0	3/10/42
Buttery, Frank	30.50	2/10/42
Carter, George R. and Maud	25.79	2/24/42
Carter, Gilbert	126.90	3/10/42
Carter, Howard	98.875	3/10/42
Carter, Howard	1.125	3/10/42
Castoff, Paul	87.33	2/10/42
Civrczak, Walter and Helen	100.0	3/10/42
Clark, Elmer	88.0	3/10/42
Clark, Elmer G.	26.00	3/10/42
Clark, Geo. A.	19.0	3/10/42
Crewe, Rudolph	0.43	2/11/42
Crown, Alexander	21.35 (A-68)	3/10/42
Crown, Alexander	21.35 (A-69)	3/10/42
Cunnard, Zellie C.	1.13	3/10/42
Dolansky, Alex./Joseph	107.0	3/10/42
DeMason, D. A.	10.0	3/10/42
DeMoson, Dorrance A.	3.75	3/10/42
Dominski, Joseph/Regina	0.69	3/10/42
Dominski, Matthew/Regina	25.02	3/10/42
Ehrhart, Clifford P. Est.	0.33	2/11/42
Forgione, Anthony	20.0	3/10/42
Freeman, Earl	41.5	3/10/42
Freeman, Earl	21.0	3/10/42
Galliher, James	0.56	2/11/42
Gieseler, Rudolph	50.00	3/10/42
Gieseler, Rudolph	19.50	3/10/42
Gieseler, William H.	51.5	3/10/42
Girard, Jefferson	8.75	2/11/42
Harold, Thomas Est.	32.80	2/24/42
Harold, Thomas Est.	1.00	2/24/42
Harold, Thomas Est.	13.20	2/24/42
Harold, Louis C.	97.00	2/24/42
Hauck, Jr., George	17.50	3/10/42

Hauck, Jr., George	10.30	3/10/42
Hauck, Sr., George	2.26	3/10/42
Hayes, James	2.025	3/10/42
Henseling, Alfred	48.0	3/10/42
Hewitt, Edna	0.23	2/11/42
Hewitt, Edna	10.00	2/11/42
Hildebrandt, Philip	26.50	2/24/42
Hill, Wallace	50.00	2/10/42
Hillman, Anna L.	2.25	3/10/42
Hillman, Elton	50.00	2/10/42
Hobbs, Elsie E.	30.87	3/10/42
Hogarth, Martha L.	84.2	3/10/42
Hopkins, Willard Est.	61.00	2/10/42
Hopkins, S. Seward	144.75	3/10/42
Hufford, Clifton	12.0	3/10/42
Jakubowski, M.	54.9	3/10/42
Jakubowski, M.	159.4	3/10/42
James, Lizzie	15.0	2/24/42
Jowdy, Sam and Drash	97.44	3/10/42
Jowdy, Sam and Drash	7.35	3/10/42
Kelly, J.W.H.	37.00	3/10/42
Kincaid, Wm. W.	152.39	3/10/42
Kneepel, Anna	11.00	3/10/42
Kneeple, Clarence	2.34	2/11/42
Kohler, William	70.62	3/10/42
Kohler, William	0.50	3/10/42
Koller, Otto	50.51	3/10/42
Kolloff, William C.	80.0	3/10/42
Kolloff, William C.	10.0	3/10/42
Kowalczyk, F.	0.83	3/10/42
Kowalczyk, F.	100.11	3/10/42
Kowalczyk, Zofia/Franciszek	22.47	3/10/42
Kyle, John H.	1.00	3/10/42
Landers, Clarence	10.26	2/11/42
Landers, Walter M.	0.26	2/11/42
Langdon, Annie	10.03	3/10/42
Lederhouse, W.	68.5	3/10/42
Lloyd, Edwin A.	25.50	3/10/42

Lloyd, Mary Diez	99.03	2/10/42
Lutts, Richard Harry	67.72	3/10/42
Marsh, William and Wife	64.0	3/10/42
Martin, Florence	20.5	3/10/42
Martin, Leon V.	170.75	2/24/42
Martin, Otis	1.0	3/10/42
Matejovic, Rudolph	50.0	3/10/42
McArdle, Harry	2.10	3/10/42
McCabe, James D.	23.50	3/10/42
McCabe, James D.	5.60	3/10/42
McCann, Joseph and Evelyn	60.0	3/10/42
McCollum, Abram Day	133.75	2/10/42
McCollum, Donald L.	60.0	3/10/42
McCormich, Webster John	3.75	2/24/42
McGrath, Wm. and Durk, J.C.	59.00	3/10/42
McGraw, Gertrude B.	98.25	3/10/42
Meigs, Lila M.	0.709	2/11/42
Meitz, Edgar G.	0.41	3/10/42
Meronto, Sam	206.00	2/10/42
Model City Union Christian Church	0.18	2/11/42
Modeltown Pres. Church	0.33	2/11/42
Morris, Francis C.	58.5	3/10/42
Moss, Duane	103.4	2/24/42
Myers, Clarence	95.0	2/24/42
Myers, Laura	49.75	2/24/42
NY Central RR Co.	24.50	2/24/42-3/10/42
Nichols, Philip	22.2	3/24/42
Nichols, Philip	8.00	2/24/42
O'Brien, Edmund	50.0	3/10/42
Olejarczyk, Stanley	30.0	3/10/42
Paul, Calvin	20.0	3/10/42
Pletcher, Fannie	100.50	2/10/42
Pletcher, Irving	95.0	2/11/42
Rafajac, John	45.71	3/10/42
Rector, Fletcher	12.0	3/10/42
Robertson, Stanley and Matie	97.0	2/24/42
Robinson, Anna M.	39.42	3/10/42
Robinson, George W.	26.0	3/10/42

Robinson, -vin A.	2.72	3/10/42
Rogina Est., Mike	42.81	2/10/42
Rogzinski, Frank	50.00	3/10/42
Russell, Wm. & Anna	20.0	3/10/42
Schmidt, Albert F.	25.0	3/10/42
Schmidt, Mable E.	25.0	3/10/42
School #11 Town of Porter	0.4	2/10/42
Sievert, Mary et. al.	3.54	2/11/42
Simpson or Sanborn, Clara	10.00	2/11/42
Smithson, Mary B.	66.66	2/10/42
Smithson, William M.	139.5	3/10/42
Strablow, Elwood F.	15.0	2/24/42
Strassner, Joseph	50.0	3/10/42
Sutherland, Benj. H.	51.00	3/24/42
Sutherland, Benjamin	4.30	2/11/42
Sutherland, Minnie	20.00	2/11/42
Swan, Grace P.	17.1	3/24/42
Swan, Grace P.	6.2	3/24/42
Swan, Milton	40.00	3/10/42
Swann, Ralph	42.5	3/10/42
Talerico, Santo	52.50	2/24/42
Taylor, Hurk	4.19	3/10/42
Taylor, Hurk	18.91	3/10/42
Tower, Fred	67.5	2/24/42
Tower, Kenneth and Lucy A.	17.50	3/10/42
Truesdell, Geo. and Ellen	83.33	2/10/42
Truesdell, Est., John W.	100.0	2/24/42
Truesdell, Howard & Mabel	100.0	2/24/42
Truesdell, M.A. and C.E.	50.5	3/10/42
Trusedell, Leonard	114.9	3/10/42
Unknown	0.13	2/11/42
Van Luven, -ev, M.	9.00	3/10/42
Van Luven, Levi H.	23.40	3/10/42
Wager, Adda Est.	1.43	2/11/42
Wagoner, Elmer	196.56	3/10/42
Walch, Mary A.	100.0	3/10/42
Wardell, Bertie J.	1.00	3/10/42
Watson, A. C.	27.64	2/11/42

Watson, A. C.	2.67	3/10/42
Watson, A. C.	7.50	3/10/42
Watson, A. C.	19.33	3/10/42
Widmer, Ruben A B	20.00	2/11/42
Wills, Theresa	1.00	3/10/42
Wiseman, John	38.8	2/11/42
Wisner, Dorr	28.85	2/10/42
Wisner, Jr., D.	47.97	3/10/42
Zimmerman, John and Marg.	78.5	3/10/42

Source: "Order for Immediate Possession Lake Ontario Ordnance Plant," United States Western District Court, filed February 9, 1942.

Niagara County Farm Bureau's agricultural defense committee set up an information office in the Lewiston town highway building[49] on Model City Road with the cooperation of a number of organizations including the Federal Land Bank Production Credit Association to assist dispossessed residents. Howard Meyers and Stanley Robertson of Ransomville, Rev. Paul Voigt and Mrs. Gordon (Cora) Gushee of Youngstown, Harry O. Aiken of Cambria, and Harvey Bradlee of Lewiston were part of an advisory committee that assisted the Farm Bureau. The hardship to land owners was multiplied due to the fact that compensation from the government was to take at least six months and the issue that some felt the price was not fair market value.[50]

Howard Baker, A.D. McCollum, and Elbert Robertson were among the group of farmers with large land holdings that were impacted by the project. They left homes and farms that were in their families for three or four generations. Most of the farmers including McCollum, Arthur Broeker, and Howard Truesdell quickly purchased other farms in the area.[51] According to the Army Corps of Engineers' Buffalo District website 5,000 acres was declared excess in 1945 and "transferred to the General Services Administration for disposal to private landowners."

The LOOW plant closed in July 1943, but the area became part of the history of environmental issues from the storage of radioactive waste by the government from the Manhattan Project. Later, Bell Aerospace, Olin Mathieson Chemical Corp., Hooker Chemical Corp., and Chem-Trol Pollution Services acquired and used part of this area. The site continues to be a source of controversy and concern due to the belief of a significant negative health impact on the surrounding community.

One of the families impacted by the proposed ordnance plant was the Burton Carney family. They moved to Porter in 1936 and lived across the road from Rex Harding's hot dog stand on Creek Road.[52] "At Harding's there were spaces in between the floor boards and we used to stick gum on the end of a stick to get the money that fell between the slats," Joan Holland chuckled. "We lived there until 1942 when the government took our property."[53]

Joan held a keepsake photo taken in the winter of 1936 of her siblings with Harding's in the background and a single Texaco gas pump in front of the restaurant. "I remember when gas was twenty-five cents a gallon. Our backyard was Four Mile Creek and the flats flooded. My father grew melons there as part of our truck garden. People came down from Niagara Falls to get our vegetables," Joan said. Her father and John Tower rode together to their jobs at Kimberly Clark. Burton also worked for John on his farm on Youngstown-Wilson Road. He took Tower's truck to pick up POWs from Fort Niagara. Joan said, "My father told me how happy they (the POWs) were and how hard they worked. Sometimes I would see them."

"We often listened to the radio. I liked *Amos and Andy*, but things weren't like today. Harry Lutts and Levi Van Luven came over to play cards with my parents several nights a week and talked about the war, but not to us. That is how I learned about what was going on. Sometimes I could hear what they were saying through the chimney that came up to my room," Joan said. She was in tenth grade at Youngstown High School in 1942 when the Carney family home became part of the LOOW history. The family moved to Lake Road and their home eventually was moved into the village of Youngstown on Lockport Road.[54]

While living on Lake Road, Joan watched from the front porch as the soldiers marched. "Once or twice a week I could see them. The officer blew his whistle and the soldiers ran through the hedge apples. They came out on the other side with large prickers," she said in amazement. At the end of the school year the family moved to Niagara Falls and Joan attended LaSalle High School then Kelly Business School.

Joan went to work at the Ration Board Office, near the United Office Building, from 1943 until 1945. "Ration coupons were allotted by the number of people in the family for things like butter, sugar, and meat. Gas depended on where you worked. The big problem was not enough meat. People were very honest and turned in their unused butter and gas stamps. If you had a good excuse like going to a funeral you could ask for more gas stamps," she said.

Joan reflected on her experiences living through war and the lesson from her mother. "Everyone hated the Japanese because of Pearl Harbor, but when the atomic bomb was dropped I thought of all the people who were killed. There were some small protests in the city after the first bomb was dropped. Today, the world is going too fast and kids have too much. My mother told us to love everyone and to remember that people impact people."

THE COLD WAR ~ The world became smaller for a local boy, part of the fall-out from the war's end. Robert Myers was born in the family house on Ransomville Road in the Hamlet of Ransomville. Ruth Clark Myers was in labor on July 23, 1938, when her husband Loren went over to Doctor Plain's to get help. Doc put his suit coat on and walked over to the Myers' home to deliver a baby boy, Robert. He charged Loren $25.00 for the delivery.[55] Doc lost two cherished sons during the war.[56]

Robert Myers was about ten years old when the POWs were at Fort Niagara. He said, "We drove by and gawked at the prisoners." Robert's dad worked for the Works Progress Administration (WPA), and helped build Fort Niagara's rifle range. His uncle, William E. Myers, was serving overseas and was killed in Italy on June 28, 1944. Elric Myers, another uncle, served in the Pacific.

Twelve years later, in 1957, the impact of the Soviet Union's place among the Allies and its occupation of East Germany became part of Robert's life story. He was serving in Germany in the Third Battalion of the Fourteenth Armored Cavalry with the Seventh Army, part of the Border Patrol during the Cold War.

Robert was stationed in Bad Hersfeld, and later sent to Bergen-Belsen for training.[57] Bergen and Belsen are two small villages in Germany northeast of Hanover. "I was in the Army for three years. We were part of the border patrol between the east and west, the Iron Curtain.[58] We were always armed. There were some rough experiences with the Russians. Watching them made me feel bad. There was a ten meter open strip at the border and a barbed wire fence. We always had more food and fruit than we needed so we would set a box of food and fruit then leave it in the open strip and hide. The Russians soldiers would sneak out to get the food. We took photographs to identify their rank and weapons. Sometimes, we gave chewing gum and candy bars to the children when they came to the fence. When the Russian soldiers saw the kids eating, they would make them spit it out."

While off duty the soldiers brought a few beers, rented some kayaks, and went swimming in the Fulda River near Bad Hersfeld. A pretty blond German Fraulein, Gertie, caught Robert's eye. Later Gertie and Robert married in Basal, Switzerland. Gertrud "Gertie" Dorn was born in 1940.[59] Her grandfather fought in WWI and did not like Robert because he was an American. Her father was in the Luftwaffe during WWII and did not want to talk about the war.

Gertie's parents met while her father was stationed at Fulda. Her mother, Anna, was a nurse's aide during the war. Gerhard Fietze, her father, enlisted in the German Army in 1932 and trained in Dresden. Later, after the United States entered the war, Gertie's uncle, Unter Offizier Wilhelm Schlott, was captured and became a POW in a camp in Oklahoma.

Gerhard was a career soldier and after serving for a time in the infantry became a pilot in the Luftwaffe. He flew one hundred and thirty-five missions to the Ukraine and Russia and was awarded the Iron Cross 1st Class on March 27, 1943, on behalf of the leaders and Supreme Commanders of the Wehrmacht by the Commander of the eastern Luftwaffe (Air Forces).

After the war Gertie's father returned to his hometown to take care of his mother and widowed sister and her two children and became a doctor of architecture. Gertie's grandfather, a former police officer, was in prison in Dresden. The family was living in Uttrichshausen. When the Americans first came to town in 1945 "we had to give up our homes. It was right at Easter. We climbed out of the back windows. The G.I.s took anything of value. The Germans tried to hide everything," Gertie said. When Germany became divided after the war, Gertie's parents divorced.

After the war "things were very unsettled. Bridges and railways were down. I stayed with my grandparents on the farm. We grew our own vegetables, but there were shortages of oil and sugar. We didn't have chocolate. Today, I still love chocolate! We had coffee only on special occasions. People who could get out did. No one had cars when I left in 1960," Gertie said.

Robert tried for years to encourage his father-in-law to talk about the war. "The men didn't want to talk about it," he said. One day near the end of his life Gerhard showed his son-in-law a graveyard of German soldiers. It was his explanation of why he did not want to speak of the past. Gerhard passed on his military memorabilia of insignia patches, photographs of Gerhard with a Junker JU-88, and medals to his son-in-law.

After Gertie and Robert married they returned to Ransomville to live. Gertie went to work for John Tower to help deliver eggs to customer's homes. Tower's chicken barn on Youngstown-Wilson Road was built with German POW labor during the war. Bill Tower, John's son, said that his father hired the Shuman brothers from Lockport to oversee the construction because they could speak German. The lives of people halfway around the world became significant to this small Town of Porter.

FLYING TIGERS AND CHENNAULT ~ Frank Serchia and his wife, Gerianne Simon Serchia,[60] live at 3739 Lower River Road in Youngstown in a home that was part of the Johnson-Hunt Estate. The property on Lower River Road is rich in its family connections to local and military history. One of the earlier residents, Margaret Robertson Johnson, daughter of Col. Edgar B. Robertson, called herself "an Army brat." Colonel Robertson, Ninth U.S. Infantry, graduated from West Point in the 1870s, and was the Commanding Officer at Fort Niagara from July 2 to September 25, 1902.[61] Lindley Johnson, Margaret's husband, was the son of Tellico Johnson, a Civil War soldier, and a descendant of Capt. Ebenezer Johnson who fought in the Revolutionary War. Lindley's sister, Edith, married Col. William E. Hunt in 1907 while he was a lieutenant stationed at Fort Niagara. Edith and William's sons, Richard Hunt a West Point graduate, and William Hunt, both served in WWII.

John and Salome "Sally" Simon purchased the property in the mid-1960s and eventually resided in the large home at 3735 Lower River Road where Edith Johnson Hunt was born, married, and died. The house was known as *Birch Cottage* and renamed *Dunrovin* by Colonel Hunt and his wife, Edith, when they returned to the area after Colonel Hunt's retirement from the military. Sally Simon was fond of saying that she prayed to Edith and felt her presence in the house. Edith was also the great-granddaughter of Samuel Wilkinson, the mayor of Buffalo who helped to rebuild the harbor front after the War of 1812. The Johnson family was also related to Dr. Ebenezer Johnson, the first mayor of Buffalo.

War brides, youthful antics, stories of an older sister, and an uncle who served with Lt. Gen. Claire Lee Chennault of the Flying Tiger's were the heart of Frank's war stories. Like many others this one started years earlier with family, immigration, and neighbors that knew each other. Frank began his family story half way around the world. "There was no work in Italy in the 1920s. The family lived in Ovindoli, east of Rome in the mountains. My father, Americo Serchia, and grandfather came here in 1921. My grandfather's name was Benedito Serchia. My other grandfather, Frank Elia, was a masonry contractor and ran a grocery store,"[62] one of five grocery stores on Ashland Avenue. "They were the richest family in the neighborhood."

In addition to family photographs and memorabilia was a copy of a War Bond. "Third War Loan" was printed across the top of the bond and "September 1943" at the bottom. It read "On behalf of the United States Treasury War Finance Committee for New York State this certificate acknowledges that Americo Serchia, #360 has 'Backed the Attack' with War Bonds."

Frank's mother, Amelia Elia Serchia, had her own part in helping the war effort. Amelia wrote to her brothers, Joseph and Albert Elia, and all the Ashland Avenue boys. The replies to her letters were attached with the "V-Mail" sticker and a censor stamp marked "passed by Army Examiner" with a number in the center. June 10, 1943, a letter arrived from "Somewhere in New Guinea." One paragraph summed up what many wrote home.

It's good knowing that all is fine with you and yours, and thank the Lord, I am still in good health, I'd like to tell you just what I am doing, but sorry – the censor. I can say, though, that my work is essential, and I am 'damn' proud to know that I am doing my part in winning this horrible war, and not sitting around doing nothing. You know yourself, Amelia, that many don't even realize that a war is going on, yes, it is lonesome, and it is hell out here, but all there is to do is to take it on the chin and try to grin, some day, all will turn out okay… keep on writing…[63]

Even in wartime children liked to play make believe and dress up. Louie Pasquale and Jeannine Pasquale, the neighbor's children, smiled for the camera. They stood proudly in their miniature handmade soldier's uniforms. Frank thought his mother might have sewed the outfits. "We played war games and took turns being the Germans or the Japs. We used to look for saboteurs and used sticks for guns and bayonets. In Art class we drew pictures of Japanese Zeroes and German planes on the blackboard."

"We (children) talked about different things like the Japs burying prisoners in the sand up to their necks. I remember the Bataan Death March. And there were the posters: 'Rosie the Riveter' and 'Loose Lips Sink Ships.' Today, the newspapers have too much freedom. Everything was for the war effort then," Frank continued.

The recycling program was another way that Frank and other children were involved in the war on the home front. At the Seventeenth Street Elementary School, Frank stood in front of the class and collected money for War Savings Stamps that were used for postage. The Boy Scouts ran newspaper drives to recycle paper. The children's playground at Haeberle Field, enclosed by a six foot fence, was used to deposit aluminum pots and pans for recycling.

The Serchia and Hank Merletti families went to see a captured Japanese submarine that was shown around the country during the war. Eight-year old Frank was very impressed with the two-man suicide submarine of the Japanese Imperial Navy captured off Oahu Island on December 8, 1941, the day after Pearl Harbor was attacked. He held the postcard with the image of the seventy-foot long sub that marked the family outing.

Frank's treasured ticket "admit one" to the fourth War Bond Drive Rally dated January 31st (no year) was for a rally held at the Senior High School. The featured draw was "Franchot Tone noted film star and assisting artists." Tone also appeared during the summer at another drive at the Hyde Park Stadium in Niagara Falls. Franchot Tone was a local boy born in Niagara Falls. His father was Dr. Frank Jerome Tone, President of the Carborundum Company.

"There was a silk red, white, and blue colored banner with a braid on top hung on the door. It meant that someone from the family was in military service, one blue star for each person who served. If there was a gold star, it meant someone died. I remember the first gold star. It was for Chester Tacconi." It was a somber memory as Frank continued.

"Americo Rosati was a warden. He came from the same town in Italy as my father. Americo walked around checking the neighborhood. Two or three people walked together. All the lights had to be out or we would get a citation. I remember the ration stamps. I was nine years old. My mother told me to go and get five pounds of sugar. There was not much on the shelf in the Red and White store on Fifteenth Street off Ashland. I gave Louise Sigmundi the ration coupon. She said 'you can't have it. The sugar is sold.' I went home and told my mother. She told me to go across the street to Rudy Maida's store," Frank said.

The family photographs told the war brides' story. Most of the photographs were taken in front of St. Joseph's Roman Catholic Church on Pine Avenue in the city. The grooms stood in their uniforms next to their brides. John Lucianni posed with his bride Jeanne Roberts. Frances Serchia was the maid of honor for the wedding party of Marge Roberts, Jeanne's sister, who married Tony Onasi. Karl Garlock and his bride, Virginia Chiasera, were photographed in Lockport. The one unforgotten message from the pulpit at St. Joseph's was to make sure to write to any family in Italy to tell them to vote against the Communists.

Frank's uncle, Albert D. Elia, Jr., served in the European and North African Theaters. One of the family stories was that "Uncle Albert worked on the Normandy Invasion with Eisenhower because Albert was an engineer." Joseph C. Elia volunteered and entered the Army Air Corps[64] in 1942 after completing his medical training and went overseas in June of 1943. A number of news articles reported the announcement by the Public Relations Office of the Fourteenth Air Force that Maj. Gen. Clair L. Chennault awarded the Air Medal to Maj. Joseph C. Elia. He was later decorated with the Distinguished Flying Cross, the Asiatic-Pacific Theater Ribbon with two Bronze Stars, the Purple Heart, and four battle stars.[65]

Joseph was the flight surgeon for Chennault and the Flying Tigers. Chennault kept in touch with Joseph until Chennualt's death.[66] His last Christmas gift to "Dr. Joe" was a pair of cufflinks. One of the pair was engraved in Chinese with the word "success" and the other "good health," Frank said. During Joseph's military service he wrote to area friends and to the local newspapers about the history of China and its national celebrations.[67]

Frank kept undated newspaper clippings with photographs of groups of area soldiers under the title "With the Services." Soldiers fighting in the Pacific on Okinawa and on the Russell Islands were Angelo Conti, Michael Colucci, Patrick O'Sullivan, Joseph A. Forcucci, Anthony Amantia, Angelo Fracassi, Silvio Sepielli, and Charles Sicurelli. Another group of Niagara Falls area native sons met while serving in China: Maj. Joseph C. Elia, Norman Yarrington, Adam Schultz, John Gimieli, Americo Del Zoppo, and John Beltrani. Roy G. Crogran, of the *Gazette* Staff, photographed four Del Zoppo brothers home on leave: Rocco, Vincent, Adolph, and Albert Del Zoppo. Two other brothers, Americo and Thomas, were also serving their country.

A touching memory of his youth with half a dozen other kids involved ice cream. "The railroad tracks were ten sets wide where we played. It was across from Carrigan's Niagara Dairy. One day there were hundreds of troop cars getting ready to be shipped out. Some of the guys asked us to get ice cream for them at the dairy. After a couple of trips back and forth, we were asked: 'What are you doing?' When we explained the ice cream was for the soldiers they gave it to us," Frank said.

"My sister Frances knows a lot about the war. You should speak with her," Frank proudly shared. Frances Serchia, a young woman living in Niagara Falls, joined the nationwide movement organized in 1941 to provide support and hospitality to the troops, another chapter of the war story at home. Frances and other local volunteers entertained soldiers at Fort Niagara and the USO Club in Youngstown to provide a "home away from home."

NOTES

[10] Tony Clark, interview by author, Youngstown, NY, May 30, 2006.

[11] "History of WWII in Europe Timeline," The History Place, http://www.historyplace.com/worldwar2/timeline/ww2time.htm [accessed March 8, 2007].

[12] Renata Holody Sikoski, interview by author, Youngstown, NY, May 24 and June 8, 2006.

[13] The Ontario House, a historic structure, was built in 1842 by Alexander Lane on the site of the Old Hathaway Tavern, which burned during the War of 1812.

[14] "Civilian Forces Join Military in Protection Plan," *Niagara Falls Gazette*, December 8, 1941.

[15] Frank Gilson, interview by author, Fort Niagara State Park, NY, December 12, 2006.

[16] About twenty percent of the acreage was transferred to the Manhattan Engineering District (MED).

[17] Frank Gilson was a Boy Scout during the paper drives.

[18] Ronald Quiett, interview by author, Youngstown, NY, June 6, 2006.

[19] Oakland Rural Cemetery is also known as Hosmer Cemetery by the local citizenry.

[20] David Dickinson, "County's German Invasion Detailed," *Union Sun & Journal*, September 7, 1996.

[21] "Nazi Prisoner Dies at Work," *Niagara Falls Gazette*, September 7, 1945.

[22] Survey by author and Raymond Dietz of the National Woodlawn Cemetery, Elmira, NY, June 29, 2006, and re-interment permits.

[23] Doug Tower, interview by author, North Collins, NY, July 10, 2006, and Youngstown, NY, August 3, 2006.

[24] Governors of NY, http://www.ny.gov/governor/nygovs/ [accessed March 8, 2007].

[25] Macedon is east of Rochester, New York.

[26] 4-F classification – not able to serve due to a physical disability.

[27] Olga Wermuth, interview by author, Youngstown, NY, July 18, 2006.

[28] John Rolfe, interview by author, Youngstown, NY, May 26 and September 15, 2006.

[29] Maj. Franklin J. Hillson, USAF, "Barrage Balloons for Low-Level Air Defense," *Air Power Journal*, Summer 1989, http://www.airpower.maxwell.af.mil/airchronicles/apj/apj89/sum89/hillson.html [accessed March 5, 2008].

[30] Rolfe described the impact on the British people from German radio propaganda.

[31] *How Green was My Valley* was named the Best Picture of 1941 and starred Walter Pidgeon and Maureen O'Hara, Reel Classics, http://www.reelclassics.com/Movies/HGV/hgv.htm [accessed March 8, 2007].

[32] "The History of Shipbuilding in the Northeast," *BBC News*, http://www.bbc.co.uk/nationonfilm/topics/ship-building/background.shtml [accessed March 27, 2007].

[33] "Rare images recall wartime blitz," *BBC News*, http://news.bbc.co.uk/1/hi/england/wear/4434123.stm [accessed March 27, 2007].

[34] Ellen Graves Truesdell, interview by author, Ransomville, NY, March 21, 2007.

[35] Durham is about eleven miles from Shiney Row. The Durham Cathedral, known as one of the finest examples of Norman architecture in Europe, was built as a Shrine for Saint Cuthbert. Construction began in 1093 and took forty years for its completion. "Cathedral

History," *Durham Cathedral,* http://www.durhamcathedral.co.uk/history [accessed March 22, 2007].

[36] Duane Truesdell passed away in 1984.

[37] Mary Wieland, interview by author, Youngstown, NY, June 26, 2006.

[38] "Order for Immediate Possession Lake Ontario Ordnance Plant," United States Western District Court, original copy filed February 9, 1942, by May C. Sickmon, Clerk.

[39] Order for Immediate Possession, 3.

[40] Ibid., 5-11.

[41] "Great Area North of Ridge will be turned into Munitions Plant," *Niagara Falls Gazette,* January 5, 1942.

[42] "War Plant Site under fire by County solons" and "Voice Objections to Munitions Plant Site," *Niagara Falls Gazette,* January 6, 1942.

[43] Mr. Scovell was a neighbor of the author's family on Lower River Road, Lewiston.

[44] "Ordnance Site Case re-opened by Andrews," scrapbook of newspaper clippings, Cornell Cooperative Extension, Lockport, New York, 1940s. Scovell presented the grievances to Rep. Walter G. Andrews of Buffalo.

[45] The New York Central was known as the R. W. & O. and ran through Model City.

[46] "Retain Hope Plan For New Arsenal May Leave Creek Road Untouched," *Niagara Falls Gazette,* January 9, 1942.

[47] "Towns of Lewiston and Porter to Lose $790,000 In Assessments by Erection of New Federal Arsenal," *Niagara Falls Gazette,* January 8, 1942.

[48] "War Department Will Acquire Land by Fair Appraisals, Engineers Says," *Niagara Falls Gazette,* January 15, 1942.

[49] The Town of Lewiston razed the building in 2008.

[50] "Another Location Nearby Urged for Huge New Arsenal," *Niagara Falls Gazette,* January 6, 1942, and "Creek Road left open under modified TNT Plant Project," Niagara Falls Gazette, January 10, 1942.

[51] "Most Lewiston and Porter Folk Seek New Homes in Nearby Area," *Niagara Falls Gazette,* January 13, 1942.

[52] Harding's Restaurant expanded several times and in recent years was operated as a restaurant by Gene Parrone. In 2008 the restaurant was renamed Old Harding's Bar & Restaurant operated by Kevin and Catherine Jeffords.

[53] Joan Carney Gray Holland, interview by author, Youngstown, NY, February 21, 2007.

[54] The Town of Porter Assessor's office does not have any information documenting the homes that were moved from the LOOW tract.

[55] Robert and Gertie Myers, interview by author, Ransomville, NY, July 11 and August 24, 2006.

[56] Military files, Ransomville Historical Room, Ransomville, NY.

[57] Anne Frank died in the Bergen-Belsen concentration camp.

[58] The *Iron Curtain* refers to the physical and ideological boundary that divided Europe from the end of WWII until the end of the Cold War.

[59] Gertie used her mother's maiden name as her surname.

[60] Gerianne Simon Serchia is one of the author's nine sisters.

[61] "List of Commanding Officers at Fort Niagara, 1797-1945," National Archives, Washington, DC. Source: Niagara Frontier State Park Commission, Niagara Falls, NY, list that ref-

erences the Archives.

[62] Frank Serchia, interview by author (sister-in-law), Youngstown, NY, July 11, 2006.

[63] Cpl. R. Finley to Mrs. A. Serchia, June 11, 1943.

[64] The United States Army Air Corps, USAAC, still legally existed as a branch of the Army when Congress created the United States Army Air Forces, USAAF, on June 20, 1941, under the command of Gen. H. H. Arnold. Technically, all WWII airmen served under the USAAF.

[65] "Doctor 'Joe' dies at 93," *Reno (Nevada) Gazette*, November 27, 2003.

[66] Lt. Gen. Claire Lee Chennault died July 27, 1958 and was buried at Arlington National Cemetery.

[67] Capt. Joseph C. Elia, "Ageless China Retains Ancient Customs in Midst of Modern War and Sees Glorious Future Ahead," *Niagara Falls Gazette*, 1940s.

CHAPTER 2

YOUNGSTOWN RED CROSS AND THE USO

THE RED CROSS moved into the St. John's Episcopal Guild Hall on October 7, 1942. Red Cross uniforms, scissors, and other supplies were stored at the hall.[68] It was built in 1942 at 115 William Street in Youngstown for about three thousand dollars. The hall was offered as a meeting place for the soldiers and families of Fort Niagara and the U. S. Coast Guard. Twenty-five members of St. John's congregation served in the military.[69]

The War Council Conference and local Red Cross representatives discussed a casualty station midway between Ransomville and Youngstown, and the possibility of designating additional first-aid posts at a joint meeting on October 23, 1942. Present at the meeting were County Deputy Director Col. William E. Hunt; Assistant Deputy Directors First Lt. C. B. Nichols and Mrs. J. P. Mies; Mrs. Daniel L. Wilson; Edwin L. Howard, vice president of the Red Cross branch in Youngstown; James Davison, chairman of the Red Cross Disaster Committee and co-chairman Harry C. Yale; Supervisor Frank L. Lutts; Mrs. Irma Ames, and Mrs. William Chestnut of Ransomville.[70]

Prior to the opening of the Guild Hall the Youngstown Chapter of the Red Cross conducted drives for the years 1927-1938 and each year from 1941-1945 to support war relief efforts in Europe. In 1941 there were one hundred twelve donations and one hundred ninety-eight in 1942. President Roosevelt called the 1943 drive the "greatest single crusade of mercy in all of history."[71]

TABLE 2.1
Collectors for the 1943-1945 Town of Porter Red Cross Drives

Collector	1943	1944	1945
Adams, Mrs.		X	
Blossom, Vida	X	X	
Borem, Mrs. Bertha		X	

Collector	1943	1944	1945
Britton, Ida	X	X	X
Brown, Elizabeth	X		
Canfield, Mrs. D. Kenneth	X		
Comerford, Marjorie	X	X	
Condren, Mary	X	X	X
Duncan, Mrs. C. L.			X
Faulkner, Mrs.		X	X
Freischlag, Mrs. E. P.		X	
Gaskill, Alice	X		X
Hays, Mrs.	X	X	
Henderson, Mrs.	X		
Howard, Mrs. Edwin	X		
Jeffords, Violet		X	
Kelley, Bernetta	X	X	X
Kinzie, C. J.			X
Kolloff, Mary		X	
Lutts, Donald	X	X	
Magavero, Miss			X
Martin, Anne		X	
Messinger, C.			X
Moon, Mrs. Chester			X
Morell, Annette	X		
Hays, Mrs.	X		
Hays, Nelle	X		
Palmer, Allene	X		
Perry, Warren		X	X
Richardson, Mrs. C.		X	X
Ripson, Edith	X	X	X
Sanderson, Ralph		X	X
Shippy, Mrs. Seward		X	
Skellen, Mrs. Thelma		X	X
Stevens, E. K.	X		X
Tower, Mrs. Geo	X	X	X
Tower, Sarah (Sally)		X	X
Turgeon, Mrs. Robert	X		
Turgeon, Pricilla	X		
Wasmund, Laura M.			X

Wiehl, Miss			X
Wilson, Dan		X	X
Wilson, Mrs. Daniel (Lucy)	X	X	

Source: *Red Cross Day Book*, Town of Porter, Town Hall, Youngstown, NY. Totals for collections in 1943 were $839.12 and for 1944 the total was $839.12. Workers for the 1941 and 1942 Red Cross collections were not listed.

Many women in the town contributed substantial hours working for the Red Cross.

TABLE 2.2
Red Cross Workers at the Youngstown Guild Hall

Red Cross Workers	Hours
Adams, Mrs. Charles	175
Allen, Mrs. Leonard	114
Blossom, Miss Vida	132
Britton, Miss Ina	156
Broeker, Mrs. Al	41
Brown, Mrs. Gerald	164
Brundage, Mrs. Eveleyn	75
Carey, Mrs. Ruby	65
Childs, Mrs. Sylvia	49
Comerford, Mrs. Kenneth (Marjorie)	158
Cothran, Mrs. G. H.	67
Cothran, Mrs. Newton	48
Courter, Mrs. Robert	316
Duret, Mrs. Arthur	38
Dutton, Mrs. Ralph	252
Eaton, Mrs. Herbert	110
Falkner, Mrs. Carl	48
Gaskell, Mrs. Alice	127
Gushee, Mrs. Gordon (Cora)	245
Haskell, Mrs. C. Ray	69
Hays, Mrs. Norman B.	189
Hediger, Mrs. Ernest	48
Hobbs, Mrs. Lelia	75

Hosmer, Mrs. John	81
Hosmer, Mrs. Merritt	60
Howard, Mrs. E. L.	175
Hunt, Mrs. William (Edith)	475
Hutchison, Mrs. Helen	81
Johnson, Mrs. Lawrence	265
Kelley, Miss Bernetta	236
Kolloff, Miss Nellie	31
Kolloff, Mrs. Jennie	68
Kolloff, Mrs. Roy	109
Krakow, Mrs. Mary	51
Mahlmeister, Mrs. A.	76
McCartin, Mrs. John	103
Mies, Mrs. J. P.	179
Nelson, Mrs. Neal	72
Perry, Mrs. Warren	101
Phillips, Mrs. Alva	74
Richardson, Mrs. Chester	115
Ripson, Mrs. Edith	108
Rodenbaugh, Mrs. Grover	89
Serba, Mrs. Edward	32
Shumaker, Mrs. Wilbur	113
Stephenson, Mrs. Helen	44
Suitor, Mrs. Harry	26
Taylor, Mrs. Ina	159
Tower, Mrs. George	99
Tower, Mrs. Ray	36
Tuttle, Mrs. George	75
VanAiken, Mrs. Irving	40
VanDitto, Mrs. Mary	30
VanWegen, Mrs. Duane	35
Wieland, Mrs. Herbert	161
Wilson, Mrs. Daniel (Lucy)	639
Yale, Mrs. Henry	34

Source: *Niagara Falls Gazette* articles and Red Cross folder, Porter Historical Museum, Youngstown, NY, 1943. Edith Johnson Hunt, wife of Col. William E. Hunt, missed only one Red Cross meeting.[72]

The USO Club building on Second Street became the Youngstown Fire Hall after the war. The building was razed in the 1970s and replaced by Marine Midland Bank, now HSBC. (Courtesy Joe Derhay)

THE UNITED SERVICE ORGANIZATIONS (USO) HALL was housed in a large stone building on the west side of Second Street in Youngstown. The Haskell Brothers sold Case tractors and Dodge and Nash Cars there in 1914. The building became a firehouse after the war and was later demolished and replaced by the Marine Midland Bank, now HSBC Bank.[73]

The Fort Niagara Orchestra played *America* for the opening dedication of the USO Club on December 20, 1942; at 3:00 p.m. Rev. Father James Lannigan gave the invocation followed by remarks from Daniel Wilson, the chairman of the program. Dr. Lewis W. Falkner, the mayor of the Village of Youngstown, welcomed everyone. Col. Floyd D. Carlock of the U.S. Army and Rev. Edmund Nixon of the Youngstown USO gave speeches. Rabbi Simon H. Shoop made a presentation of the American Flag, a gift from the Niagara Falls Jewish Welfare Board.[74]

The Program for the dedication acknowledged the governmental dignitaries in attendance: H. O. Davidson of the Federal Works Agency, Peter Kraus of the Federal Security Agency, Brigadier Harold Smith of The Salvation Army Eastern Territory USO Supervisor, and Adjutant Thomas Seaver, the USO Director of the Youngstown Club. Rev. Fred Webber gave the dedicatory prayer and benediction. The orchestra concluded the service with the National Anthem.

TABLE 2.3
USO Club Committees

GENERAL COMMITTEE
- Wilson, Daniel L., Chair
- Sealy, Joyce, Secretary
- Dutton, Ralph
- Falkner, Dr. L. W.
- Goldstein, Joseph A.
- Nichols, Harwood S.
- Rodgers, Maj. Hugh R.
- Wilkes, Henry
  Chief Boatswain's Mate

OPERATIONS COMMITTEE
- Wilson, Daniel L., Chair
- Bliss, Mrs. K.
- Danat, Alfred C.
- Dixon, Mrs. Jack
- Falkner, Carl
- Haskell, Harry
- Pierce, L. L.
- Turgeon, Mrs. R.
- Webber, Rev. Fred

INTER-CHURCH SERVICE TO SOLDIER'S COMMITTEE
- Webber, Rev. Fred, Chair
- Lannigan, Rev. James A.
- Nixon, Rev. Edmund
- Shoop, Rabbi Simon H.
- Voigt, Rev. Paul

HOSTESS COMMITTEE
- Bliss, Ms. Katherine, Chair
- Kelley, Mrs. Maude
- Seaver, Mrs. Thomas

OUTDOOR SPORTS COMMITTEE
- Pierce, L. L., Chair
- Hansen, Victor F.
- Howard, Edwin L.

INDOOR SPORTS COMMITTEE
- Falkner, Carl W.
- Herwig, Bruce
- Yaseen, Lewis

HOME HOSPITALITY COMMITTEE
- Dixon, Mrs. Jack, Chair
- Bernstein, Mrs. Louis
- Voigt, Mrs. Paul

COOKIE JAR COMMITTEE
- Turgeon, Mrs. Robert, Chair
- Barns, Mrs. Alex
- Bars, Mrs. Walter

BUILDING COMMITTEE
- Haskell, Harry, Chair
- Hansen, Mrs. V. F.
- Mies, Maj. J. P.

Source: Dedication Program of USO Club, Youngstown, New York, December 20, 1942.

Outside the Youngstown USO Club, soldiers and local girls enjoyed the live musical entertainment. (Courtesy Joe Derhay)

The Sad Sacks were a popular group that entertained for their buddies at the Youngstown USO. The mural was a caricature of the group. (Courtesy Joe Derhay)

The USO offered bingo and other entertainment for the soldiers from Fort Niagara when they were off-duty in this February 1945 image. (Courtesy Joe Derhay)

The Niagara Falls AWVS group assisted Bell Aircraft and Fort Niagara military personnel. (Courtesy Frances Serchia Esser)

AMERICAN WOMEN'S VOLUNTARY SERVICE (AWVS) ~ One of the women who performed at the Youngstown USO was Frances Serchia Esser, Frank Serchia's older sister. Frances brought soldiers home for dinner, worked at Bell, sang and danced at the USO Canteen, and sold war bonds.[75] She was active in the AWVS, Motor Transports Corps, and the USO. These groups became the dominant service organizations during the war. The local AWVS unit was formed in Niagara Falls on September 19, 1941, at 107-111 Main Street in Niagara Falls across from the Cataract House. The AWVS canteen was open daily from 10:00 a.m. until 11:00 p.m., midnight on Saturdays. It was available to members of the American and Allied forces. Services provided for the troops included a dormitory, shaves, laundry, shoeshines, sewing, pool tables, reading materials, refreshments, and dancing every night.[76]

Frances' training for the "Motor Transports Corps required that we complete a course in first aid, map reading, a course in convoy, and motor mechanics before we could qualify for our insignia.[77] Motor mechanics did me in. I had a problem with camshafts! We formed a full-fledged drill corps. Shredded Wheat Company permitted us to hold our drill practice on their premises.

We marched in many parades including the Magna Carta. It was a yearly event between the United States and Canada."[78]

The Junior Hostesses presented a show in Youngstown. Show numbers included vocals, tap dances, chorus line, and acrobatic feats. The girls wrote one of the acts, *Delay In Route,* that was part of the show and performed at the Red Cross recreation room at Fort Niagara, dinners for returning veterans in the City of Niagara Falls, and at nearby service posts.[79] Frances and Betty Ciluzzi, *The Harmonets,* sang *Candy, There I've Said It Again, Smile* (when you're feeling blue), *I'll Never Smile Again*, *Trolley Song, What a Difference a Day Makes*, and the *White Cliffs of Dover.*[80]

The chorus line dancers were Lola Alvarez, Irene Cassert, Mary Ann Foster, Betty Hall, and Jessie Zilm. Eleanor Winans did a fast tap dance. Bill Millring, the accompanist, wrote some of the music for the acts. A comedy act, *The Last Word*, performed by Velia Martini and Marion Passage was also part of the USO show presented in Youngstown. It mimicked a common argument between a husband and a wife and brought hearty laughter from the crowd. The mistress of ceremonies was Helen Foley.[81]

Capt. Jake Cooper was the 712th Battalion Recreation Officer at Fort Niagara when the USO girls presented their version of a radio show known as *Blind Date.* Junior hostesses Myra Auld, Betty Ciluzzi, Nelda Martini, Rosella Neralic, and Frances Serchia were chosen for their charm and beauty as participants! The evening included several numbers performed by a chorus of forty soldiers. Lieutenant Martin conducted the orchestra. Corporal Willis Shannon wrote an original skit entitled *GI Vacation.*[82] The *Gazette* reported that the skit was an outstanding feature of the evening. "We each picked out a soldier before the program, but didn't get the soldiers we wanted. So, we switched," laughed Frances! The winning soldiers later escorted the girls to dinner and dancing.

The AWVS provided entertainment for the monthly "Welcome Home" dinners for the veterans returning from overseas duty. The Niagara Falls Lions Club, The BPO (Benevolent and Protective Order) Elks, Rotary, Niagara Falls Firemen's Toy Committee, Carpenter's Local No. 422, and the Martha Society of the Zion Lutheran Church, assisted with the festivities and dinner preparations. The veterans were presented with citations, a carton of cigarettes, and a gift of jewelry.[83]

Members of the service organizations helped prepare the dinners and waited on the veterans.

TABLE 2.4
Niagara Area Service Organization Workers

Amato, Carl	Gray, Thomas F.
Beatty, Truman	Greibner, Clarence
Beney, Reginald	Klock, Fred
Bottorf, John	Lynch, Gerard
Burns, Dr. John	McNally, J. C.
Connolly, Dr. A. E.	Outram, Edward
Cook, William	Seager, J. H.
Corriston, William	Thompson, T. E.
Crosby, E. G.	Wahl, Gordon A.
Davy, Thomas	Wardell, Bert
Dietz, John	Welby, Joseph
Evans, David T.	Westerman, William
Ferrito, Sully	Wire, W. E.
Foss, Lawrence	

TABLE 2.5
Veterans at Welcome Home Dinners in Niagara Falls

Amendola, Carl	Pedz, Karl
Braas, Claude	Perham, John
Chase, Charles	Rinker, Ray
Clark, Thomas	Rutledge, John
Collins, Thomas	St. Philip, Thomas J.
Dier, Clarence	Sattelberg, Charles
Faroge, Charles	St. Philip, Thomas J.
Fisher, William	Shattuck, Keith
Green, Joseph	Shear, Arthur
Korman, Ray	Smith, Paul
Moraca, Joseph	Tooke, Edward A.
Nichols, Floyd	Wiseman, Al
Normand, Otto	White, Donald
Paonessa, Theodore	Young, Frank W.
Pelaccio, Cornelius	

Source: Gleaned from private memorabilia collection and *Niagara Falls Gazette* articles about two dinners for returning veterans.

The AWVS also hosted seasonal parties. A "Witches Frolic" was the theme for Halloween. Invitations were sent to the service men at Fort Niagara, the Cataract Air Corps, and the Military Police stationed on Grand Island. Miss Cassandra Waterman was the chair of the invitation committee. Mrs. Betty Baker, Mrs. Dorothy Butler, Mrs. Lucy Mears, and Mrs. Gladys Tindall planned the refreshments. Arranging decorations and entertainment were Miss Anna Cirrito, Miss Ann Marie Cirrito, Miss Frances Fiorello, and Miss Vera McGahey. The Ways and Means committee was Miss Edith Brown, Mrs. Ada Diaz, Miss Angie Long, and Miss Louise Pfeifer. Mrs. Jene Campbell supervised the junior hostesses.[84]

The Blackout published by the Niagara Falls Women's Air Raid Wardens Service Force reported some of the bi-monthly activities at the service club for enlisted men from Fort Niagara. Three busloads of girls arrived at Fort Niagara to celebrate St. Patrick's Day. They were given a ghost walk that began behind the theatre. Later in the evening, Major D. W. MacLaren, the Post Morale Officer, encouraged dancing to the music of the *Fort Niagara Bombardiers* under the leadership of Joe Agro. Joe formerly played with Rev Norvo and Joe Marsala. Edward Zandy played the trumpet and George Sedola, the trombone.[85]

Dances were held at the canteen and at Fort Niagara. The belles were taken by bus from the Elmwood plant to be the guests of military personnel for a tea dance at Fort Niagara.[86]

TABLE 2.6
USO Belles Attending a Tea Dance at Fort Niagara

Anker, Betty	Keller, Doris
Beugh, Betty	Kiosko, Charlotte
Braeuner, Lydia	Kupka, Edith
Bratton, Vivian	Maciaszek, Helen
Case, Betty	Mechieview, Helen
Clark, Frances	Noel, Helen
Colby, Nancy	Onafru, Lois
DePlacid, Carolyn	Pasciak, Frances
Doebler, Bernice	Pasciak, Viola
Doebler, Dorian	Pearl, Florence
Falcone, Mary	Politylo, Olga
Horvath, Betty	Schewergert, Pearl
Johnson, Dorothy	Senfner, Helen

Serchia, Frances
Sloma, Alice
Stafford, Virginia
Stenzel, Donna
Sydor, Ruth
Turowski, Dorothy
Turty, Dorothy
Weeks, Janet
Yung, Helen

Source: "Soldiers at Fort Niagara Host Blind Date Show," *Niagara Falls Gazette*, 1944.

Other events were more informal. In September 1944 the AWVS Canteen hosted a picnic near Bond's Lake in the Town of Lewiston for some soldiers stationed at Niagara University. During the day the soldiers played baseball and sang in the evening around a campfire.[87]

Frances and many others who volunteered in these service organizations worked during the day at Bell Aircraft and other areas of support for the war. Frances was employed at the LOOW facility as a Clerk-Typist at an annual salary of $1,260.00 until her transfer on November 19, 1942, to a Clerk-Typist Position for the Engineer Department at the Chemical Warfare Service Plant, Niagara Falls, NY. Her salary remained the same.[88]

The AWVS also sold war bonds and war stamps. "A chemical warfare plant was being built by the Corps of Engineers at that time. One of the workers that I sold war bonds to was none other than Sal Maglie. He eventually became a famous baseball pitcher for the Brooklyn Dodgers and the New York Giants. In the Brooklyn vs. New York Yankees World Series, Sal pitched for Brooklyn. Don Larson pitched the perfect game and beat Brooklyn, winning the series!"[89]

The AWVS group grew to three hundred women. They carted the military brass around when needed, ran drives for recycling including collecting old keys, and turned in approximately eight thousand pounds of scrap iron to be used for war materials. The women also published a newspaper that was sent out to the servicemen.[90]

"Bell Aircraft Corporation was building war planes in round the clock shifts, including P-39 Airacobras. This meant *Camp Bell* was loaded with famous test pilots such as Joe Mashman, Tex Johnson,[91] and Chuck Yeager who later flew the rocket-powered Bell X-1.[92] The pilots were the golden boys. They walked by my office to get to the cafeteria," Fran said. "We all loved Larry Bell because he was building the planes for the war. We were very patriotic and grateful to our country. There was a wonderful spirit of patriotism," she said.

A Bell Service Training School for Army aviation mechanics began in

Ruth Brown Walsh, third from the left, sold war bonds in December 1942 at the Sterling Engine Co. Buffalo, NY. (Courtesy Nannette Simon)

February of 1942. It opened at the Cataract House in the City of Niagara Falls on April 14, 1942. In November, *Camp Cataract* became known as *Camp Bell* and was moved near the Wheatfield plant.[93]

"One of our greatest performances between Canada and the United States was beyond description. As the finale for our show, we dressed three mannequins as Hirohito, Mussolini, and Hitler. We put them on a raft and floated them over Niagara Falls to the tune of 'when the Fuhrer said we are the master race, we heil, right in the Fuhrer's face.' The applause was louder than Niagara Falls," Frances exclaimed. Mayor George Inghs of Niagara Falls, Ontario, Acting Mayor John Kellan of Niagara Falls, New York, and Lt. George Cox, a naval hero, witnessed the event. The Fort Niagara Band played the *Dead March* as the dictators' figures were sent over the American Falls from the Goat Island Bridge. The event was part of a war bond rally that resulted in the sale of $74,000 in bonds.[94]

The group went on the road to other regional USOs and presented a variety show called *Kanteen Kapers* to several hundred Navy men from Sampson Train-

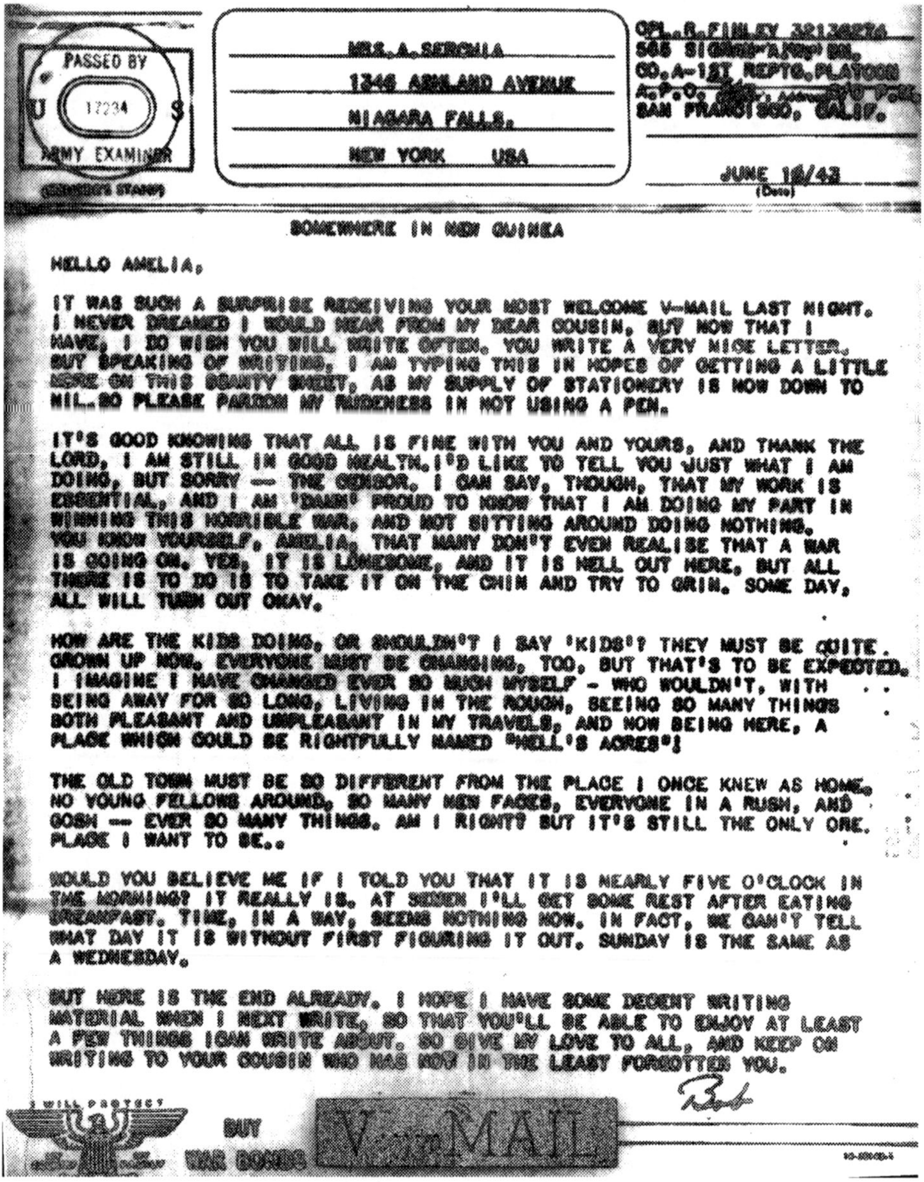

PASSED BY
U 17234 S
ARMY EXAMINER
(CENSOR'S STAMP)

MRS. A. SERCHIA
1346 ASHLAND AVENUE
NIAGARA FALLS,
NEW YORK USA

CPL. R. FINLEY
CO. A-1ST REPTC. PLATOON
SAN FRANCISCO, CALIF.

JUNE 16/43
(Date)

SOMEWHERE IN NEW GUINEA

HELLO AMELIA,

IT WAS SUCH A SURPRISE RECEIVING YOUR MOST WELCOME V-MAIL LAST NIGHT. I NEVER DREAMED I WOULD HEAR FROM MY DEAR COUSIN, BUT NOW THAT I HAVE, I DO WISH YOU WILL WRITE OFTEN. YOU WRITE A VERY NICE LETTER. BUT SPEAKING OF WRITING, I AM TYPING THIS IN HOPES OF GETTING A LITTLE MORE ON THIS SCANTY SHEET, AS MY SUPPLY OF STATIONERY IS NOW DOWN TO NIL. SO PLEASE PARDON MY RUDENESS IN NOT USING A PEN.

IT'S GOOD KNOWING THAT ALL IS FINE WITH YOU AND YOURS, AND THANK THE LORD, I AM STILL IN GOOD HEALTH. I'D LIKE TO TELL YOU JUST WHAT I AM DOING, BUT SORRY — THE CENSOR. I CAN SAY, THOUGH, THAT MY WORK IS ESSENTIAL, AND I AM 'DAMN' PROUD TO KNOW THAT I AM DOING MY PART IN WINNING THIS HORRIBLE WAR, AND NOT SITTING AROUND DOING NOTHING. YOU KNOW YOURSELF, AMELIA, THAT MANY DON'T EVEN REALISE THAT A WAR IS GOING ON. YES, IT IS LONESOME, AND IT IS HELL OUT HERE, BUT ALL THERE IS TO DO IS TO TAKE IT ON THE CHIN AND TRY TO GRIN. SOME DAY, ALL WILL TURN OUT OKAY.

HOW ARE THE KIDS DOING, OR SHOULDN'T I SAY 'KIDS'? THEY MUST BE QUITE GROWN UP NOW. EVERYONE MUST BE CHANGING, TOO, BUT THAT'S TO BE EXPECTED. I IMAGINE I HAVE CHANGED EVER SO MUCH MYSELF - WHO WOULDN'T, WITH BEING AWAY FOR SO LONG, LIVING IN THE ROUGH, SEEING SO MANY THINGS BOTH PLEASANT AND UNPLEASANT IN MY TRAVELS, AND NOW BEING HERE, A PLACE WHICH COULD BE RIGHTFULLY NAMED "HELL'S ACRES"!

THE OLD TOWN MUST BE SO DIFFERENT FROM THE PLACE I ONCE KNEW AS HOME. NO YOUNG FELLOWS AROUND, SO MANY NEW FACES, EVERYONE IN A RUSH, AND GOSH — EVER SO MANY THINGS. AM I RIGHT? BUT IT'S STILL THE ONLY ONE PLACE I WANT TO BE..

WOULD YOU BELIEVE ME IF I TOLD YOU THAT IT IS NEARLY FIVE O'CLOCK IN THE MORNING? IT REALLY IS. AT SEVEN I'LL GET SOME REST AFTER EATING BREAKFAST. TIME, IN A WAY, SEEMS NOTHING NOW. IN FACT, WE CAN'T TELL WHAT DAY IT IS WITHOUT FIRST FIGURING IT OUT. SUNDAY IS THE SAME AS A WEDNESDAY.

BUT HERE IS THE END ALREADY. I HOPE I HAVE SOME DECENT WRITING MATERIAL WHEN I NEXT WRITE, SO THAT YOU'LL BE ABLE TO ENJOY AT LEAST A FEW THINGS I CAN WRITE ABOUT. SO GIVE MY LOVE TO ALL, AND KEEP ON WRITING TO YOUR COUSIN WHO HAS NOT IN THE LEAST FORGOTTEN YOU.

Bob

BUY WAR BONDS

V-MAIL

The V-mail also known as Victory-mail was censored during the war. (Courtesy of Frank Serchia) ing School at the USO in Rochester, New York. Rose Violante's debut was a ballet number. A dance with music by Bob Bruce's six-piece orchestra followed the USO program.[95] "We gained the attention of the National AWVS-USO brass in New York City and a representative was sent to look us over. Those of us who were able to travel extensively could have applied. But (for me) there was no way an Italian momma was going to let her kid out of her sight at the age of eighteen," Frances continued.

At the end of the war on VJ Day a startling image occurred in the Serchia neighborhood. An elderly Italian woman went on her knees down Pine Avenue to St. Joseph's Church to thank God the war was over. Frances continued at Bell after the war and recollected that Larry Bell gathered the secretaries and told them to go outside. "We didn't know what was happening. The sound was so loud I thought we were under attack." It was the sound of a jet breaking the speed of sound. (On October 14, 1947, Capt. Charles E. "Chuck" Yeager flew aircraft #46-062, Bell X-1, and pushed the jet past the speed of sound at Muroc Army Air Field, now Edwards Air Force Base in California.)

Frances summed up her reflection of the war days. "This was a time of great patriotism. We licked the great depression. We loved our country and we weren't about to let tyrants take over our world. I don't remember any demonstrations against that war. There was rationing, but people didn't seem to complain. I am proud of this opportunity to serve our country – in my way as someone from the greatest generation."

THE CIVILIAN PROTECTION COUNCIL ~ The enrollment for Civil Defense in the Town of Porter was conducted by Sherlock A. Herrick, Miss Murphy, and Miss Goodreds. They registered 452 citizens; 190 pleasure cars were offered in case of an emergency. Seventy-four different occupations and Bohemian, French, German, Italian, Polish, Russian, Serbian, and Spanish languages were represented in the group.[96]

The Protection Council in Youngstown and the Sector Air Raid Wardens held a meeting at the high school on Tuesday, March 30, 1943. The representatives clarified the duties of the sector wardens and firewatchers. Instructions were given on how to function in an emergency and the council reviewed a map of the village and surrounding area. It was placed on the bulletin board at the control headquarters located in the Youngstown High School cafeteria. All air raid wardens received a first aid kit demonstrated by Mrs. Mies. The town clerk's office supplied arm bands for the air raid wardens and fire watchers. All residences and business establishments were asked to obtain a blackout instruction placard. The air raid wardens previously distributed some of the placards.[97]

Deputy County Director Col. William E. Hunt, Assistant Deputy County Director First Lt. Clarence B. Nichols, Secretary Mrs. John P. Mies, Chief Air Raid Warden David Parkhill, Chairman of firewatchers Ralph Dutton, and sector wardens Roy Haskell, Mrs. Edwin L. Howard, Donald Lutts, Ray Tower, and Mrs. Charles Ulrich were present at the March meeting.

The procedures for practice and actual air raids were revised at another meeting on April 23, 1943. The air raid signal that indicated an imminent attack was a rising and falling sound of sirens continuing for two minutes, or short blasts of whistles. Medical Depots, Emergency Hospitals, and Secondary Aid Stations were identified. Medical Depot No. 1 was located at Walmore Road at the Airport and No. 2 at Niagara University, Lewiston Road. Nine emergency medical facilities were designated:

TABLE 2.7
Emergency Medical Facilities

Emergency Hospitals	Location
Niagara Falls Memorial Hospital	Niagara Falls
Mt. St. Mary's Hospital	Niagara Falls
Carbo Coated Products	Walmore Road
Niagara University	Lewiston Road
Stella Niagara School	River Road
Lewiston Central School[98]	Saunders Settlement and Miller Roads
Ransomville School	Ransomville
Post Hospital	Fort Niagara
Ninety-third Street School	Griffon Manor

Secondary Aid Stations	
Seventy-ninth Street School	LaSalle
LaSalle High School	Hyde Park Boulevard
Niagara Falls High School	Pine at Portage Road
North Junior High School	Cleveland Avenue
Maple Avenue School	Lewiston Road

Source: "Regulations Governing Procedure During Practice and Actual Air Raids," April 1943, Niagara Falls History Library, Local History Department, WWII file.

QUOTAS AND WORKERS ~ In January 1944 the quota for the Youngstown Red Cross was 2,500 surgical dressings. Mrs. Gordon Gushee was appointed vice-chairman and assistant supervisors for the afternoon shift from 1:00 until 4:30 p.m. were Mrs. William E. Hunt, Mrs. Lawrence Johnson, Mrs. John Mies, and Mrs. Norman B. Hays. The evening group worked from 7:00 p.m. until 10:00 p.m. Assistant evening supervisors were Mrs. Gerald Brown, Mrs. Sylvia Childs, Miss Bernetta Kelley, and Mrs. Robert Ripson. By the fall of 1944 the Youngstown Red Cross made an appeal for more workers to meet the growing national needs and because the monthly quota of 5,000 dressings was missed.[99]

TABLE 2.8
1942 Red Cross Contributors

Allen, Mr. Leonard
Allen, Mrs. James
Andrews, Mr. and Mrs.
Andrews, Mr. Angus
Ayer, Miss Edith
Babyk, Hilda#
Balcom, C. E.
Balcom, Mrs. Vergil
Bedell, Mr. William
Beergdorf, Mr. William
Betts, Lt. H. H.*
Blossom, Miss Vida
Blough, Mr. Howard
Borem, Bertha
Brant, Mrs. Herbert
Britton, Miss Ina
Broeker, Mrs.
Broeker, Mrs. Arthur
Bullock, Mr. A.
Burnett, Mrs.
Canfield, Ken#
Carlock, Col. and Mrs.*
Carter, Miss Jennie
Case, Lt. M.S.*
Cathan, Mrs.
Chesterson, Capt. P. J.*
Clapsattle, Mr.
Clark, Lt. A. H.*
Clark, Mr. and Mrs. Herman
Co. B. 1213th. R.C.*
Cody, Mrs.
Coffman, Ruth
Combe, Mr. David
Cooper#
Cothran, Mr. Arthur
D'Amore, Capt. T.*
Davis, Rubert#
Davis, Lt. E. A.*
Dean, Mrs. Fred
Demmin, Mrs.
Det. DEML 1206th*
Det. Military Police*
Dietz, Mrs. Edna
Diez, Mrs. Russell
Dritschel, Mrs.
Duggan, Chaplain J. D.*
Dutton, Mrs. Geo.
Dutton, Mrs. R.
Dutton, Ralph
Eaton, Mr. and Mrs. H. B.

Falkner, Dr. and Mrs. L. W.
Falkner, Mrs. Catherine
Falone, H.#
Felders, Elizabeth
Foltz, Capt. M.E.*
Froitzheim, Lt. Col. W.*
Gassler, L.#
Gaul, Mr. Leroy
Godfrey, Mr. Harry S.
Goodnough, Capt. C.W.*
Hackett, Mrs. N. O.
Hall, Mrs. John
Hanshaw, Lt. J. G.*
Harding's Restaurant
Haseley, Lydia
Haskell, Harry#
Haskell, Mrs. Roy
Hays, Mrs.
Hediger, Mr.
Henderson, Lt. S.L.*
Herman, Col. C.J.*
Heston, Lt. R.B.*
Hill, Mr. Allen
Hogarth, Sydney
Holody, M.#
Hopkins, Mrs. F.
Hosmer, Mr. and Mrs. Jack
Houraney, John#
Houserman, Mr. Russell
Howard, E. L.
Howard, George
Howard, Mr. and Mrs. Ethan
Hq. Co. 1213th. R.C.*
Hunt, Colonel W.
Hunt, Lt.
Hutchinson, Mrs.
James, Mrs. Benjamin
Johnson Fudge Co.
Johnson, Lawrence
Johnson, Lin
Johnson, Mr. Samuel
Johnston, Gladys#
Junior Service Society – Pres. Church
Kelley, Miss Bernetta
King, Mr. and Mrs. Kermit
King, Mrs. George
Kirk, Mrs. Frank
Kolloff, Mr. Fred. C.
Kolloff, Mrs. Roy
Kolloff, Wm. C.
Krieger, Capt. G. H.*
Kulak, Mrs.
Kyle, Mr. Clyde
Lew's Lunch#
Lichtenberg, 1st Lt. Walter*
Lindhurst, Mrs.
Lutts, Donald
Lutts, F. L.
Mahlmeister, Anthony
Martin, Mrs. Anna
Martin, Mrs. N.
McArthur, Mr.
McDonald, Miss R. Jane
Med. Dept. Det 1206th*
Meland, Charles#
Mies, Miss Marjorie
Mies, Mrs. John
Miller, Mr. Lew
Mitchell, Mrs.
Monnen, Mrs. M.
Monroe, Capt. E. M.*
Moon, Mr. Wallingford
Marie's Beauty Shop#
Murphy, Arthur#
Myers, Mrs. Henry F.
Nichols, C. B.

Nichols, Mr.
Nickel, Chaplain A. W.*
Nixon, Cyris
Nixon, Rev.
Owen, Jennie#
Parkhill, David
Q.M. Det. 1206th. SU*
R. and R. Restaurant#
Red and White Store – Powers#
Regan, Lt. R. R.*
Reisdorf, Mr. Jack
Renouf, Mrs.
Ripson, Mrs. Edith
River View Hotel#
Rizzo, Lt. J. G.*
Robinson, Gavin
Robinson, George
Robinson, Mrs.
Rodenbaugh, Grover
Root, Miss Helen
Sanderson, Mr. and Mrs. R. H.
Schnoor, Mr. and Mrs. Carl
Schultz, Mr. and Mrs. Herb
Schultz, William
Schuman, Mrs.
Schwarzmuller, Capt. H.*
Shaefer, Lt. J. L.*
Shumaker, Wilbur
Slate, Miss Mildred
Smith, Capt. K. W.*
Smith, Mr. and Mrs. Charles
Stafflinger, Mr. Chas.
Steele, Lt. L.*
Stevens, Mr. E. K.
Stewart, Lt. J.*
Sutor (sic), Harry
Taylor, Mrs. Ina
Thompson, Harold
Thompson, Mr. Joseph
Thompson, Mrs. Harold
Thompson, Mrs. Vincent
Tower, George P.
Tower, Mr. and Mrs. Porter B.
Tower, Mrs. A. R.
Tower, P. E.*
Tower, Ray
Truesdale, Mrs. George
Turgeon, Mrs. Priscilla
Ulrich, C. W.
Ulrich, Dick#
Vestal, Dick#
Voight, Rev. Paul
Wagner, Mrs. William
Wall, Guy#
Walls, Mona
Wheeler, Mrs. Joseph
White, Lt. A.*
Willard, Lt. W. R.*
Williams, Lt. E. A.*
Wills, D'Lee
Wilson, Dan#
Wilson, Mrs. Florence D.
Wilson, Mrs. John
Wolfe, Mr. and Mrs.
Wright, Mrs.
Youngstown Cold Storage#
Youngstown Fire Co.
Zakary, Lt. H. L.*

Source: *Red Cross Day Book*, Town of Porter, Town Hall, Youngstown, NY.
*Listing for collections from personnel at Fort Niagara.
#Listing for collections from businesses.

When the war was over and the USO was leaving Youngstown, the Niagara Falls Salvation Army Band conducted by Bandmaster Glenn Ferris performed a musical concert at the USO Hall on Friday, December 14, 1945, at 7:30 p.m. for the Hostess Reception and Closing Program. The program for the evening gave a brief history:

Words cannot adequately describe the faithful, unstinting, and generous service given by the volunteers during the time this club has been in operation.

Needless to say, our work would have been in vain had they not played their important part in the program.

The club opened for servicemen on December 20, 1942, and until July 1945 was directed by Maj. Thomas Seaver. Capt. John Wilson then succeeded him, as the director. Statistics show that 92,265 men in the service have used the facilities offered to November 30, 1945.

During the same period 7,877 hostesses assisted with the program, serving a total of 19,561 hours.

More than 136,000 note heads have been used showing that a very favorite pastime while off duty was letter writing.

Rev. W. Edmund Nixon of the Episcopal Church gave the Invocation and Rev. Fred M. Webber introduced the speakers during the evening: Chairman Daniel L. Wilson, S. A. War Service Secretary Lt. Col. Harold R. Smith from New York City, and Mayor of Youngstown Albert Bullock. Corporal Franklin Marquardt gave a talk entitled "An Enlisted Man's Opinion." He expressed his appreciation for the photographic developing equipment, recording machine for voice records to send home, and the hospitality at the USO. Technical Sgt. Clarence Clif performed a vocal solo. Capt. Frederick de Wilde represented Col. Herbert D. Forrest, the Post Commander at Fort Niagara, who was unable to attend. De Wilde conveyed appreciation for the services of the USO. The congregation sang the National Anthem followed by the Benediction given by Rev. Herbert W. Goerss of the Evangelical Lutheran Church.

Capt. John Wilson, the USO director, assisted Chaplain Allen of Fort Niagara, and USO secretary Mrs. Luna Conger to present certificates and pins to the hostesses. Group awards were given for the Cookie Committees representatives.[100]

TABLE 2.9
USO Cookie Committee Representatives

Bars, Mrs. Walter	Lutheran Church
Baxendale, Mrs. Ernest	Salvation Army
Bernstein, Mrs. Lewis	Jewish Welfare
Bradley, Mrs. Raymond	Methodist Church
Brown, Mrs. William	Hickory College Community
Bunton, Mrs. Alex	Salvation Army
Diebold, Mrs. Edwin	American Legion Auxiliary
Hediger, Mrs. Ernest	Youngstown Study Club
Howell, Maj. Raymond	The Salvation Army
Kay, Mrs. Howard	Catholic Church
Kolloff, Mrs. Will	Presbyterian Church

Source: "USO Services Brought to Close at Youngstown; Certificates and Pins Presented for Long Service," *Niagara Falls Gazette*, December 17, 1945.

Miss Janet Weeks (Bell Aircraft girls), Miss Helen Troy (Knights of Columbus), Mrs. Mary Roberts (Lockport Defense Girls), and Miss Janet Weeks (Wurlitzer girls) represented the Junior Hostess Groups. Miss Madalyn Rodenbaugh and Mrs. Marjorie Comerford received the Senior Hostess five hundred hour awards.

TABLE 2.10
Awards for One Hundred Hours of Service

Allen, Mrs. C. Edgar	Duncan, Mrs. Ivah
Beggs, Miss Doris	Dutton, Miss Margaret
Beggs, Miss Marion	Dutton, Mrs. Ralph
Blossom, Miss Vida	Gaskill, Mrs. Alice
Bowen, Mrs. L.	Hays, Mrs. Norman B.
Brown, Mrs. Mary	Hediger, Mrs. Ernest
Carey, Mrs. Ruby	Holmes, Mrs. Dorothy
Clark, Mrs. Alice	Howard, Mrs. Edwin
Condren, Mrs. Mary	Hutchison, Mrs. Helen
Conger, Mrs. Luna S.	Kelley, Miss Bernetta
Cothran, Mrs. Arthur	Kill, Mrs. Helen

Kolloff, Miss Mabel	Perry, Mrs. Julia
Kolloff, Miss Nellie	Pierce, Mrs. Livingston
Kolloff, Mrs. Roy	Shipston, Mrs. Howard
Liddel, Mrs. Harry	Suitor, Mrs. Katherine
Lutts, Miss Marion	Turgeon, Mrs. Robert
Martin, Mrs. Norma	Tuttle, Mrs. Katherine
Messenger, Mrs. Charles	Van Wegen, Mrs. Kay
Nichols, Miss Bessie	Wright, Mrs. Grace
Nixon, Mrs. Jack	

Source: *Niagara Falls Gazette*, December 17, 1945.

An unsigned copy of a letter addressed to Capt. Wilson dated January 11, 1946, in the Porter Historical Museum files, marked the exodus of the USO.

Dear Capt. Wilson: -

As the USO is leaving Youngstown, I would like to say "Thank you for a job well done."

Three years ago Youngstown was a typical G.I. town, with very few recreational facilities to offer the boys stationed at Fort Niagara... depending almost wholly on Niagara Falls, fourteen miles away, for entertainment. The community, realizing the evils six saloons located in Youngstown, could foster, pitched in wholeheartedly when USO came to town, and helped our two very capable directors, Maj. Sever and Capt. Wilson, make the club a real success, judging from the comments of many boys who enjoyed its facilities. I'm sure a great many homesick boys felt that it truly was a "home away from home."

Now that our job is done and USO bids farewell to Youngstown...THANKS FOR EVERYTHING.

Very sincerely yours

TABLE 2.11
1945 Red Cross Contributors

Adams, Mr. and Mrs. C.	Beatty, Mr. Wm
Ayers, Mrs. Edith	Blossom, Vida
Babyk, Hilda	Blough, H. B.
Baird, Mr. and Mrs.	Borem, Mr. George
Balcom, Daisy	Bowen, Mrs. Lillian
Balmer, Miss	Britton, Ina
Balmer, Mrs. F. H.	Broeker, Mr. and Mrs. Clarence
Barrett, Dorothy	Broeker, Mrs. Alfred

Bullock, Mr. Bert
Butterfield, Mrs. C. J.
Canfield, Mrs. David
Carter, Gennie
Carter, Gertrude
Carter, Mrs. Howard
Carter, Mrs. Myra
Carter, Thomas
Chestnut, Ella
Childs, Sylvia
Clark, Mr. Herman
Clark, Mrs. Alice
Clark, Mrs. Herman
Clements, Mr. Frank
Clements, Mrs. Judith
Coffman, Mrs. Lester
Combe, Mrs. David
Comerford, Marjorie
Comerford, Mrs. Stuart
Comerford, Stewart
Condren, Mary
Conlay, Mrs. Roy
Coolan, Mrs. Grace
Coots, Mrs. Henry
Coots, Mrs. Howard
Costo, Mrs. J.
Cothran, Newton
Cothren, Art
Davis, Fred
Dall, Mr. and Mrs. Herman
Davison, Mr. and Mrs. James
Dearhorn, Mrs. Helen
Demmin, Mrs. Wm.
Dietz, John
Downey, Mrs. Joseph
Duncan, Mrs. Ina
duToi, Mrs. Jean
Dutton, Mrs. George
Dygert, Mrs. Charles
Eagle, Miss Eleanor
Eagon, Mr. H. B.
Edwards, Mrs.
Eggert, Wm. F.
Falcone, Mr. Harry
Falkner, Catherine
Faulkner, Mrs. L.
Ferguson, Bill
Fonner, Mr. and Mrs. Arlington
Frederik, John
Fritz, Mrs. Will
Gaskill, Alice
Gassler, L. L.
Gher, Mrs.
Gilson, Mr. and Mrs. James
Gorman, Herbert
Goshorn, Miss
Gushee, Mrs. Gordon
Gushee, Mrs. Wallace
Haag, Mr. and Mrs. A. J.
Hardin, Mr. and Mrs. R.
Haskell, Harry
Haskell, Mr. and Mrs. Roy
Haskell, Mr. C. R.
Haskell, Mrs. C. R.
Hayden, Mrs.
Hediger, Mrs.
Held, Mrs. H.
Henry, Mrs. Nellie
Hillman, Mrs. A.
Holody, Martin
Hopkins, Mrs. Frank
Hosmer, Mr. and Mrs. Jack
Houraney, John
Houraney, Mrs. John
Howard, Mr. Geo
Howard, Mrs. Edwin

Hunt, Col. Wm E.
Hutchison, Mrs.
Izzo, Mrs. J.
James, Mr. and Mrs. A.B.
Jaycox, Mrs. Ed
Johnson, Mrs. Alfred
Johnson, Mrs. Porter
Johnston, Mrs. Alfred
Johnston, Mrs. H.
Kay, Mrs. H. B.
Kelley, Bernetta
Kelley, Louis J.
Kelly, Mrs. Earl
Kinghorn, Mrs. James
Kinzie, C. J.
Kinzie, Charles N.
Kirk, Mrs. Frank
Kobler, Mr. and Mrs. J. F.
Kolloff, Albert C.
Kolloff, Mrs.
Kolloff, Mrs. F.
Kolloff, Mrs. Will
Lindhurst, Mrs. Elwood
Lloyd, Mrs. James
Lutheran Ladies Aid
MacArthur, Mr. John
Magavero, Santina
Mahlmeister, Mr. A.
Martin, Alma
Martin, Mrs. Norma
McCartin, Mr. and Mrs. J.
McClelland, Mrs. Frank
McCormick, Mrs. Gordon
McGrath, Mrs. Lydia
McNinch, Mrs. David
Messinger, C.
Metzgar, Ernest
Misener, Mr. and Mrs.
Moon, Irene
Mulvihil, J.
Murphy, Art
Murphy, Mrs. Harriet
Nelson, Mr. and Mrs. C.
Neuman, Lillian
Newton, Mrs. Shepard
Nichols, Mr. and Mrs. C. B.
Nieburg, Mrs. Angeline
Nixon, Rev. and Mrs. Edmund
Parkhill, Mr. and Mrs.
Parry, Warren
Pearson, Elijah
Perry, Mrs. Sarah
Phillipps, Park
Pilcher, Mrs. Pres
Pound, Clyde
Premus, Martin
Presbyterian Service Guild
Red and White Store
Reed, R. B.
Reisdorf, Mrs.
Renouf, Mrs. Wm.
Rice, Mr.
Richardson, Mrs. C. H.
Ripson, Edith
Robinson, Mr. and Mrs. Wm
Robinson, Mrs. George
Rodenbaugh, Mrs. Grover
Root, Miss Helen
Rose, Mrs. Tran R.
Sanderson, Mr. and Mrs. Ralph
Schnoor, Carl
Schultz, Herbert
Schultz, Mrs. Pearl
Seaver, Mr. and Mrs. T.
Shippy, Mrs. Grace
Shumaker, Louis

Shumaker, Wilbur
Skellen, Thelma
Smith, Mr. and Mrs. Charles
Smithson, Glenn
Stevens, E. K.
Stone, Ben
Suitor, Mrs. Ida
Thompson, H.
Thompson, Mrs. Anna
Thompson, Mrs. Jos.
Tower, Donald
Tower, George P.
Tower, John R.
Tower, Mr. P.
Tower, Mrs. P.
Tower, Nelson H.
Tower, Porter B.
Tower, Ray C.
Truesdale, George and family
Truesdale, Mrs. Leonard
Truesdell, Mrs. Homer
Ulrich, Mr. and Mrs. Herman
Ulrick, R. J.
Van Kill, Mr. and Mrs.
Vestal, Dick
Wagner, M. D.
Wall, Guy
Wasmund, Mrs. L. N.
Webber, Carol M.
Webber, Fred M.
Wegen, D. Van
Wheeler, Mrs. Winifred
Whittaker, Mrs. Wilford
Widman, Mrs.
Wiehl, Betty
Wilkesmore, Mrs. Fred
Wilkins, Mr.
Wills, Mr. and Mrs. D. M.
Wilson, Daniel L.
Wilson, Mrs. John
Wright, Al
Wright, John
Wruk, Frank
Youngstown Fire Co.

Source: *Red Cross Day Book*, Town of Porter, Town Hall, Youngstown, NY. The size of typical individual contributions rose to $5.00 and $10.00 from the $1.00 and $2.00 contributions in 1942.

The Youngstown Red Cross produced 105,202 dressings from 1941 to November 1946. Workers were reluctant to stop their service so the supervisors encouraged the volunteers to move on to the sewing and knitting branches of the Red Cross. Bradley Haskell contributed *The Honor Roll*, which was placed temporarily in the post office.

High school students Nancy Adams, Carol Anderson, Jane Davison, Martha Davison, Ruth Haskell, Judy Howard, Betty Jeffords, Betty Kephart, Annie Martin, Betty Nelson, Marilyn Nelson, Helen Tweed, Harriett Ulrich, and Willa Wright also performed service hours for the Red Cross.[101]

In addition to efforts by the Red Cross and USO area residents made efforts to support the troops at Fort Niagara. On Christmas Eve 1944 residents from the Lewiston and Youngstown areas brought foodstuffs and gifts for the servicemen. The officers accepting the "Christmas Cheer" were Lt. Ansel Tupper, Commanding Officer Battery A, 44th Battalion; Lt. Gerald Baker, 56 Operational Security Detention; Richard Carpel, Chief Warrant Officer, 44 AAA Headquarters Battalion; and Carlos Lemos, Warrant Officer, 336 AAA Gen. Battalion. Mrs. Howard Scott, Jr. was the chairman of the endeavor assisted by Samuel B. Noyes. Mrs. Merrill Eldridge coordinated the posters and Mrs. Chester Richardson decorated the gift boxes. The Youngstown Lions club collected the donated gifts from drop off stations at the business establishments of James W. Davidson and Kenneth Comerford. Mrs. John Dundon, Mrs. John Hosmer and Mrs. Robert Johnson, coordinated the Youngstown area collections. Coulson's Pharmacy, Michael's, and Vaughn's stores donated Christmas tree lights to the camp.[102]

Beyond volunteer service many in the community became part of the dramatic almost overnight change in the industrial sector from peacetime civilian enterprises to defense industries.

NOTES

[68] "Youngstown Red Cross Has Produced 105,202 Dressings Since Inception," *Niagara Falls Gazette,* November 20, 1946.
[69] "New Guild Hall Nears Completion as St. John's Church Year Ends," unidentified newspaper clipping, 1942.
[70] "Hold Conference, War Council and Red Cross Groups, Meet at Youngstown," *Niagara Falls Gazette*, October 26, 1942.
[71] "WWII Accomplishments of the American Red Cross," *Red Cross Museum History*, http://www.redcross.org/museum/history/ww2a.asp [accessed March 12, 2007].
[72] Red Cross folder, Porter Historical Museum, Youngstown, NY. Colonel and Mrs. William Hunt resided at 3735 Lower River Road in the Town of Porter.
[73] Author, *Porter*, 29. A local resident remembered a dance studio on the second floor of the building.
[74] Program for the USO Club Dedication, Porter Historical Museum, Youngstown, NY.
[75] Frances Serchia Esser, telephone interview by author, and correspondence July 11, 19, 2006.
[76] "Proud Record Compiled by Niagara Falls AWVS," *Niagara Falls Gazette*, May 7, 1945.
[77] Officers from Fort Niagara taught the AWVS courses. Mrs. Augustus G. Porter was the chair of the AWVS Niagara Falls Branch of three hundred members in February 1942. Mrs. Porter addressed the Youngstown PTA committee of Mrs. Fred Lloyd and Mrs. Kolloff, co-chairs, assisted by Mrs. Byron Powell, Mrs. J. Vincent Thompson, Mrs. William Kolloff, Mrs. Clarence Broeker, Mrs. Charles Ulrich, Mrs. Lawrence Condren, and William H. Bergdorf.
[78] Speeches by Frances Serchia Esser, Palm Springs Air Museum, May 3, 2003, and May 7, 2005.
[79] " AWVS Canteen Show at Youngstown," *Niagara Falls Gazette*, 1940s.
[80] Esser, telephone interview.
[81] "AWVS Canteen Show at Youngstown," 1940s.
[82] "712th Battalion Hold Blind Date Show," *Niagara Falls Gazette*, 1940s.
[83] "Veterans given 'Welcome Home' at Dinner Here," *Niagara Falls Gazette*, 1940s.
[84] "Witches Frolic given at AWVS," *Niagara Falls Gazette*, 1940s.
[85] "Niagara Falls Women's Air Raid Wardens' Service Force," *The Blackout*, Vol. 1, No. 4, March 20, 1942.
[86] "Soldiers at Fort Niagara Host Blind Date Show," *Niagara Falls Gazette*, 1944.
[87] "Unique Program at AWVS Canteen," *Niagara Falls Gazette*, September. 1944.
[88] Appointment by Transfer, War Department Report of Field Personnel Action by R. M. Williams, Capt., Corps of Engineers, Assistant; War, Engineer Department at Large, Buffalo, NY; March 22, 1943.
[89] Esser, speeches.
[90] Esser, speeches.
[91] Tex Johnson became an executive with Boeing.
[92] The historic flight was October 14, 1947. Yeager flew faster than the speed of sound.
[93] Bell Aircraft Corporation, *An Aviation Story The History of Bell Aircraft Corp.,* Tenth Anniversary Edition. (Buffalo: Bell Aircraft Corporation, July 1945), 265-266.

[94] "Dictators over Falls," *Niagara (Ontario) Review*, October 1, 1942.

[95] "Local AWVS Canteen USO Presents Novel Program at Rochester USO," *Niagara Falls Gazette*, 1940s.

[96] "Over 450 Enroll for Civil Defense at First District, Town of Porter," *Niagara Falls Gazette,* January 12, 1942.

[97] "Fire Auxiliary of Youngtown Meets Tonight," *Niagara Falls Gazette*, April 1, 1943.

[98] In 2007 this is the Colonial Village Elementary School, part of the Niagara Wheatfield School District. During the war, Lewiston-Porter was not a centralized school.

[99] "Youngstown Red Cross Aid Needed," *Niagara Falls Gazette*, October 1944.

[100] "USO Services Brought to Close at Youngstown; Certificates and Pins Presented for Long Service," *Niagara Falls Gazette*, December 17, 1945.

[101] "Youngstown Red Cross Has Produced 105,202 Dressings Since Inception," *Niagara Falls Gazette*, November 20, 1946.

[102] "Lewiston, Youngstown Folk Bring Christmas Cheer to Army Camps," *Niagara Falls Gazette*, December 26, 1944.

CHAPTER 3

BELL AIRCRAFT

WHILE THE SENIOR CLASS of the Youngstown High School finished the school year and prepared for final exams, the war was spreading in Europe. On May 10, 1940, the German troops began their sweep through Belgium, Holland, Luxembourg, and France. Holland's defenses were unable to stop the German Luftwaffe aircraft attacks and the Dutch surrendered on the fourteenth. Three days later the Panzer Division, German armored tanks, crossed the Meuse River and in June a major drive was launched into central France. A few days before graduation in Youngstown on June 22, 1940, the French signed the armistice with Germany.[103]

The Youngstown High School celebrated its Fourteenth Commencement when Rev. Charles Kieffer, C.M., of Niagara University addressed the seventeen graduates on June 25, 1940. "Where hatred exists there can be no peace nor happiness in the world or in the home. Leave from your lives things that destroy," Father told the graduates. Referring to the European war Father Kieffer said, "There was little cooperation among the Allied Powers before the war and that it was only when in danger that there was any real cooperation…this present war would not have happened if the Allies had in their hearts a little spirit of cooperation."[104] The graduating Class of 1940 was Norma Drinkwalter, Marjorie Brown, Eva Broeker, Adaline Pawlowski, Norma Allen, Olga Holody, Pat Maloney, Marge Rodenbaugh, Mary Schultz, Kenneth Diez, Roderick Tower, William Johnston, Freddy Nelson, Richard Jones, George Kathan, Milton Kulak, and Joyce Hardison.[105]

Some of these Youngstown graduates helped to bring an end to the war on the battlefields and through defense industries on the home front. Kenneth Diez reminisced about the efforts of his classmates. "Richard Jones served in the Army Air Corps and flew P-40s in China. Freddy Nelson was in the Army. Pat Maloney married a soldier from Fort Niagara and lived in the big house on River Road, the Pillars. George Kathan helped to test aircraft."

William D. "Budd" Johnston passed away in Omaha, Nebraska, on January 1, 2007. His obituary in the *Lewiston-Porter Sentinel* included entries from a family history album about Budd's military service. He served in the Coast Guard from July 1941 to July 1946 fighting in nine Pacific campaigns, and then enlisted in the Air Force in 1950 retiring in 1968. "He served on the *USS Wakefield* in the Pacific and on the *Callaway* as a radioman and ended up taking a kamikaze off Manila in 1945...for his service to his country, Budd received a Purple Heart and thirteen medals."

While Ken's classmates served on the battlefields, he and many others became part of the mammoth war effort at home.

VALEDICTORIAN ON THE BELL FLIGHTLINE ~ The Rev. Paul O. Voigt, Pastor of St. John's Lutheran Church, delivered the invocation at graduation. Kenneth George Diez, son of John and Edna Diez, gave the valedictorian address for the Youngstown High School Class of 1940. Ken was awarded the Alumni Award for scholarship presented by Miss Nellie Kolloff and the Principal's Award for Citizenship by Mrs. Edith T. Ripson. In less than a year Ken's recognition of citizenship activities expanded into an essential part of the war effort. Ironically, it was a war initiated from the homeland of his ancestors, his paternal grandparents.

Ken was born in the c. 1870 farmhouse at the corner of Youngstown-Wilson and Lutts Roads in the Town of Porter. His grandfather, Johann Friedrich Diez, emigrated from Germany to the town in 1867. Friedrich, his wife Anna Barbara, and their ten-month-old son Jacob, arrived via train in Lockport from New York City after a difficult journey across the Atlantic on the *SS Union*. One of the family stories about Friedrich was that he was trying to avoid military service in the imminent Franco-Prussian War by coming to America. But other ancestors served in the military. Jakob Friedrich Diez and Johann Friedrich Diez died serving with Napoleon during a terrible Russian winter in 1818.[106] Ken's great-uncle, Johann Albrecht Diez, fought with the Eighth New York Heavy Artillery at the Battle of Cold Harbor, and was buried at Arlington National Cemetery in Washington.[107] Ken wanted to enter the Army Air Corps, but did not pass the vision tests.

On his eighteenth birthday, February 18, 1941, Ken joined the war effort at the Bell Aircraft Plant on Elmwood Avenue in Buffalo. After several months he asked to be transferred to the plant on Niagara Falls Boulevard to be closer to home.[108] The Bell plant was building the P-39 Airacobra. "P" identifies the kind of plane, pursuit, and "39" indicates the plane was the thirty-ninth in the

A Bell Aircraft photo of P-39s lined up at the Wheatfield Plant. (Courtesy Kenneth Diez)

series of this type of aircraft. Eventually, pursuit aircraft were designated fighters, "F". Many American pilots gained their first experience of a single-seat high-performance aircraft in a P-39.[109] Ken worked attaching the wings and machine guns for the P-39s. Part of his work was to pre-flight the aircraft by checking the fuel oil and running the engines.

The United States Air Force Museum fact sheet describes the Bell P-39 as one of America's first-line pursuit aircraft in December of 1941. It made its initial flight in April 1939 at Wright Field and saw combat throughout the world, particularly in the southwest Pacific, Mediterranean, and Russian theaters. Because its engine was not equipped with a supercharger, the P-39 performed best below 17,000 feet, and was often used at lower altitudes for ground strafing missions. When the P-39 production ended in August 1944, Bell had built 9,584 Airacobras, 4,773 for the Soviet Union.

Ken was part of a four-man team that checked the aircraft on the flight line. The key man was Walt Zeihm, a mechanic, about fifty years old, Paul Downs about sixty years old, and a younger boy. Many of the P-39s were flown to Alaska, and then to Russia after being checked out, Ken said. Some of the P-39s were disassembled, crated and then shipped overseas. Ken continued to work at the Bell plant until early 1945 when production began to slow down and there were layoffs.

From left to right, Test Pilot Lt. Claude W. Rockabrand, Paul Downs, and Kenneth Diez checked out the P-39 at the Wheatfield Plant in this Bell Aircraft Photo. (Courtesy of Kenneth Diez)

The young farm boy was unaware of the labor issues taking place in the Bell plants. About 10,000 employees of Bell Aircraft's Wheatfield and Buffalo plants settled a contract dispute on December 12, 1941, in the interest of the nation. By July 4, 1943, 32,226 people were employed in the plants, which operated seven days a week, twenty-four hours a day.[110] The Niagara Frontier was a major cog in the war machine and "the sixth largest industrial production center measured by defense contract dollars, according to United States War Production reports."[111]

After the aircraft was checked on the ground, test pilots took it up and then reported any problems to the ground crew. One of the pilots was Lt. Claude W. Rockabrand. Ken called "Rocky" his friend and wanted to go up in the single-seat P-39 with him. They tried one day. Rocky took off his parachute and sat on Ken's lap. "Our feet were too big and Rocky couldn't use the rudders," with a smile of admiration Ken retold his dream to go up in the P-39 with his friend, the test pilot.[112]

A TEST PILOT ~ Claude Walter Rockabrand was born August 26, 1920. He played football and basketball while in high school in St. Charles, Illinois, and after graduation attended the University of Cincinnati to study engineering. Military recruiters came to the campus in 1940 looking for potential pilots. Rocky commented, "There were about four hundred people that took the test. You needed eighty percent to pass. Some tried three times. There were questions on algebra, physics, chemistry, English, and social sciences. They were looking for engineering types. Only fifty-eight passed the test."[113]

Rocky passed the test with flying colors and entered the Army Air Corps at Peoria, Illinois. He started as an aviation cadet in March 1941. His primary flight training was in Muskogee, Oklahoma, then on to Brady, Texas, for basics. Later, he was stationed as a Flying Cadet at Kelly Field, Texas, for advanced training. During training there was a mid-air collision as Rocky dove through a mushroom cloud. Rocky said, "The tail was hit. I bailed out with my pant leg on fire and landed in a ravine in some water!" Rocky broke his nose and was bleeding badly. Some ranchers saw the collision and came to carry him out of the water. The ranchers put Rocky on a horse and transported him from the ravine to their farm. "Every bone in my body ached. A lady took one look at me and passed out. The daughter said to me 'drink this. It is straight bourbon.' The other pilot bailed out too. He was shook up and had some cuts and bruises. He was also transported to the farm on a horse. When he got to the farm, the horse threw him off, and he broke his shoulder."

The medical staff at the hospital wanted to amputate Rocky's leg, but he wouldn't let them. His buddies helped him escape from the hospital and hid him in an abandoned WWI barracks. Eventually he went home to recuperate for a few weeks. When he returned, the commanding officer put him through extensive maneuvers in the air. "They put me up in an AT-6 for a check ride,"[114] Rocky said. The Colonel's first words to Rocky when they landed were: "you are not going to be a fighter pilot. You are too good of a pilot. We are going to make you a test pilot! You are going to Curtiss-Wright (Buffalo, New York)."[115]

One day Rocky and another pilot were flying over the Fort Erie racetrack in a C-46, the Curtiss Commando. With binoculars the pilots could see the #4 horse win the race. They called the control tower in Niagara Falls to place a bet with the bookies in Buffalo and in New York City on #4 to win. In those days the race results were delayed by thirty minutes over the wire service. "The Commanding Officer found out what we did and gave us hell!" Rocky said.

From Curtiss-Wright, Rocky went to Bell Aircraft, later known as Bell Aerospace. He tested more than 150 different aircraft in one month. Some of the missions were at night and during snowstorms. Rocky's favorite plane was a stripped P-63 King Cobra. "It climbed real fast, turned well, did dives well, and had a lot of fire power!" he said. During his military career he tested aircraft built by Boeing, Lockheed, Bell, and Curtiss including the P-40, P-36, P-51, B-25, B-24, B-17, C-46, P-47s, and the XP-59, the first jet.[116]

The Air Force museum's fact sheet noted Bell Aircraft's role in the development of the P-59, as America's first jet-propelled airplane. Bell built the aircraft and GE built the engine. The first P-59 was completed in mid-1942 and on October 1, 1942, it made its initial flight at Muroc Dry Lake.[117] The following year it was ordered into production to be powered by I-14 and I-16 engines.[118]

Bell produced sixty-six P-59s. Although the airplane's performance was not spectacular and it never got into combat, the P-59 provided training for Army Air Corps personnel and invaluable data for subsequent development of higher performance jet aircraft.

TABLE 3.1
Specifications of P-59 Airacomet

XP-59A	3 built, first AAF jet aircraft
YP-59A	13 built, service test aircraft
P-59A	20 built
P-59B	30 built, improved P-59A

Specifications of P-59B

Span	45 ft. 6 in.
Length	38 ft. 10 in.
Height	11 ft. 11-3/4 in.
Weight	10,532 lbs. loaded
Armament	One 37mm cannon and three .50-cal Machine guns
Engines	Two General Electric (GE) I-16s of 1,650 lb. thrust each
Maximum speed	450 mph
Cruising speed	320 mph
Range	440 mi.
Service Ceiling	43,400 ft.

Source: Reprinted by permission from the "Bell P-59 Airacomet," Fact Sheets, *National Museum of the USAF*, http://www.nationalmuseum.af.mil/factsheets/factsheet.asp?id=2215 [accessed March 5, 2008].

While at Bell, Rocky flew under the Rainbow Bridge at Niagara Falls, but was caught. "I have the pictures to prove it," he said. One time he decided to buzz a farmer who was pulling a manure spreader. Someone reported Rocky and he was called in to see Larry Bell. "Larry Bell grabbed me and said, what are you doing buzzing the farmers?" Remembering the incident with a chuckle, Rocky said he denied it to Bell as he walked out on the flight line to inspect the airplane. There was manure on the oil coolers at the leading edge of the wing. Bell reported this to Rocky's commanding officer.

There was more than testing Bell aircraft for Rocky and the other pilots. On January 6, 1942, Rocky, in uniform, sat in a movie theater in Buffalo. He enjoyed telling the next story. "There was a girl with gorgeous, long, black hair sitting in front of me in the theater. I pulled her hair! We went out to dinner after the movie. I was the most fortunate guy to get her address." In September 1943 Rocky married Arline, the girl with the long black hair.

Rocky was transferred to Alaska and on to Russia to help the Russians solve their cold weather problems with the P-39s. The Russian pilots only had about fifteen to thirty hours of flying time and then were pushed to the front, Rocky said. The winters were so cold the pilots were unable to get the engines started. Rocky told the Russians, "let them (the engines) run all night! Who cares?" So the Russians did, and that solved the problem.

About half of the P-39 fighters produced were shipped to the Soviet Union. The executives at Bell were soured on their Soviet ally after the chief of Bell's Russian office turned out to be a secret agent. He attempted to bribe the Bell librarian for blueprints.[119]

On June 16, 2006, Rocky sat with his son, Steve C. Rockabrand, and a friend, Michael T. Ellis. More than a half-century had passed since Rocky's test pilot days at Bell Aircraft. Rocky looked back on the events of the war and his lifetime. He spoke of Roosevelt as a great president. "He brought the country out of the depression. Truman's decision to drop the atomic bomb saved lives. It was the greatest decision. Reagan helped to 'tear the wall down'[120] and Jack Kennedy got the country united to send a man to the moon." These were Rocky's choices for outstanding American presidents.

When Rocky was asked by his son, Steve, "What do you think about spaceflight?" he replied, "I didn't think we would ever land on the moon. Now we have technology that blows your mind. We are going to go farther than the moon. We are going to go to outer space and other planets!"[121]

At the end of the war, Rocky was honorably discharged with the rank of Captain. He served in the Reserves and retired as a Major. There were many other test pilots, military and civilians. "We lost a lot of them. I am ashamed that the United States did not recognize the test pilots who were killed or wounded. There were no medals for them. Those guys were heroes. Aviation came a long way because of those guys!"

Claude W. "Rocky" Rockabrand passed away January 11, 2007, in Thousand Oaks, California.

P-39s FOR THE FRENCH ~ For a moment it was as if the history of the forty-foot wingspan of the Wright 1903 Flyer reached across the sky and came face to face with the birth of jet-powered flight, and the nose of the then secret XP-59! Five special people during the course of the later weeks of August in 2006 shared the evolution of Larry Bell and the aircraft industry: A. Joseph Marchese, Michael Locurcio, Roberta Henderson, Audrey Schillo, and Hugh M. Neeson, a young boy during the war. They held positions of loftsman, design engineer, inspector, keypunch operator, liaison officer, project manager, vice-president, general manager, teleprinter operator, and executive secretary during their careers at Bell.

"We lived in the backyard of the Curtiss plant. I graduated from high school and wanted to go to Albany State, but my parents couldn't afford it. So I went to Bryant and Stratton (Business Institute) instead."[122] Roberta began her story of a myriad of jobs at Bell as the aircraft industry evolved. She was hired immediately from the interview and worked initially in the telegraph department. "It was an ordeal to get to work. My dad let me take his 1937 Packard." Eventually, Roberta bought her own car to drive to work, a 1936 Ford convertible that cost $300.00 from Muck Motors.

The day after Pearl Harbor, December 8, 1941, the roof of the Bell Elmwood plant was covered with armed soldiers for security. Roberta began to recount the early Bell story. "The first order for the P-39s was from the French. When the French surrendered, the British took the order over. 'What do you need for initial funding?' they asked (Larry) Bell. He told them $50,000. They sent 50,000 pounds instead of dollars! Nothing would satisfy them," remembering the British dislike for the P-39s. One of their objections to the P-39s was the tricycle landing gear. "But the Russians were desperately in need of airplanes. They were the only ones that liked them (the P-39s)," Roberta noted. The Soviet aces were very effective in using the P-39s and accomplished the majority of their kills using that airplane.

Roberta carefully held the photograph album that told her life story and career at Bell. Some of the images were photos of her and other women at the teleprinters. This communication device had a large printer that received and typed the incoming telegraph. It dwarfed the typewriter keyboard at its base.

One day Larry Bell was waiting impatiently for news to come through the teleprinter from Wright Field. Roberta explained to Bell how it took a great deal of time for the messages to get through. "He was more patient after the explanation," she said. Some of the telegrams received were for relatives of people working on the floor. The dreaded message began: "We regret to inform you…." Roberta did not deliver any of these telegrams. She said, "Someone at Bell who knew the person brought them the painful news."

The poster of "Rosie the Riveter was funny, but true," said Roberta about women's expanded role in the war and in the workplace. "Women were treated well (at Bell). We were paid the same as men. But for the most part, women were looking for the end (of the war). In the meantime you could have a lot of fun. Bowling was big during the war," she said. One of her photographs was of a Bell Christmas party. "Bob Woods liked to play Santa." Roberta sat on his lap in the photograph apparently giving Woods her Christmas list, maybe a design for a new airplane. Robert J. Woods was the leading design engineer at Bell. Prior to Bell, he worked at Consolidated as their chief fighter design engineer and designed the Consolidated A-11s.[123]

Roberta mentioned Arthur Young, Floyd Carlson, and others who worked to develop helicopters at Gardenville.[124] "There were thirty-five employees. It was like a miniature factory. We ate lunch at Schmolz's across the street."[125]

Roberta turned the pages of the album and her life, and photos of soldiers dancing with her and other women at *Camp Bell.* The music of *I'll Never Smile Again* and *When the Lights go on all over the World* were some of the songs of the evening. Remembering the dances with soldiers Roberta remarked, "They were nice looking and nice to talk to. And they were homesick."

Other names from the past were part of the conversation: Bob Stanley, Jay Deming, Frank "Bud" Kelly, and Joe Cannon. Roberta also took dictation from Fran Dunn and typed the thirty-five-page speech that Leston Faneuf gave to The Newcomen Society at the Buffalo Club in Buffalo, New York, on May 15, 1958.[126] The address was entitled "Lawrence D. Bell A Man And His Company Bell Aircraft." Roberta's career also encompassed being the "Second girl in Bill

Gisel's office. I reminded him when the bank notes were due," she said. William G. Gisel was the President of Bell from 1960 to 1985.

Like so many others at the time, Roberta's brother served overseas in Germany. "He served in the Third Army as a truck driver. I would have held it against the Germans if he had been killed." Roberta continued about Bell Aircraft. "It was a big friendly company," remembering her career from c. 1940 until 1992. "As long as the war had to be, I was glad to come out of it with some firm friends," as she looked around her living room and smiled at Hugh Neeson and Michael Locurcio.

Roberta C. Henderson passed away February 12, 2007.

X-1 SUPERSONIC FLIGHT ~ Joe Marchese and Mike Locurcio were born and raised in Buffalo, both sons of Italian immigrants. "We lived in 'The Hooks.' It was a block off Main Street, the ghetto," and Mike chuckled. Joe grew up on the east side off Seneca Street near Chef's, a popular Italian Restaurant in Buffalo.[127] Mike was part of the secret jet development while Hugh Neeson was in grade school reading current events and placing stars on a world map.[128]

Joe signed the copy of *A Brief History of Bell Aircraft Corporation*, the 50th Anniversary Booklet 1947-1997 of Bell Aircraft's X-1, the world's first supersonic airplane. He wrote in 1997 that the sponsoring X-1 committee hoped that the narratives "will generate a reawakening of proud memories for all in our Western New York area, and especially for those who contributed in the design, building, and testing of this world famous airplane, the Bell X-1."[129]

The anniversary booklet featured an image of all the representatives of the departments involved with the design, building, and testing of the X-1: Dick Frost, Jerry LaVenture, Harold Dow, Herman Schneider, Ben Hamlin, Clarence Quillan, George White, Bill Smith, Steve Elggren, Julius Domonkos, Jack Strickler, Larry Bell, Leston Faneuf, Harvey Gaylord, Ray Whitman, Stanley Smith, Bob Woods, Roy Sandstrom, Paul Emmons, Joe Marchese, and David Devine. Larry Bell wrote on the original photo: "Best regards to Joe, Larry Bell 4/15/49."

Joe educated himself through home studies and correspondence courses. In his early working career Joe worked as a liaison man in the design, assembly, and installation of specialized restaurant equipment. Prior to this position, he worked in the manufacture of ladies apparel then transferred his skills into the aircraft industry when he started at Curtiss, first at Vulcan Street then Elmwood Avenue. He spent three years at Curtiss in one of the design groups. "I worked on the P-40, other small fighter airplanes, and the Curtiss XSBC-1. As the liaison engineer I got to work with different departments."

In 1937 one of the Curtiss project engineers left and went to work at Bell. Joe followed him a short time later and started at the Elmwood plant. "I looked at it as a new age!" Joe described Larry Bell as "a human being. He stopped and said hello to everyone and asked, 'How are your kids?' He was a likeable guy." Bell gathered all the employees for announcements and also enjoyed bringing prominent people into the facilities. Joe remembered one of those days when Franklin and Eleanor Roosevelt visited the plant. "It was really nice to see a president."

Joe worked at Bell in Liaison Engineering. He made certain everything in the operation from design to production went well, coordinating all the steps. If there was an inconsistency in part of the process, Joe ensured the problem was addressed at the right level. The workforce included women. "Women were no different than the men; just another worker. Women pilots volunteered and were recruited to deliver airplanes up to Alaska (for the Russians). They were never recognized by the government during the war," he said.

Joe was the Assistant Project Manager of Bell Aircraft's X-1. In the story of this first supersonic aircraft Joe's bio stated: "Experienced in all aspects of the management processes of transforming engineering designs into flight hardware and its subsequent testing."[130] As Joe was doing his job on the X-1, Larry Bell walked behind him. Bell watched again during the historic moment as A. Joseph Marchese carefully placed the Bell insignia on the X-1. He mentioned some of the later alterations made to the rocket airplane. "There were very important modifications to the horizontal stabilizers so the pilot would have the ability to change its angle of attack in flight," he said.

"Joe pounded on the table" to get people's attention to take control of the problems that arose during development and production, Mike remembered and smiled as he said, "It worked." Joe looked back on his life's work and said, "I am most proud of being in the aircraft industry at that time and especially being with Bell Aircraft, a pioneering company in the industry. Bell encouraged his designers to think and promote designs for aircraft that would go higher and faster than any other airplane." Fortunately, Bell Helicopter survives to this very day being one of the largest manufacturers of rotary winged aircraft in the world.

A. Joseph Marchese of Williamsville, New York, an aviation pioneer at Bell Aircraft, passed away December 1, 2006.

After the war Bell hired Gen. Walter Dornberger. "Dornberger was a constant advocate of space flight," Hugh added. During the war Dornberger and Dr. Wernher von Braun worked on the development of the German V-1 and V-2 rockets at the Peenemünde Rocket Research Center.[131] "V" for Vergeltungswaffen or reprisal weapon was also known as a "flying bomb." During this time Bell did pioneering work on spacecraft designs i.e. Dyna-Soar (Dynamic Soaring), guided missiles, and liquid rocket engines for space vehicles.

TOP SECRET XP-59 ~ Mike Locurcio began to chronicle his role in the Bell story.[132] He was attending Burgard Vocational High School in Buffalo, New York, in 1939, one of five students chosen by Michael Steffan for a summer program at Bell with the condition that the students would return to school and finish their studies. Mike completed a Lofting Course from Emio P. Grenier at Burgard doing the geometry of full-scale aircraft. Lofting is the development of full-sized drawing patterns using analytical geometry and wood battens, held down by lead "Ducks." This generated varying curves on a flat surface. Lofting evolved from shipbuilding skills developed in the early 1800s, Mike said.

Mike returned to Burgard to finish his senior year in January of 1941 as part of the Class of 1941. After graduation he went to Bell to apply for a job. There was a job for Mike on the assembly line if he wanted it, but he didn't. "I accumulated my own drawings, which they looked at," during Mike's interview for a position with the Chief Loftsman. He was grilled with questions about the geometric lines and mathematics, and then hired.

A new airplane was developed and built in great secrecy by Bell Aircraft at the former Ford Assembly Plant on Main and Rodney in Buffalo. "We had two badge passes, one to get in the building, and one for the floor where we worked on the airplane. It was top secret," he said. Mike continued, "I knew it had to be a jet because there was no room in the nose for the prop. One of the first jobs I worked on was to prove analytically that the skewed axis landing gear would in fact retract. We worked out the geometry by lofting," as he explained how the lofting lines were scribed on the wood floor. "It was design work that was done in a humidity and temperature controlled room. The room was about twenty-four feet by sixty feet." The designs gave birth to the XP-59A, also known as Airacomet, the first jet propelled fighter airplane in the Unites States.

Mike admired the Bell built XP-77. "It was an all wood military fighter airplane and it was beautiful!" He continued, "Bell built the B-29 wing panels at the Main Street plant. The B-29 was a Boeing design; however, the government divided the production between Glenn Martin Corporation and Bell. B-29s were produced at the Bell plant in Marietta, Georgia." Mike also spoke highly of Larry Bell. "He cared for human interest before anything else and asked about your kids, school, your family life, and also started up the retirement plan," Mike said with appreciation.

Mike worked at Bell for four and a half years until he was drafted in 1944 and began basic training on June 28, 1944. Training continued at Camp Swift in Texas for the ski and parachute troops. "In 1945, we were shipped over to Korea to rebuild bridges, but I only shouldered a rifle. We thought we would need to get ready for Japan and then the bomb was dropped." When Mike returned home he used the G.I. Bill to attend the University of Buffalo and obtain his degree in Mechanical Engineering.

After the war years Larry Bell was committed to do research on airplanes, guided missiles, and helicopters. The new models of aircraft were pushing the state of art as Joe, Mike, and Hugh discussed the post-war aviation industry and Bell. They agreed that Larry Bell was an effective leader and let people know they were working on the right thing. It was an important motivating factor and the contributions of these Bell employees soared through the development of airplanes, helicopters, missiles, and rockets. They enjoyed their individual roles working for a dynamic leader, participating in the development of the industry, and the significant role that Bell Aircraft and its employees in Western New York played in the history of the war.

OFF WE GO INTO THE WILD BLUE YONDER ~ Audrey Schillo's narrative began as a sales person at J. N. Adams Department Store in downtown Buffalo for $14.00 a week after graduating from Mount St. Joe's High School in a college prep program.[133] She worked her way up to assistant buyer at $20.00, but it wasn't enough money. A friend of Audrey's started working at Bell for $34.80. "It was big bucks. People were pouring into Bell from all over. Bill Fuller interviewed me with some others. Some of us were told to come back; not me, but I did anyway. He asked me 'Did I tell you to come back today?' I told him 'yes' and was hired and then trained to be an inspector."

Her inspector role was to check the camouflage paint on the wings. The top was painted green and light gray on the bottom so it would be less visible from the ground. Audrey also checked the horizontal stabilizers and later the tail cone for the B-17. The airplanes were loaded with decals and were checked to be sure they were in the right place. One morning Audrey reported to the night supervisor, "The paint is upside down." The paint was removed before repainting since two coats made the assembly too heavy.

On May 8, 1943, Audrey and all the workers received a certificate of high honor that acknowledged their contribution to the war effort. The employees were also given an Army - Navy "E" White Star Award pin, a long held treasure. The "E" stood for excellence. Hugh added that the certificate and pin were just one part of the massive efforts directed at employee morale.

The Schillo household heard news of the war from their radio. Roosevelt's "Fireside Chats" and Father Edward Flanagan's radio broadcasts were favorites of the entire Schillo family. "Roosevelt had a wonderful delivery. I still think he was the best president we ever had because he introduced Social Security," Audrey said. The family lived on Deerfield in Buffalo. Audrey's father, Charles Schillo, was a railroad man. "He designed the yards at the Central Terminal as well as other New York Central facilities," Audrey said.

Audrey worked at the Elmwood plant during the war. "There were three shifts a day. Between each shift we sang, "Off we go into the wild blue yonder…," and Audrey and Hugh sang it again. Her stint as an inspector lasted three months; then, she went into production control until the end of the war coordinating the shipment of spare parts. "One wing for the P-39 was $5,000," she said recalling an order. Eventually, "IBM came in and taught us how to keypunch. I became the supervisor of the keypunch operators." Hugh remarked, "It was the beginning of automation in the industry. Bell was one of the first companies to purchase IBM computers for engineering usage. Every time IBM came out with a new computer Bell purchased it."

"Women wore pants when we worked on the floor. I was so happy later on when I worked in an office position so I could wear a dress again. There was a class distinction between the women in pants and those in dresses," she said. More than half a century later Audrey still enjoys her lady-like attire that she carries well on her regal stature.

On VJ Day Audrey went downtown with her mother to Shelton Square. "It was where Kleinhans Men's Clothing Store used to be. We joined the celebration and flag waving." Audrey continued relating her life long career at Bell. "When Larry Bell died on October 20, 1956, his death was a loss to not only the Air Force, but the nation. She drove her pink Cadillac to the funeral home and was surprised that her car was waved into the parking area because there were so many people present. Audrey found out later that Ray Whitman also owned a pink Cadillac and that her car was likely mistaken for his! Whitman was the First Executive Vice President and Manager of the Niagara Frontier Division.

Audrey studied at Bryant and Stratton Business School after the war through a Bell sponsored program for higher education. In 1957 she became a secretary for Lionel Shub in the electronics-engineering department. "Electronics was becoming the dominant force in the industry," Audrey noted. Bell was working on automatic aircraft carrier landing systems, which are installed on all United States Navy Carriers today and will be for the foreseeable future. Audrey retired from Bell in 1980, but her work in the aircraft and aerospace industry continues to be part of her life as the secretary for the Buffalo Aero Club, a position she has held since 1983.

THE EVOLUTION OF BELL AIRCRAFT ~ For Hugh M. Neeson it took a decade after the war before his career began at Bell Aircraft. The war began for him when the Japanese bombed Pearl Harbor. "I can paint a picture of where I was sitting on that day. My father was cutting my hair after Mass on Sunday. The GE clock radio, that I still have, was on top of the refrigerator."[134] Hugh was in grammar school at Winchester #8 in the West Seneca School System. Richard Ferrand was the Principal.[135] When the war broke out Mr. Ferrand placed a world map in every classroom. Students were required to read the *Buffalo Evening News* at night and listened to WBEN in the morning, the Clint Buehlman's "AM MC CB Show."[136] The next day in school, students marked the battle or other event locations on the map with stars as the war progressed.

Hugh's father, Hugh, was an Air Raid Warden on their street, Olean Avenue in Winchester, West Seneca. In addition to having lights off at a certain time "men's smoking pipes had to be turned upside down while smoking, and there was no lighting up outside!" The massive evidence of war production was just outside the Neeson family's door. They lived across from the railroad tracks. "We had a deep appreciation of the military arsenal. There were whole trains loaded with military trucks and armored cars from Pennsylvania via the Lehigh Valley Railroad. Many evenings my dad would drive out to the Curtiss-Wright Plant at the Buffalo Airport and watch the test flights of the P-40s," Hugh said.

Like many first generation Americans and immigrants, the Neesons had family overseas. Hugh remarked, "We lived the war. We had relatives in Scotland. Mother Winifred made up care packages with cookies and so forth to send to our family." The Neeson family kept abreast of the war news reading the morning *Courier Express* and the *Buffalo Evening News*. Hugh's father was well read and Winston Churchill's writings were prominent literary works in the Neeson household. Hugh retold the current events news reports of the fall of the Philippines, the Battle of Midway, the Bataan March, D-Day, VE and VJ day, and later the Marshall Plan and the Berlin Airlift. But it was not until after the war that the news of what happened in the concentration camps and in Japanese POW camps began to be reported at home.

The Neeson family's connection to twentieth century military history began with Hugh's Uncle Titus who served in the British Artillery in WWI. He was killed in the Battle of Somme, one of the bloodiest battles of that war. The British Commonwealth suffered about 420,000 casualties during the campaign

Bell Aircraft and military officials gathered for this Bell photo during an inspection in December 1942. (Courtesy Niagara Falls (New York) Public Library)

near the Somme River in France.[137] Later in the war, Hugh's father, and his uncle, Charlie, were pulled out of the induction line by the examining Army doctor who told them to "stand aside, one is enough, go home (referring to Titus' sacrifice)," which probably saved their lives.

Early in the 1940s there were family trips to visit Mary Kerestory at the George Olmsted summer home on Lower River Road in Lewiston. The outing also featured 'going out' to Bea and George Doody's farm on Balmer Road not far from the McCann family farm, and to visit Mary Sullivan in Youngstown. Bea Doody and Winifred, Hugh's mother, worked for the Olmsted's on Windsor Avenue in Buffalo and at the summer home.[138] Hugh saw the Army trucks with a guard in the rear traveling on River Road during the family ride. Mrs. Doody told the Neeson family that the truck was filled with POWs from Fort Niagara going to work on the nearby fruit farms.

Providence directed the rides down the escarpment and the old Lewiston hill for those visits while Hugh and his family traveled through the Village of

Lewiston. Marilyn McCann was growing up in the house on Center Street next to Tops Market. After Pearl Harbor, Marilyn, her parents, Joseph and Evelyn, and her brother James (Jim) were forced to move to Lewiston after their farmhouse on Balmer Road, west of Lutts Road in the Town of Porter, was taken by the United States Government to allow for the construction of the LOOW plant. Other families in Porter including the Doody's were forced from their homes and farms.

The McCann family raised dairy cows and workhorses on their eighty-acre farm, which included forty acres of peaches. Marilyn and Jim attended Rural School No. 11, a one-room schoolhouse on Lutts Road, until their life was turned upside down when the government mandated the family move within a week. Joseph McCann was compensated $12,000 for his farm including the house, barn, small sheds, and acreage.[139] By 1943 a federal committee was established to examine the issue of over building ordnance-plant capacity. Harry S. Truman wrote in his memoirs that the committee found the cost of building and the number of ordnance plants excessive and unnecessary.[140] Thus, despite all the travails of the Porter township families TNT was produced in the Model City facility for only about nine months.[141] In the 1950s, 1960s, and 1970s Bell Aircraft used the Model City area for rocket engine testing.[142]

Jim McCann wrote to some local boys serving overseas. One young man, the son of Curly Woodard, the family's hired man on the farm, served in the Pacific and died in Bataan. When the war was over, the McCann's and other families found that most of their homes and barns destroyed. The government offered the family the opportunity to buy back their farm at the same price, but the house and barn were gone, orchards neglected, and scrub brush overtaking the fields.

For Hugh, the end of the war was most memorable! "We were vacationing in Orillia, Ontario. My father loved horse racing and earlier in the week picked up a copy of the *Toronto Star* to check on the race results. A photograph of the Hiroshima bombing covered the entire front page. On the way home we began to see people coming out of their homes celebrating and waving their flags all along the Queen E.[143] My father stopped and asked, 'What's going on?' The answer was 'the war is over – Japan surrendered!' The celebration continued as we crossed into America at the old Lewiston-Queenston Bridge."

Ten years later in 1955 Hugh graduated from Canisius College in Buffalo, New York, with a Degree in Physics. Father Growney, the pastor of St. William's Parish in West Seneca, asked his long-term altar boy a question. "What are you going to do now Hugh?" The question charted a flight plan for him to

Bell Aircraft. Father knew Lyle Watt, the head of the engineering employment department at Bell, and told Hugh, "I'll call Lyle tomorrow." Within a week Hugh joined the Bell family and became part of the fabric of the aerospace history. He was assigned the employee Pin #91103. In the main engineering room where Hugh sat at his first desk "there were four hundred people, desk next to desk, and with only one telephone for each twenty or thirty people. After the war, Larry Bell continued to bring famous people through the plant including Lucille Ball and Desi Arnaz," Hugh said.

Hugh resumed the story of the growth of Bell Aircraft. "In the late 1930s President Roosevelt was becoming aware that America needed to become ready for entry into the war that erupted in Europe. He began to organize the government and get industry on board. One of the most famous programs was the Lend Lease Project. In 1935 Larry Bell formed his company." Bell Aircraft was incorporated on July 10, 1935. Lawrence "Larry" D. Bell and Robert J. Woods, the Chief Design Engineer, moved into offices at 1807 Elmwood Avenue in Buffalo. Bell also leased the former site of the Consolidated Aircraft Corporation plant at 2050 Elmwood Avenue. The factory area was forty thousand square feet of a nearly two million square feet facility.[144]

In September 1935 Bell received a contract from the Army to install Allison engines in the Consolidated A-11 attack airplane. By the end of the year there were fifty-six employees. The following year there was an announcement in February of a contract with the Navy to manufacture wing panels and some parts. Bell leased an additional 40,000 square feet of floor space and in May a contract was received for the XFM-1, the Airacuda, a two-engine fighter aircraft. Near the end of the summer 105,000 square feet of space was leased from American Radiator and by December 31, 1935, the number of employees grew to 642.[145]

Bell built thirteen Airacudas, which Hugh said were somewhat cumbersome; in particular bailing out of the pusher aircraft was not a prospect that excited the "boom-gunners." Then, Bell Aircraft began designs for a front-line fighter, the P-39 Airacobra. It was an all-metal medium altitude pursuit fighter. About the same time Curtiss-Wright developed the P-40s in Buffalo. "America went to war with the P-39 and P-40. Together almost 25,000 were built in Western New York. The P-40 was more highly regarded and attained more notoriety. The Army Air Corps thought that most combat would be below 20,000 feet, so the supercharger was not approved for the Airacobra and the P-40. They were also over burdened with armor plating to protect the pilots, which sacrificed agility and made the airplane logy. The Japanese didn't care about pilot safety, hence the Zero was highly maneuverable. Chennault compensated for his P-40 aircraft de-

Jary Johnson ferried this P-40 from Buffalo to Fort Myers, Florida. (Collection No. mss250.30.6, Courtesy The Women's Collection, Texas Woman's University, Denton, TX)

ficiencies with tactics to beat the Zeros. The Russians did the same with the P-39s." Hugh continued about the history of the Airacobra. "It was a myth that the P-39 was not good as a fighter. Half of the kills by the Russians were with the P-39s. The Russian representatives stationed at Bell were regarded as potential spies. We gave them minimal radio equipment on the P-39s."

TABLE 3.2
Specifications P-40E Warhawk

Span	37 ft. 4 in.
Length	31 ft. 9 in.
Height	12 ft. 4 in.
Weight	9,100 lbs. loaded
Armament	Six .50-cal. Machine guns; 700 lbs. of bombs externally

Engine	Allison V-1710 of 1,150 hp
Cost	$45,000
Maximum speed	362 mph
Cruising speed	235 mph
Range	850 mi.
Service ceiling	30,000 ft.

Source: Reprinted by permission from the "Curtiss P-40E Warhawk", Fact Sheet, *National Museum of the USAF*, http://www.nationalmuseum.af.mil [accessed March 5, 2008].

In September 1940, Bell signed a lease with the City of Niagara Falls to use the airport and construction began for the adjacent Bell plant. When Ken Diez of Youngstown was transferred from Elmwood to Wheatfield, he helped pour concrete until production began at the new facility. On October 12, 1940, the first production P-39 Airacobra was delivered to the Army Air Corps at Wright Field. The workforce grew to 4,339 employees by December 31, 1940. The following year there were orders for more than 2,000 P-39 airplanes.[146]

On September 4, 1941, Gen. Henry "Hap" Arnold called Larry Bell to Washington and said, "Bring your best engineer." Great Britain knew that Germany was building a jet aircraft. The British had their own concept for a jet, which was revealed to General Arnold. Subsequently Bell Aircraft was given a secret contract for America's first jet. The aircraft was to be powered with two jet propulsion engines being built by GE in Schenectady, New York.[147] It was classified Top Secret. Bell, concerned with the Russians in the Wheatfield plant, leased the former Ford Motor Assembly Plant on Main and Rodney. (In later years it was the Trico plant.) After the jet was built, Hugh noted that "for security purposes the aircraft was disguised with a wooden propeller and inlets covered such that spying eyes couldn't tell it was a jet" when it was taken to Muroc Lake. Chief Test Pilot Robert M. Stanley tested the XP-59A October 1, 1942, and later piloted the more powerful XP-63, the Kingcobra, in its first flight.[148] The P-63 succeeded the P-39 later in the war and featured a turbo charged engine and a four bladed propeller. The Kingcobra was a much improved war airplane and after the war went on to win the famous Thompson Air Races in Ohio.[149]

On December 13, 1941, Bell Aircraft entered a seven-day week production schedule. The following day Larry Bell received the news from Washington that Bell Aircraft was chosen to build the B-29s and on December 23, 1941, the first group of women started on the production line in Buffalo. The number of employees almost tripled to 11,082.[150]

Hugh continued the discussion of wartime aircraft development. "There was a troubling experience with high performance fighters, the P-51 Mustang and the P-47 Thunderbolt. During high speed dives turbulence was encountered and there seemed to be something preventing flying faster than the speed of sound. In some cases the aircraft came apart. Bob Woods began to work on the top-secret X-1, which featured a bullet like fuselage and rocket propulsion. As was mentioned earlier, the aircraft featured an all-moveable horizontal stabilizer. At first it was pre-set on the ground, later made moveable in flight by the pilot. It became a key factor in allowing the X-1 to break the sound barrier. The principle of an adjustable horizontal stabilizer became a critical feature on all American jet fighters. 'Top secret' was quickly stamped on the design. The Russians didn't find out about the stabilizer until some F-86s were shot down. The Brits were mad too that they were kept in the dark as to this critical development."[151]

The workforce at Bell Aircraft was growing at an astronomical rate. By January 1, 1943, there were 29,953 employees, and by May women made up about forty-seven percent of all Bell workers.[152] The excitement of a young boy watching the testing of the P-40s during WWII was resurrected and vibrant in the voice of the retired Vice-President and General Manager of Bell Aerospace. "The hallmarks of the aerospace industry that evolved from the legacy of Larry Bell and his company are in the Smithsonian in Washington, DC: the XP-59, America's first jet aircraft and the supersonic X-1 flown by Maj. Charles "Chuck" Yeager, and the Bell 47D-1 in the Guggenheim Museum of Modern Art in New York City. Few people realize how well served we Americans and the world have been by our government and the aviation industry," as Hugh commented on these developments and aviation history.

Hugh remarked about Larry Bell's atypical hiring practices of that era. "Bell's policy was to hire only the best, the top ten percent of the class." He hired women and other minorities more than two decades prior to Affirmative Action. By 1941, more than ten percent of the workforce in the Niagara Frontier included persons with disabilities, and women headed up sub-sections in the aerodynamics departments.

Hugh's first assignment was on the Rascal Missile in 1955. The Rascal, the GAM-63,[153] was a major project for the United States Air Force. Hugh said that it was part of a huge United States effort to re-arm in the 1950s. Rascal was one of eight major strategic programs being sponsored by the United States Air

Force. The missile was going to be nuclear armed, launched from a bomber one hundred miles from the target allowing the aircrew to escape the blast, therefore the apt nickname "Crew Saver."

Beyond the aircraft and design projects there was time for a love story underway in the Bell Wheatfield facility. Marilyn McCann was a graduate from the last senior class at the Lewiston Red Brick School in 1952.[154] Her secretarial studies at Bryant and Stratton prepared her for the day that she dressed up with gloves and hat, boarded five different buses from Buffalo to Niagara Falls to arrive at Bell for an interview. Marilyn was first assigned to Bell's "Wallpaper Plant" in Niagara Falls then transferred to the security department at the Wheatfield plant as a secretary. Hugh pursued her, initially unsuccessfully. He joked that Marilyn knew more about him since she had complete access to his employment file. On April 28, 1962, after wooing her, Hugh and Marilyn were married in the historic St. Peter's Catholic Church on Plain Street in the Village of Lewiston. Reflecting on the war years and his life, Hugh is thankful today for forty-four years of marriage, four children, nine grandchildren, many memories, and his career at Bell.

While women were making strides in administrative positions, working in traditional male roles on the production lines in Bell and other facilities, outside the factory doors on the runways, women climbed into the cockpit and began an extraordinary chapter in aviation history.

WOMEN AIR FORCE SERVICE PILOTS ~ The strength in her voice resonated through the telephone lines and reflected an astonishing piece of aviation history. Betty Jane Williams was born and raised in eastern Pennsylvania. She was an honor student throughout her formal education with a concentration in Fine Arts. Then, Betty caught an aviation bug during the depression. She was the sole female competing with fifty males for a scholarship in a federally sponsored Civilian Pilot Training Program. Betty won the scholarship and received her pilot's license in June of 1941.[155] But her flying career came to an abrupt halt after the attack by Japan on Pearl Harbor. Civilian aviation on both coasts was grounded, but Betty was determined to stay airborne and became an airline stewardess with the Canadian Colonial Airlines. This was the only airline that did not require stewardesses to have a nursing degree. Betty commented that she was hired because she could speak French "and being a pilot."[156]

Earlier in 1939, Jacqueline Cochran, a very accomplished pilot, proposed using women pilots in the United States military. At the suggestion of Gen. Henry "Hap" Arnold, commanding General of the Army Air Corps, Cochran

Betty Jane Williams just landed at Randolph Field in San Antonio, Texas, after a test run in a P-40 in the fall of 1944. (Courtesy of Lt. Col. Betty Jane Williams, USAF Ret.)

became a consultant to the Ferry Command in 1941 to study the issue of women in the Air Corps. General Arnold wanted to know what kind of problems the British encountered using women pilots. The women pilots in England ferried aircraft from the factories to the squadrons across the English Channel. Cochran studied administration of the British program to gain knowledge that would be useful if her program using women pilots was adopted in this country because at that time, the military cockpit was male domain.[157]

Betty continued to describe the history of women pilots during the war. Cochran recruited twenty-five pilots in the United States for the British Air Transport Auxiliary (ATA) pilot program to assist Pauline Gower in England. The female ferry pool was known as the "ATA" girls. The women pilots performed ferry duty in England with the approval of General Arnold in early 1942. The demand for American pilots more than tripled during that year.

By September 1942 an experimental squadron, under the direction of Nancy Harkness Love, a highly efficient and competent pilot, was organized and assigned to the ATC for ferrying duty at New Castle Army Air Base near Wilmington, Delaware. The Women's Auxiliary Ferrying Squadron (WAFS) was composed of twenty-eight women flyers in its initial squadron. Most of the women had commercial licenses. Almost simultaneously, the Women's Flying

Training Detachment was created under Cochran. The first group of twenty-eight trained at the Municipal Airport in Houston, Texas. The two organizations merged on August 5, 1943, into a single unit, the Women Air Force Service Pilots, WASP. Cochran was named the Director of Women Pilots and Love was named the Executive of the Ferrying Division of the Air Transport Command.[158]

Betty noted that eventually the operations were moved to Avenger Field in Sweetwater, Texas. It was the only field where all the military training of primary, basic, and advanced occurred in one place. Numerous male crews were attracted to the field and requested emergency landings. Cochran ordered no more forced landings and the field was dubbed "Cochran's Convent."

In mid-1942 Betty was selected by the Canadian Colonial Airlines to attend Northeast Airlines Pilot Training at the University of Vermont in Burlington. She became a licensed Link Trainer Instructor and served in the Wartime Training Service to teach military pilots the art of navigation. "The WASP served stateside. We did not fly across the ocean, only in the Continental United States," Betty said. A year later, on January 8, 1944, Betty entered the WASP training program, graduated on August 4, 1944, and was assigned as an engineering test pilot at Randolph Field in San Antonio, Texas, flight-testing advanced trainers and the P-40 fighter aircraft.[159] The National Museum Air Force website identified the P-40 as America's foremost fighter when the US entered the war and served in many combat areas. The museum has a P-40E on display.

The WASP program was deactivated on December 20, 1944. Subsequently, Betty earned her commercial pilot's license, flight instructor's rating, and was given a direct commission into the Air Force Reserves in 1947 when the USAF became a separate service.[160] She was hired as director of the Instrument Flight Instruction Program for North American Airport Corporation located at the Westchester County Airport in White Plains, New York; the sole female pilot hired. In 1948 she was hired as a technical writer for North American Aviation and wrote the Flight Operation Manual for the B-45 four-engine jet bomber. Betty also wrote and directed a training film on the emergency procedures for the F-86 jet fighter that saved many a life during the Korean War. Betty's creative film, *Sabre Sam*, starred a sassy pilot cat based on the cat's nine lives to teach pilots the importance of engaging emergency procedures when they encountered a problem rather than bailing out. Wires and letters from pilots during the war attested to the success of Betty's motivational film.[161] The F-86 fighter aircraft engaged and shot down 792 Russian MiGs with a loss of 76 Sabres. An F-86A is on display in the National Museum of the United States Air Force in its Modern Flight Gallery.

Betty continued in the forefront of aviation. CBS-TV in New York televised her program "Let's Go Flying" to help allay people's fear of flying and promote the expanding airline industry. During the Korean War Betty was recalled to active duty and served in the Air Force Reserves for twenty-eight years. Concurrently throughout those years she was a writer, director, and producer for the aerospace industry, missiles as well as commercial and military aircraft. It was a unique position in the Marketing Department of Lockheed California Company, Burbank, California. She promoted the Lockheed L-1011, F-104, P-3, and others through film production.[162] The *Air Force Print News* on March 27, 2006, acknowledged Betty's leadership roles as one of the initial organizers of the post-war WASP organization and leadership in the continuing WASP organization.

The Women Air Force Service Pilots flew more than sixty million miles in seventy-eight different types of military aircraft from the smallest to the largest including the B-29 Superfortress. They ferried new aircraft from the factories to waiting squadrons, towed targets for training raw recruits to shoot live ammunition at a moving target, instructed pilots, did administrative flying, flight testing, robot-type flying, and any other missions except combat.[163]

Thirty-eight women pilots made the ultimate sacrifice. No life insurance was ever issued on the lives of the WASP even though they put their lives on the line every single day. Lieutenant Col. Betty J. Williams commented on this blemish of history in the Air Corps. "Their surviving families never received even a copper penny. It was a terrible injustice to a very successful pioneering program."

The WASP program provided competent military pilots at a critical time of need in our country 1,102 pilots initially. Less than three hundred are alive in 2006. In 1977, Congress passed Public Law 95-202 Title 38-Veterans' Benefits. Finally, on March 8, 1979, the government announced that WASP service was active military service for the purpose of all laws administered by the Veterans Administration. This recognition took more than thirty-four years.[164]

Some of the WASP pilots transported aircraft from Bell Aircraft to Montana, the first leg of their journey to Russia. One of these pilots, Violet Cowden, who flew Bell airplanes, became a life-long friend of Betty.

LOVE FIELD, TEXAS ~ Violet Thurn Cowden was born in 1916 in a sod House in Bowdle, South Dakota. She was six or seven years old when her dreams to soar through the clouds like a hawk started. This began her love affair with flying.[165]

Vi became a first grade school teacher in Spearfish, South Dakota, after graduating from Black Hill University. Before her teaching day began, Vi rode a bicycle to the airport for private flying lessons. "My students always knew the days I had flown. When I asked them how they knew, they told me that I was very happy. I think they tried to take some advantage on those days," she said.

"A Barnstormer taught me how to fly. I learned in a 172 Cub and an Aeronca." Vi, like many of her male counterparts during that era, didn't own an automobile or have a driver's license, but raced around the skies. She earned her private flying license before the war broke out. After war was declared, Vi wired Washington, DC, that she had her pilot's license and was available to help her country. It took a year before an answer came from Jackie Cochran inviting Vi to apply to the Women's Flying Training Detachment.

"I was the first born in my family and did things on my own. My mom did not worry until I got into the service. Dad thought it was good because I liked what I was doing, but my grandpa thought women shouldn't do those kinds of things. (Vi's grandparents were immigrants from Odessa, Russia, and came to South Dakota on a land grant.) I have my mom's spirit, and the gentleness and thoughtfulness of my father," Vi said.

Vi was part of the Class of 43-4, the first class to graduate at Avenger Field in Sweetwater, Texas. "The first three classes trained in Houston, Texas, and some finished with us. Our primary training was in a PT-19, basic training was in a BT-13, and advanced in an AT-6. We also trained in a UC-78, a twin engine. It was fun! I loved it and didn't have to pay for gas!" Vi became one of the 1,074 women to earn her military wings.

Vi was stationed at the Air Transport Command Center, Love Field, Texas. "I delivered planes to Newark, New Jersey. From there we took a military transport plane, or train, or sometimes a bus to get to the Buffalo plant depending on how many of us were at Newark and what was available." Vi flew nineteen different types of aircraft including all of the Pursuits, except a P-38 because there never was one where she flew, Douglas A-20s, A-24s, PQ-14, C-47s, UC-78s from Wichita, and P-51s from Long Beach. The WASP mission was to ferry new aircraft from the factories to debarkation points at Newark, New Jersey, and Long Beach, California, or to training fields across the country. Vi commented about an unusual aircraft that didn't have a propeller. "It was the YP-59, a jet. Ann Baumgartner was the first woman to fly it at Wright Field."

The biggest challenge of flying different kinds of aircraft according to Vi was landing. She said, "Anyone can take-off, but not anyone can land. While I was in the air I practiced all the landing procedures on the clouds while transporting the airplane. We picked up planes for Bell Aircraft in Buffalo and then flew to Great Falls, Montana. From Montana American male pilots flew the P-39s to Fairbanks. Russian male pilots picked up planes in Fairbanks and then to Russia. It was difficult to fly the P-39s because of the tricycle landing gear. I was used to the tail-draggers and more hands-on flying. We received very good service from the Bell Aircraft mechanics. All the personnel at Bell were very professional and nice. I liked the P-63s better than the Airacobras."

"I also flew P-51s. It was my favorite airplane! I was the first woman to fly a P-51 and transported it to the Tuskegee Airman. Only once did I encounter a problem. A locked wheel on a P-51 created a small fire, but I safely landed the airplane." Vi flew from March 1943 to December 20, 1944. "We delivered eighty percent of all the aircraft. This released men so they could fly in combat. When we were deactivated it was so sad to not be able to fly afterwards." Vi went to work for TWA working at the ticket counter. On VE Day "we celebrated and had a ball out in the streets. I was dating a serviceman."

"We gained the respect of the men because they knew we could do the job. Sometimes there were comments, but I didn't let it bother me. One time when I landed a P-51 a guy jumped up on the wing and asked 'Where's the pilot?' I said, 'Where do you think? Do you think he jumped out and I jumped in just now,'' Vi exclaimed! The WASP were best known for their role as ferry pilots, but also served as pilot instructors and transport pilots.

"One of my classmates, Ah Ying (Hazel Ah Ying Lee), and myself had orders to fly from Bell to Gray Falls, Montana. We were flying P-63s. It was Thanksgiving 1944; Ah Ying was bringing in her aircraft for a landing. Another plane was also coming in overhead and didn't have a radio, so the pilot could not hear the traffic controller's message to pull-up. The planes collided and Ah Ying died a few days later from her injuries." Ah Ying Lee was with the Third Ferrying Group of the Air Transport Command stationed at Romulus Army Air Base, Romulus, Michigan.[166]

Dorothy Mae "Dottie" Nichols, a graduate of University of California at Los Angeles, was a member of the first class to graduate at Avenger Field. Nichols was assigned to the 6th Ferrying Group at Long Beach Army Air Field, California, and was ferrying a P-39 from Bell Aircraft. On the way to Montana Nichols refueled near Bismarck, North Dakota, and was killed just after takeoff on June 11, 1944.[167]

Vi's wartime experiences and flying career changed her forever and was the momentum to live her life to the fullest. Vi has been married to her husband, Scott, for fifty years and they have a daughter, Kim. "My husband and family are very supportive of my passion for aviation and what I did during the war.

As a result of my life experiences when I see an injustice I don't stand back, I try and fix it. I miss flying everyday especially when the clouds are so beautiful." On February 25, 2006, Violet Cowden at the age of ninety relived the dreams of her childhood that inspired her to fly and made a jump at 12,000 feet with the United States Army Golden Knights parachute team!

HOOKER ELECTROCHEMICAL COMPANY ~ Another local company recognized very early for it's war efforts was Hooker Electrochemical. The "E" award recognized the volume of war output and an industrial attitude that existed in all areas of the organization. Hooker received the production award on September 8, 1942. Dr. Alan Valentine, President of the University of Rochester, presided over the ceremonies. Chaplain J. W. Hrdlicka from Fort Niagara offered the Invocation. Maj. Gen. William N. Porter presented the flag and Commander R. R. Smith, United States Navy, presented the "E" pins for the 1,019 employees to Ralph Binkley, Chairman of the Hooker Company Employees' Representation Association. The Niagara Falls Concert Band, under the leadership of Dr. Edward D'Anna, provided the musical entertainment for the program. Other dignitaries included Eugene Butler, Mayor of Niagara Falls, and Col. Harry A. Kuhn.

The Airacobra, a jeep, an Aquacheetah, an Army scout car, equipment used in laying down gas screens, and several incendiary bombs were part of the exhibits provided by Bell Aircraft, Amphibian Car Corporation, and the United States Army, and guarded by MPs.

Hooker operated twenty-four hours a day producing about ninety chemicals going directly into the manufacture of war products including high pressure lubricants, tires, and anti-freeze.[168]

PRODUCTION SOLDIERS ~ Western New York's strong industrial base shifted quickly from civilian to defense manufacturing. The *Buffalo Evening News* reported on July 25, 1941, that there were thirty-five Buffalo area subcontractors to the aircraft industry. "Help Wanted, Female" ran across the top of page eighteen in the *News* Classified Ads on January 2, 1943. Curtiss Wright made a dramatic plea for workers: "What American Women do in industry during 1943 will determine the number of boys who will die in this war!"[169]

Dr. Mark Barner titled women's response to the need for workers as "Production Soldiers: Western New York's Working Women of WWII." Barner's video production tells the story of the contribution of some of the Porter area women involved in the war effort. Women in the Western New York work force almost doubled in 1943 as mothers and wives became welders, riveters, and truck drivers.

Some of the production workers living in the Lewiston-Porter area Barner interviewed were Verna Poss and Cecile Fuerschbach who worked in the Drafting Department at Curtiss Wright. Emma Neubauer emphasized the need to do something to help and the impact of seeing friends leave school to enter the service. Marge Stratton called the war years a "pause in our lives. The voice of President Roosevelt declaring war was frightening," she said, but going to work and receiving a paycheck for the first time was exciting women.

Jean Borgatti, Lead Lady at Bell Aircraft, wore overalls and a kerchief to keep her hair from catching on the drills and handed her paycheck to her mother and father who gave her a few dollars in return, but with no timc to spend it. Rita Murphy McMahon drove a truck at the LOOW facility. Mildred George was proud to make a contribution as a nurse at Bell treating the cuts, bruises, and falls. Mary Kalita took classes at Burgard Vocational to read blueprints and spot weld for an Inspector's position at Curtiss Wright. Harriet Jean Price worked at Aerco Speers Graphite in shipping. Vivian Blixt turned down an office position at Bell to work directly with the aircraft as an inspector.[170] Barner's video highlighted the role of women's contribution to the successful production of defense industries. More than seventeen million volunteers and draftees who served from 1941 through 1945 took up arms and were supported by industries like Bell Aircraft across the country.[171]

Who were the men and women who took up arms? What were their lives like, and what happened to them after their Induction at Fort Niagara and forts around the country?

NOTES

[103] France capitulates and signs the armistice with Germany at Compiègne.

[104] "Seventeen Given Diplomas at 14th Commencement at Youngstown High," *Niagara Falls Gazette*, June 26, 1940.

[105] Photograph of Youngstown High School Class of 1940, private collection.

[106] Professor Albert Schule, *Heimatbuch Der Gemeinde Dettingen Unter Teck*, (Dettingen unter Teck, Herausgegeben von der Gemeinde: 1981) 123, 124.

[107] The government anglicized Albrecht Diez's name. The military records and the marker at Arlington Cemetery were in the name of Albert Dietz.

[108] Kenneth G. Diez, interview by author (daughter-in-law), Youngstown, NY, April 26, 2006.

[109] Frederick A. Johnsen, *Bell P-39/P-63*, (Minnesota, Specialty Press: 1998) p. 59, 60.

[110] "Supplement on WWII," *Niagara Falls Gazette*, May 30, 1976.

[111] "WWII: On the Home Front," *Buffalo Evening News*, August 29, 1989.

[112] Ken Diez also mentioned Douglas Muir, another test pilot.

[113] Claude W. Rockabrand, telephone interview by author, April 26, 2006, and *A Test Pilot's Tale,* Part 1 DVD.

[114] Check ride is the final test to qualify for the aircraft by performing specific maneuvers.

[115] Curtiss Wright built about 14,000 P-40s during the war at Plant 1 on Kenmore and Vulcan, Town of Tonawanda, and Plant 2 on Genesee Street adjacent to the Buffalo Airport.

[116] Aircraft designation: P – pursuit, B – bomber, C – cargo, XP – experimental pursuit.

[117] Muroc Dry Lake became Edwards Air Force Base, California.

[118] The I-14 and I-16 engines were improved versions of the original I-A. "Bell P-59 Airacomet," Fact Sheets, National Museum of the USAF, http://www.nationalmuseum.af.mil [accessed March 5, 2008].

[119] "WWII: On the Home Front," *Buffalo Evening News*, August 29, 1989.

[120] The Berlin wall was built in 1961 creating a physical barrier between East and West Germany.

[121] Claude W. Rockabrand, *A Test Pilot's Tale*, DVD.

[122] Roberta Henderson, Hugh Neeson, and Michael "Mike" Locurcio, interview by author, Buffalo, NY, August 15, 2006.

[123] Bell Aircraft, *An Aviation Story The History of Bell Aircraft Corp.,* 15, 23.

[124] Gardenville, in the Town of West Seneca, is the post office address for the Bell helicopter factory.

[125] The West Seneca Historical Museum did not have any records to confirm the spelling.

[126] Leston Faneuf, "Lawrence D. Bell A Man and His Company," Speech delivered at at the "1958 Niagara Dinner" of The Newcomen Society in North America, Buffalo Club, NY, May 15, 1958), 4.

[127] A. Joe Marchese, Michael Locurcio, and Hugh Neeson, interview by author, Buffalo, NY, August 15, 2006.

[128] Hugh Neeson, interview by author, Lewiston, NY, August 12, 2006.

[129] Aero Club of Buffalo and Bell News Association, *First Supersonic Flight: Western New York's Salute to the Bell Aircraft X-1 50th Anniversary 1947-1997 Breaking the Sound Barrier,* (Cheektowaga: Aero Club of Buffalo, 1997), 6.

[130] Aero Club, *First Supersonic Flight*, 5.
[131] V-1 was a jet propelled unmanned aircraft that carried explosives. The V-2 was a ballistic missile developed by the Germans based on Dr. Werner von Braun's design.
[132] Locurcio, interview.
[133] Audrey Schillo and Hugh Neeson, interview by author, Youngstown, NY, August 23, 2006.
[134] Neeson, interview.
[135] "Ferrand is very active at the great age of ninety-five in Albuquerque, New Mexico," said Hugh Neeson in August 2006.
[136] AM MC CB – Anti-Meridian Master of Ceremonies Clint Buehlman.
[137] "Battle of the Somme: 1 July – 13 November 1916," *BBC*, http://www.bbc.co.uk/history/worldwars/wwone/battle_somme.shtml [accessed September 30, 2006 and March 5, 2008].
[138] The Doody and McCann families lost their farms to the United States Government for the ordnance works project and moved 'into town' in 1941.
[139] James McCann, telephone interview by author, August 27, 2006.
[140] Harry S. Truman, *Memoirs 1945 year of Decisions*, (Garden City: Doubleday & Co., 1945), 179.
[141] "About the LOOW site," U.S. Army Corps of Engineers Buffalo District, Missions, http://www.lrb.usace.army.mil/derpfuds/loow/index.htm [accessed June 8, 2008].
[142] Neeson, interview.
[143] Queen Elizabeth Way is a freeway in southern Ontario named for the Queen Consort of King George VI.
[144] Bell, *An Aviation Story The History of Bell Aircraft Corp.,* 259.
[145] Ibid., 260-261.
[146] Ibid., 263.
[147] Neeson, interview and Bell, *An Aviation Story,* 263.
[148] Bell, *An Aviation Story,* 266.
[149] Neeson, interview by author, Lewiston, NY, September 4, 2006.
[150] Bell, *An Aviation Story,* 264.
[151] Hugh Neeson, interview by author, Lewiston, NY, August 12, 2006.
[152] Bell, *An Aviation Story,* 267.
[153] GAM ~ guided air missile.
[154] Hugh Neeson drove past Marilyn's home on Center Street during the war.
[155] Lt. Col. Betty Jane Williams, USAF Retired, telephone interview by author, September 1 and October 16, 2006.
[156] Williams, *Women Airforce Service Pilots WWII – 1942-1944*, July 1991, and Williams, telephone interview by author.
[157] Williams, interview.
[158] Williams, interview.
[159] Williams' speech, Seventeenth Annual International Women's Conference, March 25, 2006; Lt. Col. Betty Jane Williams inducted into Pioneer Hall of Fame.
[160] The National Security Act of 1947 established the United States Air Force. "Air Force History Overview," *United States Air Force*, http://www.af.mil/history/overview.asp [accessed March 15, 2007].

[161] Williams, interview.

[162] Williams speech, Seventeenth Annual Women's Conference, Nashville, TN, March 25, 2006. Lt. Col. Betty Jane Williams was inducted into the organization's Pioneer Hall of Fame.

[163] Williams, *Women Airforce Service Pilots WWII – 1942-1944*, July 1991.

[164] Williams, *Women Airforce Service Pilots,* 1991and Williams, interview.

[165] Violet Cowden, telephone interview by author, October 9 and October 27, 2006.

[166] WASP, Women Air Force Service Pilots Collection D810.W7 G67 1996, Texas Woman's University Library, Denton, TX.

[167] Dorothy Mae Nichols, Biofile Collection, WASP Collection; Texas Woman's University Library, Denton, TX.

[168] Personnel Department of the Hooker Electrochemical Company, *For High Achievement*, Niagara Falls, NY.

[169] The address given for Curtiss Wright was Training School, Genesee and High Streets, Buffalo, NY.

[170] With permission of Dr. Mark Barner, "Production Soldiers: WNY's Working Women of WWII," video, 2004.

[171] Ann McBride examined the history of local women's role entitled "Women Vital to War Effort" in the *Niagara Gazette* on September 5, 1999.

CHAPTER 4

AMERICAN KRIEGES

NO TICKER TAPE PARADE ~ There was no parade for many of the millions of soldiers returning home. Lady Liberty stood alone at the harbor in tribute to the men and women returning from the war. For some of the soldiers this was the first time they saw the Statue of Liberty. The lone Red Cross worker was barely visible amid the throng of soldiers at the dock. "There was just one woman, a Red Cross worker, who greeted more than a thousand soldiers," he said.[172] Most of these soldiers were ex-POWs.

He settled back in the chair to share his story. It was more than a half-century old, but the words came out with a sharpness and clarity as if it happened yesterday. There were brief pauses not from a loss of memory, but a respect for being a part of world history. The quiet spaces between the words recognized the honor of the ultimate sacrifice of so many and the pain of the worst of times from man's inhumanity to man.

John Mark Jircitano, son of Anthony and Ida, Italian born immigrants, was born at home in the city of Niagara Falls on November 22, 1919. Julie Ianni, his wife of fifty-nine years, called him "Johnny" and leaned forward as the story began to unfold. Jeff sat at attention behind his father. During the pauses in John's story, Julie and Jeff volunteered pieces of the account, as they knew it, to ensure nothing would be left out to honor John's part in WWII. Their efforts to fill in the details emphasized their pride and the importance of one man's contribution and a time quickly slipping away.

It was supposed to be the last mission for John, but the required number of missions was about to be increased from twenty-five to thirty. This was his twenty-fifth mission. Before dawn on July 31, 1944, he learned their target was a ball-bearing plant in Mannheim on the east side of the Rhine River across from Ludwigshafen about sixty-two kilometers south of Frankfurt, Germany. But, instead of being the final chapter in John's military service, it became the beginning of another painful chapter that separated him from his country and family for nine more months.

John has lived in the Village of Youngstown for fifty-two years. His experiences during the war were unknown to most of his fellow townspeople.

John was a senior at Niagara Falls High School on the morning of March 12, 1938. He could not hear the heavy sounds of the boots of the German Wehrmacht and the Schutzstaffelor Protection Squad known as the SS crossing the German border into Austria that set the course for world events and John's future.

Decades later in 1966, Joan Jircitano, John's eldest child, was required to take United States History, an eleventh grade Regents course. World War II, an essential part of the syllabus, was a significant part of her father's life. Joan, followed by her siblings, Mark, Alan, Wendy, and Jeff, learned that during the course of the war it took government authorities some time to recognize the distinction between a Nazi and a German. They studied the words represented by the acronyms of Nazi, SA, SS, and a first-hand account of the war by their father.

A Nazi was a member of the National Socialist German Workers Party or Nationalsozialistche Deutsche Arbeiterpartei (NSADP). Sturmabteilung (SA) was a paramilitary unit of the party known as storm troopers. The SA was known for its strong-arm tactics and wore brown uniforms, distinguished from the SS, an elite group within the SA.

The Jircitano household on Jerauld Avenue did not have a radio in the 1930s and John did not hear the broadcast on the thirteenth of March 1938 as Adolph Hitler announced the Anschluss, the annexation of Austria into the German Reich, in Linz. The terror and blood, which would be spent from the vibrations of that moment, moved westward and impacted the lives of millions with the ravages of a tsunami.

The fraternity style pledging for freshman at Niagara University in September of 1938 was a distraction from the world events as a crisis in Czechoslovakia threw Europe into turmoil. The Treaty at Versailles following World War One created Czechoslovakia in 1919 out of the old Austrian-Hungarian Empire. Carved out of several nations, Czechoslovakia's population of about fourteen million included three million Germans, seven hundred thousand Hungarians, five hundred thousand Ruthenians, and a smattering of Poles and Gypsies. The Germans lived in the Sudetenland region part of the western border with Germany. Hitler was determined to put all Germans under his umbrella. The major powers in Europe were concerned about a military conflict with Germany. After a meeting in Berchtesgaden and then Bad Godesberg, Germany, France, Britain, and Italy gathered for a third meeting in Munich.

Czechoslovakia was not invited to the conference, nor was the Soviet Union, which greatly angered Stalin.[173]

The Munich Agreement that followed the meetings was an attempt to appease Hitler and avoid the dark cloud of another world war. But, it was a futile effort to remedy the bitterness and harsh economic realities of the Treaty of Versailles that separated German-speaking people and inflicted unattainable reparations on Germany.

John finished his freshman year at Niagara in the Reserve Officers' Training Corps (ROTC) program with a major in chemistry. He did not imagine how valuable his two years in ROTC would become.

During the next school year tremors from the weight of German tanks rolling into Poland and the blitzkrieg tactics burst into a wave of after-shocks. Early in the morning on September 1, 1939, nine armored divisions of German troops invaded Poland. Great Britain followed by France declared war against Germany on September 3, 1939.[174] On October 16, 1940, the selective service draft registration began in the United States.

WHERE IS PEARL HARBOR ~ The Associated Press wires clicked out the story of the attack on Pearl in an empty Niagara Gazette newsroom and newsrooms across the country on December 7, 1941. Edward F. Joseph,[175] known as Eddy Jo, sang *The Autumn* accompanied by pianist Ernie Whistler at WHLD, the local radio station, when announcer Al Fox broke in with the news of the Japanese attack on Pearl. "Where is Pearl Harbor?" was a question asked by people across the country when they heard the news.[176] President Franklin Roosevelt declared December 7, 1941, as "a day that would live in infamy." Japan did the unimaginable and bombed Pearl Harbor. The following day the police made a quick survey of the City of Niagara Falls and inspection of the hotels. Police Superintendent Thomas J. Holohan announced that there were "no Japanese nationals in the city."[177] Four days later on December 11, 1941, Germany declared war against the United States. It was John's senior college year.

John and Julie remembered how the country supported Great Britain and France before the United States entered the war, although there was a strong sentiment to avoid being drawn into another world conflict. A Gallup poll found that eighty-five percent of all Americans in June of 1940 were against entering the war.[178] Germany and Italy declared war on the United States on December 11, 1941, and Congress reciprocated declaring war on Germany.

"My father was very upset when he heard that Mussolini was supporting Hitler," Julie said. The evening war was declared, the anti-Fascist Mazzini Society applauded the news at the Como Restaurant in Niagara Falls. South of the ridge in Lewiston, the Tuscarora Nation voted for war against Italy and Japan. It was a moot point since the Tuscarora Bear Clan Mother refused to ratify the treaty at the end of WWI because it did not exclude the torture and burning of Kaiser Wilhelm. So technically the Tuscarora Nation was still at war with Germany. During WWII, Pvt. Silas William Chew of the Tuscarora Nation was killed in the Battle of the Bulge and Pvt. Emmett K. Printup shortly after that battle.[179]

"College science majors were not drafted. We were allowed to finish our education," John said. On May 1942 he graduated from Niagara University with a Bachelor of Science degree in Chemistry. Several months later on October 3, 1942, John received his draft notice. A short distance north from home John found himself at the Induction Center at Fort Niagara in Youngstown. He was twenty-two years old, brown eyes, black hair, ruddy complexion, and sixty-nine inches tall.

The first barracks were tents set up on concrete pads. John shivered as he told about the cold October nights before being moved into heated quarters. The typical induction lasted for a few days, for the issuance of clothing and receiving a physical, prior to a transfer for basic training. But unexpectedly, days became weeks. "I felt like an Army veteran when I was given a job of issuing clothing to new inductees," as he waited. John's training was held up for missing paperwork, a birth certificate. His father, mother, and Aunt Rose gave affidavits testifying to his home birth to obtain a birth certificate more than two decades later!

In November John was sent to Mitchell Field, Long Island, then to the Classification Center in Nashville, Tennessee. "We were given extensive testing in eye-hand coordination, reaction time, depth perception, etc., to determine whether we were qualified for pilot, navigator, or bombardier training." He said that the greatest demand was for pilots and his scores qualified him for all three classifications.

Training was composed of four schools: preflight, primary, basic, and advanced; two months of training for each school. During preflight and later overseas, John's undergraduate degree in chemistry prepared him for the role of tutor. Other men who were in training with John came to him for academic help. His students included a roommate, doctors, and a fighter pilot. College level classes in science and mathematics were part of the academic studies.

Preflight training was in Montgomery, Alabama. The primary flight school followed in Clarksdale, Mississippi. The lighter side of the life and death training was evident in the depiction of John's first solo. It was an open cockpit aircraft with an upper and lower wing, a PT-17. John soloed on April 17, 1943, with goggles and grease on his face to protect from frostbite, and a scarf of nylon from discarded parachutes. He practiced stalls at 2,500 feet, spins at 3,000, steep turns at 1,000, and lazy eights at 2,000 feet. He smiled, "I concentrated so hard on my touch and go landings (when my instructor waved me on), that I wasn't distracted by a persistent tugging on my neck. It was only after my final landing that I realized I lost my scarf, Snoopy style!"

Prayer became an essential part of basic training in a BT-13A in Newport, Arkansas. The BT-13 had a powerful engine and "required the student pilot to use two-way radio communications with the ground, operate landing flaps and a two-position variable pitch propeller."

TABLE 4.1
Specifications BT-13 (BT – basic trainer)

Span	42 ft. 2 in.
Length	28 ft. 8-1/2 in.
Height	12 ft. 4-3/4 in.
Weight	4,227 lbs. loaded
Armament	None
Engine	Pratt & Whitney R-985 of 450 hp
Crew	Two (instructor & student)
Cost	$20,000
Maximum speed	155 mph
Cruising speed	130 mph
Range	880 mi.
Service ceiling	19,400 ft.

Source: Reprinted by permission from the National Museum of the USAF, Fact Sheets, Vultee BT-13B Valiant, http://www.nationalmuseum.af.mil/factsheets/factsheet.asp?id=481 [accessed March 5, 2008].

"The sky was almost completely overcast except for a hole directly above the airfield," he said. After an hour of practice of slow rolls John began his descent for the downwind leg of the landing pattern when he realized the airfield was the wrong field. The break in the clouds drifted. He thanked God as he remembered his instructor telling him of another airport thirty miles north of Newport, which helped him to navigate. Later on, John's advanced flying school instructor admitted he lost his orientation. John used what he called the "flying equivalent to the stop and ask directions method. I used the water tower navigation method (reading the name on a tower then finding it on a map)." July and August 1943 were at George Field, Lawrenceville, Illinois. The flight record identified further flight training in the AT-10 (AT-Advanced Trainer). More than half of the Army Air Force's pilots received training from single to multi-engine aircraft in the AT-10s.

TABLE 4.2
Specifications AT-10 (AT – advanced trainer)

Span	44 ft. 0 in.
Length	34 ft. 4 in.
Height	10 ft. 4 in.
Weight	6,465 lbs.
Armament	None
Engine	Two Lycoming R-680-9 radials of 295 hp. Each
Maximum speed	Approx. 190 mph/165 knots
Range	Approx. 660 statute mi./572 nautical mi.
Service Ceiling	Approx. 20,000 ft.

Source: Reprinted by permission from the National Museum of the USAF, Fact Sheets, Beech AT-10 Wichita, http://www.nationalmuseum.af.mil/factsheets/factsheet.asp?id=483 [accessed March 6, 2008].

Graduation was August 30, 1943, after almost four months of crew training. In September John was assigned to the Second AF Second Bomb Fifteenth Wing Twenty-Ninth Group Forty-Third Squadron. Practice was in a B-24E (B-bomber) and the Link Trainer. The B-24s were called the Liberator. Comforts were absent in the aircraft. At high altitudes there were sub-zero temperatures. The crew relieved themselves in a metal tube.

From Gowen Field Boise, Idaho, to Wendover, Utah, and Tonopah, Nevada, training continued in the B-24H. The point of embarkation (POE) was from Hamilton Field in San Francisco, California. During January of 1944 John and his crew flew on their own as they leap-frogged across the country and to Europe towards their destiny: January 17, 1944, Hot Springs, California; January 18 Midland, Texas; January 19 Memphis, Tennessee; January 20 Morrison Field at West Palm Beach, Florida; January 23 Trinidad; and January 25, 1944, Belem.

January 22, 1944, prepared to leave West Palm Beach, Florida, for England. Standing from left to right, Harold R. Skinner, Roy T. Jerome, Magnus V. McHarque, John E. Treadway, Robert E. Crosby, and Edward B. Cox. Kneeling from left to right, Dave Manker, Willie Wilson, Jim McQuaid, and John Jircitano. (Courtesy John Jiricitano)

TABLE 4.3
Specifications B-24E

Span	110 ft. 0 in.
Length	64 ft. 4 in.
Height	17 ft. 11 inc.
Weight	56,000 lbs. loaded
Armament	Ten .50-cal. And 8,000 lbs. of bombs
Engines	Four Pratt & Whitney R-1830-65 (or -43) supercharged radials of 1,200 hp each (take-off power)
Maximum speed	303 mph
Cruising speed	200 mph

Range	4,600 mi. (max. ferry range) 2,850 mi. w/5,000 lbs. bomb load
Service Ceiling	32,000 ft.

Source: Reprinted by permission from the National Museum of the USAF, Fact Sheets, http://www.nationalmuseum.af.mil/factsheets/factsheet_media.asp?fsID=2465 [accessed March 6, 2008].

Flying to Belem was a particularly challenging leg of the journey because it occurred during a solar eclipse. Belem is a port city in northern Brazil on the lower Amazon River near the equator. Days and nights seemed to blend together due to the concentration and strain of the arduous flight and as they continued on to Fortaleza in Brazil, Dakar in West Africa, Marrakech in French Morocco, then navigated around Spain because of its neutrality, and finally landed in Swansea, South Wales on February 3, 1944. The group was assigned to the 8th Air Force 96th Combat Wing 458th Group and 753rd Squadron.

The war was getting closer now for John and the crew. A large arrow on the ground in Ireland pointed to England, but it wasn't enough to keep them on course. "When we arrived in England, the radio signals from the barrage balloons (helium filled balloons with chains to deter German bombers) completely disoriented us. We were lost. A mosquito bomber (British twin-engine fighter) appeared from nowhere to escort us to the airfield at Swansea, Wales. I can still remember the landing instructions in a heavy Polish accent from the control tower. 'You are nomber wahn (sic). You may pancake.' Pancake to the English is a normal landing, but to an American it means to land with the wheels up. Dave and I elected to land with the wheels down."

The flight to Holyhead, England, was February 13, 1944. As John and the others waited for their first mission, they lined up bombers in preparation for take-off. After taxiing the airplanes to the end of the runway the men were directed to drive a jeep to the next airplane. John's college education did not include a driver's license. He only knew how to use the joystick steering wheel, but jumped in the jeep anyway for his first drive!

THE FIRST MISSION came on the morning of March 16, 1944, for the twelve men. The target was Friedrichshafen near the Swiss border. The B-24H limped back with punctures to the fuel tank and landing wheel, and minus a wingtip. John chuckled, "We were met with a shot of whiskey when they saw the condition of our plane!" March 22 the target was Berlin. March 26 it was

Sira Court; and March 27 it was Biarritz, France.

The briefings were in the early morning and took about half an hour. For a moment John was distracted and poked his buddy sitting next to him. "Look over there" as he recognized another soldier. "It was Jimmy Stewart!" and he smiled.

On April 1 they were transferred to the 564th Squadron, 389th Group, 2nd Combat Wing. They took their B-24Hs up and practiced in the Link Trainer. "The British pilots flew missions at night and the American pilots in the morning," John said. The Allies targeted factories, refineries, and transportation sites. Hitler's attacks on British cities and its civilians appalled John, like many on the home front. The missions continued: April 8 Braunschweig, April 13 Oberpfaffenhofen, April 18 Rathenow, and April 22 the marshalling yards at Hamm.

TABLE 4.4
Transfers to the 389th Bomb Group March 27, 1944

445th Bomb Group
Avery, 1st Lt. Baldwin C.
Lawson, 2nd Lt. John A.
Hasselbach, 2nd Lt. Orland H.
Moore, TSgt. Ralph W.
Syverud, TSgt. Clifford S.
Jacobson, TSgt. Ralph O.
Chamberlin, SSgt. Walter C.
Zimmerman, SSgt. Robert W.
Sipes, SSgt. Franklin B.

446th Bomb Group
Bertelsen, 2nd Lt. Robert E.
Campbell, 2nd Lt. David F.
Weller, 2nd Lt. George F.
Barsczewski, Sgt. Peter P.
Bosley, TSgt. Irvin R.
Uretta, SSgt. Sam F.
Roberts, SSgt. Joseph L.
Yant, SSgt. Charles M.
454rd Bomb Group
Tolly, 1st Lt. Alfred P.
Guild, 2nd Lt. Franklin A.
Strait, 2nd Lt. Maurice L.
Vogan, TSgt. Everrett W.
Reiner, SSgt. Sam S.
Wise, SSgt. Kenneth W.
Maxwell, Sgt. Winifred G.
Kardos, Sgt. George F.
Desantel, SSgt. Henry D.

458th Bomb Group
Lamb, 1st Lt. Robert E.
Jircitano, F/O John M.
Lodinger, F/O Herman
Koch, SSgt. Louis F.
Miller, SSgt. Carl E.
Tharpe, SSgt. Marshall A.
Morello, Sgt. Francis J.
Koussa, Sgt. Michael
Cayford, SSgt. Everett M.

Source: Assignment Order, private collection, March 27, 1944.

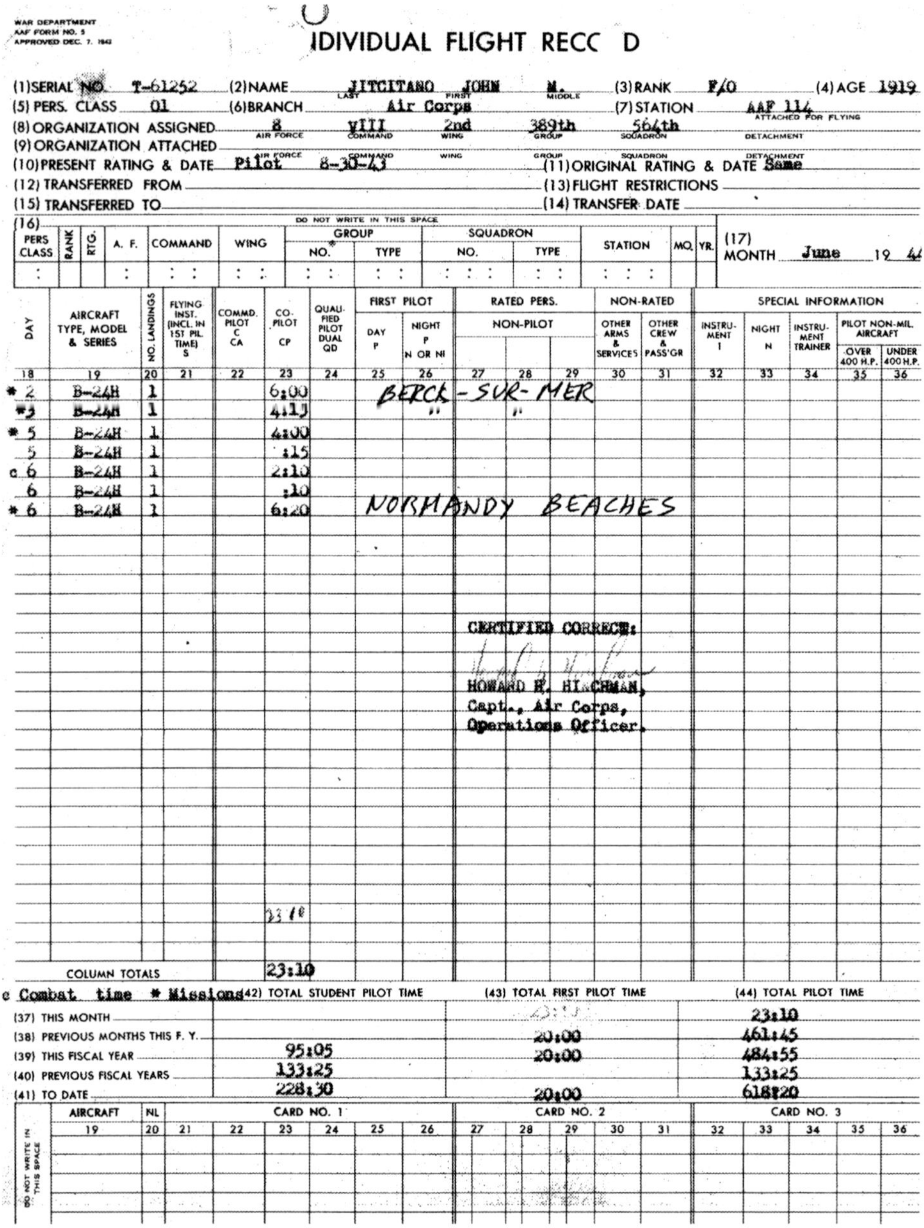

WAR DEPARTMENT
AAF FORM NO. 5
APPROVED DEC. 7, 1942

IDIVIDUAL FLIGHT RECC D

(1) SERIAL NO. T-61252 (2) NAME JITCITANO JOHN M. (3) RANK F/O (4) AGE 1919
(5) PERS. CLASS 01 (6) BRANCH Air Corps (7) STATION AAF 114
(8) ORGANIZATION ASSIGNED 8 (AIR FORCE) VIII (COMMAND) 2nd (WING) 389th (GROUP) 564th (SQUADRON) (DETACHMENT)
(9) ORGANIZATION ATTACHED
(10) PRESENT RATING & DATE Pilot 8-30-43 (11) ORIGINAL RATING & DATE Same
(12) TRANSFERRED FROM (13) FLIGHT RESTRICTIONS
(15) TRANSFERRED TO (14) TRANSFER DATE
(17) MONTH June 19 44

Day (18)	Aircraft Type, Model & Series (19)	No. Landings (20)	Co-Pilot CP (23)	Remarks
* 2	B-24H	1	6:00	BERCK-SUR-MER
*3	B-24H	1	4:15	" "
* 5	B-24H	1	4:00	
5	B-24H	1	:15	
c 6	B-24H	1	2:10	
6	B-24H	1	:10	
* 6	B-24H	1	6:20	NORMANDY BEACHES
			23 10	
COLUMN TOTALS			23:10	

CERTIFIED CORRECT:
HOWARD H. HINCHMAN,
Capt., Air Corps,
Operations Officer.

c Combat time * Missions

	(42) TOTAL STUDENT PILOT TIME	(43) TOTAL FIRST PILOT TIME	(44) TOTAL PILOT TIME
(37) THIS MONTH			23:10
(38) PREVIOUS MONTHS THIS F. Y.		20:00	461:45
(39) THIS FISCAL YEAR	95:05	20:00	484:55
(40) PREVIOUS FISCAL YEARS	133:25		133:25
(41) TO DATE	228:30	20:00	618:20

Pilot John Jircitano's flight record of his B-24H for June 2-6, 1944, of Berck-Sur-Mer and Normandy beaches. (Courtesy John Jircitano)

Hamm was a seven-hour mission, but the weather caused a delay. The B-24s arrived back at the English coast in darkness. "Realizing the American crews were not trained for flying at night, the Luftwaffe sent up fifteen Me410s (Messerschmitt Luftwaffe fighters) to follow the planes back to England. Nine B-24s were shot down while in the landing pattern. English AA (Anti-aircraft) guns destroyed one plane. When we realized we were being followed across the channel, Bob and I decided to continue to fly to a field in the western part of England. We spent the night there and flew back to our base in the morning."

It was overcast. John piloted the lead bomber and the only one with radar. The screen was teeming with blips of the ships and airplanes. Clouds broke as the B-24s came closer to land and the sight of the ground troops. John and his team commented on how the infantry performed the most difficult task. June arrived and the horrific losses at the Normandy beaches followed. June 2, 3, and 5 their mission target was Berck-Sur-Mer and June 6, D-Day 0620 hours, Normandy Beaches. The missions for the last days of June were Saarbrucken and Kothen. Then, in July, the B-24s bombed Munich on the eleventh, Saarbrucken on the sixteenth, and Bremen the twenty-ninth.

THE FINAL MISSION ~ The day arrived, July 31, 1944; it was to be their last mission. Home appeared close for a fleeting moment, just before the tour of duty was raised from twenty-five to thirty missions. The target was a ball-bearing plant in Mannheim, across the Rhine River from Ludwigshafen. This day was etched in John's mind, as the past became the present again, "...an overcast sky was forecast over the target area, visual bombing was not attempted. The Pathfinder squadron of the 389th Bomb Group, with radar and crewman trained in its use, was created specifically for bombing under these conditions. Our plane and crew from this squadron was scheduled to lead the 458th Bomb Group. The radar equipment, contained in a dome situated just behind the bomb bay, replaced the ball turret. The dome was lowered manually after take-off and raised before landing. Each Pathfinder crew was composed of a radar bombardier, a radar navigator, and a command pilot in addition to the ten regular crewmembers. The 458th Group command pilot usurped my copilot's seat, and I became tail-gunner and formation controller. Because there was no visibility to the rear from the cockpit, it was my responsibility to relay information to Bob who then adjusted air speed to keep the formation intact. There was a narrow speed range between flying slow enough to keep the planes on the outside of the turns from falling behind, but fast enough to keep the inside planes from stalling."

John relived the twenty-fifth mission: "At this point, German fighters presented no problem. The destruction of oil refineries created a fuel shortage that crippled the Luftwaffe. I never saw a German plane within four or five miles of our group except during one of our earlier missions when our escort was a few minutes late. The Luftwaffe pilots waited for gaps between escort shifts. Usually with little else to do, our escort pilots tucked their fighters into the bomber formation and grinned at the crews. This was a welcomed break from eight and sometimes ten hours of tension during the missions."

"The carefully drawn lines on the map in the briefing room neatly routed our group around all known flak (anti-aircraft gun) positions, except for those near Mannheim. As the formation neared the target, we began a methodical turn every fifteen seconds. The anti-aircraft shells took twenty seconds to reach our 22,000 feet altitude, which meant the gunners 'lead' us by one mile. Once the bomb run was started, evasive action was abandoned because precision bombing required a straight-and-level run of about thirty seconds. This half-minute was the most vulnerable part of the scheduled seven-hour mission. Flak bursts were heavy, and a shell fragment ruptured a fuel line in the bomb bay, and ignited the escaping fuel. Koch reached for his chute, but pulled the ripcord instead of the chute handle. This spread the flames until they were beyond control. Koch and Tharpe, the radio operator and the engineer, both went down with the plane."

"When the bail-out order was given, I didn't wait for the waist gunners to open the door between the waist and tail sections. This door was part of a partition designed to keep the cold air (thirty degrees below zero) that entered the open waist windows away from the tail gun position. I went through the plastic partition and pushed out the gunner through the waist gunner window and followed in tandem," John said.

John wrote about the bailout in his log. "Punctuated by the jolt which removed my boots, pulling the rip cord transformed bedlam to a tranquility of clouds, sky, and white nylon. The illusion was enhanced by the solid under-cast and erased any hint of reality. Through the fading drone of airplane engines, I could hear the whisper-soft sound of air passing through the opening at the top of the chute. That sound was the only indication that I wasn't suspended motionlessly in space. I awakened from a sense of security to the realization that my rate of descent was much more apparent at 100 feet than it was at 22,000 and that I was headed directly toward electric power lines. A few quick prayers and an 'A' in ground school resulted in a safe landing with only badly sprained ankles." John was carried piggy back by other able soldiers until he could walk again.

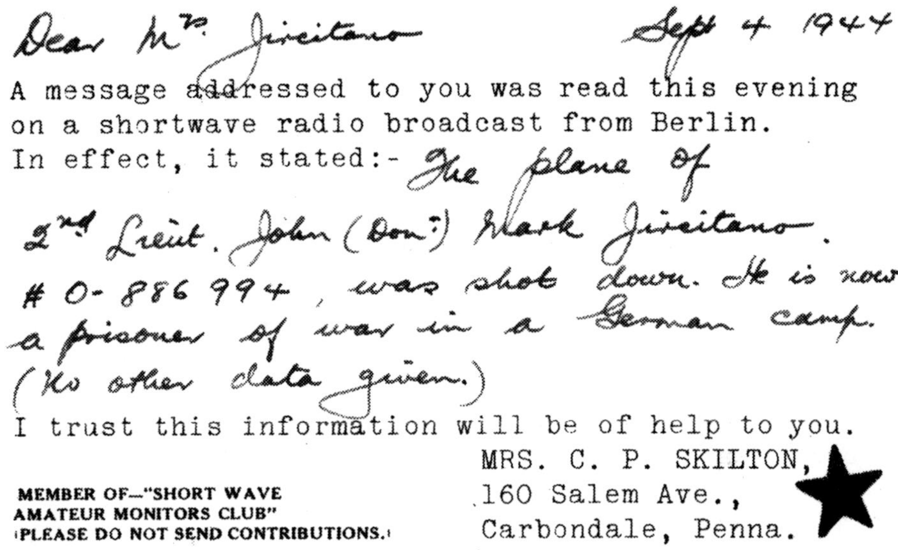

Dear Mrs. Jircitano Sept 4 1944

A message addressed to you was read this evening on a shortwave radio broadcast from Berlin. In effect, it stated:- The plane of 2nd Lieut. John (Don?) Mark Jircitano. # 0-886 994, was shot down. He is now a prisoner of war in a German camp. (No other data given.)

I trust this information will be of help to you.

MRS. C. P. SKILTON,
160 Salem Ave.,
Carbondale, Penna.

MEMBER OF—"SHORT WAVE AMATEUR MONITORS CLUB"
(PLEASE DO NOT SEND CONTRIBUTIONS.)

Several months often lapsed between the time a family was notified their son was missing-in-action and the report that he was a prisoner of war. Short wave radio operators often picked up broadcasts out of Berlin of the POW status before the government telegram reached home. (Courtesy John Jircitano)

The surviving crew was taken to a local jail near Mannheim. John and the radio operator bailed out from the waist window of the plane. The pilot used the most dangerous bailout exit, the top hatch, and was burned. His face was covered with bandages. The last mission became the beginning of their life as prisoners of war.

PRISONER OF WAR ~ July 31, 1944, at 1:00 p.m., John landed in a cow pasture near Mannheim. John's log read, "Landed a few yards from Buck. We both fell in water up to our waists trying to hide from the Jerries.[180] Judging from the smell of the water, we weren't the only things that fell in. The best place we could find was a clump of reeds about a foot high growing along a stretch of swampy ground in the middle of an open field."[181]

As he uttered a prayer of thanksgiving for surviving, John was chagrined as a group of irate farmers and villagers armed with pitchforks and shovels scurried to find the survivors. He said, "I don't know, but I was rather amused over the fuss they made. They kept on yelling and running around like a bunch of scared animals until, eventually, one of them practically stumbled over us." The civilians seemed intent on beating the men who had just rained bombs in their direction. The military arrived to "save them." The survivors were rounded up and taken to a local jail near Mannheim. John was carried again by his buddies as dreams of returning home quickly evaporated.

August 2, 1944, John and the other survivors arrived at the interrogation center at Oberursel near Frankfurt, Germany. The jolt into life as American POW No. 7034 began with three days in solitary confinement. They were questioned and began an adjustment to German cuisine: black bread and a gruesome looking soup, which John remarked, "tasted surprisingly good." There were threats of being treated as spies if only name, rank, and serial number were given. Shoes were taken each night and returned in the morning to prevent escape attempts. The deathly quiet of solitary was broken by chimes, which rang on the hour and the quarter hour. John found himself fascinated by the counterpoint of the sound against the silence.

On August 5, 1944, John was held at the Dulag, a Reception Center, near Wetzlar for about five days. The view from the camp of the countryside and fairly good chow was a pleasant diversion for John. On August 13, John and the surviving crew arrived at Stalag Luft III at Sagan, a small town about one hundred miles southeast of Berlin, adjacent to the Bober River, a tributary of the Oder. John was placed in barracks in the north compound of the camp with five British and two Canadian officers, prisoners for the past two to three years. Earlier that year on March 24, seventy-six prisoners escaped from this compound through tunnels. Three eluded capture and reached England. Most were recaptured and the remaining fifty were murdered. This was *The Great Escape* that became a classic and popular war movie.

"During my stay at Sagan, the digging of escape tunnels was still going on," John discovered later. He remarked that the security was so tight only the POWs directly involved knew of the efforts to continue digging. Back in the states the Jircitano family was about to receive a telegram.

August 14, 1944, Western Union delivered a telegram addressed to Anthony Jircitano, 2186 Jerauld Avenue, Niagara Falls, New York.

THE SECRETARY OF STATE DESIRES TO EXPRESS HIS DEEP REGRET THAT YOUR SON LIEUTENANT JOHN M JIRCITANO HAS BEEN REPORTED MISSING IN ACTION THIRTY ONE JULY OVER GERMANY. IF FURTHER DETAILS OR OTHER INFORMATION ARE RECEIVED YOU WILL BE PROMPTLY NOTIFIED. {Signed} J A ULIO THE ADJUTANT GENERAL.[182]

Many people in the country felt concern and anguish for the fate of the soldiers. Short wave radio operators wrote to the Jircitano family. They heard Berlin broadcasts that John was a prisoner of war and hoped to assuage some of the suffering of the family. John was one of twelve children, eight boys and four girls. Two of John's older brothers served during the war. Jim was a navigator in the Pacific and Rossie was in the regular Army. One of the younger brothers, Artie, was part of the occupying Forces at the end of the war.

On August 25, 1944, more news arrived via Western Union.

REPORT JUST RECEIVED THROUGH THE INTERNATIONAL RED CROSS STATES THAT YOUR SON SECOND LIEUTENANT JOHN M JIRCITANO IS A PRISONER OF WAR OF THE GERMAN GOVERNMENT LETTER OF INFORMATION FOLLOWS FROM PROVOST MARSHALL GENERAL. {Signed} J A ULIO THE ADJUTANT GENERAL.[183]

John envied his British roommates when the mail call came. Some of the other officers were prisoners now for several years. Conditions changed in the camps as the Allies began to destroy and cut off transportation routes for the Germans. The desire for news from home was never satisfied for John. He did not receive any of the letters or packages sent by his family while he was a prisoner.

John's family saved his letters. But he did not receive a reply to the letter he wrote home on October 30, 1944. He wrote:

Dear Sis,

Still haven't heard from you, but expect to, any day now. The fellows in my room have been POWs for nearly two years, & I envy them every time the mail comes in.

I'm getting along as well as ever. I play football and soccer every now and then. We have a very well organized sport program here. They play rugby here too, but I'm not particularly fond of the game. To use an English expression, the game looks like a bloody shambles to me, even though it isn't as rough as our American football.

I don't know whether I have mentioned it before, but I would like to have some photographs from home. Send as many as you can. I didn't have any when I went down.

Let me know how I can get in touch with Georgie as I can't write to him directly. Let me know how every thing is at home. Give my love to all.

Your loving brother,

Johnny[184]

George "Georgie" Richards and John grew up together and were best friends. They met in London the week before John was shot down and planned to meet the following weekend. Georgie joked, "If you don't show up it'll mean you were shot down." Later when he learned what happened to John, Georgie felt terrible and thought he jinxed his friend.

Adding to the loneliness of being captured, German soldiers taunted the prisoners with, "Your wives and girlfriends are dancing with our soldiers in your POW camps at home." News of the war came over a hidden radio. If a guard approached, the prisoners sang to disguise their efforts to listen to the radio reports. After the earlier escape tunnels were discovered, the guards punctured the cans of fruit and vegetables from the Red Cross. They didn't want the prisoners to stockpile the food. John smiled remembering their efforts to preserve some food by pouring candle wax into the hole.

The British POWs established a school to catch up on the education that was interrupted because of their military service. Their command pilot, Major Low, was a teacher in civilian life. He drafted John and two others to teach algebra courses for the American POWs. The three "teachers" planned an outline of the curriculum and on January 23, 1945, the semester for algebra classes began. School was disrupted after the first session as the Russian troops advanced towards the camp and into eastern Germany.

It was still dark and during a bitter winter snap when the evacuation of the camp was announced on January 28, 1945, to "free us from the Russian menace." Stalag Luft III was a large camp composed of a number of compounds. When the evacuation began, there were more than ten thousand airmen at the camp. The prisoners marched all day until about 6:00 p.m. John continued, "We found ourselves in an open prairie and in the teeth of a freezing gale. We slept in a barn that night, or rather we tried to." The temperature dropped below zero. A few blankets and some straw did little to keep the men warm. "Other krieges[185] continued to march about twenty kilometers beyond our position. A handful of the prisoners froze to death. Some of the men lost hands and fingers due to the exposure."

Many of the German guards were in their forties and fifties. They carried full packs and rifles. In spite of their perilous condition the POWs helped some of the older guards with their packs. For those brief moments it was not prisoner vs. guard, but all men against the elements. As the prisoners continued to march, German civilians in the towns extended acts of compassion. "They were very friendly. They came out with hot coffee every time we stopped, and sometimes while we were still going." John wrote about the incident in his journal "A Wartime

Log for British Prisoners," a gift from the War Prisoners' Aid of the Young Men's Christian Association (YMCA), 37, Quai Wilson, Geneva – Switzerland.

January 29, 1945, it was 9:00 a.m. and still snowing, but a little warmer than the previous day. At 8:00 p.m. they arrived at Muskau, a glass factory. It was the first time since they left Sagan that there was a warm place to sleep and even hot water. When the British krieges were separated from the Americans, John said goodbye to the soldiers who were his roommates for the past six months.

Two days later they left Muskau on icy roads. Flocks of refugees on horse drawn carriages shared the roads with them. By nightfall they stopped at a small farm eight kilometers from Spremberg. The next morning John looking longingly at a bushel basket of boiled potatoes on the back porch of the farmhouse asked the farmer, "What are the potatoes for? The farmer offered some, but asked us to save some for the pigs. I thought I never would be hungry enough to share food with pigs!"

February 1, 1945, was a day of rest from marching. The POWs traded cigarettes for some bread from the German civilians. The Red Cross parcels of meat were added to potatoes and carrots for a stew. The farm wife let them use her kitchen stove to cook when their culinary efforts were cut short as they were forced to move on and gulped their stew down. The eight kilometers to Spremburg seemed like eighty as they plowed through the darkness and three-inch deep water that caused the soles of John's shoes to fall off in pieces.

The next day, the POWs crowded into the railroad cars, fifty men to a car. They were given four Red Cross parcels for each group of five men to last for the three days and two nights on the train.

February 4, 1945, at 6:00 p.m., the train arrived at Nuremburg.[186] The sun had just set during a heavy downpour as the prisoners entered their new camp at Langwasser, Stalag XIIID. Conditions deteriorated. Air raids, fuel shortages, fleas, and bed bugs were the order of most days. John found solace from the bed bugs by sleeping on a wooden table.

The Red Cross food parcels were intended to supplement the rations supplied by the Germans. Now, the Germans used this as the sole source of food. Fortunately, John said, "things were different while we were on the move from one camp to another. We traded cigarettes from our parcels for food, and some sympathetic civilians even allowed us into their homes to cook the food we acquired. Once, we were given one dozen eggs for two of us!"

February 20, 1945, was a daylight raid and heavy bombing of Nuremberg.

February 27, 1945, RAF raid, cookies (bombs) dropped. Rations were cut. John recorded his rations per week that included two hundred grams (seven oz.) of meat (usually horse meat), a loaf of sour bread, and an ounce of moldy cheese. The bread was very dense. John heard that the Germans used sawdust to give it bulk.

March 14, 1945, was a big day in camp. Trucks arrived from Switzerland with 3,600 Red Cross parcels and news that more were on the way.

April 4, 1945, the Nuremberg camp was evacuated and they set out for Moosburg about ninety-two miles away. Air raid sirens and the tremors of the earth as the bombs exploded signaled the American forces were advancing from the west. The American Seventh and Third Armies thrust into Western Germany signaled hope to the POWs.

The days passed as they continued to march toward Moosburg. John's log marked the days:

April 4, 1945, arrived at Postbauer.
April 5, 1945, left.
April 6, 1945, passed thru Berching then on to Plankstetten.
April 7, 1945, continued on at 8:00 p.m.
April 8, 1945, was a Sunday, reached Pondorf.
April 9, 1945, left Pondorf and on to marching.
April 10, 1945, crossed the Danube and reached Mühlhausen.
April 13, 1945, after several days at Mühlhausen continued on to Unelsdorf.
April 17, 1945, twenty-five kilometer hike to Holtzhausen.
April 19, 1945, on to Obermunchen.
April 20, 1945, reached Gammelsdorf.
April 21, 1945, arrived at Moosberg's Stalag VII-A.

They traveled 147 kilometers, about 92 miles.

April 29, 1945, the Fourteenth Armored Division led by General Patton's Third Army fought with the Germans for several hours. Two tanks entered the prison camp as the long awaited liberation was at hand. At 1235 hours the American flag was raised! The camp was ecstatic at the sight of the swastika being torn down and the entry of Patton and his troops. "But it would be more than a week before we began the journey home," John said.

Wednesday, May 9, 1945, reveille sounded at 0630 hours. At 0820 hours the freed prisoners left Moosburg on trucks and arrived at the airport at Straubing about noon. They boarded C-47 transports and took off at 1300 hours. The military time marked the beginning of the last leg of the journey recorded in John's prisoner log. He was held as a prisoner for nine months and lost thirty

Above, the Third Army Fourteenth Armored Division liberated Stalag VIIA at Moosburg on April 29, 1945. John Jircitano wrote in his log that at "12:35 American flag raised in Moosburg after few hours skirmish with Germans. Two tanks came into prison camp." Below, Allied POWs left the camp on May 9, 1945, and then were trucked to the airport at Straubing. At Le Havre they received a "hearty welcome from French civilians." (Courtesy John Jircitano)

pounds. The plane landed at Le Havre, France, at 1650 hours. The grateful French people tossed flowers as the trucks passed. This was the only parade.

VISION AT THE ITALIAN FRONT ~ John Maroon said, "I had two mothers: Eva (neé Wassaf) Maroon, and my grandmother, Maime Wassaf, who died in 1949. I learned a lot from my grandmother. She told me 'if you ever need anything ask the Blessed Mother and be honest with people.' When I went into the Army I did a lot of praying!"[187]

John was born in 1925 in the City of Niagara Falls, New York, to Norman and Eva Maroon, immigrants from Mount Lebanon. The family operated a dry goods store on Buffalo Avenue and in 1915 moved to Pierce Avenue and Fifteenth Street. "It was a flourishing neighborhood with a confectionery, dry goods store, and grocery store. I was eighteen years old and playing basketball in high school," he said. John's athletic talents also included baseball, but his 1-A military classification, an almost certain draft status, was an impediment when earlier in 1943 he tried out for the St. Louis Cardinals. Another player with a 4-F was signed instead.[188] The war was about to interrupt John's high school education.

In November 1943, John Maroon and Vince Mazza, stood in the Navy enlistment line together. "Vince was six foot three, but rejected for military service because of a hernia! During the physical I was told to 'read these colors' but couldn't because I was color blind, and was told to go to the other line for the Army." Mazza went on to the professional football leagues from Trott Vocational High School in Niagara Falls and played in the All-American Football Conference (AAFC), for the Buffalo Bisons and Detroit Lions. He became an All Star Canadian Football League player.[189]

John was inducted at Camp Upton in Massachusetts, a former Civilian Conservation Corps (CCC) Camp about six miles south of Worchester, then sent to Fort McClelland for six months of basic training. "The war was getting bad when I was sent overseas, still a kid, to Salerno in the southern part of Italy, marching towards Rome. (The justification for the Allied invasion of southern Italy included control of the airfields for the bombers to reach Germany.[190]) I wanted to see the Pope (Pius XII). After Monte Cassino was bombed, I did get to see him from a distance."

During the fighting, "I was given a vision of the Blessed Mother and she told me 'you will never get wounded, but you will go through a lot.' After Monte Cassino we were put on a train bound for southern France as part of the invasion on June 6 and told 'don't stop' when we started to advance." The Blessed Mother's promise to John was fulfilled as he fought through four major battles.

"It was dark and we were on a hill headed towards Germany when a German tank shot at us. I hit the dirt. My rifle was shattered. The lieutenant said to dig in when I saw some men in the distance. 'They're Germans,' he said and there were a lot of them. Eventually, three of us took off to avoid capture and hid for four days with no food or water. I'd lost my shirt that caught on a tree. After the third day we could hear our own artillery and the following day I found a stream of water and eagerly stuck my head in it. We made our way down the hill when we saw our troops. We needed a rest after our ordeal," John said.

But there was no rest. "We heard over the radio 'enemy tanks coming around the bend.' I could hear a big convoy. It was the Nineteenth Army with trucks and tanks. There were over four hours of artillery bombing and three thousand Germans captured. From then on, we kept advancing. We got about seven hours sleep in seven days. The Germans fired on us as we started up a hill. There were sixty of us. I was behind a rock with our lieutenant when he said, 'It looks like we are surrounded.' There were thirteen of us left when we surrendered. If we hadn't we all would have been killed."

The day before Thanksgiving, November 22, 1944, John never got his promised Thanksgiving dinner. Instead, the day marked the beginning of his status as an American POW in Germany. "I wonder if they are going to shoot us? They checked us for weapons and pulled my prayer book and rosary beads out of my pocket. 'Are you Kathlick (sic)?' the German asked in broken English and gave me the beads and prayer book back. We were put in a cellar for three days and given only bread and potatoes to eat, then put in cattle cars and taken to the POW camp at Moosburg (Stalag VII)."

The conditions at the Camp were gruesome. More than one hundred Americans were crowded into a barrack that normally held fifteen. The prisoners slept on bunk beds, two to a bed with a straw mattress. "You slept on your side," John said. There were no athletic fields, regular religious services, beer, or a radio for news of the war. The food menu was dark bread, potatoes, and some Limburg cheese. During the five months of his captivity, John ate meat only once, a little piece at Christmas.

The POWs were given a few cigarettes that were an important commodity to trade with the guards for bread or other foodstuffs. There were no showers and little heat. The Americans dug a trench outside their barracks, the only place to relieve themselves. It was very unsanitary and dysentery was rampant with little or no medical care. "Most of the guards were older, forty-five to sixty-five. The younger German soldiers were on the front line. One of the guards told me that 'Hitler is no good. We don't want to fight anymore.' Every morning about five or six o'clock we were put in cattle cars and taken by train to Munich to fill bomb craters until about ten o'clock in the evening. Most of the time we worked and infrequently we had Sunday off."

John asked a guard, "What is that smell?" The reply was "they are burning the Jews up." Most soldiers and American citizens did not know about the concentration camps until after the war ended.

Early in April 1945, John and some other American POWs were shipped to a farm in Landshut about fifty miles north of the POW camp. "We were at Landshut for about three weeks and saw guys marching from Berlin to Munich.[191] They looked like skeletons. Then one day Americans bombers were overhead. I did a lot of praying seeing the squadrons and didn't know if the bombers knew we were there. We went nuts when the Americans came in." The next day John and his buddies were flown to northern France.

John boarded a boat for the long trip back to the states with twenty-eight dollars. He lost it all playing cards and with ten days left borrowed three dollars from another soldier to get some candy and five dollars from someone else to play more games. Dice and card playing were distractions to pass the time. "I had one dollar left and it was burning a hole in my pocket. I won fifteen dollars and paid back the other two guys what I borrowed, then won a hundred dollars. By the time the ship docked I won about thirteen hundred dollars!"

When John arrived home, ulcers and other stomach troubles forced him on a baby food diet and treatment at the medical facilities at Fort Niagara. After a furlough, he was stationed as an orderly at Fort George Meade and then at Camp Pickett, Virginia, before being discharged on November 29, 1945.[192] "I am the last one (alive) of our group. Don Strassburg was with me in the POW camp. We used to bowl together," he said.

John's prayer life, faith experience on the battlefield, and struggles as a prisoner of war evolved into more than six decades of service at church and in the community. The neighborhoods around his childhood home and the world changed since the war, but John's compassion for others and his faith have not. He has led a life of service to many children with Cerebral Palsy and other disabilities, given others hope, and raised a family. John married Margaret Agnello on September 9, 1947. They have three children: John, Jr., Deborah Leavitt, and Linda Ortiz.

Margaret Agnello Maroon passed away March 7, 2008.

POW SUPPORT GROUP[193] ~ "Don't talk to that bunch, they were in the Air Corps," someone joked as the group gathered for their weekly meeting. The spirit of brother-like competition bonded these former servicemen and their experiences as prisoners of war, and by the government's failure to believe all that happened to them. They are part of a generation of people with lost stories and a relatively unknown history.

Some men were injured bailing out of their aircraft, and others suffered from sickness and health issues due to the conditions of their confinement. "The government didn't believe what happened to us. The Germans didn't document our injuries and medical conditions." This was repeated more than once in the group and said matter-of-factly. The decades since the war and sharing within the group appeared to have healed some of the frustration and anger at the government's unbelief and lack of due recognition from society about the American POW experience.

Frequently, the airmen were reported missing-in-action (MIA) when their aircraft was shot-down over enemy territory. It was the beginning of a painful ordeal for them and for their families who waited at home not knowing if their loved one was alive or dead. It often took several months before the Red Cross confirmed their status as POWs.

Each meeting began with a sick call. John Zale reverently reported, "We lost another one." Lt. Col. Robert E. Ryan, retired, passed away in the Buffalo Veterans Hospital. Col. Ryan was part of the Texas National Guard, 36th Infantry Division, deployed to Italy in the Monte Cassino region when he was captured at the Rapido River in the Liri Valley. The mountains of Cassino overlooking the valley were a strategic defensive position for the Germans.

The group debated Gen. Mark Clark's military strategy and the cost of many lives, especially soldiers with the Polish Free Army, and also how one-quarter million German troops were able to get through the Gustav line. The line was a series of German fortifications south of Rome, which ran across Italy north of where the Garigliano River empties into the Tyrrhenian Sea, off the west coast of Italy, across the Apennine Mountains to the Adriatic Sea in the east. The center of the line was at Monte Cassino.

These POWs suffered from the ravages of war and captivity, but they survived.

EDWARD P. FEIGENBAUM I ~ held a challenge coin of the Third Ranger Battalion engraved with part of his personal history: "May 25, 1943, Licata * Maiori * Anzio * Cisterna." The test of his metal began when he was a little boy and his father died.[194] "I was small and wasn't allowed to go to the funeral, and stayed with the Allen's at their hot dog stand near the Boy Scout camp."[195] There were also good memories of his childhood; going to Mae Ellis and the Whittaker's stores,

Ulrich's Drug Store, and a hair cut from Rube Davis, the barber. After several years the family moved from Youngstown to South Avenue in Niagara Falls.

"It was the depression years. I pulled a wagon to get relief goods at the Moore Business Forms building. It used to be a chocolate factory. The Knights of Columbus gave us our one Christmas gift of candy. People were good," Edward said. He walked to Sacred Heart School for elementary and later St. Mary's for high school. Uniforms were a great equalizer "so no one knew if you were poor or not. Girls wore a plaid uniform with detachable collars and cuffs, so they didn't have to wash the whole uniform," Edward chuckled. In 1939 he began his philosophy studies at Niagara University and worked at the Hooker Chemical Company factory for forty cents an hour, then went on to work for Bell Aircraft loading the crated P-39s on railroad cars.

TABLE 4.5
Specifications of P-39 Airacobra

Span	34 ft.
Length	30 ft. 2 in.
Height	12 ft. 5 in.
Weight	7,570 lbs. normal load
Armament	One 37 mm cannon firing through the propeller hub; two .50-cal machine guns in the nose; two .50-cal. Machine guns in packets under the wing; 500 lbs. of bombs externally
Engine	Allison V-1710 of 1,200 hp
Cost	$46,000
Maximum speed	376 mph
Cruising speed	250 mph
Range	650 mi.
Service ceiling	35,000 ft.

Source: Reprinted by permission from the "Bell P-39 Airacobra," Fact Sheets, *National Museum of the USAF*, http://www.nationalmuseum.af.mil/factsheets/factsheet.asp?id=2207 [accessed March 5, 2008].

Edward was inducted at Fort Niagara on October 12, 1942, and within a month was headed overseas on a Greek ship that had been captured by the British. "Frank Duffy and I were paired buddies. I look out for you and you look out for me. This was a Ranger practice. We trained together since we joined the Third Battalion in Nemours in North Africa. Anders Arnbal was our mentor during training. He stressed this buddy system and the desire to be the best."

Edward volunteered. "I was one of four thousand volunteers, for the Third Ranger Battalion (Co. D), but only 462 were chosen. It was tough training. We practiced landings from the water carrying a weapon with live ammo and every morning did an eight-mile run before breakfast. At the fourth mile we were ordered to dump our canteen of water to condition us. I was very competitive and determined that this was not going to beat me."

In January 1943 Edward trained for the battles ahead while President Franklin Roosevelt and British Prime Minister Churchill met at the Casablanca Conference to plan for the invasion of Italy. On July 9-10, 1943, the Allies launched one of the largest operations of the war that began with the invasion of Sicily. "It lasted for twenty-eight days and they (Italians) capitulated under Marshall Badoglio," Edward said.[196] On September 9, 1943, the Allied forces began the mainland invasion. The Rangers were the first Army troops on the beach for the Italian invasion near Salerno.[197] During September the German troops moved in and occupied Rome, and rescued Benito Mussolini after a coup removed him from power.

"We held the Germans at the top of the mountain (Mount Tramonte) for ten or eleven days." It was the successful battle for the strategic heights at Chiunzi Pass. After the engagement, Edward was evacuated to a British hospital in Bougie, North Africa, for medical treatment of malaria and an infection in his spinal column. He returned to his battalion in December in time for the preparation for the fight at Anzio. Edward continued, "We were based at Pozzuoli, Lucrino, on the bay at Naples."

After the Anzio landing, the operation for Cisterna, a key Fifth Army objective, began near the end of January 1944. The Rangers put up a tremendous fight, but surrounded and outnumbered, the First and Third Battalions were unable to break through the German position.[198] There were heavy casualties. The details of the beachhead and battle to clear the road to Cisterna left life-long physical and mental scars for Edward. "We were outnumbered one hundred to one. It was a real bad day at Black Rock."[199]

Back home in Niagara Falls, Edward's mother listened to Robert St. John's radio announcement that the Rangers died fighting in Cisterna. "My mother telephoned St. John wanting to know the details of what happened to me. He sent her a copy of the news report." A fireman brought the dreaded telegram that Edward was missing to the Feigenbaum home.

Edward and his buddy Frank went through training together, the Sicilian campaign, the invasion of the mainland at Mairoi beachhead, Salerno, and now faced an uncertain future as prisoners of war. He and four of his buddies were put in a large trolley car barn's pit with more than one thousand other soldiers. "German soldiers marched on both sides of the pit holding hand grenades. We were warned that if we tried to climb out they would throw a grenade into the hole. Later, I got slapped around while we were questioned. The Italians spit at us and threw stones when the Germans marched us through Rome. We were taken to the Colosseum and thought we were going to be executed."

After the march, the American POWs were trucked to a prison camp. There was very little food for the prisoners. Edward believes hunger affects you more mentally than physically and is a real leveler of humanity. He said, "that is why mental acuity and spiritual belief play an important part in a person's well being. Survival was foremost in my mind."

At the POW camp the Americans were searched again and Germans took what they wanted. Edward and the other POWs in the camp were fed only once a day, a piece of bread and a cup of soup from dehydrated cabbage or dried peas. "We were issued half of an old wool blanket and a tin can (no handle). No can at roll call equaled no soup or no coffee. We slept on pallets covered with straw, and burnt the wooden slats to keep warm. Tobacco became non-existent, so we smoked pine needles or anything that smoldered." Depression and thoughts of suicide were common among the prisoners.

Edward and Frank vowed to each other that they would survive and somehow regain their freedom. Near the end of February they were moved from the camp to the railroad station, searched, and relieved of their belts and shoelaces, then shoved into boxcars with a hunk of bread and a can of meat that looked like dog food. In the middle of the boxcar was a small wooden barrel for the men to relieve themselves.

Edward moved along the perimeter of the car with his buddy looking for a crack or an opening. A broken strip of metal covered a joint of the wooden boards of the boxcar. They used the metal piece as a pry bar to remove some of the wooden slats and the cold air rushed in to cover the stench inside the car. The train slowed as they rushed to put the boards back in place and hold them with their bodies. Guards walked around the train, but didn't notice anything as the train resumed its journey. After what seemed like forever the train slowed again and stopped. Edward and Frank waited for their opportunity. "It was too dark to see anything through the crack. We started to move again and could hear the guards climbing back into their boxcars. The train began picking up speed.

We took off the boards and the cold night air rushed in. I looked out. Nothing was visible. Duffy bent down. I climbed on his back and slid out the opening turning over as I did. I grasped the edge and hung down (then jumped). The strain and jolt jarred my inner being, but I was out and free. I just lay there till the last car passed from sight. In a short time I heard movement as I lay still in the dark. It was Duffy stumbling my way," Edward said.

Later he discovered that they jumped the train somewhere north of Florence near a large town, which he thought was Prato. Their captivity as American POWs lasted twenty-nine days.[200] They hid in the woods of the mountains while trying to work their way south. Frank and Edward connected with the local Underground faction of the Garibaldi Brigade and worked on some of their operations. The Garibaldi Brigade was part of the Communist political party, said Edward. Another partisan faction wanted Victor Emmanuelle return to the throne and another group was part of a Christian Democratic Political party, continued Edward explaining the different partisan groups. "We traveled around Ancona, Pescara, Forli, Bologna, and San Marino in the Province of Romagna. If it weren't for Duffy and me staying close together we would never have survived." The Italians disappeared in the middle of blowing up a railroad area near Faenza when the Germans appeared, so Frank and Edward decided to leave the Underground group.

Edward and Frank ran into other escapees, American, British, Indian Ghurkas, and others, and exchanged information as they looked for American troops. Finally, they heard artillery in the distance. Frank decided to wait for the front to come to him and stayed with the local Underground partisans near Rocca Strata. Edward hid in a small ravine until he heard American voices. "I came under Allied control June 20, 1944. They put me in a jeep and took me to G-2 (War Department) in Grosseto. I was questioned then went to Civatavecchio, Naples, Africa, and then back to the United States where I was questioned again in Washington, DC. I met up with Duffy, Scotty Munro, and Bob Halliday at Fort Dix, New Jersey."[201]

At Fort Dix, Edward, an American POW, was made a guard over German POWs. He didn't understand the government's rationale for this. On October 27, 1945, he was discharged from Fort Niagara and given fifty-eight cents for travel pay (five cents a mile) to return home.

Edward returned to Niagara University to complete his education. He boxed for Niagara against Fredrick Niland, a Canisius College student. The Niland brothers' story was the basis for the WWII era movie, *Saving Private Ryan.*[202] Edward married Leocadia in 1963 and raised their three children: Michael,

Catherine, and Edward II. Edward attributes his success in life to his wife who passed away October 4, 2006.

Edward Feigenbaum I and Frank Duffy were "depression kids. We were streetwise before we came into the military. This helped us to survive." He shares his story with schoolchildren to educate them about American POWs and to pass on his survival skills for life.

JOHN S. ZALE (né ZUBRZYCKI) ~ "I was born February 9, 1922, raised in Lackawanna, New York, and enlisted February 14, 1940."[203] After a physical, John was sworn in, destined for the Philippine Islands. He wanted to go to the furthest place away and hoped to be with his buddy in Panama. John joined the Thirty-First Infantry known as the American Foreign Legion.

"I loved the Army. It was going to be my career. I volunteered for everything trying to better myself. I got three square meals a day, my own bed, and my own clothes. We were paid twenty-one dollars a month. I sent five dollars to my mother, which didn't leave me too much money for fooling around. My sister sent me a letter saying it would be good if I could send a few more dollars. Eventually, I got a promotion to a corporal; it is like being Jesus Christ. Then I got a squad and the fun stopped. I was stationed in Manila when the war broke out and the whole world changed.

The White Russians[204] living in the Philippines were trying to get out. A French destroyer was docked there for repairs, and I was supposed to go home when the bugler sounded the call to arms. From that day on it was double time and Manila was declared an Open City."[205] After Pearl Harbor, John was shipped to the Bataan Peninsula. Conditions were difficult during the Battle of Bataan. "I had to divvy up our rations, a can of tomatoes and a can of tuna between eight to ten men, a spoonful for each. I got hit in the stomach and thought that was it and my legs were gone. Body parts were in the trees and all over. I lay in a swale and prayed. It was the only prayer I ever said. I asked God, have mercy on our souls. It was the only time peace overcame me. A guy from Butler, Pennsylvania, and a Filipino scout came back for me and pulled me out. I was operated on in a schoolhouse. Word came to move the patients because the building was going to be shelled. My commander came to the hospital and said if I could get back that I'd get a promotion and another stripe to a Platoon Sergeant. A few days before the surrender came, I got malaria." John's parents received a telegram that he was wounded on January 21, 1942.

Gen. Edward King surrendered the Luzon Force to Japan on April 9, 1942. It was the largest mass surrender of United States forces, about twelve thousand American soldiers, and also sixty-three thousand Filipinos. The prisoners were forced to march from Marieveles in the southern tip of Bataan to Camp O'Donnell about one hundred miles north in intense heat and abuse by their captors. It was almost a year later that the government on March 27, 1943, sent a letter to Mr. Peter Zubrzycki advising him that John was a prisoner of war. "The Bataan March was bad. Most guys had dysentery and malaria. If I had to march another mile I couldn't have made it because I ended up in a coma for about three days. Someone else spoon-fed me. That is how I survived. I was in the Zero Ward. There was also a St. Peter's Ward. No one came out alive from there. We marched to Cabanatuan (north-east of O'Donnell) then to Bilibid Prison. It was a federal prison during peacetime."

The POWs were split up into different camps. John escaped to get supplies hidden by the medics during the battle for Bataan, and then escaped back into the camp to bring medical supplies to his fellow soldiers. John continued, "We got some quinine and sulfur. It came in handy to help your buddies that got sick. A doctor told me, that I better get out of this place. I was delirious and volunteered to go on the ship to Manchuria."

The POWs were shipped out from Manila Bay on Japanese freighters called "Hell Ships" by the prisoners. The ships were unmarked and frequent targets of Allied submarines unaware of the transported POWs crammed into the cargo holds under inhumane conditions with no light, little air, or sustenance for almost a month. Prisoners were shot trying to get out of the sinking ships. The guys who managed to get in the water faced machine gun fire from other nearby Japanese ships. "The Bataan Death March was a picnic compared to the Hell Ships. The Hell Ships were worse. We were down in the hold, no sanitary conditions, and guys full of lice. There was no food, no place to sleep. You stood or squatted; no room to lie down. When someone died they were thrown overboard. The medical supplies ended up on one of the ships that got torpedoed and were lost. I recall two torpedoes that were faulty and missed our ship. To this day I want to know which sub it was and think about it every time I see a ship. We ended up in Pusan, Korea,[206] full of lice. Everyone had dysentery. At Pusan we were loaded into trains to Manchuria."

Everything froze in their canteens during the first winter. Supplies were limited. "We moved to another camp. It was my first experience at trapping a dog, killing it, and eating it. There were no Red Cross packages. The weather was similar to home with four seasons. I think it saved my life. Near the end in 1945 we got one Red Cross package that was divvied up. The cans were punctured so you couldn't stock up." Their diet was primarily soup served in a wooden bucket.

"On one of the Emperor's birthdays we got an orange, in honor of him. It was the first thing that was delicious. We ate the entire orange, skin and all!"

The bugler blew reveille in the dark of the winter morning. The POWs were used for labor in the copper and coal mines. John worked in a textile factory. Everyday it was a five-mile march to work and back to the camp. "If you had dysentery you were not allowed to stop to go to the latrine. The workday was usually ten hours, and then we marched back. Some of the guys made out good because they were in a tanning plant and ate the molasses, but I couldn't eat canvas. When the guard was making his rounds we sabotaged the machines to make them go faster. It weakened the weave. We found out that one of the machines used peanut oil for cutting. We ate it and replaced it with water so the machines would freeze up. The poor Chinese people were getting blamed for the things we did. I threw a spring in the transformer, which burned it out. They didn't know it was me or I would have been gone. Once, we buried a lathe in the concrete. The Japs were at lunch and practicing screaming with sticks. It was our chance to do something."

Part of the daily ritual was to bow to the Emperor and the Japanese soldiers. "Humor helped us survive," John shared, remembering the few choice words mumbled under his breath to the emperor! "My first beating was from not bowing properly. He beat the hell out of me. When the Japs wanted you to admit something that was serious they beat you for four days in and out of your cell. When they saw the story wasn't going to change, it was fourteen days in solitary. An American officer, Major Hankins, witnessed any court martial. He was responsible if anyone was goofing off." Conviction for a court martial resulted in death.

The Japanese were cruel to their prisoners. "They enjoyed making themselves feel good by hurting you. In the beginning when they started winning they thought they were superior. They enjoyed kicking you. I was beat for four days after I came out of solitary. We were on a work detail. I saw a bag of brown sugar and ate a mouthful. There was sugar on my face and shirt. The head of the detail decided to punish me; he punched me instead of solitary. It was worth it. The Japs were mean to each other too. Rank was important to them."

"When we were first captured my biggest concern was for the nurses. I was worried about what was going to happen to them. They took good care of me when I was down. Our hospital was in the dirt under the trees. For three and a half years, I lost contact with civilization while in Manchuria. I became a nobody, no momma, no poppa, no Uncle Sam. Our youth was taken away from us. I got only one card in all those years, twenty-five words from my sister. "Father is the same, mother is okay, I got married and Marion is in the service . . ." John was held as a prisoner for three and a half years in Mukden, Manchuria.[207]

The Bataan Death March and Hell Ships were only part of the notorious Japanese war crimes. Japan's Biological Warfare Unit 731 promoted racial superiority and conducted lethal human experimentation on POWs and dropped weapons on several cities and towns. Germ warfare resulted in the deaths of more than one-quarter million Chinese. John was one of the guinea pigs of the plague research during his captivity.

When American bombers began to target near the camp, "the Japanese colonel wanted us to write a letter to President Roosevelt that our planes were killing American prisoners. One of the guys who lost his arm wrote to Roosevelt 'send the planes back, I have one more arm.' That is patriotism. It was a beautiful sight seeing the silver American aircraft targeting the Japanese factories!" Years later at the VA Hospital in Buffalo, John met the pilot who bombed the POW camp.

Just prior to being liberated by the Russians, a team parachuted into the camp in August 1945 to explain to the Japanese commander that the emperor surrendered and they were not to follow the standing order to kill all the POWs. Earlier, the Japanese bragged to the American POWs that they would commit Hara-Kari, also known as Seppuku, a ritual suicide by disembowelment, if captured. But when the Russians approached the camp one of the Japanese officers gave his sword to John and volunteered to surrender to the Americans rather than the Russians. John reminded him of his duty to commit suicide. The officer replied that he did not really intend to do it, so John let the Russians take the Japanese. The sword is on display in the Buffalo and Erie Naval Park, Buffalo, New York.

"The Japs lined up their weapons and now they became our prisoners. The roads were bombed so we stayed in Mukden until they could be repaired. A hospital ship[208] waited in Korea to take us back to Okinawa when a typhoon hit. My brother was looking for me at the time but we missed each other. From Okinawa they flew us back to the Philippines. The orders were 'don't bother the prisoners.' We were like kids in a candy store drinking and living it up. I finally got tired and boarded a ship for California to Letterman Hospital, and eventually a pass to go home."

After the war John worked for Bethlehem Steel for nine years, and then for the Navy on Porter Road, Niagara Falls, followed by a stint on the construction of the Robert Moses Power Project. He became a Maintenance Clerk at Fort Niagara and maintained the rifle range. When Fort Niagara closed as an active military base he helped to pack up the hospital then worked at the Missile silo. "All of a sudden around Christmas I was out of a job. Missiles were being shipped out, and we started taking care of the Reserve Centers. I retired from Fort Niagara, but my office was at Fort Drum."

John returned with his own mission to do something for the community and pass on his life skills. "I wanted to teach kids about patriotism and survival and became active in the Boy Scouts. It has been my mission in life." He continued his role during the war of helping wounded comrades and devotes his time to visiting patients at the VA Hospital in Buffalo, New York.

DOMINICK F. POLISENO was born in 1918 in Sharpsville, Pennsylvania.[209] When the mills closed Angelo[210] and Angeline Matasha Poliseno moved their family of two boys and four girls to Lackawanna. Dom grew up in the depression era raising and butchering hogs. He liked to camp, fish, and hunt. "I went into the Army from Fort Niagara and to Fort Bragg by train, and then to Butler for training as a combat engineer. After about six or seven weeks, they shipped my tail right over to Africa without a furlough. They were looking for Rangers, so I joined the First Ranger Battalion." Later the First Battalion broke up to create the Third and Fourth Battalions.

Push-ups, speed marches, running up and down the mountains, and swimming in the ocean were part of the demanding Ranger training. Four or five recruits played catch with an eight-foot telephone pole, back and forth over their shoulders then through their legs. "They kept telling you: keep going you are doing good. We were taught armed combat with a real knife. The Sergeant said 'attack me.' He took the knife away, flopped you down, and repeated 'use the knife.' We were taught how to throw a person, to use a knife to kill or to disable a person, how to bayonet, and demolition. I was a demolition expert with the combat engineers. We climbed up in the mountains using ropes and on narrow passes. We lost a guy in combat doing that and once a donkey with a whole load of machine guns and ammunition. We stretched ropes over a ravine and worked our way across with our legs crossed, and also with ropes on top and one below that you walked across."

Dom later trained new recruits who swore at him too as he marched them up and down the hills trying to prepare for combat. "They asked me if I was trying to get them out and I said, no, if you keep up with me and do this you will be alright. We turned a lot of recruits back. Near Cassino up on the mountain, in combat, we were sent two green kids, about nineteen years old. I don't know if they ever shot a rifle before, but I was told to put them on the line of the cliff. I told the new recruits to dig a trench hole, but don't go in the hole at the same time. They didn't listen. A German fighter dropped a personnel bomb in that hole. All that was left was burnt flesh. I was really mad! These kids weren't ready for this. They had basic training, but didn't have hard combat training like me. It was rough. By the way, a P-38 came by, saw the German and went after him, and shot him down. But I felt really sad for the two kids."

The Rangers chased the Germans from mountain to mountain in Sicily and on the mainland of Italy. "We chased them all the way to Messina. I was the first one in Messina. It was two o'clock in the morning when we went in and took 150 Italian prisoners. The Germans were already gone. You could see boats docked across the strait. The Sergeant and I went to the coast to meet the English. In the *Patton* movie the English come into Messina, but that never happened. Patton came later in the evening with his pearl handled pistols and the newsreel cameras. They wanted me to stand with him and get my picture taken. I gave them a few choice words. I didn't want my mother to know what I was doing and to worry. They wanted my name and where I came from for *Life* and *Look* magazines. I wouldn't let them take my picture." Dom's brother-in-law served in the Pacific. He wrote to Dom and asked him why he wanted to serve in a "suicide outfit."

The Rangers were scheduled to go to France after Anzio. "We landed first in the morning and cleared the way for the infantry to come in. We went in about five miles on the line up on Mussolini Canal and sent in a patrol. They came back with the news that one of our men was shot because he didn't give the code word. That night the Germans brought in three or four more divisions. We were three battalions, about seven hundred men, against five divisions. We got up to the banks. A German jeep came by near dawn and must have spotted something. The guard stepped out and pretended to look at the tires, but looked behind at the ditch. One of the guys said 'we have been had.' Everybody opened up on the jeep. That is when all the hell started!"

German tanks approached their position as the Rangers fired and threw grenades. At the edge of the town Dom found five of his guys inside a house taking sniper fire. "I fired a clip at the outhouse and the firing stopped. One of the guys was shot through both legs. I was so tired and must have fallen asleep and woke up to the sound of German boots. The others left me with the wounded guy. A German sergeant marching with the Rangers looked at me. I started to raise the tommy gun and my sergeant said no they would kill us. I hid the gun under the mattress and put my hands up and said 'comrade.' A soldier told us to come out." The Germans marched the Rangers to a castle for interrogation. The artillery came and everyone scattered. In the confusion Dom moved to stand with the group already questioned.

The captured Rangers were taken to the train repair station and put in the hole used to work on the engines and then trucked to an Italian camp near Florence. "The Germans lined us up. A short guy with a whip lined us up and said 'du Jewda (you Jew) when you get to Germany they will take care of you.' They took Feigenbaum too. We stayed there maybe two weeks. They gave us a little soup, and I ate some dandelions in the fields. A cat in the camp disappeared. My buddy and me walked in between the barracks and saw two English guys cooking the cat. Soup was made with horsemeat and bones. You could not see any potatoes and maybe a string like piece that could be meat. My buddy, Sergeant Fox, said 'let's go get the bones the German chef threw out. We will skin them off for vitamins then grate them on the inside for the minerals.' You will do anything to survive."

The Germans transported the prisoners from the camp by train and marched them through the City of Rome and the Coliseum for propaganda to boast that the best American soldiers were captured. Some clapped and hollered. "You could see tears in the eyes of the old women. They marched us back to the trucks and the camp in Italy, and then on trains to Camp 7A near Munich. After a few weeks it was back on the trains to Camp 2B. It took three days and two nights. About eighty of us were crowded into the rail car with a can in the middle to relieve ourselves. I pitied the guys who sat around it. The sergeant asked 'how are your feet, can you feel your feet? You better check them.' Oh my God, my feet were blue. The sergeant said to rub them to keep the circulation going. I rubbed the skin off. One guy's feet were all black. He had to have his feet cut off. That was really bad. A lot of guys had their toes cut off. You were like an animal in there. They treated you worse than an animal. Feigenbaum and another guy ripped a board off and got out when the train slowed down. They went back in the hills and fought with the Partisans."

Later, Dom was sick and unable to eat. He gave away his rations and was hospitalized with diphtheria for several months. An American medic administered the serum, which came from France, with a needle that he sharpened with the edge of a stone. "He used the same needle on all of us. When I got back to the barracks I couldn't see outside. A German doctor treated me with some eye drops. I still have the prescription he wrote." Dom weighed eighty pounds and was assigned to Oflag 64 with Pfc Frank Palumbo, an old buddy from home. They were on a work detail with twenty other prisoners in the woods along the eastern border of Poland felling trees for a sawmill operation. "They put us in an old radio shack, an observation building. Every morning we cut trees from sun up to sun down, in the snow two or three feet deep. Sundays, we were off. We didn't have any boots. We made our own hats with flaps from a blanket and sewed our own gloves. We wrapped the blankets around our feet and our legs. In the beginning the guards were nasty. I wanted to drop a tree on one of them. I knew how to cut a tree. The guard was standing with his back to us. Another kid, a Ranger from Wyoming, hollered at the guard that this big fir tree was coming down. He cursed us. I said that I don't know how to cut trees. He was a mean bastard. The guard said you better watch yourself."

Early in January 1945 the forest commandos marched back to Hammerstein as the camp prepared for evacuation to avoid the approaching Russian troops. They slept in open fields in the snow and sometimes in a barn. "One guy stayed awake. You only slept about twenty minutes. When someone died the Germans put the body on the side of the road." Infested with lice, Dom in desperation to rid himself of the pests broke through a duck pond, stripped naked, and poured the icy water over himself. At Camp IIA in Neubrandenburg, the Russians shelled the town. "The guards started to take off. I said I am going to leave. I didn't want to get taken by the Russians. Five guys came with me. We met a Russian patrol that gave us a loaf of bread. They told us where to go after we used their mobile shower. We came to a town on the rail yards. I saw a pump car and threw it on the rail and pumped like hell." Dom led his group west towards Hamburg around blown out bridges, through towns and farms, to the Elbe River where they garnered a rowboat. "None of the other guys knew how to row. I rowed and finally got to an American patrol that pulled us in. They gave us a shower and new uniforms. The next day a C-47 landed on the road and took us to Camp Lucky Strike."[211] C-47s were used to carry personnel and cargo, and in combat towed gliders and dropped paratroopers into enemy territory.[212]

Dom returned to Italy after the war and the combat sights a number of times. He spoke to students about his experiences and the war. The school children appreciated what the Rangers did in Italy. "One little girl told me that she wouldn't have been born if I hadn't fought in the war and saved their town. It was very touching."

WILLIAM J. VERONICA was born December 21, 1916, in the little town of Dubois, Pennsylvania. "My father was a coal miner and when the mines petered out we moved to Buffalo, New York."[213] Will completed a college entrance curriculum and graduated in 1937 from Kenmore High School. He hoped to attend college, but the realities of the depression forced him into the workforce at Dunlop Tire Company. Dunlop produced tires for the war effort when Will enlisted in the Army in 1941. "My dad died that year. Mom didn't speak about the war too much. My parents were happy to be in this country. My older brother worked in the CCC Camps and my younger brother, Daniel, was a test pilot."[214]

"I was part of a National Guard outfit that met at the Armory on Main and Delavan. We went to Fort Niagara as a unit, then sent to Camp Edwards, Massachusetts, as the 102nd Separate Battalion for basic training. The 102nd Cavalry still had horses then! Camp Edwards was a beautiful place on the ocean. We trained with old bolt-action rifles from WWI and were supposed to guard the airfields," Will said.

"After Pearl, I volunteered for service as a Navy gunner. About five hundred of us served with the Navy transport. We shipped out of Brooklyn on the *Old Mexico* and transported American soldiers to England. There were a lot of U-boats in the Atlantic and we lost some ships on the way over. In England, we picked up British troops for the fight in northern Africa and Italian POWs at the Suez bound for camps in Cape Town.[215] I acted as kind of an interpreter. The Italians said they didn't want the war and didn't want to fight. Some gave me letters for their relatives living in America. Mussolini was popular in the beginning because of his social programs, but when he joined up with Hitler most Italians wrote him off."

"After two years, I went in for pilot training and was assigned as a radio-operator and machine gunner on a B-17 in the 388th Bombardment Group of the Eighth Air Corps. I met my wife, Judy, in Jack Dempsey's Night Club and we married on March 15, 1944, before I shipped out for England. Our first missions were daylight bombings over Germany. We got up about 5:00 a.m. for briefings in the combat room. They put up a map and then told us where we were going to bomb. The B-17 was a big plane to us. We wore an electric suit[216] and oxygen mask because the temperatures dropped below minus fifty degrees at 25,000 feet. It was no fun." The ten-man crew struggled to move around in the tight quarters during the eight to ten hour missions.

The target for the eighth mission May 12, 1944, was an oil refinery in Brus, Czechoslovakia, part of the pre-D-day assault, when "fighters attacked us near Frankfurt, Germany, before we reached our target. We were at twenty-two thousand feet when three of our engines were hit and on fire. The order was given to bailout. We were over Hamburg.[217] As soon as we bailed, the plane exploded!" Will was hit by debris on the way down. Farm workers rushed towards him with picks and shovels and started to beat Will until the German Army intervened. "If the German soldiers hadn't come along I think they (the farm hands) would have killed me."

Worried families back home received the dreaded telegrams from the military that their sons were missing-in-action. "When the telegram came my wife was heart broken and thought I had been killed. All the worry impacted her pregnancy and she lost our twin babies born prematurely. It took six months before my family found out that I was a POW."

Interrogation followed the capture. "They tried to scare us and asked 'who is your commander? How many ships do you have? What is your mission? You must know.' But we didn't know anything and told them only our name, rank, and serial number. We were taken to Stalag Luft IV in Poland near the Baltic Sea." The Luft camp was for airmen. It took several months for Will's crew to be reunited since they bailed out at different times and were not captured together.

The reality of the camp conditions at Stalag Luft IV were nothing like the television program *Hogan's Heroes*. "Several men were killed for not conforming to camp rules," Will said quietly. "We lost two POWs playing ball near the wire fence. The guards shot them for retrieving the ball. The Germans dragged the bodies away. One guard was pretty good because his son was a POW in the states.[218] He wrote to his father that he was treated well by the Americans." There were bed checks day and night. The crowded barracks, built on stilts, were twelve feet by twelve feet with triple bunks housing twenty-four men and a pot bellied stove. Food rations created hunger and sometimes fights, but Will made a pact with some of his crew members to help each other and to share their food. Cigarettes from the Red Cross packages were used to barter for food from the German guards. "We were given one loaf of bread and a bucket of small potatoes, our daily ration for twenty-four men. I was elected room leader to cut the bread, which was mostly sawdust, into twenty-four pieces." During Will's captivity, the Germans kept most of the Red Cross packages. "We only got two or three during the thirteen months. They gave us one (package) when we went on the March.

Officers didn't work according to the Geneva Convention. "If you worked outside the camp you could grab something to eat. Russian slave laborers worked out in the fields and I got friendly with them. One day I walked out of the camp with them and tried to find my way to the Underground. I spent several days hiding and looking for food then walked back into the camp."

In January 1945 the Russians advanced and there were rumors the war would be over soon. The Germans broke up the camp of more than ten thousand POWs into groups of two hundred each and "marched us for eighty-six straight days through Germany, covering twenty-five to thirty kilometers a day. We slept in fields and barns, and a lot of men fell by the wayside. About May 23 (1945) the German guards gave up and tried to befriend us. At the Elbe River they told that us the Americans should be on the other side. A captain came over in a jeep and said, 'The war is over for you guys.' We were sent to Le Havre, France, deloused and sent back to the States on the *Queen Mary*." During his captivity and the Black Death Hunger March,[219] Will lost almost forty pounds.

He closed his story with personal reflections of current events and war. "War is hell…I hate to see people killed everyday (Iraq)… Just do the right thing…I went through the war and things happened to me that I do not want to happen to these kids…(we survived because) we had faith in ourselves. You can't give up."

RICHARD H. MORSE ~ The start of Dick Morse's high school career coincided with the beginning of the war in 1939. "I was anxious to get in the service," he said. Dick was born in Buffalo, New York, and lived in Arcade when he began his military career at the age of seventeen in the Army Specialized Training Program. He was assigned to educational classes at Syracuse University until his eighteenth birthday when he was shipped to Fort Benning in Georgia, then to Fort Jackson, South Carolina. "We were sent over as replacements for D-Day." He proudly shared the names of the ships that took him into combat as part of the Eighty-seventh Infantry Division: the *Queen Elizabeth* to cross the Atlantic Ocean in October 1944, the *Empire Rapier* on the English Channel, and a Landing Ship Tank (LST) to reach the shores of Le Havre, France. "The Allies were already in France. I was captured at Gross Réderching."[220]

DONALD MECKLE ~ "We were on our twenty-fourth mission when we were shot down over Regensburg, Germany.[221] There were two targets that day, an aircraft factory and oil refinery." Don was a gunner on a B-17 with the Fifteenth Air Corps flying out of Italy. He worked in a manufacturing plant doing some defense work in Buffalo, New York, when he enlisted in 1942. "We were shipped to North Africa for six weeks for training, then serviced planes. I was an armament specialist repairing machine guns then loaded and fused bombs on the aircraft when I heard there were openings for aerial gunners and applied. After I passed all the physicals the flight surgeon asked me, 'what are you going to do if they shoot your glasses off?' I responded that my head would be shot off. He passed me."

"We went on some tough missions and bombed Vienna three times. Sometimes the missions took from nine and a half to eleven hours in a B-17." Don said that the B-17's top speed was about 300 mph, but cruised at 155 mph while in formation. "On our twenty-fourth mission we were trying to get to the Russian lines after two of our engines were knocked out. We knew we couldn't make it back to our base in Italy. Without the two engines, we couldn't get enough altitude to go over the Alps so we tried to make it to the Russian lines. The ship was declining and the order was given to bail out before we lost power. We were close to the ground, and I just cleared the tail. In an instant, I remembered the training films as I saw the wooded area below and crossed my legs so I wouldn't get speared. My chute broke loose from the trees, and I was knocked unconscious as I hit the ground. I woke up to a German poking a rifle at my forehead." The Air Corps crew carried escape kits that contained small maps, some money, and cigarettes.

Don was taken from a transit camp to Stalag Camp IIIA in Luckenwalde, Germany.[222] He and his buddy Paul, a waist gunner, stayed together while in the camp. During desperate conditions and out of hunger some guys in the camp became scavengers and stole food from each other. "But Paul and I stuck together and it was a comfort" during the ordeal. "We heard that we were going to be taken by the Russians. They were paid for every American that was rescued and repatriated. American trucks were waiting down the road, but the Russians wouldn't let us go. We were weak and undernourished, and covered with lice from the straw bedding. An American soldier from the convoy told us to sneak out at night and no matter what just keep running towards the trucks. We did." It was April 1945. Back in the states, Don arrived in Buffalo at the Central train terminal and walked towards his home a couple of miles from the station. After walking most of the way, he was picked up and given a ride for the last leg to home. "I was glad to get home!"

BERNARD J. ADAMSKI ~ "You tried to forget and now you try to remember," he said.[223] "I was born June 12, 1924, to Joseph and Catherine Grabowski Adamczyk and have lived all my life at 703 Smith Street in Buffalo.[224] I was inducted March 15, 1943. We left on buses from the Old Post Office on Washington Street (Buffalo) headed for Fort Niagara and basic training and tests. After about two weeks, I was assigned to the Air Corps and sent to Miami Beach, Florida."

The potential radio operators took a number of tests. "We were given about one hundred fifty letters in Morse Code and asked, 'how does it sound to you, the same or different.' I studied electrical engineering course work at Seneca High School, which must have helped," Ben said. Morse Code was taught at

Scott Field, Illinois. "It was equivalent to a two year college course crammed into six months studying aircraft radio. From there we were sent to gunnery school at Tyndall Field, Florida." After a furlough in January 1944, Ben met his crew for the first time and they were assigned to a B-26 twin-engine bomber, a Marauder.

In addition to Tyndall Field, Scott Field graduates were also sent to Harlingen, Las Vegas, or Laredo.[225] Qualifications for the advanced training schools included an eighth grade education, a score of at least eighty-five on the Army Classification Test, height of six feet or less, and one hundred eighty pounds or less.[226]

"The Marauder is between a bomber and a fighter. It was difficult to fly. There was a six-man crew: the pilot was Donald Epstein; Herbert Zweig, co-pilot; Horrace Dow, bombardier and navigator; Wayne Austin, waist gunner; and John Farrell, the tail gunner. I was the top turret operator, classified as a radio operator and gunner. Flight training took place at Lake Charles, Louisiana, and Tyndall Field, Florida, and then we were given our overseas assignment. We ferried a brand new plane with no guns to be delivered to England." Like most flights Ben's crew took the southern route via South America flying in one-day intervals. After leaving Brazil, South America, they refueled at the Ascension Islands then again at the Gold Coast of Africa where the co-pilot's back problem kept them there for several days. The next stop was in the middle of the Sahara Desert. The station included four Army personnel, two small huts, one runway, and a tank set up for gasoline. Bruce Cabot, the movie star, commanded the station.

Then another delay came in Marrakech, the Casablanca area of Morocco in North Africa, when the pilot became ill. "The Army Special Services took us out tuna fishing on a tug boat through mine fields. I caught a tuna, about eighteen inches long. It was the first fish I ever caught. The guy next to me said 'I will get it in for you.' The fish hit the side of the boat and fell off! On land the natives, especially the kids, asked for gum. They ran almost fast enough to keep up with the truck. From there we flew to England and near Spain spotted some German fighters. We put some broom sticks out the window to look like guns, then landed in England and delivered the plane." A DC-6 transport took the crew to Ireland near Belfast for the final phase of several weeks of gunnery training. During the first week of June the crew received their assignment to the 385th Bomb Group 555th Bomb Squadron just north east of London, Great Dunmow, and began their missions bombing railroad bridges and other targets in France after the Normandy Invasion. "I was shot down on my seventh mission,

July 12, 1944. We took some heavy anti-aircraft fire. One engine was shot out. We drifted out of formation and lost altitude. Over the Channel on the way back we started to lose the second engine and hoped to make land. We were quite low when we spotted land and thought we could make it to England. The shortest distance across the Channel is about twenty-six miles from Calais, France, to England's coast. The navigator gave the pilot the heading to England when we came off of Calais, but if you are one degree off you flare out and can get off course." So instead of England, they approached the coast of France.

The crew saw the tracer bullets hit their ship as the pilot prepared to ditch in the water to avoid the land mines on the beach itself. Ben was near the bomb bay that still held two one-ton bombs! "We unscrewed the tips and defused the bombs just before we crashed in the water. We were taught crash landing and ditching procedures, to face towards the back of the plane and lean against the bulkhead so you don't get a whiplash and hold on to anything. I was okay until I saw the tail gunner on his hands and knees with his face covered. His headset was disconnected, so when the pilot said to prepare for crash landing he didn't hear him. I crawled on my hands and knees to warn him that we were coming down for a crash landing and to get over to my bulkhead. You could see the water. We were told distance was very deceptive. You think you are right on top of it. We didn't think we could make it back to the bulkhead. The gunner Farrel went into the tail and sat. He wrapped his legs around my waist, and we held on while the tail dragged in the water and we lost flying speed. At the first hit our hands loosened a little bit, and then when the nose went into the water, it was a big one! I don't remember anything after that. I was thrown from Farrel's bulkhead to my bomb-bay bulkhead, about twenty-five feet."

The cold Channel water woke Ben who was waist deep and unable to swim. At the tail gun opening he tried to stand, but flopped down in the water, red from his wound, unable to take another step. His jacket was torn and his face battered. He couldn't feel his legs, but pulled himself over to John who gave Ben a shove out the window into the water, then picked him up and dragged him onto the beach. "The Germans were still firing at us. It seemed like an eternity. We waved a white handkerchief and they stopped firing. They were all young kids, sixteen or seventeen years old, German soldiers, like watchmen on the beaches. We were taken to a farmhouse where we stayed overnight, and the following evening they put us on trucks again and drove until it was light. When it started to get light you could see bodies at the back of the truck. They took me to a hospital in Lille, France. My leg from my toes up to my knee was completely black and painful as heck. My ankle was swollen and the stocking cut into my ankle. I lay on a table alone in the emergency room for several hours." A French woman mopped the floors around Ben and seeing his distress returned with a pair of scissors and cut his sock, which released some of the pressure and pain. There were no doctors, bandages, or pain pills for Ben, only the kindness of a woman who couldn't speak English. The crew waited outside and carried Ben to the railroad station.

At Brussels, Belgium, Ben was sent to a new hospital and the rest of the crew went on. "I never saw them again. I hopped into the building on one leg and down a long hallway to an Army barracks behind barbed wire in back of the hospital. I was at the hospital for approximately six to eight weeks with my leg in an elevated metal rack. They never told me if the injury was from a bullet or a wound. Every morning, the German nurse came in and said to me 'nein' when I took my leg out of the rack. An elderly German nurse cared for one of the guys, a B-17 pilot. His whole face was bandaged except for his eyes and mouth. Everyday the nurse changed his bandages in the first aid room. You could hear him scream; he screamed like crazy. I used to think how heartless she was and wondered what they were doing to him." Once Ben was well enough to walk around, he helped in the first aid room to roll bandages and watch the nurse change the pilot's dressing as he screamed again. He watched her walk into a small office and cry, and again the next day. His opinion of the nurse changed as the pilot's skin healed.

The German commandant at the hospital was educated at Boston College. "He came down every morning for bed checks and correctly pronounced my name, Adamski, like in Polish. It made me feel a little like home." Ben was held in a college building in Brussels about six blocks from the hospital. "We walked up four or five stories to the top floor, an attic. There were four cells, four steps by two steps wide. I was held there for about two weeks in solitary confinement. They gave you something to eat in the morning and the evening. You were taken to wash and go to the bathroom. After almost two weeks they got you softened up pretty well. It was my first time interrogation in front of a German officer. The German lieutenant sat behind a desk and told me to sit down, opposite him. He took out an envelope and some papers and said 'Adamaski.' I said, 'yes sir.' We were told to give nothing but our name, rank and serial number and do not look him in the eyes, either look down or up. He offered me a Lucky Strike cigarette and I refused. He opened the envelope then told me everything about my life.[227] He knew when I entered the service and where I went to high school. He told me when my dad passed away and about my brother who was stationed in Buffalo as a cook. He asked, 'How does the

American government take two boys away from their mother to take care of the store by herself?' The night I was shot down I got a letter that my brother was transferred to Buffalo as a cook."

The interrogation continued with questions about the flight and the target. "He told me that I was a top turret and radio operator, and asked me what were my call signals and what frequency we were operating on. I said, 'I am sorry sir that according to the Geneva Convention I only have to tell you my name, rank, and serial number.' Up to that moment he was really nice, then, after my second refusal to answer, all of a sudden slammed his hand on the desk and said 'You know what you can do with the Geneva Convention!' Then he took a 25mm pistol and pointed it at my head. 'Who knows you are here? No one knows you are here.' I was starting to sweat. He yelled and screamed in German 'raus' get out. He got up from behind the desk. We were told to respect his rank. So I got up and saluted him. His pointed boots caught me right in the groin. Boy, it was painful. Someone helped me up."

The next stop via the trains again was Oberursel, an interrogation camp, with the same small cells, wooden bunks, straw for a mattress, and a very small window. "I saw something yellow stuck between the boards. It was a note with the word freedom and what freedom means from the back of an Old Gold cigarette pack. It was inspiring! I put the note back so someone else could read it. I was at Oberursel for a little more than two weeks and interrogated three times." Ben repeated, "no sir" to the questioning about his ability to speak and comprehend foreign languages, then was handed his Polish prayer book that he kept in his coveralls.

The British and Americans bombed the Berlin railroad yard along the route to Stalag Luft IV in Grosstychow, about late October 1944. "Bombs blew around us. We were scared, tired, hungry, and depressed as we got off the trucks at Stalag IV and walked into the camp through the barbed wire gates. The camp was divided into four sections. A British priest came once a week with the underground BBC news reports. We only received one Red Cross parcel while at the camp and it was shared with twenty-eight guys. In the morning we got a cup of tea and two slices of bread and at night a cup of potatoes. Occasionally you got some sauerkraut soup with potatoes, but no lunch."

On January 31, 1945, as the Russian troops advanced, the Germans moved the POWs out of the camp. They marched about twenty to twenty-five kilometers each day and at night slept in barns or in open fields in the cold and snow. "We grouped ourselves into four guys and shared everything and slept together. We put one blanket on the ground and three on top. One day you slept on the outside and another in the middle. On two separate occasions we were strafed, once by American pilots and once by the British, who thought we were German infantry. We jumped right in the ditch. Someone fell on top of me. One of the guys got killed and a few others wounded. We don't know what happened to them. Some guys couldn't take it and freaked out. In a little while you heard shots and surmised what happened." Off the side of the road mounds of covered beets, potatoes, and kohlrabi were buried to prevent them from freezing. Some guys were shot when they dropped out of the ranks to dig up potatoes or went to the side of the road to relieve themselves while suffering from dysentery.

Ben's socks were worn through and his boots always wet. It was Europe's coldest winter of the twentieth century. "Along the way I bargained in Polish with (displaced) Poles for a loaf of bread." One of the stops during the March was a camp just west of Berlin. Bodies of men, women, and children covered with a white powder were piled three or four stories high in a ditch. Russians, Slovakians, Poles, and others were held in the compound by nationality. The stench of decayed bodies and the moans and groans from the living dead overwhelmed Ben as he entered a Polish barrack. "One man's leg was cut off and the stump wrapped in burlap. He cried out to die from the pain. I had a sick feeling in my stomach. We thought this was the end for us, our final destination, but after five days we were out the gate and on the road again." Recently, Ben learned that the camp was Bergen-Belsen where Anne Frank died.

A British tank battalion liberated Ben and his group on May 2, 1945. He weighed ninety-seven pounds when he was liberated; he lost close to fifty pounds. At Camp Lucky Strike the freed soldiers prepared to board the ship and were given twenty-four dollars for supplies and toiletries. Many passed the time on the boat shooting dice, but not Ben. He returned to the states with his twenty-four dollars, the German flag that flew over Stalag Luft IV signed by POWs from across the country, and a new appreciation.

"I found that being with the group of men that we were with, you appreciate life a lot more."

EDWIN GRZYWA ~ "I spent my whole life in Buffalo. My parents were Frank and Julia Grzywa. We lived at 231 Wolz Avenue in the city." Ed's father was born in Poland and his mother in America. She died when Ed was seven years old. He was a machine operator at Hoodi Machine Co. making shock absorbers for defense work when he was drafted on February 23, 1943. "We did basic training at Fort Niagara for two weeks then to Atlantic City for another two weeks of training. I thought about being a truck driver, but scored well on my aptitude tests and was offered a radio operator's job in the Air Force. I was sent to Salt Lake City, Utah, for six weeks to learn Morse Code to be a radio operator. They needed men so fast and must have thought it was enough time. Then I went to gunnery in Alamogordo, New Mexico. It was the only time I handled a gun."[228]

Ed trained in Tucson, Arizona, with the 450th Bomb Group 720th Squadron and practiced about six months in a B-24. Ten men made up the crew. In December 1943, the crew went overseas and flew out of Lecchi, Italy. Ed served in Naples-Foggia, Rome, Arno, and in the Balkans. "They woke us up at two or three o'clock in the morning for briefings. We never knew where we were going until the day of the mission. I flew eleven missions pretty well safely. After our first mission we were told that one of our planes didn't return, but that it was safe in Switzerland. Our twelfth target was an aircraft factory in Regensburg. We were running low on fuel and the pilot prepared to ditch in the water then spotted land. We got up to eight thousand feet, fairly low to bail out. I sent out my first SOS and reported our position because we could not make it back to the base. We bailed out over Verona, Italy." Their altitude was low and some of the crew had been hurt swinging in their chutes against the side of a mountain, but all returned safely to the base because Verona was friendly territory.

Ed wasn't afraid to fly again after bailing out and flew his thirteenth mission with another crew, but the same target, Regensburg. They were hit by flak over the target and lost an engine. "We got as far as Yugoslavia when German fighters motioned to our pilot to bail out or get shot down. We bailed out at twenty thousand feet. I left my forty-five pistol on the plane because we could be shot if we were caught with it. A fighter pilot circled around us as we bailed out. I prayed. He didn't fire at me. We never had any training on parachutes and this was the second time in two days I bailed out. I hit the ground pretty hard and hurt my back. I hid my chute in a foot and a half of snow and tried to get back to Italy with my escape kit: twenty-one dollars, chocolate rations for six days, and a (silk) map. I came to a farm and told the farmer that I was American. He took me to the house and told his wife to fry me some eggs. I gave him the money and the chocolate to his kids. He told me to get on the wagon and then took me to town and turned me in."

Instead of reaching the Underground the farmer took Ed to face men in green uniforms with a swastika and guns drawn. "The interrogator spoke pretty good English. He told us about the plane from our group that came down in

Switzerland. He held a big book with a picture of the bomber that I bailed out of the first time. My eyes popped out and then he told me my father's name and where I went to school. They probably had spies in our country. There was an article in the newspaper when I was shot down." During the interrogation Ed was held in solitary, stripped, and kicked by the guards when he bent over to pick up his rosary. "They wouldn't let me have it."

After being interrogated he was put on a small truck and taken to a camp in East Prussia. "Breakfast was a slice of bread, lunch a bowl of broth, and supper small boiled potatoes. During the fourteen months I only got four Red Cross packages split between three other guys. The Germans punctured all the cans so we couldn't save any food if we tried to escape." The Russian offensive in the summer of 1944 threatened Stalag Luft IV, so the prisoners were placed on a ship for evacuation then a forced run to another camp. "I was shackled to another guy and he limped, but hung in there. I was afraid we would get shot if he fell down. We marched double-time in the heat of the afternoon. Some guys were bayoneted. At the camp I didn't work because I was a non-com. Privates and corporals went out on work details. It was boring with nothing to do. We didn't have anything to read. We ate from a can and you couldn't shower, only wash your face. Mattresses were straw and filled with lice."

As the Americans approached the camps from the west and the Russian lines pushed into Germany from the east, the prisoners were put in groups and marched south. Ed's group marched for fifty-six days. "February was one of the coldest months and the coldest winter for Europe. We marched and often slept in the snow and were given a ten-minute break. Sometimes we slept in a barn; it was terrible with the manure. This went on for fifty-six days. Half way through the March I developed gout in my two big toes and they swelled. The guards cut out part of my shoe so I was able to stay with the group. On April 26 (1945) we were liberated between the Russian and American lines. We walked over to the Americans as the Germans were captured." News of world events including the death of President Roosevelt came from new prisoners or the guards. "We heard about Roosevelt dying. I felt sad. He was a good president."

The emaciated men were put on a diet and stayed in Le Havre for a time. On his return home Ed's family did not recognize him, and they almost walked right by because he lost almost forty pounds. "That was the first time I saw my father cry. I stayed home for forty-five days on leave, and then reported for two weeks to Atlantic City. I didn't have enough points[229] to get discharged. During the leave I met my wife. It was love at first sight. We married on November 17, 1945. I worked as a supply clerk in South Carolina until I was discharged." Today, Ed takes four pain pills a day for the injury to his back when he bailed out.

During his captivity, Ed lived without church services and seeing the American flag. "It didn't mean too much to me when I was a kid, but this changed when it was taken away. I appreciate the American flag and what it stands for. We take so much for granted. I appreciate the young men and women who are serving our country today so that we all can have freedom. I know what they are going through. You don't know from day to day if you are going to be killed. My heart and prayers go out to them. People don't understand. War is no fun. It is horrible. Freedom is everything!"

ELWYN F. "AL" PALMERTON ~ "Coping with the living conditions in the POW camp depended on your thoughts about how to survive and changing your mental attitude." Al worked at both the Buffalo and Wheatfield Bell Aircraft plants while living in Chaffee, New York, when the war broke out. Lewis Palmerton, Al's father, served on the Draft Board. "My brother was married with a couple of children, so dad said 'you are going to go.'[230] I was stationed at Fort Niagara in 1942 and stayed there for quite awhile. Finally, they shipped me to Mitchell Field, Long Island, for about two months and then to Texas." Al received his wings and rating of second lieutenant from Blackland Army Air Field in Waco, Texas, on October 1, 1943.[231] He remained in the states while his wife, Lois, was hospitalized with complications after giving birth. Their two-week old infant son, Elwyn Jr., passed away on February 11, 1942, in Colorado Springs, Colorado. Once Lois was discharged from the hospital, Al left the states on April 14, 1944, in a new B-24 on the southern route bound for England.

"When I got to Marrakech (Southwestern Morocco) my plane was due for a one hundred hour check. Only one crew at a time checks the radios, electronics and so forth. The base power people were in there at the same time as the radio people and blew the wires out. We were told to hang on and that we are going to get another harness. For thirty-two days we lived in the French Foreign Legion quarters with our own cook and a maid. Preparations were underway for the invasion and they wanted us to get the airplane to England as soon as possible. I was asked, 'Can you fly the airplane without (electrical) power?" I said sure, why not. If you can start the engines, I can fly it. I took it up for a two-hour check. The only thing that didn't work was the servo unit on the control. We shipped to Ireland first for the crew to receive gunnery training. The four officers didn't have anything to do, so we ran around Ireland chasing whiskey bottles! Things were always happening. I did not have any power for navigation and we arrived in England at night. The pilots who had sub-control were going to pick me up about fifty miles out to guide me and leave the lights on for three minutes while I was on approach. I got it down and bounced around a little and went into headquarters and said, when you have a black out you have a black out. There were four candles on the desk."

The next morning Al received orders to take his aircraft to Liverpool to begin their missions with the 8th Air Corps, 448th Bomb Group, 713th Squadron stationed in Seething, England. At home local newspapers reported on Al's status. Yellowed undated clippings updated his status in the news. "Now overseas, 2nd Lt. Elwyn F. Palmerton, 170 Christiana Street, North Tonawanda, has participated in a course designed to bridge the gap between training in the states and active soldiering at one of the Air Services Command Stations known as control depots. His next assignment will be a fighter aircraft base."[232] Another article announced Al's status as a Liberator pilot, that he arrived in England, received a promotion to First Lieutenant, and was a graduate of Arcade High School, employed at Bell Aircraft before his induction, and the name and address of his wife. These news reports informed the public about the status of the American troops. The information also became an effective tool of the German interrogators through their newspaper clipping services. The Germans used the news clippings and other methods to intimidate the airmen with details about their background.

On the fifth mission over France, on June 24, 1944, Al's B-24 was hit twice rupturing the tanks and the wings between the fuselage, and the number two engine. "We were targeting the buzz-bomb sites that were hitting England. I was at the IP (initial point)[233] turn just before making the bomb run. I was trying to hold our position so the navigator and nose gunner had a chance to get out and fortunately they made it. Gasoline was running all over and it caught on fire. I was glad, because it wouldn't explode; we had a hot fire so we bailed out. I was the last one out of the plane. As I was coming down a German officer shot at me from the ground. There were six holes in the upper half of the chute. I walked toward him limping and minus a shoe. He put his weapon back in the holster. About twenty feet from him I stopped dead in my tracks and he stopped too. I asked him, why were you shooting at me? He responded that he saved my life because it stopped others from shooting. Then he asked why did I stop walking. I told him because I lost my shoe. He walked toward me. I wanted him to capture me. I did not want to give up. He said 'I am capturing you. For you the war is kaput.' I saw our airplane in a spiral and hit the ground about a quarter of mile away. The entire crew was taken prisoner. It took them seven days to round us up. I was caught within fifteen minutes. About two hours later the Germans caught my nose gunner. We sat in the middle of the field guarded by four German soldiers all night long. We were close to the fighting and heard the shelling from the English, and then the Germans. The ground was jumping! They put us in a 1934 Chevrolet truck that ran on wood. We stopped and were held in a vacant grocery store for three days then taken to Lille, France, for about seventeen days and held in the third floor of an old Bastille. I stood on the edge of my bunk and could see a P-47 coming right beside the Bastille shooting all the way down as the pilot landed on the street. They captured him."[234]

Back home Al's MIA status appeared in the news of missing Army Air Force personnel. "Palmerton did instructing in southern and southwest airfields and took part in the invasion and pre D-Day bombings over France. He was piloting a B-24 Liberator." Lois Palmerton received a letter from Chaplain Theodore Runyan of the 448th Bomb Group assuring her of his prayers, the possibility of Al being a POW, and the great courage and determination Al showed to overthrow an enemy "who would destroy everything we hold dear and sacred." After the Red Cross confirmed that Al was a POW his family and friends sent letters and Red Cross packages that were never received. Lois received a form letter from the American Red Cross, 698 Delaware Avenue, Buffalo, New York, that parcels were being provided for shipment overseas to newly captured American prisoners with emergency personal essentials. The parcel included a pair of pajamas, a sweater, bedroom slippers, a safety razor, three packages of razor blades, two pair of socks, a light undershirt, a pair of light drawers, six cakes of soap, two bars of laundry soap, one tin of tooth powder, one toothbrush in a container, two bath towels, two face towels, a tin of shoe polish, four handkerchiefs, a housewife, two pair of shoelaces, a box of cascara,[235] a box of vitamin tablets, band aids, and a pipe.

Al and the other prisoners were transported to Frankfurt by rail for about two weeks of interrogation. The interrogators "told us the history of our lives. My story was a lot different than enlisted people. We were in a very orderly camp at Sagan. I arrived after *The Great Escape* and things were pretty tough because the Germans tightened things up. I was the ranking officer of our room." The daily routine included three walks around the perimeter of the compound and picking up the barracks. Cleanliness was important, Al said. He cared for the mental health of the other soldiers in a unique way. "Some of the guys went over the bend. At night you heard people looking out at the window talking to their wife, their girlfriend, or their mother. I had a fella in my room from Texas, a navigator. He was badly burned while bailing out and his fingers were twisted. I took care of him, washed, and cleaned him. He was a wonderful guy. We worked together when someone in the barracks went berserk. I asked my friend to come with me to talk to the other guy who was in trouble. My friend said, 'you think you have a problem. Look at me. I can't change (burns), but you will get out of here sometime.' That straightened the other guy right up! We had to do that a lot."

Physicians were among the captured POWs, but "you couldn't even get an aspirin. Smoking was a big problem. The doctors put on seminars in the camp about smoking and taught classes on psychology and mathematics. Lawyers taught too. In my room, one fellow got up early to read a book. He was the third bunk up and opened the window to put a piece of bread on the ledge for a pigeon. This guy hid the pigeon under his overcoat when we were called to line up one morning. Some of the guys were in their BVD's and while the Germans made the count, the pigeon flew away. They tore our barracks apart thinking the bird was a homing pigeon. That night a few Germans leaned against the doorway and listened while we played Bridge. Our scouts alerted us. A couple of guys said 'did you hear the news? The pigeon got through!' The guard took off for the office." The prisoners continued to leak "information" including news that a tank division was heading their way and expected in a few days. These humorous moments kept up their spirits.

Theatrical performances provided another distraction. "Even the Germans come to watch our shows and loved them. It got to the point that they brought in cloth for us to make costumes. One thing they didn't allow was the American flag. One guy had the flag tattooed on his shoulder and did his three walks around the perimeter without a shirt so every guy who passed him could see the American flag. That raised another ruckus. The Germans couldn't figure out what was going on. They thought we were scouting for underground fences. It was morale building so you didn't go bananas. POW life was tough for us officers too, but we lived on hope and went around with a smile. We wanted to be ready to continue fighting the war if we got out."

Word came about nine o'clock one evening to get prepared to leave the camp and begin the march to Stalag VIIA at Moosburg. The prisoners were given a Red Cross parcel, which became a burden to carry, as they walked through the gate into the heart of winter. "It was rough, a wet soggy snow, and on the third day we stuffed paper into our pant legs to preserve the heat. It got to the point that you couldn't see the end of the line; it went on for miles and miles in both directions. I was in the middle. My co-pilot was worn out by the fourth day. It was cold and snowing and his feet were freezing. We got him up and changed off every hour to help keep him going." One night was spent in a Catholic Church. "We were button to button, about three thousand of us. It was one of the rare nights where we slept that was dry. The German soldiers went up and down the street into every house looking for food. We were bad off."

Another dry spell came for the POWs at the Dresden China Factory that was operated by slave labor at the time. Al and his buddies sabotaged the glazing process, which slowed down things in the plant for about a week. "A few days later, we were about twenty-five miles away when the Air Force came and blasted the city." Dresden, an industrial and cultural center, was severely damaged from the bombing raids during the war.

The day of liberation became the most moving event for Al. "When Patton came through the gates, he sent some of his men over to the headquarters to take the German flag down. Everyone watched. It was so quiet you could hear a pin drop. The camp was always loud. Then, they started pulling up the American flag. I never heard such a noise in my life. Honest to God, when that flag got to the top and unfurled, the camp went berserk! I will never forget that moment."

RICHARD DUERR, the son of Arthur and Lonia Duerr, was in the Civilian Air Patrol (CAP) when he was seventeen years old. He graduated from North Tonawanda High School and about a month after his eighteenth birthday enlisted in the Army in Buffalo, New York.[236]

Dick was inducted at Miami Beach with a group of about thirty other members of his CAP group. From Miami they were sent to different places. Dick was sent to gunnery school in Las Vegas and did very well. He turned down an opportunity to go on to Instructor's School because he "wanted to get in on the action. All I wanted to do was to fly. I was the only one in my Cadet Squad selected." After gunnery school, Dick was assigned to a crew in Florida for crew training. After four months, in September 1944, "We flew a brand new B-17 bomber overseas. We had a layover in Iceland and spent the night. The next day we continued on to Scotland and were assigned to the 303rd Bomb Group" 8th Army Air Corps based near Bedford, England. They bombed major targets in Germany.

"I was a replacement on my fifteenth mission with another crew. Their ball turret gunner was not available. It was the 300th mission of the 303rd Bomb Group. Our target was Cologne (Germany). Only a few took off because of the ice on the runway. It was in bad shape; planes skidded. We were attached to another Bomb Group." It was January 10, 1945.

During Dick's last mission, "We left the formation over Belgium because one engine was knocked out. The only working compass was on the pilot's flight panel. The other instrument panels were destroyed. The 88 caliber canon guns from the German Tiger tanks hammered us. We thought we were over France and friendly territory. We were down to one engine and the left wing was blazing with fire. The flight controls were failing. We had ten men on board. One was a Mickey operator. (Dick explained that the Mickey operator used radar to see through the clouds.) He went out the side door, the waist door. The four men in the front (of the aircraft) parachuted safely and landed in friendly territory. The other six parachuted well behind enemy lines. The flight engineer and tail gunner were killed. I hit the trees and became up ended and landed on my head. We tried to hide, but three of us became POWs. We were captured by the German Wehrmacht who were fighting in the Battle of the Bulge."

After Dick was captured he could barely walk or remain conscious. "Two captured British airmen supported me to walk. During the night we slept in a field. I looked for the British men the next morning to thank them for helping me, but they were gone. They saved my life because the Germans were shooting stragglers," Dick said. He was taken to a German hospital. "Paper was used for bandages. There was a lot of yelling and screaming because there was no medicine to ease their pain. It was terrible. I slept on the floor. We were given broth and a piece of sour bread." While Dick passed through Cologne, he saw an older woman with a little girl about four years old. There was a patch over the child's eye from an injury due to the bombings. "The woman tried to hit me. She was furious and telling me that I was a murderer. I had nightmares for years. We couldn't see from the air what happened on the ground from our missions." The sight of the injured child and human toll of the bomb damage exposed a different perspective for Dick about war.

After Dick left the hospital he was interrogated. "I was beaten and questioned. 'What was the emblem on the aircraft?' I was asked. I gave them misinformation. The camp was at Wetzlar. German cameras were manufactured there," Dick said. He was held in solitary confinement for about a week and then taken to a camp in Nuremburg. "Hunger was an ever present ordeal for all of us. I lost fifty pounds."

When the British bombed Nuremburg "we were led to a tunnel to get away from the bombing. What a show! Flak was falling from the German anti-aircraft guns. A British bomber shot down a German fighter airplane. It looked like a shooting star and exploded. Then a British Landcaster bomber was hit and blazing furiously. It spiraled into the ground where it exploded. We left there and were marched to Moosburg. It took about a week. We slept in the fields on rocky ground at night under guard on the way and also while we were at the Moosburg camp." Patton's Third Army liberated the camp. "I had managed to crawl through a hole someone had cut through the fence around the camp. While I walked down the road, I thought how it felt so wonderful to be free. You don't know how precious freedom is until you lose it. I returned to the camp and waited to be released. I thanked the Lord for letting me get through this alive."

After Dick and the others in the camp were released they were taken to a large field near Regensburg, Germany, "where C-46 cargo planes were to fly us to Camp Lucky Strike in France. While we waited, a squadron of several dozen German biplanes landed on our field escaping from the Russians."

Dick offered advice from his experiences in the war and as a POW. "Go to extremes to stay out of a war. When war is necessary, we should only bomb military targets when possible. Talk and discuss differences. We are a kind-hearted people. Hopefully, the enemy will learn from the American way."

JOHN D. "DON" GRIFFIN[237] was shot down three months before the D-Day landings. He was born August 9, 1923, to Lawrence and Arna (Shea) Griffin at Our Lady of Victory Hospital in Lackawanna, New York, and resided in the East Buffalo area for most of his life. Don attended School No. 9 and Kensington High School. He worked for Curtiss-Wright in the old Westinghouse plant when he was drafted. "My brother Gerard enlisted; he was already serving. Just before the war ended my younger brother, Cornelius, shipped out of San Francisco on the *USS Boxer* and was only two days out when Japan surrendered."[238]

Don entered military service on February 27, 1943, and was inducted at Fort Niagara. The fort was a bustle of activity. "We didn't get out while we were there. Most guys were at Fort Niagara for only three or four days. From there we were assigned to a branch of the military and sent for basic training to another site. You got a physical in the morning and then looked at the list to see where you were going. I was there a little longer. Oh the food! One of my first meals was down in the basement of those big three story buildings. Cockroaches galore! I got my tray and went through the chow line. Up in the right corner were lima beans and a cockroach. Well, you are in the Army now and you don't know how long you are going to be there, so I flicked the cockroach off and ate all my lima beans!"

About a week later during a snowstorm Don left for Miami Beach and basic training followed by armament school at Buckley Field and Lowry Field, Colorado. He enjoyed his tenure at Lowry, which included invitations to private homes for dinner and horseback riding in the mountains. After Lowry he was sent to Fort Kearney, Nebraska, for assignment to an airbase. "At this point I passed the physical for aerial gunner and was sent to Wendover, Utah, for gunner school." Wendover Army Air Base was a gunnery school in 1943. The following year at Wendover, Col. Paul W. Tibbets, Jr. prepared to drop the atomic bomb at Hiroshima. "Wendover was desolate. The only good thing in the area was the State Line Hotel where you could drink; it was not in Utah. I was assigned to a crew in Moses Lake, near Spokane, Washington, and third phase training in Sioux City, Iowa, to wait for shipping orders."

The crew split up and Don was sent to Bangor, Maine. "We were restricted to the base on New Year's Eve then went to Goose Bay, Labrador, and waited for the weather to be able to take off on a B-17. About three hours from England, we lost an engine. The pilot feathered the prop and it started to fog. We saw treetops and yelled 'pull up, pull up!' We were supposed to land at Nutts Corner, but the fog was too heavy, so we were sent to an airfield in the Hebrides. These are islands off the northwest of Scotland. We waited for ten days for another plane. Finally, it arrived and we were assigned to the Ninety-fifth Bomb group of the Eighth Air Force. After more training in February, we became operational."

Don's missions were part of the first American raids on Berlin. "While over the North Sea, there was a call to abort the mission. Was it for real or the Germans? Some of the Ninety-Fifth Bomb Group went ahead and bombed the outskirts of the city. On Sunday the fifth, Berlin was still cloud covered and on March 6, we headed for Berlin. The Germans knew and sent their fighters up. We were a little south of Hamburg and all hell broke loose. There were three groups, about fifty planes. German fighters attacked at the front and rear. Fighters hit our gang and were knocking us out like flies. Our plane got hit. I was in the ball turret in a fetal position and put my arms over the guns. If I go down, I am not going down screaming. I said a few prayers and decided to try and get out. I flipped the door open and saw the waist gunner, Leo Chaplinski (Chappie), a lawyer from Pennsylvania, holding the cables together so I could open the door and get out of the turret. The plane was on fire! I tried to jump out and got thrown back inside. The radio operator kicked me out. I was going down headfirst and couldn't breathe when I became aware that I had the oxygen mask on. As soon as I flipped my mask off I pulled the rip chord and could see civilians coming at us with old rifles. After I caught up with the co-pilot and a few others, we were put in a wagon and I started to joke. Another guy said 'Duckbutt,' my nickname, don't make fun of these people; they don't like us.' We were taken to a processing center and eventually Stalag Luft VI near Lithuania."

Stalag Luft VI was located in the north in Pomerania, Prussia. The Russians began to advance in the Baltic States and on July 17, 1944, the main group of POWs left the camp crammed into boxcars to the Baltic Sea, and then were put in a hold of a lake freighter. Water was lowered in a bucket, but most prisoners were unable to move for water, sleep, or to relieve themselves. On land, "they manacled us and forced us to run double time from the train station at Kiefheide to Gross Tychow. We called it the 'Heydekrug Run.' It was hotter than blazes in July, and we didn't get any water. If you fell down they (the Germans) jammed you with a bayonet. When we arrived at the Vorlager[239] of Stalag Luft IV at Gross Tychow, some of the guys ran to the pump for water. The guards hit their rifle butts on the guys' hands to keep them from getting a drink. Many of the guards were just kids, teens; but they were nasty."

Moments of despair and fear were part of captivity. In the middle of the night guys cried out 'momma' or 'bail out, bail out!' "I looked at the moon and wondered if my mother was looking up at the moon too. Another guy put his arms around me and said 'Duckbutt, we are going to make it.' It helped me to reassess the situation."

As the war continued, the POWs at Stalag Luft IV were divided in half. Don's group boarded the train for Nuremburg. British bombers hit the area and Allied troops advanced from both sides. "We started to march to Moosburg. We weren't mistreated, but civilians spit at us and threw stones. The British POWs were in the back of the line and when we took a break, they came by us in strict military formation. Most of the time we were bedraggled. Early in (the month of) March some P-47s strafed us and someone put the American flag out. I don't know where we got it. We arrived at Moosburg and it was very crowded. I think more than forty thousand Americans. When the word came to us that Roosevelt died, we were given permission to have a brief ceremony and someone played taps and raised the flag."

The rains of April brought Patton's troops and liberation. "We hopped the trucks and got on some C-47s to Camp Lucky Strike and were warned not to eat too much. I saw a piece of white bread. It looked like angel food cake. A liberty hospital ship carried about three hundred of us across the Atlantic. I still remember how I felt seeing the crossing and remembering the D-Day landing. I was shot down three months before D-Day. We docked at Boston harbor. At Camp Myles Standish, spinach was served on the chow line. I love spinach! All of a sudden there was a lot of commotion. Some of the guys went over the line at the servers, German POWs. I was given a sixty-day leave and flew home to the Buffalo Airport. I was one of the last to get off and can still hear my mother scream when she saw me. My sister was there too. Homecoming was good. I went back to Atlantic City and was processed for some R & R (rest and recreation) at Fort Collins in Denver. They took good care of people. On September 30, 1945, I got my discharge."

Don graduated after three years from the University of Buffalo with a Degree in Social Work through the G.I. Bill and spent his working career helping others in the Welfare Department, where he met his wife of fifty-three years, and then in the Probation Department. "I don't know how many great leaders we lost in WWII. All in all, I have no regrets. I am thankful for my upbringing and freedom. If people only knew what freedom really means. The American people don't know what they have. This is a good country!"

METRO "JIM" MARCHYN was originally from Pittsburgh, Pennsylvania. He enlisted and sat around for six months waiting to be called up. Eventually, Jim was sent to Miami and then navigation school in Texas. Training followed at Langley Field, Virginia, for the PFF (Police Field Forces) and instruction on how to bomb through clouds. Jim was a navigator with the 385th Bomber Group stationed in England. During one of the missions, he landed the aircraft after convincing the pilot someone else needed to know how to land the plane.[240]

His first mission was on D-Day. The target of their B-17 was a bridge at Rheims[241] as the massive fleets below crossed the Channel with thousands of soldiers prepared to storm the Normandy beaches. Smoke came out of the woods from the German flak guns. Jim watched the bombs hit their target. The center arch of the bridge collapsed preventing the Germans from crossing and the anti-aircraft guns were silenced.

Jim was caught in the increase in the number of missions required before returning home. On his twenty-third mission the number was raised from twenty-five to thirty, then thirty-five. "On the thirty-fourth mission the number two engine couldn't control the RPMs.[242] The next day, Wednesday, at fifteen thousand feet we couldn't see and the mission was scrubbed. On the thirty-fifth mission, we were the last ones over the target area. At six o'clock, I saw seventy German fighters. Our bomber group was scattered and not where they were supposed to be. We were hit and on fire. When I tried to bailout the plane blew up, and I was blown out, but got to the ground safely." Jim was in a free-fall from 28,000 feet when the B-17 exploded. He waited to pull the cord for his parachute until he was below the cloud cover at 8,000 feet.

Captured by the German police, Jim was taken to Stalag Luft IV, a POW camp for airmen. "When we marched from Nuremburg, three of us escaped. I gave the guard some cigarettes and asked if he wanted to come with us. We took off across the railroad tracks and were on the loose for about a month. We tried to get back to Patton's location, but were re-captured and taken to the Burgermeister's[243] house in a small town. He spoke English. We told him 'If you surrender to us, we will get to Patton and your town will not be bombed.' He agreed and then looked out the window and said, 'I can't do it.' We looked out the window too and saw five SS Troopers. The Burgermeister was afraid of the SS men and knew we would all be shot if they found us with him. We were held as prisoners again with two hundred officers captured during the Battle of the Bulge." Jim concluded, "C'est la guerre!"

WILLIAM DIBBLE was with a field artillery unit in the 1st Division 21st Infantry serving in Africa. During the invasion of Sicily he was pinned down and captured in June 1943. He spent twenty-one months as a POW and was in the forced March at the end of the war in Germany.[244]

JOHN SCHULTZ served in the European Theatre in the 103rd Army Infantry Division, 411 Regiment, Riflemen. He was captured in the Voges Mountains of France.[245]

RAYMOND BUERSTER was also taken as a POW in France. He was in an anti-tank unit with the Army Infantry.[246]

ARTHUR KLAFFKA was with the 15th Air Force, 451st Bomb Group, 725th Squadron, and flew out of Italy. He was the only survivor of a B-24, the Calamity Jane, after a direct hit on the bomb bay over an oil refinery target near Vienna, Austria.[247]

MARIANO GIUGA was born on Effner Street and went to School Number One in Buffalo; "it is not there anymore. My father, Philip, came to this country from Italy in 1915 and served for a year in WWI. My mother, Grace Dryja, was born in Italy too." Mariano Giuga was married with two children and working at Curtiss-Wright when he was drafted at the age of twenty-four in July 1944.[248]

After basic training he crossed the Atlantic Ocean on the *Queen Elizabeth*. "Glenn Miller played *Begin the Beguine* and other old time songs as we boarded the ship. It was a big boat with a swimming pool, a movie theatre, and pool tables. There were five thousand of us on board. Twelve soldiers slept in a room about six by six with bunks on three sides, four bunks to a side and our equipment stored underneath the bottom bunk; not much room to move around. We arrived in Scotland then took smaller boats to cross the Channel. Hundreds of bombed watercraft stuck up out of the water. The Le Havre harbor was crowded with GIs. Some French people threw stones and glass bottles at us as we landed and also while we marched. They were with the Germans then." After the liberation of Paris in August 1944, the Vichy government[249] went into exile in Germany until the end of the war.

Mariano arrived in France to serve with the Seventh Army's Third Division. "There were seven or eight of us that hung together since basic training. We went to get our winter boots, but they didn't have my size because my feet were small. My buddies were put on the front line the next day. I was told that they were all killed and run over by tanks. It made me sick. After I got my boots, we were packed like sardines in large trucks and taken to the front. From that day on things cooled a little. My job was to patrol our side of the river four hours on and eight hours off. We could hear the Germans firing their machine guns."

"We crossed the German border in March 1945 when I was captured. We were in a minefield and many guys were killed and wounded. It was dark and I couldn't see. We just crossed the Rhine River. We crossed it three times and there was no telling if we were in France or Germany." Mariano crawled over the lifeless bodies of his buddies and the screams of the wounded. He was cut up too and captured at daybreak. After six weeks on the front lines Mariano became a prisoner, not in a POW camp, but forced to march for the next forty-five days.

The POWs slept without blankets and marched in the rain and the snow. "Everyday I missed my kids and prayed. I tried to runaway, but there was no place to run. They took my shoes. There were a lot of (German) soldiers, older guys; they killed some guys who ran away. Near the end, about a week before I was liberated, the Germans gave me wooden shoes. It was hard to walk. Our rations were a half-cup of mint tea each day and a quarter slice of bread every other day. A couple of times we got two slices of bread for eight people and a cup of mint tea. We ate what we could pick up along the way. Sometimes there was some unidentifiable meat. I dug for snails and dandelions under the snow and encouraged the others to do the same. You will eat anything if you are hungry. I lost about fifty pounds."

During the March, the Germans shared the news of President Roosevelt's death with the prisoners. "I didn't feel good about that. He did a lot for the people. He started the CCC camps and put people to work." Mariano marched until the morning of April 27, 1945, his daughter's third birthday, when Gen. George Patton arrived on the scene. "To me, General Patton was the greatest man I have ever known. He shook my hand. We took showers and our clothes were burned. The new clothes didn't fit well, but they were clean. I was liberated on my daughter's birthday. Patton told us 'we are going to do everything we can do for you fellows.' He used a bullhorn and said mostly swear words; but he was the kind of a guy that figured if he can do it, you can do it. A lot of guys didn't like him, but to me he was the greatest guy ever. Patton saved me. He told the guys in the tank to give us all their shoes, clothing, and food for us. He didn't talk to us too long. He was all soldier. To me, he was God. He saved my life."

The POWs were asked how they wanted to go home. Mariano chose a boat ride to return to the states; it was a small boat like a barge. With nothing to do to pass the time the soldiers played cards and dice. Mariano traded a German Luger for twenty-five dollars to play dice. He won five hundred dollars that the captain put in a safe. When they landed near Trenton, New Jersey, Mariano did not see the captain and thought: "oh, oh my money is gone. When they called my name to go down the ladder the captain saw me and gave me the envelope. I wondered if he stole some of it. I didn't care and just wanted to get out of there. I had to go to the bathroom and for the hell of it I counted it. Every penny and the change was there too. He didn't take a dime. I called my wife and told her when I would be home."

Mariano arrived by train on his wife's birthday, June 8, 1945. He passed his wife, Violet, and sister-in-law going down the tunnel, but they didn't recognize him, so he called out. The reunion was bittersweet. His wife told him that Daniel, his brother, was killed-in-action on March 2, 1945. "I don't think I was half a mile away from him (in Germany). He was only eighteen when he got drafted, five years younger than me. He was one of the first to go."

Before his discharge Mariano was sent to a hotel in Lake Placid, New York. "This was the good part. Some captain told us that whatever we want we will get it for you. At the entrance to the hotel there was a glass plaque over the door: 'no pets allowed here…no Jews allowed here…no Negroes allowed here.' One of the guys was a Negro with our group. He was a friend of mine; he cried and said 'we are human too.' He complained and the next day the sign was gone."

Reflecting on his experiences Mariano said, "Its funny you know, but the worst part was when I heard about my brother. I would have stayed in Germany and fought all the Germans, if I had known."

BENEDICT L. KLINSHAW ~ "Since the Pope took my name the boys (the POWs in the support group) bow down to me!"[250] Ben's characteristic sense of humor was at the heart of his survival story as a prisoner of war. Born in South Buffalo, Ben worked at Worthington Buffalo Works with his father, a blacksmith, and his two brothers when he entered the Fifteenth Air Force in September 1943 at the age of twenty-two.[251]

The monthly *Worthington Buffalo Works News* published for the employees of the Worthington Pump and Machinery Corporation at Buffalo, New York, reported on its workers "In The Service" and production efforts to support the war including the Worthington BB-6 diesel engine and Worthington steam jet ejectors and vacuum pumps used to help prepare plasma and penicillin that was processed in a high vacuum.[252]

Ben was inducted at Fort Dix, and then sent to St Petersburg, Florida, a small town at the time, for basic training. Signs advertised the need for aerial gunners so Ben volunteered and was sent to Tyndall Field Army Air Force Gunnery School in Florida. "Clark Gable was there. We were taken up in an AT-6 and did flips and some rolls; and for the final test, the wings touched the water! If you were not sick or dizzy, you became a gunner." Training at Tyndall Field included calisthenics, marching drills, machine and turret gun instruction, practice firing at a miniature target airplane as it was towed around a circular track by a driverless jeep, and air to air firing practice. Ben graduated in the Gunnery Class of 43-5 under the tutelage of Lt. Col. James R. Luper, Director of Training; Maj. Henry H. Hunter, Commanding Officer Student Detachment; and Lt. Charles Shearn, Secretary of Training.[253]

From gunnery school Ben was sent to Keesler Field on the outskirts of Biloxi, Mississippi, where "we learned airplane mechanics to fix those big Chrysler engines," in an intensive nineteen-week course intended to "Keep 'Em Flying!" The students learned the fundamentals of aircraft maintenance for the B-24 followed by studies of airplane structures; hydraulic, electrical, and fuel systems; instruments; engines; propellers; and engine operation.[254] From New Mexico to Tucson, Arizona, Ben trained on a B-24. "Because of my size they put me in a ball turret. In order to keep the guns level you laid flat on your back. The sight is in between your legs with two fifty caliber machine guns on either side."

Staff Sergeant Klinshaw became a turret gunner and assistant engineer on a Liberator flying out of Italy. On his fourteenth mission their ship, the *Chiquita Mia*, was hit by enemy fire and the props nicked. Ben was burned, hit with a piece of flak on his left shoulder (which he didn't know at the time), and then was grounded by the Company doctor. "We were informed that we would be flying over Germany again on February 25, 1944. I went to the doctor and had my grounded order changed so I could fly with my crew."

During the next mission Ben flew with the 722nd Bomb Squadron scheduled to rendezvous with the 450th Bomber group and nine others. Over Yugoslavia they ran into flak, one of the engines caught fire, and there was a fuel leak. The plane burst into flames and the order given to bailout. "I put a chute on, when the co-pilot said 'you got my chute.' I had to change, but was still the second man out of the plane. On the way down I pulled on my chute to get close to another guy. It is pretty lonesome as you are going down." Being one of the first out of the aircraft turned out to be a mistake. The first four that bailed out got caught. The other six made it to the Underground in Italy. Ben made a splint from a pine tree branch and used the rubber bands from the chute to hold it in place to help the engineer who broke his ankle.

After being captured the POWs were taken to Ljubljana, Yugoslavia, held in a jail for several days, and then transported to Frankfurt by train. The interrogating German officer ironically grew up in Syracuse, New York. After visiting Germany in 1939, he was drafted into the Wehrmacht and not allowed to return to the states. Ben said, "I only told him my name, rank, and serial number. He opened up a book and told me about my family, where I lived, the whole history of my life." For a week the prisoners were fed bread and water, then loaded into rail cards bound for Memmel, East Prussia, and Stalag Luft VI. Like many American POWs Ben was moved several times. After a few months the POWs were marched to the Baltic Sea and put in a hold of a ship for three days, standing room only, to Swinemunde, Germany, and finally a five-kilometer run to Stalag Luft IV at Grosstychow. Ben chuckled describing a humorous moment on the railroad cars known as forty and eights. "When we were on the trains one of our guys had some Exlax. The German guard looked at it and asked 'chocolate?' The prisoner responded 'yeah chocolate.' The guard ate all the 'chocolate!' Boy, did he have a problem later."

"They treated us awful at the POW camp. I saw guys get shot and die. They were buried outside the camp with no marker. Three guys didn't wait until the bell rang to leave the barracks one morning. They just wanted to go to the bathroom." Trying to keep busy in the camp "we put on a show. There was a guy who was a producer, T. J. Edwards, from Boston; he did shows in New York City. Edwards picked certain guys to do the acting. Some guys did not want to know anything. I always think positive and know if you fight, you will make it." Ben joined the acting troupe.

The prisoners walked around the compound each morning for exercise. Ben and the others played cribbage and cards that were from their infrequent shared Red Cross package. "We didn't have a chaplain, but a couple guys would get up and say prayers and preach to us. It was the only religion. They weren't Catholics. No education programs for us. You had to keep yourself busy. We got the news on those little radios that the British made. Someone guarded the front and back door while we took turns and listened to the BBC.[255] The crystal radio sets were made from our flying suits; they were covered with wires."

The letters and post cards home bore constant themes. "Dear Mom & Dad, I am well and hope you are the same…I hope you don't worry…give everyone my regards. Your loving son." Ben advised his parents that POWs were limited to two letters and four postcards a month and requested that his family contact the Red Cross to send him needed packages. He wrote about some memories of St. Monica's Church in south Buffalo, and his desire to fulfill his Easter duty. On July 2, 1944, Ben wrote, "Everyone of you is in my prayers and at Mass. We have a Catholic priest here now and I went to Confession and Communion offering it for your health."[256]

Ben's parents wrote a letter dated October 1, 1944. They were anxious to receive mail and news from him that probably was delayed due to destroyed transportation routes and censors. It was a newsy letter about the weather, family, the new cathedral in Buffalo, Bishop John Duffy's funeral, concern for the growing paper shortage, and wishes for their son's health.

More trials as a POW came for Ben during the forced March in late January. "I saw a couple of guys die on the March. Smitty from York, Pennsylvania, got forty-five dog bites because he slowed down. I weighed about 138 pounds and went down to 90 pounds. We starved; food was really important to us."

The forced March from Stalag Luft IV near Grosstychow, Poland, began in late January 1945, and ended in Halle (Saale), Germany, in April.[257] More than 9,500 men, most of whom were Army Air Corps bomber non-commissioned officers, were forced to march almost six hundred miles. The Soviet offensive was quickly moving into Germany. These American servicemen already suffered from their own aircraft being shot down or damaged forcing the crew to bail out, and often losing their buddies who did not make it out of the aircraft. The harsh winter conditions and poor physical health of the Americans claimed its own casualties. Ben said they picked up sugar beets left in the field after the harvest, desperate for anything to calm the endless hunger. Some prisoners did not survive. Others suffered amputations or life-long medical conditions from the severe conditions on the March.

"We were liberated in late April[258] as we walked into American lines, and then were taken to Camp Lucky Strike. I remember that they gave us half a slice of white bread and how good it looked. One guy ate two or three doughnuts and died because we were in such bad shape. From Lucky Strike we were shipped to the states. I was assigned to Fort Dix as a clerk non-typist, got married, and lived off the base until I was discharged."

Ben survived captivity and the March. "People in this country don't know what war is. I try to be good to everyone, keep myself busy, and have a sense of humor. I am thankful to be alive and want to pass things on to the next generation." In spite of a quadruple bypass, insulin diabetes, a stroke, and cancer of the esophagus, he plans to live to be at least one hundred!

ROBERT E. MAC PHERSON was born in Buffalo, New York, in 1922, the son of David and Henrietta Mac Pherson. He was sent to Europe as a casualty replacement several months after D-Day and served with the 1st Infantry Division 26th Regiment Co. F. "From Southampton, England, we took a small ship over the Channel. In your mind you were thinking about what happened on D-Day as you got in the water and on the beach." Bob was digging shallow foxholes during his first combat experience and ducked under a truck during a mortar barrage. He chuckled remembering that later he found out it was a munitions truck! His company was in and out of wooded areas trying to take towns.[259]

November 1944 "we took a little town amidst some resistance and didn't expect a counterattack that night. It was a small farming village. One soldier stood on guard by a window while we slept in a building located in the front of the town. That night there was a counterattack and a German threw a concussion grenade in the window. I couldn't kick the grenade because of the four guys on the other side of the room. In an instant, I held the grenade against the wall with my feet. It blew me across the room. My combat boots were shredded and shrapnel in both feet. I was stunned and couldn't feel anything below my knees. The Germans arrived with tanks and captured about fifty of us. We were told to line up on the street, but I couldn't walk. The German guard said 'don't worry we will send an ambulance.' I thought I'd be shot if they left me. Some of the guys saw a wheelbarrow nearby and asked the guard if they could put me in it. He hesitated for a moment, and then said, yes." Bob believed this saved his life.

Bob was trucked north to Gernsheim Hospital Camp, part of a larger camp. Crepe paper was used for bandages and medicines were in very short supply. The pot-bellied stove fuel lasted only about three hours for heat in their room with fifteen bunks. Bob stayed in the hospital camp from early November to the beginning of January. Russian and Polish slave workers, from the other part of the camp, did farm work in the area. A big influx of captured Allied soldiers occurred during the Battle of the Bulge that began in December. Bob was offered a big stick to help him walk. "The guards were okay. We had wood slat beds with burlap mattresses filled with straw and issued a small empty can. You punctured two holes for a string or wire to fasten on your belt for coffee in the morning and sauerkraut soup with an occasional piece of turnip in the soup in the evening. The can was your life support. Each day eight guys got a loaf of black bread that one guy cut with a knife into eight parts. We took turns to cut it. The cutter got the last choice."

Bob carried a small booklet where he wrote the names and addresses of the fifteen guys with him in the hospital camp and a list of one hundred fifty-four different kinds of candy bars. "We were hungry and when you were not doing work everything was about food and conversations about the great dinners we had before the war. I started writing about candy bars. It was like a hobby to keep my mind off what was happening."

In early January 1945 Bob and others were trucked south towards Bonn and then marched to Stalag VIG, a temporary camp. "Eventually, they gave me some make-shift sandals out of wood. Sometimes I walked in bare feet. In Bonn we were issued a blanket to sleep on the floor. At night, we teamed up to sleep close to another guy then switched sides. There was bombing near us across the river from Bonn. The building I was in collapsed on me and three guys near me; they didn't move. I got out from the rubble and over to the air raid shelter, but the guards wouldn't let me go back. My stick and jacket were gone. I told the guards I didn't have a coat. They gave me a Russian coat. Kids threw sticks and stones at me as we walked. They hated the Russians. I tried to get in the middle so I wouldn't get hit. I fell a lot and took the lining out of my coat to wrap on my feet and then put it in my pocket to dry out to later wipe my feet again." At one point during his captivity Bob was also held for several weeks at Stalag XIIA, in Limburg.

Bob became part of the history of the Black Hunger March near the end of the war; injured, and without a walking stick, he fell to the back of the line.

"Two guys asked me if I would help them escape by distracting the rear guard. When the time came they gave me the signal, so I fell down. It wasn't unusual because I was so weak. The guard poked me with a bayonet and I managed to get up, but I saw the other two were not out of sight yet, so I fell down again. I didn't know if I could get up this time and the guard struck me again with the bayonet in my back. I managed to pull myself up knowing the alternative would be that he would have to kill me. Within a few days American tanks came down the road, and I knew we were liberated. I laid down on my back and couldn't get up. I had been going on adrenalin."

Trucks took the liberated soldiers to recovery camps. Bob was taken to a field medical facility and then transferred to a hospital in France. He lost almost half his body weight by the end of the march from 185 to 105 pounds. "They gave me a piece of white bread. It looked like angel food cake! A guy came up to me (in the hospital) and asked 'are you Bob Mac Pherson? You are the guy who made it possible for us to escape. We thought you were dead. My buddy was shipped out and we have been looking for you.' We shook hands. I didn't think too much of it at the time, but it really affected me that they spent time to find me and to thank me for helping them escape. They were worried that I was killed when they saw the guard stick me with a bayonet."

After five months of hospitalization in the states, Bob was returned to "limited service" prior to being discharged. The government rejected many cases of disability by returning soldiers to limited duty. Bob was married on January 14, 1946, to his fiancé who waited for him to return from the war. His shrapnel wounds continue to cause suffering.

Years later, Bob returned to Germany, but found no signs of the camp, only the Limburg railroad station where he was forced to work. It brought back the sounds of the war and captivity. He believes that "it pays to never give up!"

IN THE MIDST of spirited debates over whose battalion or unit was the best, if Patton was a good General, questioning Eisenhower's decision to not push further into Germany across Russian held territory at the end of the war, laughter over their starting pay of twenty-one dollars per month (less one dollar for insurance, another dollar for laundry, and twenty-five cents for the old soldiers' home) are stories of life and death, and the horrors of war. These men in their youth became a number. They were tortured, starved, and endured brutal and inhumane conditions. They went on to raise families, live productive lives, and become assets to their community.

Many other soldiers from Western New York were inducted at Fort Niagara, which became a major POW camp. John Jircitano heard the German guards telling the Americans that "our soldiers are dancing with your wives." Could it be true?

NOTES

[172] John Jircitano, interview by author, Youngstown, NY, January 26, March 24, and April 9, 2006.
[173] Margaret MacMillan, *Paris 1919*, (New York:, Random House Inc.,, 2003), 214.
[174] Bruce Robinson, "World War Two: Summary Outline of Key Events," *BBC*, http://www.bbc.co.uk/history/worldwars/wwtwo/ww2_summary_01.shtml [accessed March 19, 2007].
[175] Edward F. Joseph became the General Manager of WHLD.
[176] Supplement on WWII, May 30, 1976.
[177] "Civilian Forces Join Military in Protection Plan," *Niagara Falls Gazette*, December 8, 1941.
[178] "Air Plants Fueled War Effort," *Buffalo Evening News*, August 27, 1989
[179] Supplement on WWII, *Niagara Falls Gazette*, May 30, 1976.
[180] Jerries was a nickname for German soldier.
[181] Jircitano, interview.
[182] Western Union telegram to Anthony Jircitano, 2186 Jerauld Avenue, Niagara Falls, NY, August 14, 1944, private collection.
[183] Western Union telegram to Anthony Jircitano, August 25, 1944, private collection.
[184] John Jircitano, letter home October 30, 1944, private collection.
[185] Kriege evolved from Kriegsgefangen, the German term for Prisoner of War.
[186] Nuremberg is also spelled Nürnberg, Germany.
[187] John Maroon, interview by author (cousin), Grand Island, NY, February 22, 2007.
[188] 4-F draft status unfit for military duty due to physical disability.
[189] "Vince Mazza," NFL, historical players, http:www.nfl.com [accessed September 30, 2008].
[190] Professor Richard Holmes, "World War Two: The Battle of Monte Cassino," *BBC*, http://www.bbc.co.uk/history/worldwars/wwtwo/battle_cassino_02.shtml [accessed February 28, 2007].
[191] POWs were being moved by the Germans to avoid capture on the east from the Russians and on the west from the Allies.
[192] John Maroon received an Honorable Discharge from Company G, 143rd Infantry, on November 29, 1945.
[193] POW Support Group Thursday meetings attended by author on various dates 2007, Buffalo, NY.
[194] Edward P. Feigenbaum I, interview by author, Wilson, NY, March 12 and April 2, 2007.
[195] Camp Moss was the a Boy Scout camp, established c. 1928, west of Oakland Rural Cemetery, Lake Road in the Town of Porter, NY, near the Leonard Allen farm.
[196] Feigenbaum, interview.
[197] "Rangers of WWII," *United States Army Ranger Association*, http://www.ranger.org/html/ww2_history.html [accessed April 2, 2007].
[198] The First and Third Battalions were part of the Ranger Force known as Darby's Rangers. Lt. Col. William O. Darby was the Commanding Officer of the First, Third, and Fourth Ranger Battalions.
[199] Feigenbaum, interview.
[200] The government required thirty days of capture for benefits. Edward's time in the Underground, almost five months, and making his way back to American forces was not recog-

nized. He battled the government for five years after the war to be able to receive benefits.

[201] Edward arrived in the Boston, Massachusetts, harbor next to a fishing pier, on August 1, 1944.

[202] "The Niland Boys," *Canisius College*, http://www.canisius.edu/archives/niland.asp [accessed February 2, 2007].

[203] John Zale, interview by author, Buffalo, NY, July 23, 2007.

[204] The White Russians fought unsuccessfully against the Bolsheviks during the Russian Civil War.

[205] During war, a government may declare a city an "Open City" abandoning defensive efforts so that the opposing military will take the city without bombing or attacking to preserve the landmarks and civilians.

[206] Pusan is located in the southeast tip of Korea.

[207] Mukden is Shenyang, China.

[208] The hospital ships were known as mercy ships. The freighter *Dorothy Luckenbach* was reconverted at Bethlehem Shipbuilding Company's docks and renamed the *Ernestine Koranda.* Three Worthington Buffalo built 445 hp, 6 cylinder diesel engines, which drove the 300 kw direct current generators, powered the Koranda's operating room lights and other medical equipment. Source: *Worthington Buffalo Works News*, Vol. 3 No. 1 May 1945, 1.

[209] Dominick F. Poliseno, interview by author, Buffalo, NY, June 12, 2007.

[210] Angelo Poliseno emigrated from Castrora dei Volsci, a town in the hills of Italy less than thirty miles from Cassino.

[211] Camp Lucky Strike was located in Janville, France.

[212] "Douglas C-47," Fact Sheets, *National Museum of the USAF*, http://www.nationalmuseum.af.mil/factsheets/factsheet.asp?id=502 [accessed July 3, 2007].

[213] William J. Veronica, interview by author, Buffalo, NY, July 3, 2007.

[214] Daniel J. Veronica was killed testing a T-33A for Bell Aircraft in a mid-air collision with a tanker, KC-135A, and crashed on Rosamond Dry Lake on December 11, 1957, flying out of Edwards Air Force Base in California. Sources: Edwards AFB Accident Index 11 Dec 1957 and "Test Pilot Killed in Air Crash," *Bakersfield Californian*, December 12, 1957.

[215] Cape Town is in the southwestern tip of Africa.

[216] The electric suit was wired like an electric blanket. The crew was told to stay alert and not keep the temperature too high.

[217] Hamburg is in northern Germany.

[218] This was the desired outcome the United States government hoped for by treating the German POWs held in America according to the Geneva Convention.

[219] The Black Hunger Death March was a forced march of Allied POWs in an attempt by Germany to avoid the advancing Soviet offensive. Some groups of POWs marched more than ninety-two days and six hundred miles in brutal conditions during the winter.

[220] Gros-Rederching, France, is near the Moselle River and the border of Germany.

[221] Regensburg, Germany, is in the southeast part of the region of Bavaria.

[222] Luckenwalde is about thirty-five miles south of Berlin.

[223] Bernard J. Adamski, interview by author, Buffalo, NY, July 23, 2007.

[224] The surname was legally changed to Adamski years after Ben's father died.

[225] Harlingen and Laredo are in Texas.

[226] *Student Handbook*, T.L. 282, Scott Field, Illinois, 24, 25, n.d.

[227] Raymond F. Toliver's story of Hans Joachim Scharff, *Master Interrogator of the Luftwaffe*, identified a number of ways that Germany obtained information about airmen. Scharff received daily a copy of the *Stars and Stripes,* several days after it was in print, and accessed newspaper-clipping services from Allied publications that reported on their soldiers.

[228] Edwin Grzywa, interview by author, Buffalo, NY, July 13, 2007.

[229] A minimum score of eighty-five points was required for discharge from the service. Points were accumulated for service credit, overseas credit, combat credit, and parenthood credit. Source: "Army Point System for Discharge of Men is Announced," *Niagara Falls Gazette*, May 10, 1945.

[230] Al Palmerton received his order to report on October 12, 1942, from Local Board No. 630, North Collins, NY.

[231] Elwyn F. Palmerton, interview by author, Town of Lewiston, NY, June 27, 2007.

[232] The name of the newspaper was not on the clipping. The *Buffalo Evening News* and *Courier (Buffalo) Express* covered stories of area servicemen.

[233] IP or Initial Point is the last leg of the bomb run after which the pilot makes a turn to a heading over the target.

[234] Several decades later Al and the pilot of the P-47 met again at the wedding of Al's son.

[235] A "housewife" contained sewing notions such as needles, thread, and buttons. Cascara was a laxative.

[236] Richard Duerr, interview by author, Buffalo, NY, May 10, 2008.

[237] Don is also known as John J. Donald Griffin.

[238] J. Donald Griffin, interview by author, Buffalo, NY, July 3, 2007.

[239] Vorlager was the main part of the camp.

[240] Metro Marchyn, interview by author, Buffalo, NY.

[241] On May 7, 1945, Gen. Alfred Jodl signed the Act of Military Surrender at Eisenhower's headquarters in Rheims (Reims), France.

[242] RPM ~ revolutions per minute.

[243] Burgermeister ~ German equivalent of the position of mayor.

[244] "File unit: WWII Prisoners of War Data File, 12/7/1941 - 11/19/1946," Records of WWII Prisoners of War Series, created 1942 to 1947, documenting the period 12/7/1941 to 11/19/1946. Record Group 389, Archival Databases, National Archives, http://aad.archives.gov/aad/series-list.jsp?cat=WR26 [accessed October 8, 2007] and Allied POW program, Youngstown, NY, October 6, 2007.

[245] WWII Data File and Allied POW program, 2007.

[246] WWII Data File and Allied POW program, 2007.

[247] WWII Data File and Allied POW program, 2007.

[248] Mariano Giuga, interview by author, Buffalo, NY, July 23, 2007.

[249] The Vichy government operated from July 1940 to August 1944 following the military defeat of the Third Republic of France and a vote by the National Assembly. Marshal Philippe Pétain was President of the Council of Vichy France and collaborated with the Germans.

[250] Cardinal Joseph Ratzinger took the name of Pope Benedict XVI when he was elected on April 16, 2005.

[251] Benedict L. Klinshaw, interview by author, Buffalo, NY, July 13, 2007.

[252] *Worthington Buffalo Works News*, Vol. 2 No. 8 December 1944, 18.

[253] Tyndall Field Flexible Gunnery Class 43-5, Army Air Forces Gunnery School booklet, Ryndall Field, FL.

[254] *Keesler Field Mississippi*, San Antonio, TX, July 1942.

[255] BBC ~ British Broadcasting Corporation.

[256] Staff Sgt. Benedict L. Klinshaw, POW Number 2174, Stalag Luft IV, letters to Mr. and Mrs. A. J. Klinshaw, 258 Babcock St., Buffalo-10, NY, private collection.

[257] "Commemorating the 50th Anniversary of the Forced March of American Prisoners of War from Stalag Luft IV," May 8, 1995, Congressional Record, select Volume 141(1995), search: S6237-S6238 Congressional Record Online via GPO Access, http://www.gpoaccess.gov/crecord/search.html [accessed February 28, 2008].

[258] Ben Klinshaw's three brothers also served during the war. Robert Klinshaw, a younger brother, looked for Ben as the Allied troops moved into Germany. John Klinshaw served in the Navy and Fred Klinshaw served stateside in the Marines during WWII.

[259] Robert E. MacPherson, interview by author, Buffalo, NY, July 12, 2007.

CHAPTER 5

POWs AT FORT NIAGARA

THE GERMAN POWs ~ While John Jircitano, John Maroon, and other American soldiers were prisoners overseas in the midst of the war, their German counterparts held in the camps in the United States had quite a different experience. At Fort Niagara, according to the Cornell Cooperative Extension records, prisoners typically left for work projects to the nearby farms or factories on trucks about 7:30 a.m. They ate bag lunches out in the fields and in some instances were given additional foodstuffs and experienced acts of kindness by many of the local farm families. Officers were not used for labor unless they specifically requested work and the non-commissioned officers performed supervisory duty.

Each POW was assigned a serial number. The first part designated the theater of operation: "81" for North Africa or "31" for Europe. The letter that followed indicated the country of military service such as "G" for German, "I" for Italian, and so forth. The last number was assigned consecutively as the prisoner was captured. An earlier prisoner designation for POWs transferred to the United States was a three-part number, for example 4W-G-1425. The first component represented the division of United States military districts from 1 to 9, "W" for War Department, and the first letter of the country for which the prisoner served, followed by another number.[260] The majority of the Fort Niagara POWs were captured serving in the European Theater.[261]

It took some time before the United States distinguished a typical nationalistic German soldier from the fascists and those who supported the Nazi party. Across the country hard core Nazis dominated the camps. At Fort Niagara about six percent of the prisoners were listed as SS or SD.[262] The Nazis were a political party with a platform that was a blend of socialism, military dictatorship, and fascism. During the last free German election in 1932 the Nazis received only about one-third of the vote. Some of the German POWs were professional soldiers and others were conscripted for service in the Wehrmacht. The typical soldier was nationalistic, but not a Nazi party member. The American people and the government were slow to recognize the distinction, which resulted in the initial failure to protect the POWs from passionate Nazis.

An Associated Press article by Robert Otey brought to national attention the issue of Nazi soldiers' treatment of fellow prisoners sympathetic to the Allies. The first foreign prisoners of war executed in the United States were hanged on July 10, 1945, at Fort Leavenworth, Kansas. They were convicted at Camp Gruber in Oklahoma for the murder of a fellow prisoner. The executed Germans termed "fanatical Nazis" by Army authorities were members of Rommel's Afrika Korps.[263] Seven other prisoners, former members of Wolf-Pack submarine crews, were also convicted and executed for the murder of a fellow prisoner whom they accused of giving information of military value to the United States.[264]

Early in the spring of 1941 at Fort Niagara, the 1213th Reception Center for Army draftees and the 1206th Service Union Station Complement (SUSC) moved into newly constructed quarters consisting of six two-story frame barracks (each housing sixty-three men), two one-story recreation buildings, a guardhouse, infirmary, officers quarters, two new hospital wards, and a warehouse. A permanent garrison of four hundred men assigned to Fort Niagara received extensive combat training.[265]

By June 1943 Fort Niagara became a replacement-training unit for a few months and later a refresher unit for men of the Second Service Command. In April 1944 under the command of Col. Herbert Forrest, Fort Niagara served as a Separation Center and began preparations for holding POWs. The Walter S. Johnson Building Company of Niagara Falls, New York, constructed facilities and a fence for the prison camp on the southern end of Fort Niagara. The camp and its barracks were bounded on the east by Lake Street and the south by Jackson Street. An earlier plan to house the prisoners in the Lake Ontario Ordnance plant at Modeltown, now known as Model City, was abandoned after determining Fort Niagara would be a better choice due to space and economics. At that time, the Army was using the buildings at Model City for storage.

The first POW camps in the United States were in the south particularly Texas, Louisiana, and Florida. The Geneva Convention necessitated removing the captured troops out of the fighting zone and to safety as soon as possible. As the influx of prisoners continued, camps were established in the north and across the country in former CCC camps, high school gymnasiums, and other facilities. Construction of the camps, food products, necessary goods and services, and eventually POW labor evolved into profitable enterprises.[266]

According to a report dated August 10, 1945, by Maj. D. L. Schwieger to Fort Niagara's Commanding Officer, the camp was activated June 1, 1944, and the first POW received June 12, 1944. When the first German prisoners arrived here, the *Niagara Falls Gazette* headline on June 13, 1944, read "400 Nazi War Prisoners Arrive at Fort Niagara For Work in Farm Areas." The initial group of German POWs at Fort Niagara was part of Field Marshal Erwin Rommel's Afrika Korps and the second group to arrive in Western New York. The first group was sent to Medina to work in the H. J. Heinz food-processing plant in late May.[267]

A United States Army captain who spoke German commented that the POWs were elated over seeing the old dilapidated Depot Hotel in Niagara Falls. They believed bombs from German planes caused the missing and broken windows, and pitted walls.[268]

The prisoner population doubled to approximately eight hundred on June 13, 1944, when another contingent arrived by rail at the Tenth Street station in Niagara Falls guarded by the Military Police and transported to Fort Niagara in Army trucks. These German soldiers were previously held in a Texas prison camp and described as solid in appearance and in excellent health. Some of these prisoners were sent to branch camps in Chautauqua and Wyoming counties.[269]

By mid July, another six hundred prisoners arrived at the Suspension Bridge Station of the New York Central Railroad and were transported from the station to Fort Niagara under heavy guard by bus. They were reported captured by American forces at Cherbourg, France, on June 16, 1944. Many of these prisoners were not German. Col. John M. McDowell, in charge of the military district of Western New York, reassured the community that there would be no coddling of prisoners of war and that the prisoners would be harbored under strict and rigorous conditions.[270]

A few of the early groups to Fort Niagara arrived from other camps. About two hundred German POWs were held for less than two weeks during August 1944 at the Van Etten CCC Camp about ten miles northeast of Elmira, New York. On August 23 the prisoners were transported to Fort Niagara to help with the fruit harvest. The Van Etten camp was renamed and known as the *Small Branch German POW Camp* until the 1970s. The camp designated *The Factory* became part of the government's effort to democratize the German soldiers through a weekly POW magazine entitled *Der Ruf*.[271] The mail was sent to Fort Niagara for processing to keep the location of the Van Etten camp secret, particularly from the prisoners. Supplies for the camp were drawn from Fort Niagara and rations from the Rome Air Depot.[272] *Die PW Woche* (The PW Weekly) was one of the first POW newspapers. It began on August 14, 1943 and was printed in German, included world and local news, a pin-up picture, and sports articles. It sold for fifteen cents and was read by about seventy percent of all the POWs held in the United States[273]

Prisoners were transported from the base camp to work sites and farms in the town, and up to thirty miles away and then returned at night. This facilitated using the prisoners throughout Niagara and in adjoining counties. The Niagara County Producers and Processors Association worked with the military to assign prisoners to farms and food processing plants. Jamaican workers were also being imported to assist in the severe farm labor shortage.[274] One of the farm labor agreements in Porter was between the Processors Association and fruit grower John J. "Jack" Dietz, address R.F.D. #2, Youngstown. He farmed the one hundred acre O'Connor farm bounded on the west by Cothran Road and east by his brother's farm, Kenneth Diez.[275] Jack requested sixty man-days of labor for the month of September 1944. The Farm Labor Association Organization Agreements were casually filled out. Some of the agreements were signed by the operator such as the Ransomville Chemical Cold Storage with a general mailing address and accepted with the signature of J. C. Cornell, Assistant Manager of the Niagara Producers and Processors Association. The requested information of man-days of labor for specific months was left blank on the Storage Agreement.[276]

An additional half page form requested the farmer's name, address, telephone number, and responses to three questions. First, "What time in the morning will you want to pick up the prisoners?" Jack indicated 7:30 a.m. The second question was "Will you be grouped with another user in transporting prisoners? And Who?" He replied "maybe" and did not respond to the "who." The last question, unanswered, was "I hereby confirm agreement that I will use P.W.s as follows." The Agreement written in pencil was dated August 5, 1944. The grower was also to indicate the number of men for each week in September and October, and only a total for the months of November and December.[277]

The Farm Labor Association Organization Agreements were between the Niagara Producers and Processors Association and operators defined as "a producer, processor, or manufacturer of farm products or food supplies." The agreements stipulated the man-days per month, the rate per hour for a maximum of ten daily working hours, the deposit towards labor, redress of the government in the event of failure to pay any sums of money for wages, and the operator's obligation for transportation at his expense for workers and guards. POWs received compensation in canteen coupons. Food products, soap, and most other common items were available at the canteen. At the end of the war, prisoners were given cash for unused coupons and for some this was a sizeable amount.[278]

Supplemental Agreements by the War Department to contract for prisoner of war labor were authorized and negotiated under the First War Powers Act 1941 and Executive Order No. 9001. Town records contain twenty-one revised Supplemental Agreements with changes for rates of wages and additional job classifications with requests for various numbers of POWs. The agreements included transmittal letters from the Army Service Forces, Headquarters, District No. 4, Second Service Command Western New York Military District, 1807 Elmwood Avenue, Buffalo 7, New York, addressed to the Niagara Producers and Processors Association, Inc., c/o Mr. James Cornell, Box 79, Wilson, New York.

A special farm bureau committee organized to address the acute labor shortage in the fall of 1941 appealed to Fort Niagara for assistance. Col. F. D. Garlock granted permission for the soldiers to be released to work on the farms. More than two hundred soldiers on September 6 assisted Youngstown area growers with the harvest of the Elberta peach crop. [279]

Privates Vernon Nichols of Rochester, New York, Therby A. Colyer of Shade Gap, Pennsylvania, and Harold J. Day of Gouverneur, New York, all stationed at Fort Niagara, appeared in a photograph in the *Union Sun & Journal* working on Merritt Hosmer's farm on Youngstown-Lockport Road. Hosmer was one of the largest peach producers in Niagara County. Private Day told the reporter that it was the first time he was in a peach orchard! The soldiers helped save *Peach Sunday*, September 7, 1941, when growers expected thousands of people from Western New York to descend on the fruit belt and buy their peaches.[280] E. Kenneth Stevens told Thomas Tower that the government collected peach pits locally to use in gas mask filters during the war.[281]

The Wartime Labor used in agriculture, food processing, and allied agricultural industries involved the movement of large numbers of workers into New York State to produce, process, and preserve the 6,500,000 tons of food crops annually turned out by the farms. Farm Labor Association Records at the Town Hall and the Cornell Cooperative Extensive in Lockport, New York, noted workers from Jamaica, Bahamas, Barbados, Newfoundland, soldiers from training camps, migratory workers, and POWs. In New York State 800 POWs were used in farm labor in 1943, 4,200 in 1944, and 5,800 in 1945. But the real measure of their contribution in the data was in the "man-day contributions" of POWs as a group. In 1945 the 5,800 POWs were used for 150 days, a total of 870,000 man-days.

Hartwell J. Kennard, Major, C.M.P. Prisoner of War Officer, from the headquarters of the Western New York Military District in Buffalo and the Niagara Producers and Processors Association, Inc., in care of Daniel Dalrymple at the Federal Building in Lockport, corresponded concerning the labor agreements, requirements, and requests for prisoners of war to be used on the farms and processing plants. Farmers usually picked up the prisoners at Fort Niagara between 7:30 a.m. and 8:30 a.m. Most farmers provided their own transportation. Albert Krueger's group was transported with Holmon O'Connor and Roy Bradley's workers. George P. Tower, Nelson Tower, and B. A. James shared transportation for their POWs. Charles Holland and Alexander Henschel wanted their group picked up by the Schultz bus that serviced the area schools. Youngstown Cold Storage requested fifteen men for four months. Lyndonville Canning Co. wanted workers picked up at 6:00 a.m.

Most farmers applied for ten prisoners. Newton Cothran and Alexander Dolansky requested thirty workers during part of the harvest season. Some of the farmers without their own telephone gave a neighbor's telephone number. Louis Wills submitted the telephone number for J. P. Sanger, Ransomville 2159. Prisoners and guards typically brought their lunches provided by the United States Army. Employers were required to furnish drinking water for the workers. A deposit of one week's pay in advance was required.

TABLE 5.1
Niagara County Farm Labor Contracts for POWs

Farmer's Name	Address and other	Date of contract
Adams, Herbert E.	Ransomville	
Adams, Harry H.		
Barker Canning Co.	Ferguson & Ray Dickinson	September 8, 1944
Bewley Bros. Canning Co.	Middleport	July 11, 1945
Bigalow, Alanson C.	Wilson	August 12, 1944
Bradlee, Ira H.	Lewiston	
Bradley, Roy L.	Ransomville	August 15, 1944
Broeker, Alfred	Youngstown	June 9, 1944
Brooks, Wm J.	Ransomville	August 1945
Burrows, Albert		1945
Campbell, Daniel H.	Ransomville	June 9, 1944

Campbell, E. T.	Lewiston	June 8, 1944
Carey, Russell R.	Wilson	
Churchill Farms	Newfane	1944
Clapp Baby Food	Burt	May 1945
Colbert, Charles F.	Shore Acres Farm	
Cothran, G. H.	Youngstown	July 22, 1944
Cothran, Newton		June 9, 1944
Davis, C. G.	Lewiston	September 4, 1944
Demler, Norman	Niagara Falls	
Diez, Florence E.	Lake Road	June 9, 1944
Dolansky, Alexander	Youngstown	June 9, 1944
Dolansky, Joseph	Youngstown	July 21, 1945
Flood, Philip	Ransomville	September 2, 1944
Gabbey, Robert S.	Burt	
Gasport Storage	Gasport	June 18, 1945
Gaertz, William F.	Ransomville	August 8, 1944
Gillis, Harry S.	Ransomville	August 1, 1944
Greenwald, Carl A.	Burt	
Gursslim Bros.	Royalton	August 2, 1945
Gushee, Gordon	Youngstown	June 27, 1945
Harrington, Albert A.	Barker	August 16, 1944
Hays, Norman B.	Youngstown	June 9, 1944
Henschel, Alexander	Ransomville	August 23, 1944
Hickmann, Paul	Wilson	
Holland, Charles B.	Youngstown	August 22, 1944
Hopkins, Douglas	Youngstown	June 12, 1944
Hopkins, Seward (Harold)	Lewiston	June 9, 1944
Hosmer, John L. (Jack)	Youngstown	June 8, 1944
Hurtgam, Carl	Ransomville	August 2, 1944
Hurtgam, Edward	Ransomville	September 6, 1944
Israel, Otto F.	Barker	July 14, 1944
James, B. A.	Youngstown	June 9, 1944
Kelley, L. J.	Youngstown	
Kirk, W. Frank	Youngstown	August 8, 1944
Krueger, Albert	Ransomville	August 28, 1944
Kubala, Vincent	Youngstown	August 11, 1944
Kyle, Clyde	Youngstown	July 13, 1945
Lerch. Co-op. Cold Storage	97 Grand Street	October 5, 1944

Liddell, Kermit	Burt	August 15, 1944
Lindhurst, Elwood for Miss Ayer	Youngstown	
Lloyd, James	Youngstown	August 16, 1944
Lockport Canning Co.	Lockport	June 9, 1944
Lutts, Frank	Youngstown	June 9, 1944
Lyndonville Canning Co.	Lyndonville	August 15, 1944
Lyndonville Ice & Cold Storage	Lyndonville (Orleans)	September 20, 1944
Manning, Donald	Ransomville	
Mark, Philip C.	Wilson	July 16, 1945
Martin, Frank A.	Ransomville	June 10, 1944
McCormick A. L.	Burt	June 9, 1944
McCormick, Gordon C.	Youngstown	June 9, 1944
McKnight, Rollin	Burt	July 16, 1945
Middleport Cold Storage	Middleport	September 20, 1944
Mooney, R-	Kenmore	August 8, 1945
Morgan Bros.	Lewiston	June 9, 1944
Myers, Howard	Ransomville	June 9, 1944
Niagara Producers & Proc.	Lockport	July 22, 1944
Nixon, John G.	Lewiston	
O'Connor, Holman	Ransomville	June 9, 1944
O'Connor, R. A.	Ransomville	August 18, 1944
O'Neill, Al. O.	Gasport	August 3, 1945
Papke, W. F., Jr.	North Tonawanda	
Patterson, Homer	Youngstown	July 31, 1945
Perry, Galen M.	Ransomville	August 31, 1944
Pettit, Roy		
Pugh, - L.	Lockport	August 3, 1945
Randleigh Farm	Lockport	August 8, 1945
Rinelli, Anthony	Appleton	September 6, 1944
Sandberg, E. E.	Appleton	July 25, 1944
Sanderson, Ralph	Youngstown	June 9, 1944
Sandik Food Corp.	Lockport	June 9, 1944
Schultz, Elwood	Ransomville	August 8, 1944
Shippy, Seward	Youngstown	June 9, 1944
Shumaker, Wilbur H.	Youngstown	June 8, 1944
Silsby, Howard		
Silsby, Stephen W.	Gasport	August 20, 1945
Skurski, Mike	Ransomville	June 9, 1944

Smith, Howard L.	Ransomville	July 12, 1945
Sparks Brothers	Royalton	
Speas Company	Lyndonville	August 15, 1944
Standard Brands	Lockport	June 9, 1944
Stella Niagara by Mother Assumpta	Stella Niagara	May 15, 1945
Suday Inc./Krauss	Wilson	August 21, 1945
Thompson, Joseph L.	Youngstown	June 9, 1944
Tower, Donald R.	Youngstown	August 30, 1944
Tower, George P.	Youngstown	June 9, 1944
Tower, Harry		
Tower, Nelson	Youngstown	June 9, 1944
Tower, Perry E.	Youngstown	June 8, 1944
Tower, Ray C.	Youngstown	July 26, 1945
Truesdale, George		
Truesdale, Leonard		
Tugwell & Wiseman	Modeltown	1944
Velzy, O. M.	Lewiston	June 9, 1944
Vrooman, John	Lewiston	June 14, 1944
Wagner, Howard	Youngstown	July 3, 1944
Wagner, William	Youngstown	August 16, 1944
Ward Orchards by W. T. Ward	Olcott	August 17, 1944
Welkley Bros.	Gasport	June 9, 1944
West Somerset Cold Storage by R. A. Dickinson	Barker	
Wills, Dlee M.	Youngstown	
Wills, Louis	Ransomville	September 9, 1945
Wilson, George L.	Appleton	August 14, 1945
Wilson, Harley	Wilson	
Wilson Canning Co.	Wilson	June 9, 1944
Woolson, Isaac H.	Lewiston	September 2, 1944
W—dr-, Harold R.	Wilson	June 7, 1945
Youngstown Cold Storage by J. Van Kill	Youngstown	June 8, 1944
Dietz, John J.	Youngstown[282]	

Source: Farm Labor Association Organization Agreements, Box #13, 15-3, Folders 1-6; Cornell Cooperative Extension, Lockport, New York.

CRITICISMS OF THE POW CAMP ~ Col. Herbert R. Forrest, commanding officer, held a press conference on September 9, 1944, concerning the treatment of the prisoners at Fort Niagara and the adherence to the terms of the Geneva Convention. He addressed a group of newspaper and radiomen's questions in regards to the criticisms of the camp. Fran Skimin, a *Niagara Falls Gazette* staff writer quoted Colonel Forrest: "The Geneva treaty demands that prisoners of war housed at an Army camp receive the same food and the same quantity of food as the captors." There were complaints after an ice cream truck was seen inside the POW compound and criticisms for allowing the German prisoners cigarettes and beer. They did not like our beer, but believed American cigarettes were the best. Months later cigarettes were not available due to shortages. The final question of the day to Colonel Forrest remained unanswered for the moment. "Were the Americans, held prisoners by the Nazi government in internment camps in Germany, being afforded the same kind of treatment?"

Maj. William K. McClure, the POW camp commander, said the prisoners "are easy to handle and there has been no trouble at this camp." The prisoners did refuse to eat sweet corn calling it "chicken feed." Mess Sgt. Louis Catapario, a former Brooklyn butcher, commented that the Germans in addition to refusing to eat sweet corn didn't like steak either, but loved to eat potatoes and ice cream.[283] The POWs ranged in age from eighteen to sixty-four.

The issue of prisoner care continued to be a source of controversy in the town. In late February of 1945 Colonel Forrest again publicly responded to the criticisms and cited pertinent provisions of the Geneva Convention. Prisoners of war "must at all times be humanely treated and protected, particularly against acts of violence, insults, and public curiosity…The food ration of prisoners of war shall be equal in quantity and quality to that of troops at base camps."[284]

By April of 1945 the critical national food situation changed the diet for prisoner fare and most fresh meats, canned fruits and vegetables, and butter were eliminated. The meat diet for the POWs changed to hearts, liver, and kidneys. Oleomargarine was used in place of butter and corn syrup as a substitute for sugar.[285]

There was national concern that deviation from the terms of the Geneva Convention would result in retaliation by the German government against the American POWs held in Europe.[286] But, the government justified a work program for the prisoners to address the national manpower shortage. Colonel Forrest told the local press that prisoners were used in all types of work, except labor directly connected with the war effort. POWs picked cotton in the south, cut pulpwood in the north, harvested wheat in the west, and canned fruit in the east. Contractors paid the government for the prisoners' work.[287]

The instructions for using the POWs on the area farms, Appendix B, became a distant afterthought as relationships and trust were forged between area farmers and workers. Harry Adams of Ransomville loaned his truck to Peter Gruen, a thirty-four year old POW working on Adams' farm. Greun was involved in an accident at the intersection of Ransomville and School House Roads on July 2, 1945. The state police arrested Adams and charged him with allowing an unlicensed driver to operate his truck. Justice of the Peace, Taylor H. Austin of Ransomville, fined Adams $5.00 and Gruen was returned to the stockade at Fort Niagara.[288]

Locally, the prisoners pruned trees and harvested fruit on the farms, and worked in the canning factories and other agri-business concerns. The Comptroller of Niagara Fruit Industries, R. E. Crysler, advised Mr. J. C. Cornell of the Niagara Producers and Processors Association, by letter dated January 3, 1945, of the job descriptions and adjustments to pay rates.[289] Loaders were paid at the rate of seventy-five cents per hour and loaded full cases into railroad cars or storage. The rate of pay for Strappers and Stitchers was seventy cents to operate strapping machines to put wires on cases and staple new cartons for packaging. Two people worked together as Flippers to turn full cases into new empty containers at sixty cents. A Gluer's wage was sixty cents to brush glue onto the flaps of cartons. Pushers pushed cases onto a gravity conveyor. Rippers opened cases for the Flippers to empty and Folders folded and stacked old empty cartons. Pushers, Rippers, Flippers, and Folders pay rates were all sixty cents an hour.[290]

TABLE 5.2
Niagara Producers and Processors Association Requests for POWs

Dates	Farmers	Processors
8/21-28	50-80	20-50
8/28-9/2	70-100	70-100
9/4-9/9	340-390	160
9/11-9/16	520-580	220
9/18-9/23	315-500	220
9/25-9/30	195-225	230
10/2-10/7	175-200	210
10/9-10/14	145-170	210
10/16-10/21	70-90	150-210
10/23-10/28	50-70	150-210
10/30-11/4		50

11/6-11/11	50
11/13-11/18	50
11/20-11/25	50
11/27-12/2	40
12/4-12/9	40
12/11-12/16	30
12/18-12/23	10
12/25-12/30	10

Source: Farm Labor Association Organization Records, Notebook II, 2006.1.6a, Town Hall, Town of Porter, Youngstown, NY, 1940s.

J. J. Sugden, Regional Farm Placement Supervisor, War Manpower Division, United States Employment Service, 65 Broad Street, Rochester, New York, advised Maj. H. J. Kennard, Commanding Officer of the Army Service Forces in Buffalo, about the job classifications and rates of pay for the use of POWs in particular factories. Tugwell[291] & Wiseman, Inc., packers of canned foods in Modeltown, specified job categories for the POWs: sorting, peeling and packing fruits and vegetables, unloading cans from cars, feeding covers and catching cans from closing machine, handling of green produce in baskets, casing and piling canned goods in warehouse, and cookers' helpers.[292]

Tugwell packers reported 17,601.5 man-hours during the period from August 22, 1944 to October 23, 1944, with wages totaling $10,912.93.[293] The Warehouse Division of Niagara Fruit Industries paid $1,400.00 for wages during the first week of January 1944. POWs were rotated between the farms and industrial sites. In January 1945, the Comptroller of Niagara Fruit requested specific POWs who were exceptionally good workers, daily if possible.[294]

TABLE 5.3
Names of Prisoners Requested by Niagara Fruit Industries

Bauer, Kurt	Fritzsche, Kurt
Beyer, Heinz	Klein, Hans
Bleier, Josef	Luenemann, Johann
Boehles, Karl	Luther, Karl
Bratfisch, Heino	Malling, Ott
Dropsch, Helmet	Neurohr, Willi
Engel, Siegfried	Ohr, Johannes

Reisenbichler, Friedrich	Siegfried, Engel
Rosenthal, Alfred	Wissgott, Rudolf
Schauerte, Josef	Wuerfel, Reinhard
Schwarzkopf, Horst	Ziegler, Willi

Source: Farm Labor Association Organization Records, Town of Porter, NY.

The POWs provided needed manpower for agri-business and other industries locally and across the country in almsot every state (See Appendix D). Americans living in areas near the camp compounds watched this visible intrusion of the war into their lives. The personal encounters and memories of people in the Porter community and on the farms with the prisoners put human faces on the soldiers we called the enemy.

Agri-business entities and food processors corresponded with James C. Cornell, the Manager of Niagara County Producers & Processors Association. Cornell responded to requests for wages, details concerning guards traveling with the prisoners, registration fees, and dates requesting workers. John L. Hosmer was the President and Holman O'Conner the Secretary of the Association.[295] Wilbur Shumaker, Seward Hopkins, and Percy Morgan were the directors in 1944. Paul Roegge of Lockport was the Vice-President.

TABLE 5.4
Western New York Area Agri-Business Entities Utilizing POWs

A. A. Grinnell Co., Inc.		Oakfield, NY
Bater, Floyd		
Curtice Brothers Co., Inc.		Rochester, NY
Fort Niagara Exchange		Youngstown, NY
Genesee-Orleans Vegetable Growers Growers Cold Storage Co.	Francis H. Balke, President	Waterport, NY
Harold H. Clapp, Inc.	P. B. Duncan, Supt.	Burt, NY
Haxton Canning Co., Inc.		Oakfield, NY
H. J. Heinz Company		
Kennoak Farm	H. S. Golde, Jr., Proprietor	Wilson, NY
Letchworth Canners & Growers, Inc.		

Lockport Canning Co.	George Bewley, President	Lockport, NY
Middleport Cold Storage	James F. Holahan, Mgr.	Middleport, NY
National Grape Corporation		
N.C. Demler Cider Mill	Norman C. Demler	Niagara Falls, NY
Niagara Frontier Canning	George R. Bewley, Owner	Lockport, NY
Niagara Producers & Proc.		Niagara Falls, NY
Oakfield & Elba Growers, Inc.		Elba, NY
Ransomville Cold Storage		Ransomville, NY
Sardik Food Products Corp.	J. M. Krausz, Manager	Lockport, NY
Speas Company	Edwin L. Bush, Manager	Lockport, NY
Standard Brands Inc.	J. Thomas Schneider, Esq.	Lockport, NY
Torrey, Elbert		
Tugwell & Wiseman, Inc.	C. H. Wiseman, President	Modeltown, NY
Welkley Brothers	J. H. Seabury, Partner	Gasport, NY
W. Somerset Cold Storage	C. L. Fox, President	Barker, NY
Wilson Canning Co.	W. E. Current, Manager	Wilson, NY
W. W. Clark Co., Inc.		
Youngstown Cold Storage	Wilbur H. Shumaker, VP	Youngstown, NY

Source: Farm Labor Association Organization Records, Notebook I and II, Town Hall, Town of Porter, Youngstown, NY, 1944 to 1945. The government leased Ransomville Cold Storage for storage of canned milk and cheese.

THE GERMAN SISTERS ~ Three missionary Sisters of St. Francis of Penance and Christian Charity[296] arrived in Buffalo, New York, in 1874, at the urging of German Jesuits working among the poor immigrants on the east side of the city of Buffalo. The Sisters established a novitiate in Buffalo and in 1908 they moved to Stella Niagara on Lower River Road in Lewiston.[297]

In the 1940s there were still German born Sisters at Stella. For Sister Auxentia Gromke, a cook for the children's dining room at Stella Niagara, the prisoners were family. There is a story that Sister Auxentia's cousin was one of the prisoners from Fort Niagara and that he received some special treats from the kitchen.

One of the initiation rituals for the freshman students at that time was a treat of *O'Henry* chocolate bars hidden on the grounds at Stella. The prisoners from

Fort Niagara were working outdoors and thought the chocolate was for them. Each time they saw one of the Sisters, the prisoners gave a nod and said "danke."

Margaret "Peggy" Dineen was a student at Stella Niagara while her three brothers served in the military during the war. Eugene, a chemist, was in the Army and served stateside. Her younger twin brothers were in the Navy. John was in the Atlantic and William lost his life in the Pacific. He served on a battleship that the Japanese blew up near the Marshall Islands.[298]

Peggy watched the German POWs working at Stella. There was a lot of rain that year and the POWs were used to help cut the grass on the extensive grounds. "We were told to not interfere, but could say hello to the prisoners. We were never afraid of them," she said. The Sisters taught their students including Peggy that "the prisoners are human beings just like you. They are lonely and away from their homes and family."

MONGOLIAN POWs ~ Eugene "Gene" Pacia went to Youngstown in the summer with his mother to help their relatives at the historic *Ontario House*, known to locals as *The Stone Jug*, the bar. Alexander Lane built this cornerstone of the Youngstown village in 1842 at the intersection at Main and Lockport Streets on the site of the old Hathaway Tavern that was burned during the War of 1812.[299] "We slept on the third floor and my mother helped in the restaurant. I was working at the Temperance Farm on River Road for the Broeker family. They were a large German family. The German prisoners helped to pick fruit. I rode my bike from the farm into the village to get cigarettes for them at Mae Ellis's store. It is where Danny the barber is today.[300] The prisoners were Germans, but some of the men told me they were Mongolians. I think the Mongolians came later, maybe even after the war was over," he said.[301] As the war continued, Germany also forced French, Austrians, Czechs, Poles, Arabs, Russians, and others from the conquered areas into military service.[302]

DEMOCRACY AT THE ELWOOD SCHULTZ FARM ~ One of the most effective teaching tools of democracy and the American way of life came from an unplanned resource during the war. It was the local farmers and their families' treatment of the prisoners who were part of the farm work programs. Elwood Schultz of Daniels Road, Ransomville spoke German. Elwood and Dorothy Schultz and their daughters, Marlene and Mickey, established a special relationship that is evident in the correspondence to the family after the war.[303]

Each morning the farmers went to Fort Niagara and brought the prisoners to the farms by trucks. The men climbed in the back of the truck and a car fol-

POWs on the Morgan Farm in Lewiston, New York. According to the US Army Military History Institute records 378,156 German, 41,456 Italian, and 5,424 Japanese POWs were held in the US. (Courtesy Dorothy Boyce)

lowed in case someone tried to escape. There was always a guard and sometimes two. Fred Stupp guarded the POWs at the Schultz farm. Some of these prisoners were artists in Germany before being drafted. They talked about their families and children and were always very polite. The POWs brought their lunch with them. The Schultz family shared potatoes and meat as they ate together in the kitchen. Twelve to fifteen men helped with the production of vegetables.

For some of the prisoners working for Schultz, it was several years after they left Fort Niagara before being repatriated. The letters gave accounts of the difficult conditions of shortages in occupied Germany and requested basic necessities, and other items like artist paints or nylons. Most of the letters were written in German.

The salutation in some of the letters was an affectionate "dear uncle" and concern for the Schultz family's health. These former prisoners wrote about agriculture, inquired about the crops, and some about their hope to return to the town to visit with the Schultz family. Other words were very painful. One letter told the tragedy of a POW returning to Germany to find his wife and all his children killed. Some returned to find homes and personal belongings destroyed from the bombs.

A few of the POWs were sent to England and others to LeHavre in France to be part of the reconstruction before being repatriated. Letters arrived from

Tesinsko, Czechoslavakia; Stuttgart-Mohringen, Germany; Roydon-Essex, Great Britain; Forsbach, Germany; Hoengen, Germany; Dortmund-Hochsken, Germany "Britische Zone;" and Correspondence des prisonniers de Guerre Designation du Depot: Lager-Bezeichnung Metz (Moselle) France. The pages are yellowed now and edges frayed, but the pain and suffering of war and its aftermath were clear. These are a few excerpts from the letters.

January 3, 1948

Lieber Onkel!

How are you and your wife today Marlene and Mickey? Hopefully they are all in good health. I am alright (sic) health wise. Now again I am a free person and can do what I want. I have enough work as a locksmith, but not on farm…not enough food…I lost 32 lbs. since a prisoner…no tobacco…my little blue girl waited for me and now we want to marry in April. We will not have all the things we need for our house. We will take those hurdles as they come. One does not even get a wedding dress or suit now. If only we could get what we left overseas in America. Often then I think back on the time when I was a prisoner. I could hardly wait for homecoming. But many days I would not mind to get back to Youngstown, but now I have an obligation that one feeling can overcome all the hardships.

I have a small favor to ask of you. You know how I passionately like to paint. I am asking you for some oils because here we could not get them for years and I would see to it that I would paint you a picture.

Would it be possible to have a pair of stockings (small) for my bride and it would give her the greatest joy for that. In the hope I will hear from you I send my best greetings and wishes. Many greets to your wife and Marlene and Mickey.

2 February 1947

Honor Herr Schultz,

I will keep my promise and give you a sign that I am alive. My family are all alive and also my apartment is in tact. I hope that you and your family are healthy. Again I want to thank you for your demeanor that you showed me. My English knowledge is not enough to write in English so please excuse me. And now I am at home and am going to miss a lot of things I am accustomed to. Regards to the family.

I would be happy if I get some answer from you.

2 September 1947

My dear Mr. Schultz!

Few weeks ago I received your letter from June 5th and last week we received your packet. I will be say very much thanks to you and your family. You don't know how much gladness

Above, German POWs at the Elwood Schultz farm. (Courtesy Mickey Schultz)

Left, Fred Stump, the guard from Fort Niagara at the Elwood Schultz farm, enjoyed a moment with Mickey, Marlene, and the family dogs. (Courtesy Mickey Schultz) *you have make by myself and by my wife....Ruth like the blue dress with the white points very much. It is like a present of the heaven. The stocking are very wonderful too. You must be know we don't can buy things like that never in the last 8 years. My wife only have anguish, the stocking can not keep to long...*

May I trouble you for a pictures of us boys and from your family too. I don't have any one.

You must excuse me when I beg today for a little piece soap...I hope you stay well also your wife and Marlene and Mickey!...

My dear Mr. Schultz, I wish you and your family all the best and I thank you very very much!

8 March 1949

Dear Mrs. Schultz,

I just have to send you my greetings...I am always glad you send some greetings from you.

Everyday I ask (my husband) if he wrote to them but now I think he hasn't written for a long time. He was in a military hospital.

I think he doesn't have any homesickness for America. But for his next vacation I am going to see he spends it in America with you. He was in the Army since 1940. So my dear Mrs. Schultz don't be mad if my (husband) *doesn't write; writing is his weaker side. But he is always happy when he gets mail from you. I would really like it if you write.*

Many best wishes.[304]

SERENADING THE PRISONERS ~ People in town remember riding their bikes to Fort Niagara and giving the prisoners drop apples from the farms. Pat Hutchison Phillips was a teenager when she and a youth group serenaded the POWs at the barbed wire fence. She thought Rev. Dave Helwig of the Presbyterian Church organized the group of young people from the First Presbyterian Society and St. Bernard's Catholic Church. Pat remembers it being a lot of fun.[305]

Some of the prisoners kept pet mongrel dogs. When the locals inquired why the prisoners were allowed to have dogs the *Union Sun and Journal* ran a story that reported there was no regulation against the dogs being in the stockade at Fort Niagara.[306] When the POWs left they gave their mascot dog, Mitzi, to the Hutchison family.[307]

Pat recollected that growing up in the village of Youngstown was great with woods behind the Hutchison home at 614 Main Street. "A hermit lived in the woods behind our house in a shack there. His name was Johnny Casey. Across the street, on the west side of Main Street, was the village dump. Boys shot at the river rats from the dump with their BB guns. But we didn't run around at night, and we didn't dare disobey our parents then," Pat said.

Lt. Harold Hutchison wrote, "Soloed Ship No. 12 on April 15, 1943." (Courtesy Pat Hutchison Phillips)

The casualties of war impacted directly on Pat's family. Her older brother was called Hutch. "He graduated in 1942 from Youngstown High School and was working at Ulrich's Drug store in the village when he announced 'I am going in the service.' All the boys felt that way. I remember David Hays too."

Pat's father, Sgt. Maj. Harold Hutchison, was a career soldier and served in the Twenty-fifth and Twenty-eighth Infantries. He was stationed at Fort Niagara before going overseas during WWI and died in 1935 while serving at Fort Hayes in Ohio. Pat's mother, V. Helen Jarnot Hutchison, worked for the postal service and was assistant postmaster in Youngstown. Robert Hutchison, Pat's brother, also served in the military. "He was a Navy pilot, graduated from high school in 1943, and went right in," she said.

John Martin, Pat's cousin, was a Navy gunner on a United States destroyer in the Pacific. Martin's ship participated in the blasting of Truk, the attack on Ponape, the battle of the Marianas, and attacks on the Japanese bases at Saipan and the Bonin Islands according to a newspaper clipping from Youngstown in the Hutchison family file folder in the Historian's office.

"Hutch married (Josephine Clauser of Bloomfield, Pennsylvania) before he went overseas," Pat said. "He enlisted from here and received his pilot wings and commission at Foster Field, Texas, on October 1, 1943. His wife called to let us know he was killed. It didn't sink in right away. I answered the telephone then went to tell my mother about the call. I was thirteen when he died." Pat carefully held the photograph of a cross-shaped gravestone precisely aligned in its row in the heart of seemingly endless rows of the same. The stone is engraved: "Harold W. Hutchison 2nd Lt 32 Photo q 5 RCN GP N.Y. July 24, 1944." Hutch was doing photo reconnaissance during a mission in Italy when he was shot down. Second Lt. Harold Hutchison became the first Youngstown soldier killed in action during WWII, and was buried in the Sicily-Rome Cemetery about thirty-eight miles south of Rome at the edge of the town of Nettuno.[308]

MAC DONALD'S DAIRY ~ Area businesses supplied goods and services to Fort Niagara. D. Richard MacDonald of MacDonald's Dairy on Portage Road in the Village of Lewiston delivered milk while the POWs were held at the compound. Joel MacDonald was about seven years old when he rode with his father on the milk truck. "I went with my dad. He delivered milk there on the weekend and backed the truck up to the door at the Officer's Club. Some of the prisoners who were standing around gave me a doughnut and one put me on his shoulders. They seemed to be happy to see a young child. I waved to them as we came down the old Lake Road to Fort Niagara."[309]

WASSER, WASSER ~ From the shores of Marblehead, Massachusetts, to Youngstown the Richardson family's lives were filled with the themes of hard work, struggle, and accomplishment. Chester Richardson grew up in Lynn, Massachusetts, and was part of the Class of 1916 of Massachusetts Institute of Technology, MIT.[310]

"The government wanted technical people in WWI. My father earned a degree in Electro-Chemical Engineering and Metallurgy. He was drafted and worked in the Chemical Warfare Service Department in Washington, DC. His group tested and developed lenses in gas masks to prevent them from fogging up," Jane Richardson said.

When the war was over Chester was transferred to the Department of Agriculture. He worked in the fixed nitrogen lab and developed the process by which ammonium nitrate fertilizer was produced and used on farms. A job offer from Mathieson Alkali Works, later known as Olin Chemical Corporation, Niagara Falls, New York, put Chester on the eventual road towards the Town of Porter.

It was 1937 when Cora Gushee rode her horse on the dirt road known as *Poverty Ridge*, now East Avenue, to welcome her new neighbors, the Richardsons. "Cora was the first person to greet our family," Jane said. Cora became a key figure in the twentieth century history of the town. She was the town historian for several decades until her 100th birthday.

Jane recalled the Richardson's farm life. "We owned a team of horses called 'King and Queen.' King was seventeen hands high and Queen sixteen hands. They were a cross between a Percheron and an Arabian, a gentle natured team of horses. The team pulled the single bottom plow, wagons, the stoneboat, the sprayer, the duster, the sickle-bar mower, and even the old McCormick Deering 1020 steel-wheeled tractor out of the mud when it got stuck. It took only one horse to pull the cultivator. We always chose King to do that because he was the lazy one. He let Queenie do most of the work of getting the load started when we hollered 'giddy-up.' He also let her do the bulk of the bracing against the traces when it came to stopping the load on 'whoa' and I can remember sitting on top of the sprayer, yelling 'giddy-up,' 'whoa,' 'gee,' and 'haw.' We would go up and down the rows, turn the corners at the end, and I never picked up the reins. They did it all on the verbal commands of a high-pitched juvenile voice. Were those good horses or what? Don't make 'em like that anymore."

"After the war in 1946 we got a Case tractor with rubber tires and joined the modern age of farming. My memory of the war began with the POWs. I was about eight years old. We worked with two groups of fifteen each to help pick fruit with an armed military guard. By the third day of picking, the guards helped too. Their rifles hung in the tree while the POWs walked right by," Jane said.

"The best legacy my father left us was that he was totally impartial. He treated everyone the same. Dad was full of fun with a gentle disposition. He was at ease with everybody, and also with the prisoners. My father spoke Berliner Deutsch. He learned German in college. The prisoners could understand him. But there was always one in the group who could speak English."

The prisoners fascinated Jane and her older brother, John, who was eleven. The POWs sat under the sugar maple tree to eat their bag lunch and drink coffee from quart canning jars. Jane and John mingled with them. "We drove by the prison camp area at night and saw the barbed wire fence and floodlights."

The image of the POW camp was impressive to Jane, but her mother's perception of the camp and the prisoners was different than her children. "My mother was very nervous. She was worried her children would be held hostage in an escape. One of the men was older, in his forties. Another prisoner was only fourteen years of age. I heard that there were also Italian prisoners working on another farm."

Pearl Darcy Richardson believed that a mother's place was in the home and kept a watchful eye over her children while busy with household chores and canning. She put up 1,500 jars every year of vegetables and fruit from the two-acre house garden. Sugar was rationed, which made it difficult to can. Pearl's sisters sent her their sugar coupons from Washington, DC. There was a shortage of dairy products during the later part of the war, but their dairy cows provided the family with milk and butter. During church events Pearl carefully wrapped butter as prizes to the unexpected delight of the recipient. There were four war ration books for foodstuffs and other items. War Ration Book No. 1 was for sugar, shoes, and coffee. Three other books followed for the distribution of meats, butter, processed foods, and other items.[311]

Chester hauled the cherries harvested with the help of the prisoners to the Clinton-Bailey Market in Buffalo. He owned a Model A Ford stake truck with very worn tires and was stopped by the police on Niagara Falls Boulevard. When told by the police to get some new (rationed) tires he replied: "Tell me where to get them and I will." The officers told him: "Just be careful driving the truck."[312]

"The other POWs deferred to the oldest prisoner. One day he was sitting under a tree and motioned to us (Jane and her brother John) to sit with him. He offered to share his lunch and pulled out his wallet to show us a picture of his family, a boy and girl about the same age as us. My mother watched and this changed her feelings about the prisoners. That night when we milked the cows my mother filled four gallons of milk and set them to chill. The next day she stood at the top of the steps and asked, 'Does anyone speak English?' A prisoner came to the steps and took his hat off. Mother asked him, 'Will you please tell the men that there is fresh cold milk for anyone who wants it?' The men dumped out their coffee and ran to fill up their jars with milk," said Jane.

"I didn't see it, but dad talked about the prisoners working at the Youngstown Cold Storage. One of the guards at the Storage had a vendetta. He was very surly to the prisoners and at one point pointed his rifle. It was pretty tense," Chester told his daughter.

Jane smiled telling about her personal role on the farm while the prisoners worked. "I thought I was such a big shot. Mom sent me out with a jug of water.

Dad taught me the German word for water 'Wasser.' I would go out in the orchard with the jug and a tin cup walking up and down the rows crying out: Wasser, Wasser!"

A number of young men from the town became soldiers and served during the war. Some lost their lives and yet there appeared to be very few negative feelings in the community towards the captured German soldiers. "The Youngstown village teenage girls would ogle at the POWs at the fence. There was no animosity!" and Jane smiled.

The Richardson family worshipped at St. John's Episcopal Church of Youngstown. Jane repeated the prayers for the troops, their safe return, and an end to the war. She tried to hum and remember the hymn of prayer, "Blessed are the folks who were weary at heart waiting for the war to end, wishing…."

The day the prayers of the Richardson family and the country were answered was on VJ Day. "I remember going out to the road barefoot to get the mail. There were big tomato worms by the mailbox. I pulled the paper out. 'PEACE' in big black letters took one quarter of the page. There were pictures of tanks rolling and war scenes below the word 'peace'. I went high tailing it off to the house yelling: peace, peace, and waving the paper!"[313]

"I JUST WANT TO GO HOME" ~ John Richardson was three years older than his sister Jane. "I was nine years old and just came down for breakfast that morning of December 8 in 1941. My parents were at a party Sunday night and everyone talked about what happened. They were still talking about it Monday morning. It was a serious conversation, but didn't immediately concern me. It was my earliest memory of the war," John said.[314]

After D-day there was an impromptu school assembly including a prayer service. Johnny Johnston and about a half dozen seniors were leaving school to join the war effort. "They stood up and we honored those who were leaving." John started to list some of the schoolmates who did not return including Harold Hutchison and his neighbor, David Hays. "Johnny Johnston walked through the area around Hiroshima after the bombing. He died later from cancer from the radiation." John recalled others who served. "Bob Courter flew P-51s and Guy Myers was a tail gunner in a B-24. David Hays was flying a mission with a DC-3 on D-Day that carried glider pilots."

Children became involved in the war effort. "There was a recycling area in the ellipse in front of the school (Youngstown Red Brick) for collecting scrap iron. Someone threw the cannon on the pile in the iron yard, but it was recovered and anchored to the flag pole!" In 2007, the cannon was on the top floor of the school near the entrance to the Porter Historical Museum.

John remembered the air raid practices. "We evacuated the school and went in groups to a particular house. We played board games until the all clear signal."

One of John's images of the past was the piece of jewelry that people wore. "It said 'remember harbor.' There was a pearl in the loop of the letter 'h'. And there were little ditty rhymes children repeated and the Movietone News feeding us information all the time. It was about five minutes, fifteen minutes if there was a double feature. Once or twice we went to the movie house at Fort Niagara." A regularly scheduled transit bus went to Niagara Falls to the city theaters for western movies and actors like George "Gabby" Hayes and Alan Ladd. John smiled remembering Geraldine Fitzgerald starring with Alan Ladd in the movie *O.S.S.* and the Gypsy Rose Lee movies shown at the USO in Youngstown.

When the POWs came to work on the family farm, John was twelve years old. His father assigned him to one of the POWs. "Gustav was seventeen-years old. One day he said to me 'I just want to go home.' I realized these are people too. All of a sudden I didn't hate the Germans. After WWI it was hard for children of German descent. There was a holdover of sentiment against the Germans."

"We picked up the POWs in our Model A truck and didn't always get the same prisoners. One of the farmers wanted to get the same ones, because they were so good. The best workers were farmers themselves at home in Germany. There was only one problem that I heard about at Fort Niagara. Some of the POWs deliberately broke some of the plumbing works in the barracks," John said.

Each morning as the POWs began the day at the Richardson's farm, Chester spoke in German to them about what work he wanted them to do. Chester enrolled in German language studies while he was at MIT. He wanted to be able to read German engineering technical manuals. John said, "One of the prisoners came up to me and asked when was my father in Germany because his pronunciation was excellent." During threshing the women put on a picnic and made sandwiches for the POWs and John ran errands. The Hurtgam story was a shock he noted. "We didn't talk about suicide in those days," John said remembering the story of the POW who hung himself.

After the atomic bomb was dropped the Richardsons were thankful the war was over. Jane piped in that their father told them, "that for the Japanese people it was honorable to fight for the cause. Surrender was not acceptable. When the atomic bomb hit, the world had never seen anything like it. This allowed the Japanese to surrender and save face because it was so devastating. Without the bomb, the war would have dragged on."

John's image of VJ Day was the photograph of a seaman who grabbed a nurse in Times Square in New York City, kissed her, and then walked away. Alfred Eisenstaedt's photograph was on the cover of *Life* on August 14, 1945. "There was the story of the priest who volunteered and took a young man's place at Auschwitz after the man (Francis Gajowniczek) who was to be killed pleaded for mercy because he was married with children. Kolbe (Father Maximilian) took his place." John found it ironic that the Franciscan monastery Kolbe established in Nagasaki, Japan, survived the bomb.

John became part of our country's history of military service. He was drafted during Korea and did a tour of duty with the Eighty-Second Airborne.

DESPAIR IN THE HURTGAM BARN ~ The sound of the frogs in the swampy area of Frog Hollow Road, now Andrews Road, in the Hamlet of Ransomville was the stage for a tragic chapter of the German POWs. Mervin Hurtgam was about fourteen years old and lived with his parents, Edward and Winifred Brawn Hurtgam, and an older brother, Ronald, who helped work on the family vegetable farm.[315] Edward also operated a lumber mill.

The production of vegetables required a lot of hand labor for planting and harvesting. The Hurtgam farm, like many others, contracted for prisoners from Fort Niagara due to serious labor shortages. Area women also helped on the farm while some of their husbands were off to the war and money was short. "The women bunched vegetables and the men picked and packed them," Merv said. The POWs were not closely guarded while they worked on the seventy-nine acre farm. It was a common occurrence in the town that the guards let the prisoners work unattended.[316] Mr. Hurtgam let the POWs off at the grocery store in the hamlet, conducted his business, and then returned to pick up the prisoners. People from Ransomville commented that the POWs stood on the corner waiting for Mr. Hurtgam, but never tried to run off.[317]

"My mother always made something hot to eat and coffee for the prisoners during lunch. It was something extra to add to their sandwiches and other foodstuffs from their lunch bags. In the packinghouse my mother hung a clean towel for each man. My father spoke German to them," Merv said. His grandmother, Augusta Hurtgam, emigrated from Germany to America.

August 23, 1945, was etched in detail in Merv's mind. The war was over and the prisoners would be shipped back to Germany soon. It was the noon hour. During the day the guard took a head count, but this day was different. The prisoners were getting ready for lunch in the packinghouse around the bunching table. The guard took his usual head count and realized "Karl is gone!"

Above, Fort Niagara German POW graves in the foreground at Woodlawn National Cemetery in Elmira, New York, re-interred from the Modern Post Cemetery of Fort Niagara in 1949. (See Appendix E)

Left, Mervin Hurtgam, front row on the right, with some friends, family, local workers, and POWs. An aerial view of the Hurtgam family farm on Frog Hollow Road, Ransomville. (Courtesy Mervin Hurtgam)

Merv, his mother and father, and a neighbor, Junior Woolson, were in the house eating lunch when the guard came to the house to inform them and to contact Fort Niagara that Karl was missing. "Hell, I'll find him, he is probably in the haymow sleeping," replied Merv. Karl was in charge of the team of horses and a number of cows. He got them ready to work each morning. Merv figured Karl was taking care of the animals during lunch and went to sleep in the haymow.

Merv followed by his buddy, Junior Woolson, headed for the barn. He went to the place in the barn where hay was thrown down to feed the cows. There was a ladder leading to the haymow. At this time of the year the haymow was filled to the peak of the barn with loose hay. As Merv went up the ladder Junior Woolson was close behind. Merv climbed up about fifteen feet into the mow on the hay before he saw Karl hanging. He had put a rope over a two by four used to stop the hayfork from running off the end of the track. In horror at the sight Merv yelled to his friend that Karl hung himself and to get out of the barn. Junior never saw him. Down the ladder and out of the barn Merv kept yelling "He hung himself' as the boys ran across the barn yard and over the fence on their way to the house. They passed the packinghouse, but the other prisoners already knew what happened.

"He hung himself, he hung himself," Merv cried out to his parents and again sixty-one years later in retelling the event. "The authorities from Fort Niagara came out to the farm, and then the other prisoners cut Karl down and carried his body. I don't know if they held a funeral for him," reflecting on that tragic moment.

There was talk that Merv would have to go to New York City for an investigation, but it never occurred. Some people told Merv that Karl was a Gestapo and could never go back because Merv knew that "the Gestapo was not supposed to surrender." In other camps across the country the Nazis controlled the other prisoners. But there never appeared to be any intimidation or fighting amongst the prisoners on the Hurtgam farm.

"I can't go in the barn," Merv told his father. It was several months before Merv could return to the barn. The impression in the wooden two by four where the rope was placed left an indentation from that dreadful day in Merv's memory. "I would like to go and cut that piece of wood out of the barn, maybe I will soon," he said.

The family celebrated with the POWs on their last day on the farm. Merv's mother set out a "big spread and my father gave them beer. They got very drunk," laughed Merv. "We took them back to Fort Niagara and some of the prisoners fell out of the truck into the snow. Some did not want to go back (to Germany)," he said.

After the war was over some of the prisoners wrote to Edward Hurtgam. He mailed them their books that were left for safekeeping. No one ever came back to visit and Merv's parents never went to Germany, but they did correspond with some of the prisoners for a time.

In 1953 Merv joined the United States Air Force and taught electronics. The Hurtgam's were a patriotic family, but like most other area farmers treated the POWs with dignity far beyond what was required.

FDR AND HOWARD MYERS APIARY ~ Howard Myers owned the largest apiary in Niagara County with 3,500 hives. He also kept hives in Genesee and Livingston Counties, near Potsdam, and in Florida. Howard farmed one hundred acres at the intersection of Dickersonville and Swan Roads in Ransomville. Etta, Howard's daughter, was born in 1926 in the farmhouse where she grew up and walked about half a mile down the road with several friends to the one-room schoolhouse at the corner of Dickersonville and Ridge Roads.[318]

In 1992 Etta's grandson, Clayton Randall Stidham, Jr., recorded for history and a college assignment in History 292, some of Etta's earliest memories. The first was an event that would tie the Myers family to a public servant who was on the verge of becoming a focal point in the history of the country and the world. The Empire State Beekeepers Association was invited to the home of New York State Governor Franklin Delano Roosevelt at Hyde Park in 1931. Howard was the president of the Empire State Beekeepers Association. Roosevelt was a hobby beekeeper.[319]

Howard Myers stood next to Roosevelt at the meeting and personally introduced the members of the Association. Later Myers always insisted, "He was the first person to introduce Roosevelt as 'the next president of the United States.' Mrs. (Eleanor) Roosevelt saw that the ladies in the line were not wearing gloves, so she graciously removed hers and shook hands barehanded. One of my grandmother's (Etta) memories from that day is of Sara Delano Roosevelt (Franklin's mother) taking her by the hand into the house and getting her a glass of cool water."[320]

A decade later the country rallied behind President Roosevelt after Japan attacked Pearl Harbor. Eventually, part of the war found its way to the Myers farm. The Myers obtained prisoners of war to help with the labor shortage on their farm. The POWs worked in the orchards and helped build the frames for the beehives. "I was about sixteen and walked out of the house in shorts and a halter top. The guard told me to go back to the house and put some clothes on. These men haven't seen a real woman in a long time," Etta chuckled as she told of her 36-26-36-schoolgirl figure! Etta's mother prepared hot lunches for the POW workers. "But before they would eat it, they waited until we ate some of the food. My mother put on a pot of corn on the cob for one lunch. They never saw it before, but decided it was good after eating some."[321]

"The prisoners spoke a little English, so we were able to communicate and understand each other. We got to know them and knew about their wives and families," Etta said. After the war some of the prisoners wrote back to the Myers family. One of the earliest was dated 30.5.46. The postal stamp was from Cherbourg Manche imprinted with "CORRESPONDANCE DES PRISONNIERS DE GUERRE Kriegsgefangenenpost."[322] It was addressed to Adams & Myers Honey Farm, Ransomville, Niagara County, New York.

Dear Sir!

Maybe this letter from a former prisoner of war, who used to work at your farm, is somewhat a surprise to you and I hope not an annoyance at all. But now, after it's all over, though we have still to stay here for a little while in France, there is something I would like to say. Yes, I want to say "Thank you" to you, for the time, we spent over there, for the treatment and all we received in your country. Though a prisoner is not supposed to have a very pleasant time, I like it very much to remember this period, and because I owe it partly to you, it is therefore you, to whom I dare to address this letter. Still, there have been two other fellows here, who used to work at our farm gang, though they are now gone to another camp, they wanted me to express theyr (sic) gratitude as well as theyr greetings, and now, when I am closing, I, too greet you once again, and wish you everything for the best.

Yours truly …[323]

The German people suffered for years after the war from shortages and rationing. A letter arrived addressed to the Myers family from Germany dated January 5, 1947.

I don't know if you will still remember me. I have worked for you nailing the frames for the Beehives and Joe always put in the wires.

First of all I would like to thank you for the grand dinners we used to get and for the milk and honey we would get along with the dinner.

Well now, I hope that you had a good crop and are in the finest health. What are Etta and Pa doing? Are they still not married? You tell them it is about time they started.

I wish that I could, along with my family, come and work for you, because I don't like it here in Germany anymore.

Our rations per day are very small: 250 gram bread (… which is approximately 1/3 loaf of bread.) 20 gram sugar (about 5 teaspoons) 20 gram (illegible) 25 gram meat (not quite 1oz) 10 gram fat (about 1/3 oz.) 13 gram marmalade (about 1 oz) There is no tobacco or cigarettes, coffee as in America, is not to be had. You can imagine how much hunger we have here. My son has no shoes and it is quite impossible to buy any. I only hope that God in heaven will save you from this misery and destitution.

On the 23rd of May I arrived here to my family and you can't imagine how great our joy was to be together again.

May God in heaven prevent any such a terrible battle of the nations to come again. Well now, how was the honey crop? I hope it has been a real good one. What is Joe doing is he still painting the Bee hives? How are the chances of coming over there? I would like very much to come to America, with my family, and work for you, but I haven't the money to pay for the passage, if it would be possible for you to pay my way and then I could pay it back once I got there.

I shall be very happy to receive an answer from you, then I would know whether you had received my letter, And now I must close with the hope that this finds you just the best of health.

Our heartiest greetings send you

We would be very grateful if you could send us a little parcel of coffee and tobacco. You can believe me when I say that it doesn't give me much pleasure begging you for things. But the want and terrible distress compels me to do so.[324]

The envelope was stamped from the Deutsche Post and addressed to "Mr. Bob Davis Ransomville: New York bei Howard Meyers Fruits and Honey U.S.A." Germany Russian. Zone was the return address. The letter was dated September 16, 1947.

Bob Davis married Etta Myers on August 15, 1942.

My dear Bob and Etta!

We have received your dear lettre (sic) to-day and we are glad about the photos, that are enclosed. And now, dear Bob and Etta, I and my wife additionally wish very much fortune and all good things to our marriage. May our God always let shine the sun about our marriage and hold together in good and bad days. Thus once more all good things for our future life. As I read in our lettre you expect a baby. That's fine, for a life without children is not satisfactory for long. What have you ordered, a boy or a girl?

Dear Bob and Etta! I could not send you a present for your marriage, but a gift for your little baby I have made. As soon as, we may send by mail a small chest of about six pounds will be arriving at you. Now dear Bob, do you still angle, or do you not?

You don't put forward, how we are glad, that it's allowed to come there, for fit work with you. I hope, you succeed in receiving our passport for America and I pray daily, it may succeed. Thus, dear Bob and Etta, don't sell your caravan, that I have a lodging.

How does Jo do? He also becomes older. Please greet him from us.

I also thank you again for the parcel, I received from you.

I find no words to express, we are glad about it. Now I close my lettre (sic).

Dear Bob and Etta we wish good health and hearty salute you

Yours

Dear Bob and Etta! Don't badly think about us: But I should be very glad, if you or Etta's parents would send us such a precious parcel again. The expenses I give willingly back you![325]

STARVATION IN FRANKFURT ~ The postage stamp on the envelope read "Deutsche Post." It was postmarked "GrossKarben" on January 25, 1947. On the left side was a large circular stamp from the United States Civil Censorship Germany Passed 21244. The envelope was addressed to Mr. Jakob Hosmer, Fruit-Farm, Youngstown, Niagara – New York. The letter was typed:

Dear Mr. Hosmer,

It is now several months I have come back home, and I want to ask you whether you and your family is well. I hope you are alright (sic), and will always be. I wish also to thank you once more for all you have done for me when I was there.

Fortunately I found my wife and my child well. They thank you too for the nice things you gave me for them. They needed them badly, for it is absolutely impossible to buy anything here.

I am glad to be home and free, only the life should be more endurable. The want of food, clothes and fuel in my country is greater than you may imagine. It is a catastofe! (sic) Many people is starving, particularly in these extremely cold winter-days.

I work as a mason, which is my profession, at Frankfurt, an hour's trip by train to make twice a day. George and Sepp were with me til to the end, but I don't know whether they have come back home or not. A great many of my comrades had to remain in France or England.

No I repeat my good wishes, hoping to hear from you once, and if you can do something for my family I should be very thankful to you. I beg to greet your workers Stenlein and his colleague from me.

Allow me to send you and your family kind regards.[326]

OTHER POW CAMPS IN THE UNITED STATES ~ John Kohl sat in the museum of the Historical Association of Lewiston on Plain Street in the Lewiston village and shared about the search for his German roots. It appears that those who have a passion for their genealogy also love history. Ancestors come alive in the context of the pivotal moments of time and world events. A letter arrived in 1998 from John's discovered family connection in Germany and brought a personal story of how a young man's life was changed when his country set its path on war.[327]

The letter arrived on March 17, 1998. The writer shared his excitement and interest about discovering family. After a few paragraphs of introduction the story of war from the German perspective and its impact began to unfold.

In 1936 we were told that we would have to leave our farm. My parents – old, sick people – couldn't muster the strength and died within six weeks. Then in 1937 with the help of the "Ruges" (German Relocation Authority) *I bought a farm… I went out there, but only worked a short time – because then came the second stroke of fate. The district farm manager wouldn't release the place and so I had to go back* (home) *again. Luckily my sister was still* (there)*…I bought my farm…My sister didn't go with me…She married…*(Then in 1939) *I got married myself…Everything would have been fine again, but in January 1942 came the call-up by the Army to Zewen in North Germany for training. After training I went to a unit in Rotterdam, Holland. We took care of the whole North Sea Station. We went out in ships, small transports, and trains…exposed to the bombs of the flyers and were always underway. In 1943, I went into the Navy Artillery and then to Korfu, Greece. In September all hell broke loose. We were being shot at from all sides. The fight went on until the leader himself was wounded. The battery was blown up after we had gotten ourselves to safety. Then the Italians entered into it as well, first fighting with us, and later against us. We got through an opening and down a hill to the harbor. We tried to reach the harbor during the night, intending to use the boats in the harbor to escape. But unfortunately the Italians were there and we didn't have enough equipment.*

The war was over to us. Then came the Partisans.[328] *We were to line up and every eleventh person was to be shot and those remaining to become prisoners…so went their orders. Then after long negotiations they withdrew the orders, but demanded that we were to be guarded by them as long as we were in Kofu* (sic). *Almost nothing to eat, no water, 10 days exposed to the elements. Then we were shipped off and brought to Brindisi, Italy. There we were guarded by the Italian Army. At the gate everything was taken from us… pictures, rosaries, wedding rings, etc. When I saw that, I put my wedding ring in my mouth and in so doing was able to smuggle it through. The camp was filthy and full of disease. Rails for beds, shoes for pillows—water with a few noodles. In the evening a piece of raw squash. The captain of the camp was a Jew. He let the water run for a few minutes a day. As in Korfu we couldn't wash. Then came the worst. Dysentery spread because of the unclean water and within a very short time, there were many dead. We gave up hope. We hadn't been reported to anyone—not even to the*

Red Cross. After 20 days came our salvation. We had to line up in front of the barracks and were filmed by a man with a camera. To our question of who he was, he gave no answer. Then on the next day, we were picked up. We were then taken to Malta by ship. There for the first time we could wash ourselves again. After nine days, we were off again to Bizzerta to a large transit camp. There we got some real food. We were very hungry. After eating we got terrible bellyaches. Our stomachs were greatly shrunk due to the long time without food—we had to begin with small amounts of food. In Bizzerta we were reported to the Red Cross.

My wife hadn't had any word from me in a long time. In the meantime she had received a notice that I was missing. The transports leaving Bizzerta went alternately first one to Russia and the next one to America. I got lucky and came to America. On 3 November 1943, we left for America.

I think that should be enough for today. A person doesn't like to talk about the bad times as much as the good times. The next time—more about the subject of America….[329]

Excerpts of another letter to John gave insight into the experiences of life at an American Prisoner of War camp.

Now to continue with my incarceration in America. On 24 November 1943 we arrived in Norfolk, from there on to Camp Indianola Nebraska. I had nothing, only that which I carried on my body. We had to give up our German uniform and got an American uniform with red letters P-W (Prisoner-of-War) on front and back. After a while when we had recovered a little from the ordeal at Korfu, a US soldier came into the barracks which were occupied by fifty men. A farmer needed 8-10 men. Anyone who wanted to work could go with him. I volunteered at once because I wanted to get out of the camp and I was lucky. A German farmer named Ruf had to pick us up everyday with a guard and bring us back. The farmers, Ruf the older and Ruf the younger, could speak good German and soon noticed that we were very hungry. We had to harvest corn, because at the time there wasn't any harvesting machine for corn. Ruf worked together with a neighboring farmer. One day their wives came and brought us some sandwiches. After we had eaten, the women said to us that Farmer Ruf wanted us to sing a marching song—otherwise they wouldn't leave the field.

They were large fields that we had to work. We worked the field on the Ruf farm until Christmas. I can still see it today as I describe it. Old Farmer Ruf, who had emigrated came up to us and asked us about everything in Germany. Then he asked us to sing two Christmas carols – "Silent Night" and "O Du Froehliche". That we did gladly. Tears of joy ran down the old man's cheeks, because he was hearing a German Christmas carol again after so many long years.

Then when we went back to the camp, Ruf brought us a Christmas tree with a few decorations. He said that he was very satisfied with our work. He wanted to make Christmas away from home a little bit easier with the Christmas tree. We thanked him, but had to tell him that the guards in the camp would take the tree away. Ruf said that we should leave it up to him. Ruf didn't leave as he usually did, but stayed with the guard until we were in the camp. As we had told him, the guard took everything away from us. Then Ruf went to the captain while we waited. Later both came back to the guard. Now the guard had to give everything back. When we came into the camp, our fellow prisoners rejoiced with us. And so it was a little more like Christmas in the camp.

Later we worked for another farmer. This one gave us no water to drink. For a short time I also picked cotton. That wasn't nice work.

Then we went on to Arizona. We were separated into groups of Army and Navy. In Tempe we went to the camp Papago Park. A gloomy camp, where there were only the men from the Navy. The atmosphere was a lot harsher there. We couldn't talk with other people and they couldn't talk with us. The "big Nazis" were taken out and put in a separate camp. The US Army was worried about these people and therefore they were guarded more stringently. They were not allowed to work, but we had to. I was in Camp 2 and went to Water Insses (sic). *In summer we had to mow the ditches and in winter we had to shovel them out. We still had a civilian guard who was not well disposed towards us. If somebody tried to speak to us, he immediately directed him to leave.*

Later the pressure was increased. Each one had to complete many, many meters of ditches. We didn't finish. The next morning the guards came and took out 120 men. I was among them. We went to Camp "Pima." This was a camp for prisoners of war. There were 28 days of bread and water, then 3 of warm food. This cycle repeated itself. We endured this for a time. While we were at work we always had blocks of ice around, because it is so hot in Arizona. Then we gave it up and went to work again on the ditches. Sometimes we finished the job, sometimes we didn't. Then I got away from the ditches and had to work in a laundry. The people who wanted to talk to us were afraid—others looked at us like we were criminals.

After that, Camp 2 was transported to California. Fortunately I was among them. A camp was being filled in Palm Springs. There we had to work in the kitchen for the US soldiers coming back from the Pacific. Everyday we had to take off our P-W clothes and put on white clothing like the American soldiers. There were two kitchen bosses—Willi, the son of German emigrants and Robert, a combat veteran and also a captain. They both had a very different view of things from those who only guarded the prisoners. They were our support.

I had to work there in the bakery wing with Baker John. Baker John was a civilian from Poland. It wasn't long before we were good friends. He showed me everything and after a while we were a team. He had only one fault. He was not an early riser. There were do-nuts (to make) *everyday. Usually I had these already made when he came in. He liked that.*

What wasn't eaten came back to the bakery. I had to throw the baked goods in the garbage. That broke my heart. One time I told John that my fellow comrades would be so happy if they could have a piece of "Kuchen" like that. He advised me to tell the captain. Later when the captain came into the bakery I go up the courage and asked him. He told that if I promised not to sell any goods off the base, then he would allow it. I told him that I couldn't begin to sell anything, since I never go to leave the camp. A great weight fell from my heart. We got 80 cents per day in camp wages. That was a nice job, but we never got out of the camp.

Then in September 1945 came the promised journey home. We were brought by train to the Transit Camp "Schenks" (sic) in New York. [330] *We were addressed over the loudspeaker. The last sentence was, "Anyone who doesn't come along has to stay here". Everyone paid attention, so as not to miss the connection. Then came the bitter disappointment while we were on the high seas. We would still have to spend a year in England. There we worked for some farmers. Security, however, was looser.*

Finally, in September 1947, we got to go home. After Hamburg we spent 2 days in the camp at Dachau near Munich, until I received my discharge papers. I still keep them stored away safely today. For me, returning home was another readjustment. To the children I wasn't Daddy anymore, but a strange man. Nobody, much less the general public, acknowledged my situation. … What I needed was time. When I think back on it, everything was crazy.

I haven't written much about my wife as yet. She didn't have it easy during my absence. She really worried about me. I was reported as 'missing'. She didn't know anything about me. She had to take care of the children and the farm. And then the constant air raids alarms. After a few happy years, she got sick and died on … at the age of 56. It was a hard blow for me… I want to end my letter,

with best wishes and greeting to the Kohl family and Cousin Dianna." [331]

Sergeant Georg Gaertner, a POW at Camp Deming, New Mexico, was assigned to the Panzer Artillery Regiment of Field Marshall Erwin Rommel's Afrika Korps when he was captured during the Battle of Tunis on April 13, 1943. Gaertner was afraid of being shipped to Russia at the end of the war. He escaped alone from the POW camp and evaded capture by the F.B.I. for decades. When the war ended the War Department was unable to account for only a dozen prisoners of the more than 372,000 German POWs held in the United States.[332]

Gaertner wrote with Dr. Arnold Krammer in *Hitler's Last Soldier in America* that news of the concentration camps and treatment of the Jews sickened him and many of the other German soldiers that fought for a government that would commit such atrocities. But to the guards in the POW camps in America the prisoners were simply "Nazis." How America treated the Nazis at Fort Niagara was a reflection of the government's efforts to follow the Geneva Convention in the hopes that American soldiers held overseas would be treated accordingly. The inspection reports of Fort Niagara and the branch camps confirmed those efforts.

NOTES

[260] Arnold Krammer, *Nazi Prisoners of War in America* (New York: Stein and Day, 1979), 64.
[261] "Detention Rosters, Ft. Niagara, NY," Records of the Office of the Provost Marshal General; Record Group 389, Entry 461; National Archives Building, College Park, MD.
[262] The SS or Schutzstaffel was the elite Nazi guard, a security and military organization of the Nazi Party, which carried out many of the plans of the Final Solution. SD or Sicherheitsdienst was the security intelligence organization of the Party. SA or Sturm Abteilungen, the Storm Troopers, was the predecessor to the SS to protect senior Nazi leaders. Holocaust Resource Center of Buffalo, vocabulary reference, http://www.holocaustcenterbuff.com [accessed February 19, 2007].
[263] Robert Otey, "5 Germans Hanged for Killing Companion," Associated Press, July 10July 10, 1945.
[264] James Swartz, Jr., "7 More Germans Die for Traitor Slaying," AP, August 25, 1945.
[265] "History of New Fort Niagara," *Youngstown Centennial Magazine,* 1954.
[266] Dr. Arnold Krammer explained the evolution and profitability of POW camps at the Axis POW program, First Presbyterian Church, Youngstown, NY, May 5, 2007.
[267] "Prisoners of War to be Housed at Fort Niagara while working on Farms," *Niagara Falls Gazette,* June 2, 1944.
[268] "German Prisoners See 'Bomb Damage' at Falls," *Buffalo Courier Express,* June 13 , 1944, 1.
[269] "German Prisoners Allowed Dogs," *Union-Sun & Journal,* June 16, 1944.
[270] "More Prisoners Arrive at Fort," *Union-Sun & Journal,* July 15, 1944.
[271] Der Ruf ~ The Call.
[272] Alfred G. Hilbert, "Van Etten CCC Camp Housed Nazi POWs," *The Chemung Historical Journal,* 2709-2710.
[273] "Die PW Woche," *YANK The Army Weekly,* December 31, 1943.
[274] "400 Nazi War Prisoners Arrive at Fort Niagara for Work in Farm Areas," *Niagara Falls Gazette,* June 13, 1944.
[275] John Dietz and Kenneth Diez, brothers, spelled their surnames differently.
[276] Farm Labor Association Organization Agreements, Notebook II, Historian's Office, Town Hall, Town of Porter, Youngstown, NY.
[277] Farm Labor Association, Notebook II, NY.
[278] Dr. Arnold Krammer, WWII Axis POW Conference.
[279] "Soldiers Help Eases Crisis in Orchards," *Union-Sun & Journal,* September 6, 1941.
[280] "Soldiers Help Eases Crisis in Orchards," 1941.
[281] Tom Tower, conversation with author, April 18, 2007. Tom is one of the many descendants of Peter Tower, an early settler in the town.
[282] Farm Labor Association Organization Records, Notebook II, 2006.1.13, Town Hall, Town of Porter, Youngstown, NY. Other area farmers did use POWs on their farms including Kenneth G. Diez and John Tower, but were not listed in the Lockport records. Roderick Tower told the author that farmers shared the POWs.
[283] "Nazi Prisoners Refuse Sweet Corn," *Union-Sun & Journal,* September 9, 1944.
[284] "Prisoners Worked," *Niagara Falls Gazette,* February 26, 1945.
[285] "Army Changes Prisoner Fare," *Union-Sun & Journal,* AP, April 24, 1945.

[286] "Prisoner Care Follows Treaty," *Union-Sun & Journal*, February 26, 1945.

[287] "Prisoners Worked," *Gazette*, February 26, 1945. During Dr. Arnold Krammer's lecture he explained that the POWs were paid any unused balances for their wage compensation at the end of the war.

[288] "Captive Nazi Listed as Driver in Accident," *Union-Sun & Journal*, July 3, 1945.

[289] Niagara Fruit Industries was located at 722-752 Third Street, Niagara Falls, NY.

[290] Letter from Niagara Fruit Industries, Inc. to Mr. J. C. Cornell of the Niagara Producers and Processors Association, January 3-4, 1945, Farm Labor Association Organization Records, Notebook II, 2006.1.65, 2006.1.66, Historian's Office, Town Hall, Town of Porter, Youngstown, NY.

[291] Rexford Guy Tugwell, Charles Tugwell's son, was the Assistant Secretary in 1933 and Under Secretary of Agriculture 1934-37 for President Franklin Roosevelt. Rexford grew up in Wilson, NY, and became part of Roosevelt's "Brain Trust."

[292] Tugwell & Wiseman, Inc. Job classifications, Notebook I, Farm Labor Association Records, Historian's Office, Town of Porter, Notebook I, 2006.1.45, October 28, 1944.

[293] Farm Labor Association Records, 2006.1.46, November 1, 1944.

[294] Comptroller of Niagara Fruit request for POWs, Farm Labor Association Records, Historian's Office, Town of Porter, Notebook II, 2006.1.68, January 16, 1945.

[295] Farm Labor Association Organization Records, Notebook I, Town Hall, Town of Porter, Youngstown, NY.

[296] The Sisters left Germany in the midst of the difficulties of life under Chancellor Otto von Bismarck known as der eiserne Kanzler, the Iron Chancellor.

[297] "History," *Sisters of St. Francis of Penance and Christian Charity*, http://www.franciscans-stella-niagara.org [accessed March 5, 2008].

[298] Margaret "Peggy" Dineen, telephone interview by author, February 9 and November 3, 2006.

[299] Author, *Porter*, (London: Arcadia, 2005), 30.

[300] Ibid., 27. Note: This brick structure on the west side of Main Street at the intersection of Water Street was constructed by B. D. Davis c. 1854 and operated as a general store by the Davis and Haskell families well into the twentieth century.

[301] Eugene Pacia, interview by author, August 21, 2006.

[302] Krammer, *Nazi Prisoners of War*, 149.

[303] Mickey Schultz, interview by author, January 10, 2006.

[304] Elwood Schultz, family correspondences from POWs who worked on the Schultz farm, names omitted.

[305] Pat Hutchison Phillips, interview by author, Youngstown, NY, July 31, 2006.

[306] "German Prisoners Allowed Dogs," *Union-Sun & Journal*, June 16, 1944.

[307] Phillips, interview.

[308] "World War II Databases," *American Battle Monuments Commission*, http://www.abmc.gov/cemeteries/cemeteries/sr.php [accessed February 28, 2008].

[309] Joel MacDonald, telephone conversation with author, November 1, 2006.

[310] Jane Richardson, interview by author, Youngstown, NY, July 6, August 10, and September 1, 2006.

[311] "Rationing Program," *Niagara Falls Gazette*, May 7, 7, 1945.

[312] Jane Richardson repeated her father's story about being stopped by the police because of

worn tires, unable to get new tires because of the rationing.

[313] Jane Richardson shared her memory of VJ Day.

[314] John Richardson, interview by author, Youngstown, NY, August 10 and September 1, 2006.

[315] Ronald Hurtgam was given a farm deferment.

[316] Mervin Hurtgam, interview by author, Ransomville, NY, May 27, 2006.

[317] Harold Denny, telephone interview by author.

[318] Clayton Randall Stidham, Jr., "Grandparent Essay: Etta Davis," April 28, 1992, 1.

[319] Ibid., 6.

[320] Ibid., 6.

[321] Etta Myers Davis, telephone interview by author, June 6, 2006.

[322] Translation ~ Correspondence of prisoners of war.

[323] Letter addressed to Adams & Myers Honey Farm, May 5, 1946, Etta Myers Davis papers, names of sender omitted.

[324] Letter to Myers family, Etta Myers Davis collection, names of sender omitted, January 5, 1947.

[325] Letter to Bob Davis, Howard Myers Fruits and Honey Farm, September 16, 1947. Etta Myers Davis papers, names of sender omitted.

[326] Hosmer notebook, Porter Historical Museum, Youngstown, NY.

[327] John Kohl, conversation with author, Lewiston Historical Museum, July 24, 2006.

[328] Partisans were anti-fascist resistance movements, which fought against the occupation of the Axis forces.

[329] Letter to John Kohl, March 17, 1998, Lewiston, NY, name of sender omitted, translated to English from German by Dianna M. Winsor, April 10, 1998.

[330] Camp Shanks (Orangeburg, Rockland County, NY) was a staging area for troops going overseas. After the war it was used as a staging area for German POW repatriation. "Camp Shanks," *New York State Military Museum*, http://www.dmna.state.ny.us/historic/mil-hist.htm [accessed March 5, 2008].

[331] Letter to John Kohl, July 17, 1998, Lewiston, NY, name of sender omitted, translated from German by Dianna M. Winsor, April 10, 1998.

[332] Georg Gaertner with Arnold Krammer, *Hitler's Last Soldier in America* (New York: Stein and Day, 1985), 15, 21, 49-54.

CHAPTER 6

INSPECTIONS OF FORT NIAGARA

Parker W. Buhrman from the Department of State accompanied Emil Greuter, the representative of the International Legation of the Red Cross of Switzerland, for the initial inspection of Fort Niagara on July 29, 1944. Maj. William K. McClure was the camp commander, Executive Officer Capt. Charles Becket, Medical Officer Lt. Jakob S. Arnoff, and Camp Spokesman Bruno Tachen.[333]

TROUBLE MAKERS AT THE FORT ~ Greuter's report dated September 16, 1944, identified the camp as situated in the southeast corner of the "Fort Niagara Falls Military Reservation." The compound was 350 yards by 450 yards with an adjacent athletic field of 100 yards square surrounded by a double fence of barbed wire. Buildings were theater of operation construction and the barracks were furnished with steel cots and cotton mattresses, electric lights, and heated by coal stoves.[334]

At the time of this inspection there were 70 non-commissioned officers and 2,117 other enlisted men in Fort Niagara and the branch POW camps. Greuter acknowledged that there were no complaints by the prisoners about their treatment. Fifty-six patients were being treated at the station hospital, and the general health of the POWs was good. A physician and an Army dental surgeon were on duty in the dispensary of the stockade.

TABLE 6 .1
Work Details for Agricultural Labor and Food Processing at the Branch Camps

Attica Camp	112
Cobbs Hill (Rochester)	107
Dunkirk	107
Hamlin Beach	210
Letchworth Park	220

Medina	164
Newark	135
Oakfield	212

Source: Greuter Report, September 16, 1944.

Grueter cited the recreation facilities as deficient and attributed this to the fact that the camp was recently activated. The camp administration was also criticized for the lack of educational resources and for the fact that some American newspapers were withheld on occasion. A Catholic priest from Stella Niagara and a civilian Lutheran minister (neither minister's name was given in this report) held regular religious services. Both clerics spoke fluent German and attendance was good at religious services. About fifteen hundred of the prisoners were regularly employed in a pay status on post and on agricultural details pruning trees, working at a floral nursery, cleaning out old orchards, cutting cord wood, repairing barns, painting silos, spreading manure, building fences, and digging draining ditches.

Each prisoner received three dollars a month in canteen coupons. The canteen stocked a limited supply of cigarettes and no beer or soft drinks during the first inspection. Greuter commented again on the lack of awareness by the camp administration to utilize the canteen as an important morale builder for the prisoners.

Pay rates for POW labor varied based on work classification. The government gained the difference in the actual pay from the per diem rate paid to the POWs of eighty cents. These monies provided significant revenue of millions of dollars to the federal government.

TABLE 6.2
Area Producers, Hourly Wages, and Overtime Paid for POW Work

Harold Clapp, Inc.	65 cts.	1.5 after 14 weeks
Lockport Canning Co.	60 cts.	No overtime
Lyndonville Canning Co.	65 cts.	No overtime
Norman Demler	60 cts.	No overtime
Sardik Food Products	70 cts. 75 cts. after 30 days	1.5 overtime
Speas Company	65 cts.	No overtime
Standard Brands, Inc.	65 cts.	1.25 overtime

Tugwell & Wiseman	60 cts.	No overtime
Welkley Brothers	70 cts.	No overtime
Wilson Canning Company	60 cts.	No overtime
Youngstown Cold Storage	60 cts.	No overtime

Source: Farm Labor Association Organization Records, Notebook II, 2006.1.6a, Town Hall, Town of Porter, Youngstown, New York.

One of the stories passed down through the years concerned the conduct of the prisoners at the camp when they first arrived. The coffee shop talk was that there were serious disturbances until some of the POWs were shipped out. Another story was about the segregation of the troublemakers in an inner barbed wire area of the camp, and that some POWs were not allowed to leave the stockade. Under the Geneva Convention officers were not required to work. This could account for the sight of POWs remaining in the camp while others left to work on the farms.

Greuter determined that the source of the unsatisfactory atmosphere of the camp, considerable internal friction, and disturbances were from about seventy non-working non-commissioned officers (non-coms) who were constantly bringing pressure on the enlisted men to slow down or to refuse to work. The Red Cross delegate believed that the punitive attitude on the part of some of the administrative officers was not conducive to a spirit of cooperation. Thirty prisoners were cited for disciplinary action due to insubordination and being disrespectful to officers.

Greuter also expressed his displeasure about the attitude of the posted officers that the prisoners were criminals instead of soldiers in detention and that this was contrary to the spirit of the Geneva Convention. He recommended that the non-working non-coms officers should either be isolated or removed from Fort Niagara.

TABLE 6.3
Numbers of Enlisted Men in New York at POW Camps, July 1, 1944

FORT NIAGARA ~ Major Camp	256
Newark	112
Rochester	91
Dunkirk	100
Letchworth	195

Hamlin Beach	173
Oakfield	100
Medina	116
PINE CAMP ~ Major Camp	329
Fair Haven	88
Clyde	88
Port Byron	88
Geneva	123
Harrisville	177

Source: The weekly report on Prisoners of War, Earl L. Edwards, Lt. Col., C.M.P., Assistant Director, Prisoner of War Division Report;. Record Group No. 389; NWCTM Ref. Collection; July 1, 1944; National Archives Building, College Park, MD.

TABLE 6.4
Numbers of POWs at Penal and Medical Institutions, July 1, 1944

	Halloran General Hospital, Brentwood, NY	Mason General Hospital, Staten Island, NY
German officers	12	12
German enlisted men		109
Italian officers		8
Italian enlisted men	7	199
Japanese enlisted men		1

Source: The weekly report on Prisoners of War, July 1, 1944; National Archives Building, College Park, MD.

LIBRARY BOOKS ~ Subsequent inspections were positive in regards to the treatment of the POWs.[335] The reports were sent from the Special War Problems Division, the Department of State, to General Bryan.

Mr. P. Schnyder, another representative of the International Red Cross Committee, inspected Fort Niagara on October 8, 1944, and its 767 German prisoners, 4 non-coms, 2 members of the sanitary personnel, and 761 privates. The spokesman for the POWs was Cpl. Manfred Siemsen.

Fifty men were quartered in each barrack. One large building and several

POW barracks were purchased by area farmers and used in labor camps after the war. (Courtesy of Old Fort Niagara Association)

smaller ones were designated for the kitchens and mess hall. Other barracks housed a canteen, post office, recreation hall that also served as a chapel, and an infirmary for minor medical issues. Thirty-five German patients with infections and some cases of malaria were treated at the military camp hospital. The POWs requested German physicians.

Schnyder found that the food was excellent, but the library poorly equipped. The International Red Cross Committee provided several dozen books; 150 books were from the Young Men's Christian Association (YMCA), and another 150 books from an unidentified source. There were few amusements, limited musical instruments and footballs during this inspection, and no motion picture shows available to the POWs. They requested notebooks and hand towels to be available in the canteen, letter paper, a German chaplain, and winter clothing. Religious services were well attended; 200 men went to Mass regularly and 80 men attended Protestant services.

Overall Schnyder concluded that the camp made a good impression, but that several misunderstandings spilled over to the labor detachments. The prisoners requested a classroom building, more room for the barber, a shoe repairman, a tailor, and wood for the carpenter.

Substantial educational courses were offered for the prisoners when the fort was inspected on March 8, 1945. Fifty prisoners were enrolled in the five classes in elementary English, twelve in elementary and advanced French, and four in Spanish. Arithmetic, algebra, geometry, German Literature, and biology were very popular. Other courses of Technical Drawing, Physics, Statistics, building, bookkeeping, agriculture, and vocational classes were also offered. The University of Chicago sponsored extension courses in English, Accounting, and Biology.

ANTI-NAZI PROPAGANDA ~ Dr. Rudolph Fischer, another Red Cross representative, accompanied Leonard L. O'Bryan of the Special War Problems Division, Department of State, for a visit on February 15, 1945. Maj. William K. McClure was still the camp commander, Capt. L. M. Noble, the senior officer, and Franz Feik, the camp spokesman.[336]

The report's count of POWs at Fort Niagara in early 1945 included 5 officers, 11 non-coms, and 1,810 enlisted men. The seventy non-coms who caused trouble at the camp had been sent away to an undisclosed location. There were no problems afterwards. Three German non-certified doctors answered sick calls under the supervision of an American doctor and two German dentists. Lack of cigarettes was still an issue, but tobacco was available for the POWs to roll their own.

The POWs were annoyed because the Assistant Executive Officer confiscated books from the library and replaced them with books written by authors whose writings were condemned in Germany. Feik told Fischer that "Such an evident form of attempted indoctrination was stupid and that they (the POWs) recognized immediately such ill-concealed propaganda." Feik maintained that the men had the right to be treated as prisoners of war and not as political prisoners, and that they lived too long under Gestapo methods not to recognize when it was being used on them. "This may be anti-Nazi propaganda but it is certainly not the American way of doing things and does not lead to an appreciation of American institutions,"[337] Feik said.

BRANCH CAMPS OF FORT NIAGARA ~ Andre Vulliet inspected Fort Niagara and its branch camps on March 8, 1945. At that time the branch camps were Newark, Dunkirk, Letchworth Park, Hamlin Beach, Attica, Medina, and Sodus Point, all in New York State.[338]

Vulliet was struck by the substantial improvements at the camp since his first visit during last August. Now, there was a library, reading room, carpenter's shop, artist studio, and small music room, movie hall, chapel, theater, classrooms, canteen, and athletic facilities.

Werner Sachs, a German POW, drew this sketch of Ernest Wille's art studio. Wille painted the mural on the east wall of the Officer's Club Building. (Courtesy of Niagara County Historical Society, Lockport, NY, being held in trust for Old Fort Niagara)

Father William Heim, a German-speaking priest and chaplain for the Sisters at Stella Niagara on Lower River Road in the neighboring Town of Lewiston, said Mass for the Catholic POWs.

Father Heim was born in Friedrichshafen, Germany. He attended the seminary at Rottweil and studied at the University of Tübingen. Father Heim was urged to come to America by his uncle Rev. Frederick Fricker, a pastor in Honesdale, Pennsylvania.[339] Father Heim passed away August 4, 1956.

Army Post Chaplain Allen served the Protestants. He did not officiate, but his assistant played the organ and three German-speaking civilian pastors took turns at the services and preached the sermons. All of the pastors seemed to be very popular. This was the largest attendance at church of any prisoner of war camp the inspector was aware of at a base camp. Church services were held in the theater hall.

The library expanded substantially to about 900 books: 200 classics, 600 novels and short stories, and 100 sundries. Several hundred books were in circulation among the branch camps. The POWs requested additional books written in English by contemporary American authors for those studying the English language and some books in French.

Twelve all-male faculty taught classes. Three were professional teachers and the lead educator was a university professor in zoology and biology. Classrooms were open from 7:00 a.m. until 10:00 p.m. About 200 men took advantage of the education programs.

A former German radio band conductor led the POW orchestra. Three of its members were professional musicians. Three violins, two trumpets, two saxophones, a drum set, a guitar, and a piano were available. The prisoners organized a thirty-two-man choir and several athletic teams for each company, but there was not enough sports equipment.

A professional artist promoted new artists and woodcarving. His name and the names of the two other professional artists in the camp were not mentioned in the reports. Some of the German soldiers took up painting as a hobby at Fort Niagara and in the branch camps. A theatrical group of about fifteen men performed plays each month with a special feature of Bavarian and Tyrolian dancers.

The Signal Corps loaned the camp a projector to show films rented from an unidentified Buffalo firm in addition to the YMCA's German film service. There were five or six radios in the camp. Copies of the *New York Times* and *Christian Science Monitor* were available.

Doctor W. Bubb, Red Cross representative, and Mr. J. L. Toohey, Department of State, visited the base camp on August 17, 1945. Their report noted that the camp was a former reception center area for Fort Niagara.

American officers named in the report were Capt. Lew M. Noble, Executive Officer, and Lieutenant Colonel McClure. At this time there were 131 American enlisted men, 689 prisoners or war, and six certified enlisted protected personnel. Prisoners performed off-post work on a recent day: 112-farming, 99-food processing, and 60-Army work on other posts. One detail of sixty-nine prisoners was rained out and twenty-four were assigned to permanent light duty.[340]

The camp was deficient concerning available reading materials, but complimented for a "splendid shoe repair shop with power equipment." The station hospital averaged about thirty-four POWs per day, which included men brought from the branch camps for hospitalization.

POWs complained of only one pound of salt per hundred rations, no winter underwear, socks wearing out, and that no movie pictures were shown in the past few weeks; but there were no formal complaints.

MEDINA CAMP ~ Mr. P. Schnyder of the Red Cross visited the Medina, New York, camp of Italian prisoners in November 1943 and on October 10, 1944. The camp moved to a different location in the town. Corporal Heinz Eilsholz was the spokesman for the 157 German POWs. The mess hall was divided into two parts by a large curtain: one side for the American plant workers and the other for the prisoners.[341]

An arrangement was made with the library of the City of Buffalo to provide reading materials from their extensive selection of German books. In the fall of 1944, the POWs at Medina worked solely at the Heinz canning factory. The day shift was from 7:00 a.m. to noon and 1:00 to 5:00 p.m. The night shift worked from 5:30 to 10:30 p.m. and from 11:30 p.m. to 3:30 a.m.

Doctor Bubb and Mr. J. L. Toohey, Special War Problems Division of the Department of State, visited the Medina camp located in the migrant workers' barracks of the H. J. Heinz plant, on August 27, 1945. Lt. Glen D. Overton (spelled Glenn Oberton in another report) was the Commanding Officer for the 17 American enlisted men, 126 prisoners of war, and 3 enlisted Protected Personnel. The majority of the POWs in the month of August still worked at the Heinz facility.[342]

Supplies and clothing were drawn from Fort Niagara and a local contracted physician provided medical attention. There were no complaints. Bubb and Toohey concluded that Medina was a very clean and well-run camp.

THE DUNKIRK BRANCH CAMP was established on June 26, 1944, located on the Chautauqua County Fairgrounds. Fort Niagara post engineers erected the security fencing to surround the existing buildings. The Food Processors' Association of Fredonia, the contractor, was responsible for building and interior maintenance. Most of the POWs worked in the food processing plant and a small group worked on area farms.[343]

The commanding officer at the Dunkirk Camp on August 24, 1945 was First Lt. Robert S. Carnahan. A medical officer arrived weekly from Fort Niagara. Seriously ill prisoners were transferred to Fort Niagara's hospital when necessary. Doctor W. Bubb found Dunkirk to be an excellent camp, but in need of more fat for cooking and an additional football.

HAMLIN BEACH CAMP consisted of five barracks and seventeen tents and was established in June 1944. Hamlin Growers and Processors Inc. maintained the buildings and water supply from the mains at Brockport. During the August 28, 1945, inspection there were 31 American enlisted men, 322 POWs, and 2 enlisted Protected Personnel. First Lt. William B. Houston was the Commanding Officer. Complaints were made to the Red Cross Delegate about the absence of replacements for worn out socks and not enough food for those working in the extreme heat of the unpopular foundry detail.[344]

AT LETCHWORTH PARK a detachment worked on farms and at a canning factory. Letchworth was a former CCC Camp originally organized for road building and park maintenance. The POW Camp was established in June 1944. On October 10, 1944, Pfc. Siegfried Zimmerman was the spokesman for the 215 German prisoners.[345]

The October inspection pointed out that there were fewer opportunities for entertainment than in the other camps and no movies, but their well-equipped canteen provided even a few luxury articles. Religious services were conducted for the Catholic POWs, but no Protestant services. Overall the POWs enjoyed the breathtaking scenery of the park.

The Labor Report by First C.M.P. Pearlie B. Lupo at Letchworth for the period ending August 6, 1945, listed the POW personnel positions at the camp as follows: a spokesman, clerk, fireman, cook, cook's helper, baker, seven KPs, canteen clerk, barber, two medical officers, medical aid man, plumber, carpenter, painter, and two gardeners. Off-post ten POWs worked at Kelly's Nursery, five at Elster Fruit Factory, and eleven at Maloney's Nursery.

THE ATTICA CAMP, a former CCC camp, was in the midst of an agricultural district located near the Town of Attica about seven and one-half miles from Batavia. Private First Class (Pfc)[346] Wolfgang Kirschegger represented the 149 German POWs. Farmers contracted for POWs for work in the production of potato and corn crops. Some of the prisoners worked in canning factories.

Mr. Schnyder noted the prisoners' requests for musical instruments and footballs. Clothing was inadequate and in poor condition and the camp lacked correspondence forms and library books, but the canteen was well supplied. American Army chaplains held religious services. Under the Medical Services category some of the prisoners "suffered from the effects of an unpleasant, but not serious rash caused by a poisonous plant, poison ivy." Overall the camp made a good impression on Schnyder.

The Labor Report for the period ending August 6, 1945, for Attica by First Lt. George H. Hodges Commanding was similar to the Letchworth positions for camp overhead. Thirty-five prisoners worked at the East Pembroke Canning Corporation and ten at Rogerson Cold Storage Company in Leroy, New York.

OAKFIELD CAMP ~ Oakfield's commanding officer for the two hundred POWs on August 1945 was First Lt. Paul D. Stogdale. The Haxton Canning Plant employed fifty-five of the POWs and twenty-four other prisoners performed camp labor as clerks, firemen, cooks, cooks' helper, bakers, kitchen police (kp), tailor, barber, canteen clerk, medical aid, spokesman, carpenter, and painter.

GENESEO CAMP ~ On October 18, 1945, 290 POWs were assigned to the branch camp at Geneseo, New York. General Food Corporation employed 110 of the Geneseo camp's prisoners. Bishop & Babbin employed twenty POWs. The prisoner overhead included one camp spokesman, five cooks and helpers, seven kps, one latrine orderly, two fireman, two company clerks and interpreters, one carpenter, one medic, one supply person, and three post engineers. Several prisoners worked in the canteen and the bakery.[347]

The October daily status report also accounted for the American personnel: one officer and thirty-six enlisted men including a First Sergeant, Company Clerk, Supply Sergeant, Mess Sergeant, six Stockade Guards, and twenty-four POW Chasers. Two enlisted men were sick in the hospital. The commanding officer of the camp was Capt. John T. Simpson.

FBI INVESTIGATION ~ John Edgar Hoover, the Director of the Federal Bureau of Investigation, received a letter from a resident of Geneva, New York, concerning the POWs.

We have a fine situation in this neck of the woods on which some of our patriotic minded politicians or military officials should straighten out.

First over at Seneca Ordnance Base, which covers many square miles (directly across from Geneva, New York) there are hundreds of thousands of shells and ammunition needed for our war effort and which should be in trustworthy hands. Instead they have 110 Italian war prisoners doing work on the grounds and wandering around with nothing but an armband (which can be torn off easily) ...and in any case should not be doing work at U. S. Ordnance Base.

Secondly, there have been quite a number of German prisoners brought up around here to work on farms. The result is that the farmer cannot watch these prisoners and they are escaping everyday. Result is five have disappeared from farms around here inside of a week. Latest two to escape was from a farmer north of here near Newark, New York, on Wednesday of this week. Why should these German prisoners be put out on farms without proper guards and allowed to escape and God only knows what damage they can do before they are caught? Please get after it.[348]

The writer requested that his identity not be divulged by Hoover. Hoover forwarded the letter to Col. L. R. Forney, Assistant Chief of Staff, G-2, War Department, Washington, DC, and copied the Intelligence Liaison Section, to address the concerns.

MORE REPORTS ~ Maj. D. L. Schwieger and Capt. Charles E. Tremper, Office of the Provost Marshall General, inspected Fort Niagara on August 9 and 10, 1945. The stockade administration was cited for failure to post the required notice of "Safeguarding German Prisoners of War," for not making available to the prisoners a German translation of selected Articles of War, an excess of POW Camp overhead positions, marking of "PW" on outer garments worn by the prisoners was inadequate at all the branch camps except Attica, which was noted as above average, and that labor contracts written since June 1, 1945, made no provision for payment to the government of $1.50 per day for each prisoner whose labor was not fully utilized.

The POW Morning Report for the 1206th SCU (Service Command Unit), POW Camp at Fort Niagara, on October 18, 1945, listed 659 POWs at Fort Niagara's base camp, which included 17 in the hospital, 12 in sick quarters, and 1 private in detention. First Lt. F. W. Shields remarked in the above report that Gustav Klostermeier, 4W-G-4311, Ogfr, was transferred from Medina, identified as detention number five, to Letchworth Park, detention number four. Captain Werner Roessler, 31G-17330, was transferred from Letchworth to Westfield. No reason was given for the transfer. Juergen Thoeming, 31G-364392, a civilian, and Kurt Vornholt, 81G-226185, a soldier, returned from the station hospital to duty. One hundred forty-four prisoners returned from the Dunkirk branch camp to Fort Niagara on the date of the inspection. A week later prisoners were still being transferred to the base and branch camps late into 1945. Fort Niagara's POW camp had 131 American enlisted personnel.[349]

Pine Camp, also a major POW camp in New York State, was authorized December 24, 1942. Its branch camps in 1945 were Fair Haven, Clyde, Fort Byron, Geneva, Fayetteville, Rome, and Slaterville. German prisoners were also being treated at the penal and medical institutions of the United States Disciplinary Barracks (USDB) Green Haven, Halloran General Hospital, and Mason General Hospital, Long Island, New York. Italians were being treated at Mason Hospital and there were Italian Service Units at Elmira (Horseheads), Fort Jay (Governor's Island), Fort Hamilton, Camp Shanks, and Staten Island.[350]

TABLE 6.5
1206th SCU at Fort Niagara POW Camp, October 20, 1945

Name	Rank	Primary Duty
Adam, Douglas G.	Capt.	Security & Intelligence
Bacon, Thomas F.	1st Lt.	Hq. Det.
Bruning, Joseph H.	Capt.	Cons. Mess Officer
Carnahan, Robert S.	1st Lt.	CO Dunkirk
Cobb, Norman S.	1st Lt.	CO Westfield
Coffey, Clarence W.	1st Lt.	CO Co. B
Ditchfield, Arthur W.	2nd Lt.	CO Sodus Point
Griffin Frederick J., Jr.	1st Lt.	Adjutant
Houston, William B., Jr.	1st Lt.	CO Hamlin Beach
Jamieson, Charles P.	1st Lt.	CO Marion
Lesaius, Adolph V.	1st Lt.	CO Newark
Lowe, Charles R.	Capt.	CO Attica
Lupo, Pearlie B.	1st Lt.	CO Letchworth Park
Martin, Daniel H.	1st Lt.	Asst. Supply & Mess
McClure, William K.	1st Col.	Commanding Officer
Morris, Landis D.	1st Lt.	CO Brocton
Nestel, Arnold	1st Lt.	Asst. Ex. Officer
Noble, Lew M.	Capt.	Personnel Adjutant
Overton, Glen D.	1st Lt.	CO Medina
Schulz, Eldor J.	1st Lt.	Supply Officer
Shields, William F.	1st Lt.	CO Co. A
Simpson, John T.	Capt.	CO Geneseo
Stogdale, Paul D.	1st Lt.	CO Oakfield
Tracey, Walter J.	1st Lt.	Abs. Sick Gen Hospital
Wolfson, Joseph M.	1st Lt.	CO Hq. Det.

Source: Headquarters Army Service Forces Office of the Provost Marshal General, semi-monthly Report on Prisoners of War as of October 1, 1945.

NATIONALS FROM OTHER COUNTRIES ~ The Enemy POW Information Bureau Strength Reports for the Second Service Command in the Archives Questionnaire Folder held copies of Form R-5127 dated August 15, 1945, used to ascertain German POWs of Russian origin and letters from the Prisoner of War Operations Divisions about the issue of nationals from other countries pressed into service by the Germans. In addition to the standard name, rank, and serial number, the POW was required to give his residence and army service for Russia; German army service and if volunteered or drafted; and if a Soviet citizen, did he desire to return to Russia and if not to provide an explanation.

The "German POWs" were screened for potential citizens of other countries including Poland, France, Czechoslovakia, Holland, Belgium, and Luxembourg. Colonel S. V. Constant, Director Security and Intelligence Division, sent a secret communication to the Commanding Officer at Fort Niagara dated April 21, 1945, in regards to screening of POWs for Polish origin. Erwin Kleinert #93049 and Felix Nowroth #93175 were interviewed and their files reviewed. They were questioned with due caution taken so that the purpose of the interview would be kept secret due to concerns about repercussions from other prisoners. Kleinert and Nowroth were questioned to determine if they were true citizens of Poland, impressed into the German Army, physically qualified for service in the armed forces, and held political beliefs in accord with the tenets of the United Nations to determine if they were suitable for replacements in the Polish Armed forces.[351]

Another request in the file was for PW Erich Langner, #54317. The review of his file and a personal interview determined that he was born in Szopinice in Polish Silesia, served in the Polish Army from March 1935 to May 1936, and was impressed into the German Army in 1945. The conclusion of the interview on June 1945, determined that he was a "true citizen of Poland not Czechoslovakia."

On April 30, 1945, Major McClure, the commanding officer, responded to the Commanding General, Second Services Command, that the interviews and investigation indicated that POWs Kleinert and Nowroth were believed to be true citizens of Poland and also fulfilled the other requirements.

Col. A. M. Tollefson sent another letter dated August 27, 1945, to the Commanding General of the Second Service Command that camps at Fort Dix, New Jersey; Fort Dupont, Delaware; and Mitchell Field, Fort Niagara, Pine Camp, Camp Upton, and West Point in New York confirmed holding nationals of other countries than Germany. Fort Niagara held one POW from France and three from Belgium.[352]

TABLE 6.6
Fort Niagara POWs of Belgium Origin

Name	ISN	Unit	Rank
Hermanns, Josef	54197	Miscellaneous Unit	Gefr
Kriescher, Richard	31G-726276		
Scholl, Willi	051858		

Source: "Camp Labor Report – 2nd Service Command, Delaware to NY," Enemy POW Information Bureau Reporting Branch, Subject File 1942-46; Record Group 389, Entry 461; National Archives Building, College Park, MD. Kriescher and Scholl did not appear in the Detention Rosters. This could be due to an error in the recording of the names.

Eighty-two POWs from Fort Niagara claimed Czechoslovakian origin. Questionnaires in the Czech language were sent to Fort Niagara in September 1945 for the interviews with a request for their return to the Provost Marshal General by October 31, 1945. On November 7, 1945, a letter by Colonel Tollefson to the Commanding General requested transfer of the prisoners of Yugoslavian origin from Fort Niagara.

TABLE 6.7
Fort Niagara POWs of Yugoslavian origin

Name	ISN	Unit	Rank	SS or SA
Grill, Josef	81G-26799	Misc. Unit	Sold	
Mlinaritsch, Alois	8W-G-2018	756th Inf. Div.	Sold	
Piewetz, Alois	8W-G-24296	334th Inf. Div.	Gefr	
Supanek, Anton	31G-12220	17th SS-Panzer Gren. Div.	Osold	SS
Tschoritsch, Nikolaus	31G-12208	2nd SS-Panzer Division "Das Reich"	Ogefr	SS
Udvari, Lorenz	31G-11992	17th SS-Panzer Grenadier Div.	Sturmmann	SS

Welker, Christian	31G-12259	2nd SS-Panzer Division "Das Reich"	Ogefr	SS

Source: "Camp Labor Report – 2nd Service Command, Delaware to NY," Enemy POW Information Bureau Reporting Branch; and "Detention Rosters, Ft. Niagara, NY," Record Group 389, Entry 461, National Archives Building, College Park, MD.

Colonel Tollefson reported in writing dated December 10, 1945, about the issue of POWs claiming Czechoslovakian origin. The military attaché of the Czechoslovakian Embassy in Washington informed the Prisoner of War Operations Division that a roster of POWs who claimed Czechoslovakian citizenship did not have a valid claim.[353]

TABLE 6.8
Numbers of POWs at Fort Niagara and Branch Camps, October 24, 1945

Camp	Officers	Non-coms	Enlisted Men	Protected Personnel	Totals
Attica		2	67	2	71
Brocton		22	155	2	179
Dunkirk		1	252	2	255
Geneseo		7	306	2	315
Hamlin		8	337	2	347
Letchworth	1	8	311	2	322
Marion		23	185	1	209
Medina		3	229	2	234
Naples		16	250	1	267
Newark			255	3	258
Oakfield			187	2	189
Sodus Point			129	1	130
Westfield	1	21	330	1	353
Fort Niagara	2	24	1062	5	1093
Totals	4	135	4055	28	4222

Source: Capt. Lyle T. Dawson, Office of the Provost Marshal General, of Prisoner of War Camp, Fort Niagara, New York Report; Other Inspection Reports

A guard watched from the tower, in the foreground, on the east side of the POW compound at Fort Niagara. The automobile traveled north on Route 18F known as Lake Road. (Courtesy of Old Fort Niagara Association)

Folder, Fort Niagara, New York; Record Group 389, Entry 461; October 24, 1945; National Archives Building, College Park, MD.

CLOSING OF THE FORT ~ Capt. Lyle T. Dawson, Office of the Provost Marshal General, of POW Camp Fort Niagara, on October 24, 1945, was informed that a plan would be made about November 1, 1945, for the deactivation of the camp. The *Niagara Falls Gazette* reported on November 26, 1945, that according to Army authorities the prisoners would probably be moved that week. It was unknown if the POWs were to be sent to Germany or to another camp. The correspondence to Porter residents from POWs after the war confirmed that many of them were used for reconstruction efforts in England and France, and were not repatriated for several years following the end of the war. Preparations were made to abandon Fort Niagara as an Army post on December 31, 1945, and the 712th Military Detachment, which was stationed at Fort Niagara for the previous two years, had already left. The station complement and the POW guard detachment remained at the post.

The government letters from the Prisoner of War Operations Division to the Commanding General of the Second Service Command in the National Archives files opened locally unknown pages of the makeup of the "German"

POWs at Fort Niagara and some of the history of Germany's forced conscription of conquered peoples into its service and also likely support of Hitler beyond Germany's borders.

There were mixed feelings in the Porter community from curiosity to fears about the "Nazi" soldiers housed in the POW camp at Fort Niagara while the war took local young men far from home, some never to return. Most of the American soldiers inducted at Fort Niagara and across the country returned home and never talked about what happened to them during the war. After more than a half a century, some veterans began to give glimpses into the history of their experiences to end an unimaginable evil and save the world. Some were first generation Americans and some were from other towns, but their lives intersected with Fort Niagara and the war. How did they arrive at this global moment in history, and what was their role in the war?

NOTES

[333] Emil Greuter Report to Prisoner of War Camp Fort Niagara Falls, New York; Record Group No. 389, Entry 461, September 16, 1944; National Archives Building, College Park, MD. The reports identify the fort as "Fort Niagara Falls." Fort Niagara is not in Niagara Falls. The fort is located in the Town of Porter about fifteen miles north of the City of Niagara Falls.

[334] Report, September 16, 1944; 2.

[335] Red Cross Legation of Switzerland Inspection Reports of the POW camp Fort Niagara Falls, New York, for visits on October 9, 1944, February 15, 1945, March 8, 1945, and August 27, 1945; NWCTM Ref. Collection; following and are in The National Archives Record Group No. 389, Entry 461; National Archives Building, College Park, MD.

[336] Red Cross Report, Inspection February 15, 1945.

[337] Report, Inspection February 15, 1945.

[338] Report, reports March 8, 1945.

[339] "Rev. W.A. Heim, Veteran Stella Chaplain, Dies," *Niagara Falls Gazette*, August 6, 1956.

[340] Red Cross Report, August 27, 1945.

[341] "Medina, New York, Labor Department under Fort Niagara visited on October 10, 1944, by Mr. P. Schnyder," Other Inspection Reports Fort Niagara, NY, Folder; Enemy POW Information Bureau Reporting Branch, Subject File 1942-46; Record Group 389, Entry 461; National Archives Building, College Park, MD.

[342] "Medina, New York, Labor Department under Fort Niagara visited on August 27, 1945," Other Inspection Reports Fort Niagara, NY, Folder; Enemy POW Information Bureau Reporting Branch, Subject File 1942-46; Record Group 389, Entry 461; National Archives Building, College Park, MD.

[343] "Work Detachment, Letchworth Park, New York detached from Fort Niagara visited on October 10, 1944 by Mr. P. Schnyder," Other Inspection Reports Fort Niagara, NY, Folder; Enemy POW Information Bureau Reporting Branch, Subject File 1942-46; Record Group 389, Entry 461; National Archives Building, College Park, MD.

[344] "Prisoner of War Camp Hamlin Beach, New York August 28, 1945," Other Inspection Reports Fort Niagara, NY, Folder; Enemy POW Information Bureau Reporting Branch, Subject File 1942-46; Record Group 389, Entry 461; National Archives Building, College Park, MD.

[345] "Work Detachment, Letchworth Park, New York detached from Fort Niagara visited on October 10, 1944, by Mr. P. Schynder," Other Inspection Reports Fort Niagara, NY, Folder; Enemy POW Information Bureau Reporting Branch, Subject File 1942-46; Record Group 389, Entry 461; National Archives Building, College Park, MD.

[346] The report used the German rank of Gefreiter followed by the identification of Pfc (Private First Class).

[347] "Daily Status Report for guards and POWs at Branch Camps," Location Geneseo, NY; PMG Inspection Reports Niagara, NY, Other Inspection Reports Fort Niagara, NY, Folder; Enemy POW Information Bureau Reporting Branch, Subject File 1942-46; Record Group 389, Entry 461; National Archives Building, College Park, MD. PMG ~ Provost Marshal General.

[348] John Edgar Hoover, Director, Federal Bureau of Investigation to Assistant Chief of

Staff, G-2, War Department, Washington, DC, Attention: Col. L. R. Forney, July 22, 1944; Record Group 389, Entry 461; National Archives Building, College Park, MD.

[349] Report of Inspection by Capt. Lyle T. Dawson to the Commanding Officer, Fort Niagara, NY as of October 24, 1945; Record Group 389, Entry 461; National Archives Building, College Park, MD.

[350] Headquarters Army Service Forces Office of the Provost Marshal General, Washington 25, DC, "Semi-monthly Report on Prisoners of War as of October 1, 1945," from the National Archives Record Group No. 389 OPMG, Entry 461, National Archives Building, College Park, MD.

[351] "German Prisoners of War Claiming Czechoslovakian Origin," Letters from Prisoner of War Operations Division to the Commanding General, Second Service Command, Governors Island, New York; Folder Second Service Command; Enemy POW Information Bureau Reporting Branch, Subject File 1942-46; Record Group 389, Entry 461; National Archives Building, College Park, MD.

[352] "Camp Labor Report – 2nd Service Command, Delaware to NY," Enemy POW Information Bureau Reporting Branch, Subject File 1942-46; Record Group 389, Entry 461; National Archives Building, College Park, MD.

[353] Headquarters Army Service Forces Office of the Provost Marshal General, Washington 25, DC, "Semi-monthly Report on Prisoners of War as of 1 October 1945," National Archives Record Record Group 389, Entry 461 Box 2707, National Archives Building, College Park, MD.

CHAPTER 7

HONOR TO THE SOLDIER

"Honor to the Soldier, and Sailor everywhere, who bravely bears his country's cause," Abraham Lincoln.[354] These are a few recollections of the men and women who bore our country's cause.

MEDICS AT FORT NIAGARA ~ Joe Derhay is from Jersey City. He was inducted at Fort Dix, New Jersey, in April of 1943, and then sent to Pine Camp, later renamed Fort Drum, near Watertown, New York, for basic training. He was a medic at Fort Niagara from 1943 until the spring of 1945.[355]

"I remember the bus trip on our way to Fort Niagara. Someone cried out, 'Here is our town!' We just passed the business district of Main Street, and I asked, where is it? The response was that we just passed it." Joe laughed remembering his first impression of the Village of Youngstown. Soon after he arrived, Joe boldly asked Col. William J. Froitzheim for a pass home to get his accordion to play at the picnics in the park at Olcott, New York. Surprisingly, the answer was yes.

There was a lilt in his voice as Joe spoke about his time at Fort Niagara. "Fort Niagara was almost like home to me. On Saturday night we played at the USO for all the dances. We were an informal group, not a military band. The formal group was known as the 'Sad Sacks.' When they were shipped out we took over. Young people came from the town and danced with the G.I.s. There was a piano too and a dark room to develop photographs in the hall." Joe and his group played the music of Glenn Miller, the Andrew Sisters, and jazz pieces. Some of the popular songs were: *Long Ago and Far Away*, *Sentimental Journey*, *Shore Harbor Lights*, and *Chattanooga Choo Choo.*

"We also played and danced to *In The Mood, Beer Barrel Polka, Don't Sit Under the Apple Tree, Deep In The Heart of Texas, Sweet and Lovely, My Blue Heaven, Tea For Two, For Me and My Gal, Peg of My Heart, Lilly Marlene, Dream, All Of Me, White Christmas, I've Been Working On The Railroad, Stardust*, and many that Glenn Miller's Band played and those we heard from the juke boxes," Joe said.

Above, on bivouac a few miles from Fort Niagara, Joe Derhay was first in line for chow. Below, the soldiers enjoyed the town's delicious apples. (Both courtesy Joe Derhay)

TABLE 7.1
Fort Niagara 1940s Medical Corps Roster of Enlisted Men

Amico, Pvt. Samuel J.
Atley, Pfc. Robert B.
Barron, Pvt. Francis J.
Beauchemin, Pvt. Raymond F.
Bennett, Pfc. Stuart H.
Biddle, Pvt. Donald J.
Bieck, Pvt. Louis F.
Boyd, Pfc. Paul E.
Boyle, Pvt. Benedict J.
Brann, Pvt. Joseph A.
Brown, Pfc. Oliver J.
Buchsbaum, Pfc. Aaron J.
Burnett, Pfc. Edward C.
Butler, Pvt. Jack
Cain, Pfc. Edward J.
Carroll, Pfc. Charles M.
Carroll, Pvt., Charles J.
Cheer, Pvt. Nicholas V.
Christie, Pvt. Donald M.
Connors, Sgt. Cyril P.
Cooper, Pvt. Donald E.
Cooper, Pvt. Leon L.
Coppersmith, Sgt. Frank R.
Cripps, Pfc. George W.
Cronk, Pvt. Carl A.
Curtis, Pfc. Clifton R.
Daley, Tech. Sgt. Roy M.
Degone, Pvt. Albert J.
Edick, Pvt. Howard H.
Elliott, Pvt. Walter R.
Ellis, Cpl. Seward T.
Epke, Pfc. M—ton O.
Fahey, T/4 James M.
Fitzgibbon, Pvt. George C.
Goodfellow, Pvt. Raymond B.
Grossman, Pvt. Myer
Harvey, Pvt. John I.
Hayes, Pfc. Denton E.
Horton, Pvt. John A.
Hotchkiss, T/4 Clair E.
Humbert, Pvt. Frankin C.
Joseph, T/4 Carl J.
Juergens, Pvt. Karl A.
Kerr, Pfc. Grant W.
Langworthy, T/5 Donald C.
LaPoint, T/5 Richard W.
LeGault, T/4 Albert F.
Lichtenstein, T/5 Meyer
Marquart, Pfc. Ralph E.
McCabe, Pvt. Carl J.
Midey, Sgt. Anthony P.
Moat, Pvt. Warren H.
Nightingale, Pvt. Walter E.
Norman, Cpl. Edward L.
Northrup, Pvt. Thomas D.
O'Rourke, Pvt. Paul J.
Ontko, Pvt. Stephen T.
Perreault, Pvt. Leo H.
Repsick, Pvt. Joseph
Rice, Pvt. Kenneth M.
R—man, Pfc. Harold S.
Robinson, Pvt. Edward C.
Rodrigue, Pvt. Louis P.
Ross, Pfc. Myron
Sahlen, Sgt. Joseph L.
Schur, T/5 Ronald J.
Sharpe, Pvt. Harold R.
Simmons, Cpl. Kenneth J.
Slavin, Pvt. Richard J.
Solometo, T/4 Solomon J.

Spallino, Pvt. Peter J.	Warney, Pfc. Frank J.
Stucker, T/5 Charles F.	Watts, SSgt. Edgar J.
Walzer, Sgt. George G.	Wilcox, Pvt. John R.

Source: Medical Corps Roster, private collection, no date. Some of the men in the table are also listed in the Christmas 1943 and 1944 rosters with a higher rank, so it could reasonably be concluded that this was an earlier roster possibly 1942. Lt. Col. William J. Froitzheim, Medical Corps Surgeon, and 1st Lt. Lois H. Alfred, Chief Nurse, were in a December 1943 photo array of the Medical Department Detachment of Fort Niagara's Station Hospital.

The menu for Christmas dinner at the Fort in 1943 was fruit cup, stuffed olives, stuffed celery, mixed sweet pickles, roast turkey, cranberry sauce, sage dressing, giblet gravy, whipped potatoes, candied yams, asparagus tips, peas, sliced tomatoes, salad bowl, sliced cucumber, parker house rolls, raisin bread, mince pie, pumpkin pie, fruit cake, ice cream, chocolate cake, mixed nuts, hard candies, assorted fresh fruits, coffee, and cigars. The roster for the Station Hospital was on the reverse side of the Christmas menu.

TABLE 7.2
Fort Niagara 1943 Medical Corps Roster of Officers

Alfred, 1st Lt. Lois H.	Jaworski, 2nd Lt. Helena M.
Banzer, 1st Lt. Joseph H., M.C.	Kicinski, 2nd Lt. Harriet P.
Beetem, Capt. Luther F., M.C.	Levine, 2nd Lt. Pearl
Black, 2nd Lt. Elizabeth Allan	Loughlin, 2nd Lt. Margaret M.
Bloor, 1st Lt. Robert J., M.C.	Lowery, 1st Lt. William C., M.C.
Bonnell, 2nd Lt. Mary E.	Maslansky, Capt. Manuel M., D.C.
Campbell, 2nd Lt. Mary C., Dietician	Neary, 2nd Lt. Thomas E.
Cataldi, 2nd Lt. Hugo A.	Orlansky, Capt. George J., M.C.
Darrow, 2nd Lt. Russell E.	Phelps, 2nd Lt. Mary E.
Earle, 2nd Lt. Barbara E.	Prince, 1st Lt. Sidney, D.C.
Foran, 1st Lt. John M., D.C.	Roadruck, Capt. Roscoe D., M.C.
Froitzheim, Col. William J., Surgeon	Saleman, 2nd Lt. Frances M.
Gastinger, 1st Lt. Leona	Schneer, Maj. Jacob B., D.C.
Giardina, Maj. Anthony L., M.C.	Szall, 2nd Lt. Mary J.
Gould, 2nd Lt. Lillian	Thayer, 2nd Lt. Eleanor M.
Graybowski, 2nd Lt. Gertrude D.	Velkoff, 1st Lt. Abraham S., M.C.
Herrington, 2nd Lt. Mildred E.	

Source: Station Hospital Roster, December 25, 1943, private collection. M.C. ~ Medical Corps, D.C. ~ Dental Corps. Following WWII and during Korea other area physicians and dentists stationed at Fort Niagara's hospital included Dr. Peter Marra, Dr. Paul Haber, and Dr. Gerard Cacio.

TABLE 7.3
Fort Niagara 1943 Medical Corps Roster of Enlisted Men

Abend, Pvt. Lester I.
Aleksa, Pvt. Frank C.
Alesi, Pfc. Joseph T.
Amico, T/4 Samuel J.
Atley, Sgt. Robert B.
Baker, Pfc. Francis M.
Baldwin, Pvt. Harold J.
Barcliff, Pfc. Eldred L.
Barron, Cpl. Francis J.
Beauchemin, Cpl. Raymond F.
Bender, Pvt. Robert J.
Bennett, Sgt. Stuart H.
Biddle, Cpl. Donald J.
Bieck, Pfc. Louis F.
Boyd, T/4 Paul E.
Burnett, T/5 Edward C.
Butler, Pfc. Jack
Cancellier, Pvt. Joseph H.
Cheer, T/4 Nicholas V.
Clark, Pvt. Kenneth W.
Clift, Pfc. Clarence M.
Coleman, Pvt. Harold S.
Collins, Pvt. Vincent R.
Connors, SSgt. Cyril P.
Cooper, Pfc. Leon L.
Coppersmith, TSgt. Frank R.
Cramer, Pvt. Oties H.
Cripps, SSgt. George W.
Curtis, Sgt. Clifton R.
Daley, MSgt. Roy M.
Davis, Pvt. Harry W.
Degone, Pfc. Albert J.
Derhay, Pvt. Joseph M.
Dewey, Pfc. George M.
DiStasi, Pvt. John
Durchslag, Pfc. Harry J.
Edick, T/5 Howard H.
Elliott, T/4 Walter H.
Epke, SSgt. Milton O.
Erteld, Pfc. Dwight D.
Evers, Pvt. Louis T.
Fahey, T/3 James M.
Ferro, Pvt. Frank E.
Fisher, Pfc. Elmer
Fitzpatrick Pfc. Joseph
Genser, Pvt. Henry
Gouldine, Pfc. William T.
Gurnee, Pfc. Robert W.
Havens, Pfc. Karl E.
Hill, Pvt. Allen T.
Hillyer, Pvt. Charles F.
Holden, Pvt. Jack
Horton, Pfc. John R.
Humbert, T/4 Franklin C.
Iacovazzi, T/5 Peter S.
Johnsten, Pvt. Earnest L.
Joseph, SSgt. Carl J.
Juergens, Cpl. Karl A.
Kerr, Sgt. Grant W.
Langworthy, SSgt. Donald C.

LaPoint, Sgt. Richard W.
Linn, Pvt. Jay J.
Locastro, Pvt. Manuel
Makowski, Pfc. Arthur J.
Manfred, Pfc. Ernest A.
Mehler, Pvt. Norman L.
Meyer, Pfc. Severein G.
Mihalik, Pvt. Joseph
Mourtzikos, Pvt. Peter
Murphy, T/4 Gerald J.
Nightingale, Cpl. Walter E.
Norman, Sgt. Edward L.
Northrup, Pfc. Thomas D.
O'Rourke, Pfc. Paul J.
Pecker, Pvt. Jack
Perigo, Pvt. Raymond C.
Perreault, T/5 Leo H.
Privitera, Pfc. Albert D.
Rank, Pvt. Stanley M.
Repsick Pfc. Joseph
Roach, Pfc. David H.
Robinson, Pfc. Walter H.
Rodman, Sgt. Harold S.
Rodrique, Cpl. Louis P.
Ross, Pvt. Robert P.
Samek, Pvt. Walter B.
Santasero, Pfc. Nicholas
Sarkin, Pvt. Marvin
Schauman, Pfc. Robert W.
Schott, Pvt. Carmen F.
Sechrist, T/5 Preston F.
Seeberg, T/4 Harry
Sharpe, Pfc. Harold R.
Slavin, Pfc. Richard J.
Smith, Pfc. Robert R.
Smith, Pvt. Kenneth M.
Solometo, SSgt. Solomon J.
Spallino, Sgt. Peter J.
Taylor, Pvt. Sidney
VanOrden, Pvt. Peter J.
Verilllo, Pfc. Armand A.
Whitmire, Pvt. Robert L.
Whitney, Pvt. Arthur F.
Wilcox, Cpl. John R.

Source: Station Hospital Roster, December 25, 1943, private collection. Karl Juergens acted as one of the interpreters for the POWs.[356]

On Sundays Father Ferdinand Ward, a Catholic priest, said Mass; then, Joe entertained with his accordion at the Communion breakfasts. "We also played in town. Clarence Clift sang, and I played the accordion for Mr. and Mrs. Christian Nelson's twenty-fifth wedding anniversary celebration on March 28, 1944, at their Main Street home. Clarence was a cousin of the actor, Montgomery Clift."

The traditional roast turkey was served at the Christmas dinner menu in 1944 with some changes from the previous year: shrimp cocktail, stuffed olives, stuffed celery, mixed sweet pickles, cranberry sauce, oyster dressing, giblet gravy, snowflake potatoes, candied yams, asparagus tips, candle stick salad, parker house rolls, butter, mince pie, pumpkin pie, fruit cake, ice cream, mixed nuts, mint candy, assorted fresh fruits, coffee, sweet cider, and cigars.

Above, Fort Niagara's theatre, one of the few remaining structures from the World War II era. Below, the interior of the theatre. (Above courtesy Joe Derhay, below courtesy Mary Wieland)

TABLE 7.4
Fort Niagara 1944 Station Hospital Roster of Officer

Beetem, Capt. Luther F.
Bellinger, 2nd Lt. Evelyn M.
Black, 2nd Lt. Elizabeth A.
Cohen, Capt. Moses, M.C.
Cooper, 2nd Lt. Edith J.
Darrow, 1st Lt. Russell E., M.A.C.
Foran, Capt. John M., D.C.
Froitzheim, Col. William J.
Gastinger, Capt. Leona
Gluck, Capt. Roland, M.C.
Hendler, Capt. Hyman B., M.C.
Ibbott, 2nd Lt. Edith E.
Jaworski, 2nd Lt. Helena M.
Kartman, Capt. Jules D., D.C.
Landsman, Capt. Harold M. M.C.
Lapin, Capt. Samuel B., M.C.
Lawrence, Capt. Salvatore A., M.C.
Lobo, 1st Lt. Joseph M., D.C.
Longhlin, 1st Lt. Margaret M.
Lorys, 2nd Lt. Michael, M.A.C.
Maraski, 2nd Lt. Michael, M.A.C.
McCarthy, 2nd Lt. Regina M.
McGinnis, 1st Lt. Hannah D.
Muraski, 2nd Lt. Edwin A., M.A.C.
Schaefer, Maj. Leo J.
Slattery, 2nd Lt. Marguerite R.
Szall, 2nd Lt. Mary J.
Vasilake, 2nd Lt. Connie M.
Willner, Capt. Victor, M.C.

Source: Station Hospital Roster, December 25, 1944, private collection.

"We wore white uniforms in the hospital. The nurses were all officers, lieutenants or captains. Some of the soldiers being treated were shell-shocked. The hospital wards were supposed to be 'quiet' but there were enormous sounds from morning reveille and the rifle range, which was close to the hospital ward. Bell Aircraft tested the guns (on the fighter aircraft) over Lake Ontario everyday and that also added to the noise," Joe said. Fort Niagara was renowned for its soldiers' marksmanship and its excellent 1,000-yard rifle range. "I was classified expert at the rifle range, which amazed the officers, because I was '4-F,' not fit for combat."

It was an eight-hour day with three square meals in the mess hall, Joe said. "The cooks were all Greeks; one was from Rochester. Most of my buddies were from there, also Elmira and the Finger Lakes region. There was a rotation for K-P and furnace duty. The older buildings were heated by anthracite coal that we banked up at an angle so it wouldn't burn so quickly during the night. It was very important to the Mess Hall because the water had to be very hot for coffee. Once, someone on furnace duty had not shoveled enough coal so the coffee wasn't hot the next morning, and there was some hollering about that!"

"I remember the German and Italian prisoners being at Fort Niagara. They

The pit for the rifle targets on the 1,000-yard firing range. Fort Niagara's soldiers were known as some of the world's best marksmen. (Courtesy Joe Derhay)

kept asking us for cigarettes. There was no fraternization with the POWs. They were not at the USO and didn't dance with the Youngstown girls," Joe said, clearing up an old misconception in the town. The POWs compound was separate from the hospital wards. "We didn't have much contact with the prisoners, but they did try to get cigarettes from us. We also watched them play soccer in the fields."

TABLE 7.5
Fort Niagara 1944 Station Hospital Roster of Enlisted Men

Alesi, T/5 Joseph T.	Bender, Pfc. Robert J.
Amico, T/4 Samuel J.	Bennett, Sgt. Stuart H.
Anderson, SSgt. Ashley K.	Bernard, T/5 Ralph
Baldwin, Cpl. Harold J.	Biddle, Cpl. Donald J.
Barber, Pfc. Arthur T.	Bieck, Pfc. Louis F.
Barber, Pfc. Arthur T.	Butler, Pfc. Jack
Beauchemin, Cpl. Raymond F.	Cancellier, Pvt. Joseph H.

Cheer, T/4 Nicholas V.
Cingire, Pvt. Anthony A.
Clark, Pfc. Kenneth W.
Clemens, Pvt. Floyd H.
Clift, Pfc. Clarence M.
Connors, SSgt. Cyril P.
Curtis, Sgt. Clifton R.
Dalmaris, T/4 Steve
Davis, Pfc. Harry W.
Degone, Pfc. Albert J.
Derhay, Pfc. Joseph M.
Dewey, Pfc. George M.
DiStasi, Pfc. John
Durchslag, Pfc. Harry J.
Edick, T/5 Howard H.
Elliott, T/4 Walter R.
Erteld, Pfc. Dwight D.
Fahey, T/3 James M.
Fisher, T/5 Elmer
Fitzpatrick, Pfc. Joseph E.
Fulmer, Pfc. Lewis A.
Gouldine, Pfc. William T.
Hansen, Pvt. Knud E.
Havens, Pfc. Karl E.
Horton, Pfc. John A.
Humbert, T/4 Franklin C.
Indgin, T/5 Louis
Joseph, SSgt. Carl J.
LaCapra, Pfc. Joseph A.
Langworthy, SSgt. Donald C.
Lanphear, Pvt. Milton E.
Linn, Pfc. Jay J.
Manfred, T/5 Ernest A.
Martucci, T/5 Sam F.
Mihalik, Pfc. Joseph
Mourtzikos, T/5 Peter A.
Murphy, T/4 Gerald J.
Nightingale, Cpl. Walter E.
Norman, Sgt. Edward L.
O'Rourke, Pfc. Paul J.
Parrott, Pvt. Arthur J.
Perigo, Pvt. Raymond C.
Prendergast, TSgt. Leo J.
Privitera, Pfc. Albert D.
Rank, Pfc. Stanley M.
Repsick, Pfc. Joseph
Roach, Pfc. David M.
Robinson, Cpl. Walter H.
Rodman, Sgt. Harold S.
Schauman, Pfc. Robert W.
Schott, Pvt. Carman F.
Sharpe, Pfc. Harold R.
Smith, T/5 Robert M.
Spallino, Sgt. Peter J.
Steele, Pvt. John M.
Sullivan, Pvt. John F.
VanOrden, Pfc. Peter G., Jr.
Verillo, Pfc. Armand A.
Whitney, Pfc. Arthur F.
Wichrowski, T/5 Anthony
Wilcox, T/4 John R.
Zank, Pvt. Allan M.

Source: Station Hospital Roster, private collection.

TABLE 7.6
Fort Niagara 1944 Station Hospital Civilian Employees

Alaimo, Rose	Horst, George
Alongi, Lilyan	Howard, Judith
Barrett, Vern	Mahon, Rita
Boyle, Helen	McGuire, Elizabeth
Cebula, Josef	Ricotta, Marie
Crowley, Virginia	Robinson, Virginia
Fix, Melba	Rodenbaugh, Grove
Gibson, Anne	Shipston, Mary M.
Gieseler, Rudolph	Simonds, Patricia
Hart, Beatrice	Wilson, John
Hayes, Dorothy	Zulke, Henry

Source: Station Hospital Roster, December 25, 1944, private collection.

In the late spring of 1945 Joe was transferred to Miller Field, Staten Island, New York. "Some of the girls from Youngstown wrote me letters and poetry, and reminisced about the times at the USO. They sent me an invitation to their graduation exercises from the Youngstown High School. While I was at Miller Field, President Roosevelt died, then I was sent to Boston, Massachusetts." Joe and the band group arrived at the Boston harbor before dawn and met the Victory Ships returning with the troops from Europe. As soon as it was light they played happy music accompanied by a large welcome home sign. There was pride in Joe's voice as he told about the returning troops. "We played five to six hours until all the G.I.s got off the boat."

After Boston, Joe was sent to Los Angeles, California, and then discharged. He and his buddy, Cpl. Bill Brayford, decided to hitchhike home. It took three weeks and seventy-seven rides via Phoenix, El Paso, Mexico, Houston, New Orleans, Tallahassee, and Miami to journey the 4,750 miles home to Jersey City.[357]

Joe returned to Youngstown several times after the war to enjoy the annual Youngstown Firemen's Labor Day Parade and visit friends that he met while stationed at Fort Niagara. He celebrated his eighty-third birthday in the fall of 2006 and with his band continues to regularly entertain others.

Soldiers after Mass walking in front of the Fort Niagara chapel. In 1948, the chapel was moved to the corner of Second and Hinman Streets in Youngstown under the direction of Rev. Andrew Pronobis for St. Bernard's Roman Catholic Church. Father Pronobis was an Army chaplain attached to the 323rd Infantry Division of the 81st Division and later to the 56th Evac Hospital Division, both in Italy. He received the Purple Heart for his wounds during the Anzio landing. (Courtesy Joe Derhay)

STATION HOSPITAL ~ A banner with four blue stars hung on the front door of the Slattery home in Middleport, New York.[358] Two stars represented sons and the other two for daughters Esther and Marge. They were part of an historic effort by more than 59,000 women nurses who served during the war.[359] Francis, their brother, served with the Fifth Division Marines and was wounded at Okinawa, and another brother, Charles, served stateside in Tennessee.[360] Two other siblings were at home.

"My mother and all my aunts were teachers. I wanted to be something different," said Marguerite "Marge" Slattery Dyer about her career path. Marge and her sister both trained at Mount St. Mary's Hospital on 6th Street, Niagara Falls, New York. Esther was in the graduating class of 1941 with Mary Cavanero.[361] Marge went to work at Union Carbide as an industrial nurse before enlisting in 1943. Esther, at twenty-one years old, became the youngest nurse with the Twenty-Third General Hospital Unit at Buffalo General Hospital.

Wartime was wrought with fragile and painful moments. "I took the train to visit Esther while she was in basic at Fort Meade, New Jersey. While I was there, we went to dances. One day you danced with an airman, the next day he was shipped out, and then you found out he was killed. One of the pilots named his aircraft, *Slats*, for my sister. He was shot down over France during the invasion. Esther went over with the troops on the old *Queen Mary* wearing a life

Above, hospital ward buildings at Fort Niagara.

Below, the Station Hospital administration building is in the background behind the dispensary. (Both courtesy Joe Derhay)

Above, actor Guy Kibbee visited wounded soldiers being treated at the fort's medical facilities.

Below, Nursing Corps at Fort Niagara. See Table 7.4 for roster. (Both courtesy Joe Derhay)

jacket all the time as the ship navigated around the German subs until landing at Casablanca. She went through the war overseas: the invasion of Italy, the Battle of the Bulge, and liberation of France, following the combat troops in a field hospital. My sister was adventurous, but afterwards she didn't want to talk about the war."

Women were not drafted like the men, but there was pressure to enlist because nurses were needed. As the war progressed the shortage grew. President Franklin Roosevelt, during his State of the Union address on January 6, 1945, proposed that the Selective Service Act be amended to include a draft to address the urgent need for nurses.[362] "My initial physical was at Fort Niagara followed by basic training in Atlantic City. We took over the hotels on the boardwalk for living quarters. Ten-mile marches included a full pack and aircraft drops of bags of flour to simulate bombs," Marge said.

After basic she was sent to Fort Niagara to recruit other nurses from local hospitals.[363] Teas were held to recruit more nurses. Lieutenant Col. William J. Froitzheim was the Medical Corps Surgeon at Fort Niagara at the time. "He was old Army and very formal. Our Captain McGinnis, an older woman, was regular Army. One of the other nurses was lifted-off at Corregidor with Gen. Douglas Mac Arthur. She was a thirty-year veteran."

The nurses' quarters were across from the Officer's Club building. "Meals at the club were very plush. One of the POWs was painting the mural then.[364] POWs waited on us and laid white napkins across our laps when we sat down. They were very polite. I went to the PX for toilet articles, sugar, and other things, so I didn't need my ration cards and gave them to my mother. A Second Lieutenant earned ninety dollars a month." Marge was promoted to the rank of Captain at discharge.

"Some of the doctors wanted us to baby-sit their children, since they didn't know anyone in town. Captain McGinnis wasn't in favor of that and issued an Order that none of her nurses were to baby-sit." Off-duty the nurses enjoyed movies at Fort Niagara's theatre and dances in the ballroom at the Officer's Club. "We used to go to the *Fort Inn* and the *Ray-Ott Club* in Niagara Falls."[365]

Two guards with machine guns stood outside the POW officer's hospital ward. Some of the prisoners were Storm Troopers. "The POWs had their own corpsmen; they gave baths and changed beds. We only went into the POW hospital rooms to distribute medicine or give treatment. I tried to give one of the German colonels a shot of penicillin. When he refused to turn over, I responded: 'you are afraid of a shot? I thought you are the super race!' He jumped up and the guard pointed the machine gun at him and said 'go ahead and I will

Marge and Esther Slattery were part of the 59,000 American nurses who served in the Army Nurse Corps. (Courtesy Marge Slattery Dyer)

shoot you.' The officers were very arrogant." Marge served at Fort Niagara for about eight months until she received Orders for China-Burma, but was sick and unable to go.

After recovering from pneumonia, Marge became part of the 1247 Mitchell Field Train Unit. "The decks for the wounded were three high on the trains. Pants became part of our uniform because we climbed up on the decks to treat the returning wounded soldiers being transported to the hospitals. We helped the Red Cross workers load cigarettes that they passed out to the men." The trains were to transport the injured to a hospital in the state where the soldier came from to be near their family, but it didn't always work out. Marge's brother, Francis, was hospitalized in Georgia.

The nurses pulled twelve-hour duty shifts on the hospital trains. The trains had their own cooking cars and refrigeration. While traveling via civilian trains on leave "Someone always picked up your check in the dining car, because you were in the service. Everyone was patriotic," Marge said. Marge traveled across every state in the Union treating the returning wounded and served until 1947. She made a training film about medical care on hospital trains.

The best thing about those days for Marge was that "everyone was involved. I haven't seen such patriotism since then." The most difficult thing was that "so many people were killed or wounded that you knew."

Marge's sister, Esther, married Dr. John W. Simpson in 1948. Simpson was a key figure in the development of the atom as a source of energy in nuclear power. He contributed to applications of nuclear theory in marine and space propulsion, and generation of electrical power. Simpson worked at Westinghouse on electrical equipment that was used in Navy vessels during the war.[366]

D-DAY UTAH BEACH ~ The Hamlet of Ransomville is on the east side of the Town of Porter. For the first quarter of the twentieth century Ransomville was the heart of agri-business in Porter until a devastating fire in 1924 destroyed much of the business district,[367] but not the patriotism of its native sons.

Burdette Jeffery Harris and Janet Peterson Harris and their children lived on the corner of Harris Avenue and Route 93 in the hamlet. Route 93, Youngstown-Lockport Road, is the main road running west to east from Youngstown to Ransomville in Porter. Ruth Lucille Harris, Burdette and Janet's youngest daughter, was in eighth grade when war was declared. Ruth recalled her teacher at the Wilson school, Mrs. Lydia Southard, as part of the details of the day unfolded. "Someone brought a radio to school that day. All the girls were crying. I knew my two brothers were going to be called up. It was sad and a scary time. I was frightened they (the Germans) were going to come over here."[368] Reeve "Bud" Carlton Gates, Jr. recollected hearing the news on Jack Armstrong's radio program.

Ruth's story was similar to her husband Bud's. Their fathers were air raid wardens in Ransomville during the war and like many others in the town. The death of a POW on the Hurtgam farm was a vivid memory for Ruth. Bud watched for enemy aircraft on top of Burly's store[369] and on August 30, 1946, saw the tragic fatal crash of a P-39 flown by Bell test pilot, Jack Woolams, over Lake Ontario.

Ruth worked for the Lafler family in their store on North Ridge. She said that "rationing was a big thing and we were also dealing with a shortage of cigarettes. *Life* magazine was our Bible. It was our vehicle of knowing what was going on during the war. We gathered milkweed pods. The kapok was used for life vests.

I also wrote to Willard (her brother) making my letters like a newspaper. But the letters were censored."

Near the end of his life on July 8, 2000, Willard Ransom Harris decided to share the story of his experiences during the war with his sister, Ruth Harris Gates. Ruth transcribed the story of Willard's military service to honor her brother. She wrote, "Willard helped to preserve the freedom we enjoy today by serving our country in WWII."[370]

Willard Ransom Harris was born January 27, 1920. Shortly after his twenty-second birthday, on February 5, 1942, his parents drove him to the Newfane Draft Board in their Model A Ford coupe. A bus took the inductees from Newfane to the Induction Center at Fort Niagara. At Fort Niagara the soldiers were given winter uniforms and a heavy overcoat. They purchased their own toiletries at the PX. Willard brought a small Norton Camera from home that was made in Lockport, New York. Willard told Ruth, "They didn't give us any toilet articles…we bought all of them at the PX, except for a few things I took from home."

The induction process at Fort Niagara included orientation films watched at the movie theater. Then it was on to the Whirlpool Train Station in Niagara Falls. The New York Central Train transported Willard and the troops to Camp Lee, Virginia. Three other local soldiers made the same journey through the war with Willard: Clyde Jacobs from the Tuscarora Nation, Roy Campbell from Ransomville, and a Hausman from Newfane.[371]

Camp Lee was a training camp for medics. Willard was assigned to the Twelfth Infantry Regiment Medical Detachment and his three buddies to the Fourth Medical Battalion. Their training included how to drive an ambulance, pick up injured soldiers, and how to bandage their wounds. A respite from the basic training included a weekend in Richmond, Virginia. A group of the soldiers went to see Mario Lanza. But "other than that, it was training all the time…no fun," Willard told Ruth.

There was more training at Camp Gordon, which was about fifteen miles from Augusta, Georgia, of thirty-mile forced marches during one hundred plus temperatures with a full pack, a gas mask, and an extra pair of shoes. Maneuvers continued in the Carolinas with the motorized division then back to Georgia. Willard's story continued with a parade at Camp Gordon "before all the Generals, (Dwight D.) Eisenhower, (Charles) de Gaulle, (and) Lord Louis Mountbatten to observe the Fourth Division on parade."

The next stop was Camp Gordon Johnston, originally named Camp Carrabelle, on the Gulf coast south of Tallahassee, Florida.[372] Willard's unit was put through extensive amphibious training for several weeks. They practiced at Dog Island carrying everything over their heads. "Medics didn't carry guns. The Red Cross on our helmet was our protection. There was an international agreement that said that no one could fire at us. Some honored it and some didn't. I was one of the lucky ones!"[373]

There were a few leaves back to Ransomville via an airplane flight to La-Guardia and a train ride from Grand Central Station in New York to Buffalo. Willard's mother was receiving treatment at Roswell Park Cancer Center at the time. His father had only "A" gas ration coupons.[374] Willard told Ruth how the community helped his family. "Farmers at home gave Obbie Goodfellow, he ran a gas station across from the Legion Hall, their extra coupons so dad could get enough gas to get to Buffalo to see her. I took a bus from Buffalo to Niagara Falls and then I took Les Schultz's bus to Ransomville."

Camp Kilmer, New Jersey, was an Army Post Office (APO) shipping point for overseas mail. It took about a week to cross the Atlantic Ocean. Willard was on the *Europa*, a prize German ship captured in WWI. "Our whole regiment was on it – like sardines packed in a can! The bunks were below deck. We were all scared to death. The Chaplain couldn't believe the gambling going on…The *Missouri* was out in front with destroyers, sub chasers and aircraft carriers. The French sent their *USS Normandy* over to the United States for safe-keeping. It was being used in the convoy as a troop ship. So was the *Queen Elizabeth* from England."

There was a six month wait in England and hikes to keep in shape. Then, after a train-ride on June 5, 1944, the unit arrived in South Hampton. General Eisenhower and Lt. Col. Teddy Roosevelt, Jr., the Assistant Division Commander, greeted them. The soldiers were loaded onto a LCM.[375] "We were scheduled to cross the channel (English Channel) on that day – June 5, but the water was way too rough. The boats were going under the waves instead of over them! So they took it slow and maneuvered the craft around and we (the Fourth Infantry Division) arrived at Mitchell Point, off shore from our landing spot in Normandy, on the coast of France, on June 6, 1944, at six o'clock in the morning. Some of the boats got it from the German U-boats – We could see them blow."[376]

The greatest military invasion from the sea on the beaches of Normandy left an indelible mark on Willard as he described landing on Utah Beach after the LSTs[377] arrived. They reached the beach on a British landing craft. It took them about ten minutes to go ashore. "We ran like hell to get away from the beach. Everything was zeroed in right there. We surprised the Germans in the pillboxes.[378] They guessed that we were coming across from Dover, England, as it was the shortest route – only twenty miles. We out maneuvered them!"

Willard was attached to the Twelfth Infantry Antitank Company. They received support from the 101st and 82nd Airborne. The human carnage was almost incomprehensible that day. Willard shared with his sister that "a lot of guys were killed that day. The damn beaches had barriers of railroad irons and fencing. We waited for these to be blown up by combat engineers. Things worked out as planned, but an awful lot got killed. There were dead all over the beach. Couldn't help any of them. They were long gone."

Willard's combat experience against the German army continued for 103 days and nights through the French towns of St. Mère Église, Cherbourg, Avranches, and Saint Lot. Overhead were the Eighth Air Force and the British bombers. Willard explained how the Americans were pushed back twenty miles, as far as Bastoyne. "The Germans caught them (the Eighty-Third Infantry) at a weak point and formed a bulge...General (Anthony Clement) McAullife was waiting at Bastogne. The Germans wanted him to surrender and he told them, 'Nuts!' Also waiting were Patton's Third Army, Bradley's (Gen. Omar Nelson Bradley) First Army, and the British. Patton was at the bottom of the 'U'. Our regiment (originally part of the First Army) got separated and became attached to Patton's Third Army for the rest of the war. Couldn't have been a better general. Patton got things moving."

Willard's account included how their regiment liberated Paris in August of 1944. Frenchmen told the soldiers that the worst thing the Germans could have done to them was to destroy their wineries. They beseeched the soldiers to save the wineries. Willard also became a primary source of the horrors of the concentration camps. "Some people say the Holocaust never happened. They were dead wrong! I saw it with my own eyes."

The Germans called Willard's division the "Terrible Green Cross" because their artillery was so accurate. He was wounded in the Battle of the Hurtgen Forest[379] near the Belgium-German border and received the Purple Heart. On July 4, 1945, Willard boarded the liberty ship, *USS Seabass*, headed for home. At Fort Dix, Willard Ransom Harris was discharged.[380]

MEMORIAL SERVICE IN RANSOMVILLE ~ A Service of Gratitude and Memory was held at the Methodist Church, coordinated by the mothers of service men, Sunday evening, February 27, 1944, at 7:30 p.m.

TABLE 7.7
Memorial Service in Ransomville, New York

Prelude	Mrs. Delmar Sherlock
Invocation	Rev. Robert Packer
Instrumental Number	Miss Ruth Smithson
Scripture	Twenty-Third Psalm
Solo	Mrs. B. Addison Rising
Offertory	Miss Mary Schweitzer Mrs. Delmar Sherlock
In Memoriam	Rev. John A. Mann
Candle Lighters Procession	Miss Dolores Magill Miss Susie Curtis Miss Ruth Conger Miss Jean Sweigert
Address	Mrs. Florence Reef
Violin Solo	Miss Mary Schweitzer
Benediction	Rev. H. J. Farrington
Postlude	Mrs. Delmar Sherlock

Source: "Candle Glow" program, Military archives files, Ransomville Historical Room, Ransomville, New York. Mrs. Reef's address was entitled *The Battle on the Home Front.*

TABLE 7.8
In Service Overseas on February 27, 1944

Arnold, Sgt. Elwin E.	Cornell, Sgt. Raymond
Bale, Sgt. Ray L.	Demin, Pfc. Carson
Bonnett, Pfc. Daniel	Demin, Pvt. Elton
Bonnett, Pvt. Melvin	Drinkwater, S1/C James
Britt, Sgt. Jack	Figura, Paul
Campbell, Cpl. Roy	Figura, S2/C Harry
Canfield, Pfc. Lewis(Louis)	Fredericks, Pfc. Clarence
Canfield, Sgt. Rex	Furman, Clarence
Caraglin, James	Furman, Pvt. Gerald
Chestnut, Sgt. John	Golding, Cpl. John
Colliver, Cpl. Calvin C.	Goodman, Cpl. Lyle S.
Colliver, Cpl. Ray L.	Goodman, F2/C Malcolm

Goodman, Lt. Janet
Harris, Pfc. Willard
Hildebrandt, Pfc. Philip E.
Hillman, Cpl. Eugene H.
Hochhadel, Sgt. Leonard
Ingraham, Sgt. Max
Johnson, S1/C Jack C.
Kagel, Kenneth
Lederhouse, Pvt. John
Lindsay, Warren
Lisman, Pfc. Francis
Lyndhurst, Lt. Harold
Mann, Capt. John A.
Mann, Pvt. Reginald
Masters, Pvt. Leslie
Mattice, Donald
Moose, Sgt. Raymond
Myers, Cpl. Henry
Myers, Elric
Myers, Pvt. Wm.
Nagy, Pvt. Frank
Pedley, Cpl. Lamont
Petit, Pfc. Jarvis
Reese, Lt. Wilbur
Ryan, Pvt. Leland
Schultz, John
Schultz, Pfc. Howard
Schultz, Pfc. Robert
Seefeldt, P.O. 3/C Bernard
Seefeldt, Howard
Smithson, Cpl. Raymond D.
Smithson, S2/C Donald
Smithson, S2/C Jack T.
Stevens, Pfc. Alfred
Sutherland, Ronald
Thielman, Francis
Upper, Alvin Franklin
Velsey, Cpl. Gordon
Vince, S2/C M.P., Jr.
Warren, Lt. Gertrude
Whitt, Cpl. Richard
Wills, Cpl. John

Source: "Candle Glow" program, Ransomville, New York.

TABLE 7.9
In Training in the United States, February 27, 1944

Albright, Arthur Austin
Ames, A/S Wm. T.
Atherton, Geo. T., Jr.
Austin, Cpl. Harold
Austin, Sgt. Wm.
Baker, Sgt. Arthur
Bale, Pfc. Richard S.
Bauer, Cpl. Albert
Blackwell, A/C Alex.
Blackwell, Lt. L. D.
Bohnstadt, Pvt. Ronald
Bowen, Cpl. Albert C.
Bowen, Pvt. Richard L.
Bowman, Harold
Bradley, Lt. Russell
Burlingame, Pvt. William
Campbell, Pvt. James
Carew, Pvt. Richard
Carter, Pvt. Kenneth
Chestnut, Pvt. James
Chestnut, Sgt. William
Clark, Cpl. Robert
Clark, S3/C Robert F.
Clement, S2/C Robert

Coleman, Cpl. Robert M.
Coleman, A/S Ronald G.
Connor, Sgt. Clifford
Cornell, Douglas
Cornell, Pvt. Roy D.
Curtis, Sgt. Howard
Dent, A/S C.W.
Drinkwater, Pfc. Robert
Drinkwater, Capt. Victor
Durfy, Sgt. James R.
Edwards, William
Farquharson, Pfc. George
Farquharson, Pvt. John
Figuro, Pfc. Bruno
Frey, Floyd
Geartz, S2/C Roger
Gentle, Sgt. Spencer
Glenn, Pvt. Benny
Goodman, Pfc. Norvel
Grzybowski, Pfc. Edw.
Hardison, S2/C Gerald
Helwig, Cpl. Erwin, Jr.
Henschel, Sgt. Paul
Holman, A/C Eugene
Ingraham, Pvt. James
Ingraham, Sgt. Richard
Jarrett, Jack
Jindra, Cpl. E. V.
Johnson, Clifford E.
Johnson, Eugene
Knapp, Sgt. Glenn L.
Knarr, Sgt. Carl
Kneeple, Pvt. Charles
Kratz, S2/C Gerald
Langdon, Cpl. Lawrence
Lederhouse, Albert
Lederhouse, Chester
Litchard, Pvt. Edward B., Jr.
Litchard, Pfc. Ernest
Mack's, Pfc. Larne
Mack's, Ralph
Mann, Pvt. Arthur
Manning, A/C Donald S.
Marcel, T.M.3/C Franklin
Masters, Kenneth
Masters, Sgt. Robert
Matthews, Sgt. Duane
McClure, Sgt. Maj. Walter
McGrath, James
McKie, Pvt. Donald
Molyneaux, Cpl. Garrett
Molyneaux, Lt. R.L.
Moore, Cpl. Charles
Moore, Pfc. Willis
Moss, A/C Kenneth
Moxham, Pvt. Howard
Myers, Douglas
Myers, Lt. R. E.
Myers, Pvt. Irving
Nelson, Pfc. William
Ortt, Pvt. Gordon
Ortt, Pvt. Milford
Parker, Milford
Patterson, Sgt. James
Pless, Pvt. James
Pollow, Pfc. John
Reese, Andrew F.
Rose, Cpl. Ralph W.
Schrader, Pfc. Albert
Seefeldt, Ralph
Shultz, Pfc. Norman
Sievert, S2/C Donald
Skurski, Cpl. Benny
Smithson, Pfc. Richard, Jr.
Sutherland, Kenneth
Theis, Archie

Theis, Sgt. Wm.	Wasmund, Pfc. Norman E.
Tower, Everett	Whyte, Sgt. George
Tower, Cpl. Gerald	Wiepert, S2/C Louis
Truesdell, Pfc. Donald	Woolson, Nathan
Truesdell, Lt. Merton	Zeitz, Pvt. Wallace

Source: "Candle Glow" program, Ransomville, NY.

Ralph Dutton, Clerk, wrote in the *Minutes of Session* of the First Presbyterian Church of Youngstown for November 20, 1944, that a decision was made to join with St. John's Episcopal Church in a united "V-E Day" Service at the Presbyterian Church. There were no other entries in the Session books related to the war during the period from 1941 to 1946.

TABLE 7.10
St. John's Episcopal Church Roll of Honor

Andrews, James	Mies, Louis M.
Barber, George A.	Morris, Lewis L.
Buck, George	Myers, Guy
Carsen, Ronald	Nixon, Donald O.
Clark, Lela	Nixon, Oliver
Comerford, Kenneth	Powley, Frank
Comerford, Stuart	Powley, Edward
Cothran, Arthur	Powley, Eugene
Dehay, Arthur	Riesdorf, Jack
Devinney, William	Sparling, Gorden
Grimes, George	Stuart, J. G. W.
Harvey, Albert	Tauscher, Robert A.
Harvey, Alfred	Tausgler, Norman D.
Herrick, Sherlock A.	Taylor, Paul G.
Herrick, Sherlock A., Jr.	Taylor, Charles S.
Holstein, Charles C.	Thompson, Richard
Hunt, Richard J.	Tiefenbach, William
Hunt, William H.	Tower, Jean
Jones, Richard	Tuttle, George M.
Kathan, George	Wagner, John
Lundquist, Whay	

Source: Plaque at St. John's Episcopal Church, Youngstown, New York.[381]

On July 14, 1946, the community gathered again for another memorial and also for the dedication of an electric organ at the Ransomville Baptist Church on the south side of Route 93. Rev. Anthony E. Jefferson gave the Invocation and Katherine Davis sang *Let Not Your Heart Be Troubled.* Rev. Robert Packer offered a memorial message after prayers and a reading with the Benediction of Peace. The community left the Sanctuary in Silence to *Choeur-de-Pelerin.*[382]

Gardner V. Plain, Roger Plain, John A. Chestnut, James Ingraham, William R. Burlingame, and Raymond D. Smithson from Ransomville were remembered during the service. First Lt. Gardner V. Plain attended the Citizens Military Training Camp of the CCC, at Fort Niagara for four years. He was later assigned to Army recruiting duty at Newark, New Jersey, and then stationed at Fort Benning, Georgia, where he was commissioned in December of 1940. Lieutenant Plain was attached to the parachute troops unit of the 502nd Regiment when he was killed in an Army transport plane crash on August 15, 1942. Gardner was survived by his bride of six weeks, Eleanor Sophia Lare.[383]

Gardner's brother, 2nd Lt. Roger Plain, was with the 133rd Regiment in the anti-tank gun division. He entered the service on February 1, 1942, and was killed in an accident in North Africa on July 29, 1943. Gardner and Roger were sons of the local family doctor, John C. Plain.

Sgt. John A. Chestnut entered the service on July 17, 1941, went overseas October 8, 1943, to North Africa as an Air Force Gunner and Engineer on a B-17 and was killed on his fourth mission November 10, 1943. William and James Chestnut, John's brothers, also served during the war.

Pvt. James Ingraham entered the service on February 25, 1944, and left for Europe in September 1944. He was killed on March 15, 1945, and buried at St. Avold, France.

Staff Sgt. William R. Burlingame was a gunner on a B-17 *Flying Fortress* with the 366th Bomber Squadron 305th Bomb Group of the Eighth Air Force. He completed more than twenty bombing missions over enemy territory and served as the right waist gunner when he was killed January 1, 1945, during a mission over Magdeburg, Germany. He was buried the next day at Kläden, Germany, and re-interred in an American military cemetery at St. Avold, France, in July 1945.

Cpl. Raymond D. Smithson was a member of the 505th Parachute Infantry Regiment. His regiment was one of the first to reach France during the Normandy Invasion. Corporal Smithson was killed in action January 21, 1944.[384]

An unidentified yellowed newspaper clipping, in the Ransomville Historical Room, covered the story of another soldier killed in action in Italy. Private William E. Myers was with the Twenty-seventh Armed Forces, the Fifth Army.

He entered the Army in March 1942 and did his basic training at Fort Barrancas in Florida. Myers was sent overseas in March 1943 assigned to the Twenty-seventh Armed Forces Fifth Army. He served in North Africa and on the Anzio beachhead. There was no date in the article.

TABLE 7.11
Honored Dead from the Town of Porter

Bowman, Seaman Harold G.	Ransomville
Burlingame, SSgt. William R.	Ransomville
Canelli, Sgt. Tarcisio	Youngstown
Canfield, Louis (Lewis) C.	Ransomville
Carlock, Sgt. Floyd D.	Fort Niagara
Carrara, Ship's Cook 1c Malcolm A.	Youngstown
Chestnut, Sgt. John A.	Ransomville
Doty, Seaman 1C Howard Fred	Youngstown
Eaton, Pvt. William J.	Ransomville
Fredericks, Sgt. Clarence E.	Ransomville
Hays, Lt. David S.	Youngstown
Hutchison, 2nd Lt. Harold	Youngstown
Ingraham, Pvt. James	Ransomville
Mann, Corp. Reginald W.	Ransomville
Mobley, Sgt. Oscar E.	Youngstown
Myers, Pvt. William E.	Ransomville
Plain, 1st Lt. Gardner V.	Ransomville
Plain, 2nd Lt. Roger	Ransomville
Serba, Pfc. Frank M.	Youngstown
Smithson, Cpl. Raymond D.	Ransomville
Tower, Cpl. Everett L.	Ransomville
Doty, Cpl. Walter J. (MIA)	Youngstown

Sources: *Buffalo Evening News Almanac and Fact Book, 1947 WWII – List of Honored Dead,* subtitled "Niagara County Dead," Buffalo, NY, 1947. Military archives files, Ransomville Historical Room, Ransomville, NY. WWII Registry, Navy Department files, National Archives and Records Administration, http://www.wwiimemorial.com/ [accessed June 27, 2008].

Nagebe Fadel and other mothers waited anxiously for their sons to return home. Edmund Fadel served in the Pacific Theatre. (Courtesy Tom Fadel)

PRAYER AT IWO JIMA ~ Marine PFC Edmund L. Fadel was twenty years old serving overseas with the Fourth Marine Division in the Pacific Theater. He was the son of Leo and Nagebe Fadel, Lebanese immigrants. The Fadel family lived at 206 Fifty-Eighth Street in Niagara Falls, New York. On Thursday, March 1, 1945, the *Gazette* carried an AP Wire photo by Joe Rosenthal under the headline: *Falls Marine Prays During Lull in Iwo Battle.* Edmund knelt and prayed the rosary surrounded by the carnage from the Battle at Iwo Jima with two buddies, Pvt. Walter Sokowski and Pvt. Nicholas Z.A. Zingaro, both from Syracuse.[386] Rosenthal's historic photograph of raising the Stars and Stripes was also taken at Iwo Jima on Mount Suribachi, the southern tip of the island.

Intense fighting on the battlefield resulted in substantial casualties on both sides, but in the end the United States gained control of the island and the airfields. Iwo Jima was a strategic site because the airfield allowed the American B-29 bombers to land and refuel on their missions to Japan. Iwo Jima is a volcanic island in the Pacific Ocean about 1,100 km south of Tokyo.

Edmund L. Fadel passed away September 24, 1969.

SERVED WITH DISTINCTION ~ Letters arrived at the Ransomville Post Office that no mother or father wanted to receive. Mrs. Jessie Canfield, RFD #3, Ransomville, NY, received her letter dated October 28, 1944. It was not the first such letter that arrived in Ransomville, nor was it the last.

My dear Mrs. Canfield,

I presume by this time that you have already been officially notified by the War Department that your son Private First Class Lewis G. Canfield, 32670090, Company G 112th Infantry was killed in action while serving in France.

I desire to extend to you my sincerest sympathy together with that of the officers and men of this organization in your hour of bereavement. Your son served with distinction and was a credit to his family, the service, and the United States. He was a splendid soldier and held in high regard by all members of this command. His loss is deeply felt.

I am prohibited by exigencies of the services from disclosing the location of the American military cemetery in which your son is interred, however full information in this respect may be had by writing direct to the Quartermaster Gen., Washington, 25, D.C.

Your son made the extreme sacrifice in order that the families of free men might remain free. Those of us who remain are determined to do everything in our power to achieve the ultimate victory for which he was so heroically striving that he shall not have died in vain.

Most sincerely yours,

Carl L. Peterson, Lt. Col., Infantry, Commanding.[385]

THE HAYS BROTHERS ~ It was a long arduous journey from out west that brought Norman Brownson Hays to Youngstown. In 1915 he became a cowboy and lived in a sod hut on the prairies of Alberta near Calgary. He moved there with his parents from Elizabeth, New Jersey. Four years later he returned briefly to Western New York and married Harriet Sage from Middleport. The newlyweds returned to the ranch in Alberta where Harriet gave birth to Grace, their first child.[387]

The cattle and wheat ranch in Alberta failed, so the family moved with Norman's father and mother, Norman and Florence (neé Brownson) Hays, to Oregon where they remained for several years. Two children, David and Harry, were born there. After several years the Hays family returned east to Gasport, New York, and Norman began his studies at the Rochester School of Optometry. In 1932 Doctor Hays and his family resided in a large brick home and farmed a one hundred acre fruit farm on Church Street in Blairville.[388] Harriet told her daughter, Grace, that at one time it was the summer home of Millard Fillmore, the 13th President of the United States.[389]

Brothers David, Harry, and Paul Hays in front of their home on Church Street, Youngstown, NY. (Courtesy of Lt. Col. James O. Hays, USAF Retired)

Norman and Harriet Hays were the parents of Grace, David, Harry "Brownie," Paul, James "Jim," and Sidney. "While growing up we helped by working on the farm. I remember when we took breaks every hour with my mother and the other women who worked packing prunes. David never took a break; instead, he ran down the road a piece and back. He was in excellent physical condition. I think David was born to be a soldier," Harry said.

"After Pearl Harbor, Brownie and David went to work at Bell Aircraft. David worked at Bell for a month, and then he enlisted to become an air cadet. ("After he got his wings," added Harry.) The doctors discovered a medical problem as a result of childhood typhoid that caused him to lose his hearing at high altitudes, so he re-enlisted and became a glider pilot with the Eighty-second Airborne because gider-glider pilots maintained low altitudes.[390] While David was overseas, a local girl, Jane Service waited back home for him. Jane lived in the village on Lockport Street across from Ken Stevens' house. Her mother, Laura, was my fifth grade teacher," said Jim.

The traditional small banner with blue stars hung on the door of the Hays' home during the war.

Jim was about ten years old when "we used to ride our bikes into the village over to Fort Niagara. There was a sign 'Do not stop under penalty of law!' The soldiers hollered at us when we came near the barbed wire fence," he said. Some German POWs held at Fort Niagara worked on the Hays farm. "They were hired to pick apples and were very pleasant and polite. My mother said that sometimes on a clear night when sound carried she heard the German men singing," Grace said.

"At Christmas time the young people of the Presbyterian and Episcopal churches caroled the POW compound. The prisoners responded with carols of their own. I think both they and we were very touched," Jim said.

In March of 1945 the graphic nature of war was brought to the Hays doorstep. It was the final airborne and glider assault of the war across the Rhine River onto German soil. During *Operation Varsity*, crossing the river on March 24, 1945, "there were almost three thousand airplanes that went over the Rhine that day. David was in the second wave and leader of the second squadron. The gliders landed in the pasture of a dairy farm. The field was crowded with other gliders so David landed on the edge of the pasture. While he and the other three crewmen unloaded a jeep a German soldier came out of the cover of the field with a repeating pistol and shot them all. David was killed. The other crewmen survived their wounds," Harry said. David's co-pilot told the story of what happened that fateful day in a book that Harry read after the war. [David's parents received a letter about what happened. It was different than this account. See *A Mother's Memory*.]

David's brothers all performed some military service. Paul was a torpedo technician in the Navy and served in the Aleutian Islands in the fall of 1943. The battle for the Aleutians was launched simultaneously with the Battle of Midway. Harry, known as Brownie, also worked at Bell Aircraft in the Wheatfield plant riveting wings and then cleaned up on the main assembly line. "Fourteen months later on January 27, 1943, dad dropped Jim and Sid off at the high school and took me to Buffalo to be sworn in."

Harry served in the Army Air Corps for twenty-five months at Tonopah Army Air Base, Nevada, servicing heavy bombardment bombers as part of the west coast defensive units. He was reassigned to the infantry and received training in anticipation of being shipped to Germany. But after a medical detour he was assigned to an anti-aircraft artillery outfit on Iwo Jima in preparation for the invasion when Japan capitulated.

When the news that Hiroshima was bombed reached Youngstown, there were mixed reactions. Ralph Sanderson knocked on the Hays' door with a petition to stop any further use of atomic bombs.[391] "He (Ralph) may have been among the first to understand the power and danger inherent in nuclear weapons. Ralph and my father were good friends and worked together at church."[392] Dr. Hays did not sign the petition; he lost one son and another son, Brownie, was about to storm the beaches of Japan.

David Hays was buried in the WWII Netherlands American Cemetery located in Margraten near the historical city of Maastricht about eleven miles east of the German border. The large monument to all the soldiers reads: "Here we and all who shall hereafter live in freedom will be reminded that to these men and their comrades we owe a debt to be paid with grateful remembrance of their sacrifice and with the high resolve that the cause for which they died shall live." This cemetery is the resting place of more than eight thousand Americans.[393]

David Hays was awarded the Air Medal with Bronze Oak Leaf Cluster, the Purple Heart, the Presidential Unit Citation, the American Campaign Medal, the European-African-Middle Eastern Campaign Medal with one Bronze Arrow Head for initial assault troops, plus one silver and two bronze battle stars on this medal, and the WWII Victory Medal.

David's brother, Sidney, was drafted into the Army in 1957 and served as a Chaplain's assistant until May 1958 when he received an honorable discharge to accept a commission as a second lieutenant reserve commissioned officer. He served in various medical clinics as an optometrist and was granted another honorable discharge on August 31, 1964.

Jim, motivated by the service and sacrifice of his brother David, served in Vietnam and in peacetime. Jim flew 225 combat missions in Vietnam in the A1E aircraft[394] and retired at the grade of Lieutenant Colonel in 1973.

A MOTHER'S MEMORY ~ Years after the war Harriet Hays wrote her memoirs of those fragile days. It began with a story of her eldest child Grace's wedding. "The bride was lovely in a long dress with a long train." A year later, David and Brownie graduated from high school and went to work at Bell Aircraft. "The country was under great tension because of the war in Europe, and the plant was making all the planes possible for Great Britain."[395]

Harriet's memoirs continued with her memories of the outbreak of the war.

Pearl Harbor came that fall and the country was shocked. I remember the dreadful news coming over the radio that Sunday afternoon and felt a premonition of personal loss...Soon David applied for pilot's training in the (Army) Air Force. In a few days he was gone. He enjoyed it and did well until he had an ear infection and was grounded and dismissed. He im-

mediately enlisted for glider pilot training. He did well at this and was one of only two in his class who received commissions.

We went to New York to see him off to Great Britain. He was killed on the push into Germany in 1944[396]*...I find it difficult to write about this time...First we received word that David was missing in action. This was almost more distressing than the actual news of his death. There had been so many harrowing reports of the German prison camps, and my imagination ran wild...An officer friend of David's wrote us later to tell us what happened. The gliders were flying in equipment and had an assigned area in which to land. David was one of the last in and had to land outside* (the area). *When he landed and attempted to dig in, he was shot by a girl sniper from a nearby barn. Later she was found and killed.*

After David went into the service, Brownie continued to work on airplanes until he was drafted into the Army Air Corps. He had his basic training at Miami Beach, and then was shipped by train to Denver.[397] *The coaches were old ones with hard, wicker seats, and the men could not lie down for five days. Being six feet one inch tall didn't help Brownie any...before being sent to the Pacific arena he was in Washington, D.C.,*[398] *for a bit, and we visited him there. It was a very difficult time, so soon after the news of David's death, to have another son going overseas.*

As I remember, he was sent to Okinawa[399] *but on the way over they received the wonderful news that Japan had surrendered. We had three sons serving in the services all at the same time. Paul joined the Navy immediately after graduation from high school. After training as a torpedo technician, he was sent to the Aleutians. The only enemy he encountered there was the extreme cold and loneliness. When the war was over he returned home and entered Niagara University.*

My only contribution to the war effort was knitting, rolling bandages and hosting at the USO Fort Niagara, adjacent to Youngstown, was an active military post at that time and made the need for a USO great. This was an enlistment post and we saw many boys already homesick.

There was a group of German prisoners held at Fort Niagara. Under armed guard, they were allowed to go out and help the farmers, farm help being very scarce with so many men in the service. We had several such groups of prisoners work on our farm. A funny incident happened when we had the prisoners helping. At least, it is funny now. They were working in the garden beside the house. On the porch there was a gallon bottle containing a rooting solution I had been using to transplant seedlings. Later I discovered that the prisoners drank it. I was very disturbed and was relieved when there was no report of illness among them the next day.

We were close enough to the camp so that we could hear them singing in the evening. It was a lovely sound floating on the night air. I believe most of them were glad to be out of the fighting.

Harry Hays added another entertaining story of the POWs. "While they were picking fruit, there were usually one or two guards. On one occasion the guard fell asleep under the fruit tree. The prisoners took his weapon and hid it, then went back to picking. When the guard woke up, he was fit to be tied. The prisoners were obviously happy to be in the United States."

Harriet's *Memoirs* continued with stories of the rationing:

I have not mentioned the rationing of food, gas, and many other things. Living on a farm, food was not a problem to us. Sugar was in short supply, but we learned to substitute honey even in baking. If one was careful, the gas was plentiful enough for necessary trips. One of the things I did find it difficult to get was hose. If a store got a supply in, immediately a line of people formed at the door. Paint came on the market to use on one's legs to make them look as if one was wearing hose. All of this part of life was definitely linked to the war effort.[400]

PHOTO RECONNAISSANCE ~ The heritage of the aerospace industry and Bell Aircraft is treasured locally. Pat smiled as he looked up from his work on the wing of the Curtiss Jenny. Patrick A. Geelan is part of the Niagara Vintage Aircraft Restoration Group, which volunteers at the Niagara Aerospace Museum.[401] Evidence of Western New York's rich aviation history surrounded Pat in the aircraft displayed on the second floor of the Museum.

Pat graduated from LaSalle High School in 1938 and went to work at Moore Business Forms. History was about to repeat itself in the Geelan family. Pat's parents were part of the British fight against Germany during WWI. Pat was about to embark on fighting the Germans during the next war.[402]

Thomas Geelan, Pat's father, served in the Irish Regiment of the British Army. He was captured by the Germans and became a prisoner of war. Caroline, Pat's mother, told her son that his father kept his sanity in the POW camp by knitting. Thomas, like many others, never spoke about the war. His wife, Caroline, grew up in Hertford, England. She lost a brother during the war and did not hide her antipathy for the Germans because of her brother's death.

Pat became part of a unique effort to fight the Germans during WWII. He was drafted in July 1942 and inducted at Fort Niagara. He was at Fort Niagara for a week or two then assigned to the Army Air Corps. He trained in Miami Beach, which sounded glamorous, but Pat noted that at that time, "Miami was nothing but sand dunes." His military preparation included studying electronics and electrical power systems.

Pat was a member of the 827th Air Engineering Squadron, part of the Seventh Photo Reconnaissance Group in the Eighth Air Force. The squadron was stationed at Mount Farm Airfield in England. Pat worked on the maintenance of the electrical systems of the P-38s, also known as F5s. There were four squadrons with fifteen airplanes each. He began to explain the work of photo reconnaissance groups. The P-38s were built at Lockheed in California. They were one of the fastest airplanes used during the war. The airplanes used for photo reconnaissance missions had no armament and two to five large automatic cameras in the nose. Photographic intelligence was vital to the air and ground combat operations. The P-38 was an unconventional design in 1937 and was extensively modified prior to its use in combat.

TABLE 7.12
Specifications P-38L

Span	52 ft.
Length	37 ft. 10 in.
Height	12 ft. 10 in.
Weight	17,500 lbs. loaded
Armament	Four .50-cal. Machine guns and one 20 mm cannon
Engines	Two Allison V-1710s of 1,475 hp each
Cost	$115,000
Maximum speed	414 mph
Cruising speed	275 mph
Range	1,100 mi.
Service Ceiling	40,000 ft.

Source: Reprinted by permission from the National Museum United States Air Force, "Lockheed P-38 Lightning," http://www.nationalmuseum.af.mil/factsheets/factsheet.asp?id=495 [accessed April 18, 2008].

The photo reconnaissance missions captured the images and details of the German military and industrial installations. Sometimes the missions were unsuccessful due to weather or German fighters, which forced the squadron to return. The signal that the mission was a success was the sound of the P-38 at 300 mph buzzing the airfield! Pat chuckled, telling about how one pilot flew so low that he took part of the roof off the main building.

The first American photo mission was on March 28, 1943. The cameras took nine-inch square prints developed from one hundred to two hundred feet rolls of film. The images were usually taken at about 25,000 feet. The missions averaged 1,400 miles round trip. In addition to identifying key targets, the film covered the movement of enemy troops. There were about one million photographs taken across enemy territory throughout Europe and into Russia.[403] The cameras captured the city of Bremen and Nuremburg, the railroad marshalling yards at Ulm, factories at Fallersleben, the refineries at Misburg, the bridges at Cologne and Frankfurt-am-Main, and the airfields at Hesepe near Hanover. The Seventh Photo Group was the main source of intelligence for the Eighth Air Force. Heavy bomber attacks followed that wreaked havoc on the targets of the earlier photo missions. The P-38s returned after the bombing raids and navigated through the Luftwaffe to document the destruction of the targets.[404]

There were air raid alerts at the base in England, but "we were never attacked," Pat said. "Most nights we went to the pubs in town on bicycles that we bought ourselves. But the night before VE day we knew something was up. We were restricted to the base. White stripes were painted on the wings and around the fuselage of all the planes for identification purposes. Eisenhower ordered the stripes on all Allied planes too. He knew that Germany had captured some of our planes, so any plane without the stripes was considered an enemy."

Back home on May 2, 1945, front page headlines in the news proclaimed the last leg of the war in Europe: "British Nearing Luebeck...Berlin Garrison Split...Allies within Nine Miles of Cutting Off Denmark...Nazi Chancellery Stormed...Million Germans Surrender...Allied Campaign in Italy Drawing Rapidly to End...Doenitz Believed Moving Toward Last-Ditch Fight In Norway, and 1,207 Vehicles Destroyed by RAF."

Pat's unit returned to the United States at Norfolk, Virginia. Before their discharge, they were surprised when German POWs served their meals. Pat completed his honorable military career in October 1945. The Seventh Photo Group's story acknowledged the coordinated effort of weathermen who predicted holes in the clouds hundreds of miles away, the mechanics and camera repairmen; and all the related personnel that in some way contributed to the photographs which were an integral and important part of military intelligence that helped to bring an end to the war.

THE COMBAT ENGINEERS' purpose during the war was to build bridges, roads, and prefabricated buildings such as hospitals. They also cleared and removed mines and booby traps, and demolished damaged buildings, tall smoke stacks (enemy observation points), and pill boxes (fortifications). Sgt. Richard Byron was the "1st Squad leader (1st Platoon Company A) of the 171st Engineer Combat Battalion of the 13th Corps. The 171st was on the north flank of the Ninth Army in Europe."[405]

The Allied side of the Town of Linnich in the background was photographed sometime after Christmas 1944. The infantry support bridge and assault boats on the Roer River were damaged at night when two Messerschmidts, German fighter aircraft, attacked just missing Richard Byron. (Courtesy Richard Byron)

After a year at Rensselaer Polytechnic Institute (RPI) studying aeronautical engineering, Richard enlisted in the Army Reserves and became Active Duty and did eighteen grueling weeks of basic training at Camp Fannin near Tyler, Texas. Richard heard Walter Winchell's radio broadcast report that "Camp Fannin made the Marines Paris Island look like a Girl Scout camp!" Basic engineering training followed at St. Bonaventure University in Olean, New York, for a semester, and then it was on to Camp Carson in Colorado and the 104th Infantry Division pre-overseas training. At Camp Carson he was transferred to the 171st Engineer Combat Battalion.

The point of embarkation (POE) was New York City. On August 11, 1944, Richard and other soldiers boarded the *U.S.S. Hermitage.* "It was a former Italian luxury liner called the '*Conte Biancamano*.' It weighed twenty-five thousand tons and was then the twenty-third largest ship afloat. Fourteen days later they arrived in Liverpool, England. The first two weeks were spent chasing equipment and meeting the British. Then it was on to Southampton. "We built two bridges for practice over the Thames River at Henley."

At Southampton, Richard and about two hundred other soldiers boarded another ship. "We crossed the channel (English Channel) in less than a day aboard a Liberty ship and dropped anchor on the sixteenth at 2030 hours. The channel was like a pool table. We waited there for six days through air attacks and storms. The beach area was choked with ammunition and troops. Finally, it was our turn to get off," Richard said. It was September 23, 1944, on Utah Beach in France, a few months after D-Day.

About ten days later the platoon was split up and moved out on four trains. They traveled through France to Belgium. Richard's squad was assigned to guard a train while riding and living in a boxcar. While stopped at the rail yards they found some of the cars being cut out of the trains in the First Army area. "Patton's men were taking the cars with tanks and gasoline for the Third Army. Patton gloried in his publicity. Gen. Omar Bradley was top notch though and of course, General Eisenhower was great." Richard had no love for Gen. George S. Patton.

Richard's battalion was assigned to the 84th Division's 333rd Regimental Combat Team on November 16, 1944; on November 22 the battalion went with the 113th Cavalry Group, and on December 21 with the 102nd Infantry Division. During this time the engineers laid mines and trip flares. The trip flares were in front of the infantry units. He said that "in an attack, we could guide the infantry through the German mine fields and ours, cutting paths."

It was part of a typical scenario during the war for Richard and the combat engineers. "An urgent call at 0430 came from Company C of the First Battalion 333rd Infantry: attacking pillboxes of Siegfried Line, need Flame Thrower Team, having trouble. The Platoon leader is 1st Lt. Ed Greenan. He calls Sgt. Richard Byron, First Squadron Leader: 'Quick, grab a flamethrower and a satchel (20 lbs.) charge (TNT) - meet me at my jeep (with two men).' I take Tech. John R. 'Catfish' Smith and Pvt. Bob Beers. We jump into the jeep; Lieutenant G. drives. We streak down a road to a point near the infantry position. Incoming fire is too intense. We stop under enemy fire and hit the ground then leap up and run, then crawl toward our objective. The flame gun weighs eighty pounds and the satchel charge another twenty pounds. I felt as if the flamethrower was a big target strapped to my back. When the fight started, an infantryman hit the ground only a few yards from the pillbox embrasure. I

These images depict part of the mammoth undertaking to cross the Rhine River, the focal point for the invasion into Germany. The engineers constructed bridges to replace those destroyed by the retreating German forces. (Both photos courtesy Richard Byron)

couldn't squirt flame without frying him. In desperation he pulled the pin of a hand grenade, waited for the krauts to open the embrasure and lobbed the grenade into the opening, killing five and wounding ten or twelve. The rest escaped through an emergency exit."[406]

Richard continued, "While Lieutenant Ed got together with the infantry Company Commander, Al, we three went into the relative shelter of an adjoining gravel pit. I set down the flame-thrower and we talked over tackling the second pillbox. Then came (German) mortar fire. The second round hit close, a large piece of shell hit me in the back. I was numbed. Catfish, at my elbow, was hit, breaking his collarbone. A second fragment pierced his lower back, an eighth of an inch from his spinal cord. He had no feeling from the wound."

"Beers was not hit, but Catfish was uncharacteristically whimpering. I got up the nerve to feel my back. My field jacket wasn't torn! I cut Catfish's jacket away and used his wound packet (sulfanilamide powder) to bandage his shoulder and my packet for his other wound. The flame-thrower, standing upright, had been drilled by shrapnel and knocked flat, producing a twenty-foot geyser of jellied gasoline. Luckily, it requires a flame to ignite the stuff. The Germans left the larger pillbox retreating to new positions. Then, we…moved in." Many infantry troops moved in with the engineers. Richard explained, "When the battle was over, the infantry officers set up defensive positions on the top of the bluff. The pillbox was pretty full and Beers was sent with several other men to carry five or six wounded to the rear. Lieutenant Greenan left me there while he made his way back to the company for orders. Meanwhile, I was cold. I put my field jacket on Catfish. I found a dead GI outside the box, killed by a shell explosion. I took off his new unmarked field jacket. It was very difficult, as rigor mortis had set in. He was a good soldier and had a new, unused pair of socks in his pocket!"

"Lieutenant Eddie came back soon with orders for us to stay until no longer needed. He also brought the latest mail, a fruitcake from my mother. There were thirty-nine of us in the pillboxes. We cut the cake into thirty-nine pieces. The other piece of mail I received was a 'Dear John' letter from the holder of my fraternity pin! Later that night as Lieutenant Ed and I set out to return to our company there was a falling mortar shell and then another. The five-centimeter projectiles landed harmlessly less than half a dozen yards away in a patch of mud. They surely would have killed us," said Richard.

Christmas, December 25, 1944, was celebrated in the field. The dinner of creamed turkey was brought out in a weapons carrier. One of the soldiers found a lone piece of turkey in the cream sauce. "He held it up and the group cheered," Richard said.

Pontoon Bridges have been used extensively throughout history to provide temporary river crossings. (Courtesy Richard Byron)

The Roer River operation began February 5, 1945. It required construction of a footbridge, two infantry support bridges, and one treadway bridge for the tanks. It took five attempts to build the footbridge before the Ninth Army was able to cross the river. The surging currents of the river and mortar hits wreaked havoc during the construction attempts. One of the infantry support bridges was bombed out during the night. "We built another infantry support-bridge the next morning. At the end of that day two Me262s attacked, tried to destroy the bridges, but missed. I was on one bridge, watching them dive in and drop one bomb each and climb away."[407] The *Stars and Stripes* (Liege Edition) covered the crossing and described it as an "Engineer's Nightmare."[408]

The Ninth Tactical Air Force P-47Ds, Republic Thunderbolts, provided most of the air support for the operations. Once in a while when a German Tiger Tank threw 88mm fire the Thunderbolts appeared overhead and went into a 45-degree dive. Their machine guns and five hundred pound bombs destroyed the tanks.[409]

TABLE 7.13
Specifications P-47D Thunderbolt

Span	40 ft. 9 in.
Length	36 ft. 2 in.
Height	14 ft. 8 in.
Weight	17,500 lbs. maximum
Armament	Eight .50-cal machine guns; generally carried one or two 500 lb. bombs
Engine	One Pratt & Whitney R-2800 of 2,430 hp
Crew	One
Cost	$85,000
Maximum speed	433 mph
Cruising speed	350 mph
Range	Approx. 1,100 mi. with drop tanks
Service ceiling	42,000 ft.

Source: Reprinted by permission from the National Museum of the USAF, Fact Sheets, Republic P-47 Thunderbolt, http://www.nationalmuseum.af.mil/factsheets/factsheet_print.asp?fsID=520&page=1 [accessed March 6, 2008]. Richard Byron added the number of bombs.

The crossing of the Rhine River, Operation Flashpoint, was an extensive production. There was a parade of semi-trailer trucks carrying pontoons, timbers, tanks, and landing craft. The 171st was assigned the rear half of the bridge and to join their bridge sections with those built by the 1253rd Engineer Bridge Battalion. Construction began on March 24, 1945, at 0800 hours. The Rhine operation was the largest concentration of anti-aircraft fire since the Normandy landing.[410]

"After we crossed the Rhine the Ninth Army was placed under the command of Gen. Bernard Montgomery of the British Second Army during the rapid movement to the Elbe River. It was termed *The Rat Race*." Air support was from the RAF Hawker Typhoon fighter-bombers using rockets.[411] On March 25, 1945, at 0100 hours the bridge was completed and the Fifth Armored Division and the Eighty-Fourth Infantry Division began crossing the Rhine at Wesel rolling into the heart of Germany.[412]

There was occasional opposition as the troops moved through Langenhagen, Hanover, and Stendal, toward the Elbe River. Along the way the engineers made minor road and bridge repairs, and removed mines and booby traps. There were frequent attacks of ground strafing and bombing by Focke-Wulf, FW-190 fighter-bombers. "At the same time we watched the thousand plane raids of Boeing B-17s and Consolidated B-24s heading deep into Germany," Richard said.

"We were stopped at the Elbe River about sixty-five kilometers from Berlin and received orders to halt and prevent German soldiers from crossing the river to surrender to us. Our forces could have taken Berlin," he said with disappointment. Earlier, the Allies agreed at the Yalta Conference to let the Russians take Berlin.

Almost immediately the troops went into occupation duty. In their wool uniforms, standing with a Tommy gun "we kept German hausfraus in line for the food supplies!" Richard's skin allergy, aggravated by the wool uniforms, long johns, and his sleeping bag, caught up with him. Since their last fight in Germany was over, he went to the battalion surgeon, who previously wanted to hospitalize Richard at the beginning of his combat time. The surgeon immediately ordered Richard to be sent to the hospital. He arrived in Paris via a C-47 to be treated at the 198th General Hospital. It was a large building about nine stories high. "On VE day I was on the sun roof of the hospital. Music was playing. Nurses were bringing food. Down in the streets there were big snake dances and a few airplanes flew under the Eiffel Tower. Everything went crazy!"

After VE Day Richard was released from the hospital and sent back into Germany. It was a month later before he caught up to his unit in Paris. "Our unit was slated to be shipped out to Japan. We were proclaimed: experienced combat troops, not battle exhausted. We were to knock out beach obstacles in the assault on the main island of Honshu.[413] The estimate of American and Japanese casualties for the initial assault and invasion was about four million. "It would have been suicide. Then the A-bomb was dropped. The fire bomb raids on Tokyo were more devastating than the two atomic bombs." Richard emphasized that Truman's decision to drop the atomic bombs saved lives.

Richard examined the present state of the world and his concerns over the gradual destruction of our natural resources, the unraveling of the conservation works of President Theodore Roosevelt, and the world issue of overpopulation. Part of what Richard fought to protect, he sees being destroyed. Richard Byron is the Curator and Senior Historian for the Ira G. Ross Aerospace Museum opened temporarily in the HSBC Arena, Buffalo, New York, formally Niagara Aerospace Museum in Niagara Falls, New York.

THE ZERO HOUR ~ Pfc. Herbert Allen, the son of Mr. and Mrs. Jim L. Allen, was stationed in New Guinea. Jim Allen grew peaches, apples, cherries, and pears on his fruit farm on Lake Road in the Town of Porter. His peach trees produced as much as 3,000 bushels per year. The Allen family wintered in St. Petersburg, Florida, in 1944 while Mr. Allen was working on the new construction of the Florida Power Plant as an operating engineer. Herb wrote to his parents in a letter from New Guinea dated December 31, 1943, about the Japanese radio program called *Zero Hour.* The live broadcasts were intended to demoralize the troops fighting in the Pacific through intimidating commentary and playing songs like *I'll be Home for Christmas.* Herb's letter said that the radio feature had the opposite effect and bolstered the American soldiers' spirits.[414]

LETTER FROM THE FRONT ~ Roderick "Rod" Tower leafed through a box of old letters at the dining room table in his home on Lutts Road in Youngstown. One was from a friend Lt. David S. Hays dated "December 23, 1944 France. It was probably the last letter David Hays wrote before being killed. He was a glider pilot and in the class behind me at the high school. David was killed in Holland or Belgium," Rod said.[415]

Hello Roddy,

How's the big game hunter I have been doing a little of that myself. The game being wild boar, deer and Germans that haven't given up. The only boar I have seen so far is one a French man (Frog to us) caught in a snare. He only weighed about 120 lbs.

Their is plenty of tracks of boar and deer but they are hard to find. I have flown over Paris a lot of times. I prefere Brussels to it and I still have a girl back home I wouldn't trade for all the girls over here.

Well I have important report to get off. Got to keep her happy.

Your Friend, David Hays[416]

There was another yellowed letter written in German. Its fading ink told a familiar story of gratitude for an American farm family and the difficulties of post-war Germany. "After the war John and Nelson (Tower) had a German couple work for them. The wife translated the letters for us," Rod said.

Liebe familie Tower:

First, I would like to convey to you most cordial greetings from my home country. It is with great joy to inform you that I got your letter dated February 19, 1948. We were very happy to receive this letter and are happy to hear that you are all healthy. If I may ask, who wrote

POWs in front of Rod Tower's farmhouse October 5, 1945. From left to right, written on the photo: "Emil ~ carpenter ~ August 1 month John's barn very good worker, Arno June ~ 23 ~ May ~ fast worker, August Weiss ~ March best worker ~ leader farmer, Walter Krell ~ July ~ is okay, August Kleigreve ~ April ~ good worker ~ very happy go lucky ~ farmer." (Courtesy Roderick Tower)

the letter in German to us? It is written very nicely, and I assume that this person can read my letter as well. Also, I would not like to fail to congratulate Rod on his little boy. Dear Family Tower, now I would like to tell you why I have left the United States and when I was released as a prisoner of war. We left the U.S. on March 6, 1946 and arrived in Belgium on March 17. We stayed there for 8 weeks and we assumed that we would get released from there, but instead we had to go to England where I stayed for the remainder of my prisonership. We left England on Nov. 15 and on Nov. 20, 1947 we were finally free in Germany after 3-1/2 years as a Prisoner of War. I will never forget this time in my life.

Dear Family Tower, I have often thought about you and about the time I spent with you and I must say again and again that I have found a very good and friendly family in you, which helped me forget quite often that I was a prisoner of war. That is the reason why I thank you with my letter for all the good, which you did to me and for the time, which I lived with you. I believe that you as well might have been satisfied with me. I have told my relatives quite a lot about you and how friendly you were and that I found such a good farmer and I can only say good things about you and what I saw in the U.S.

Dear Family Tower, now I would like to tell you how things are at my home. I was not allowed to see my father again, as he died on January 17, 1947 while I was a prisoner of

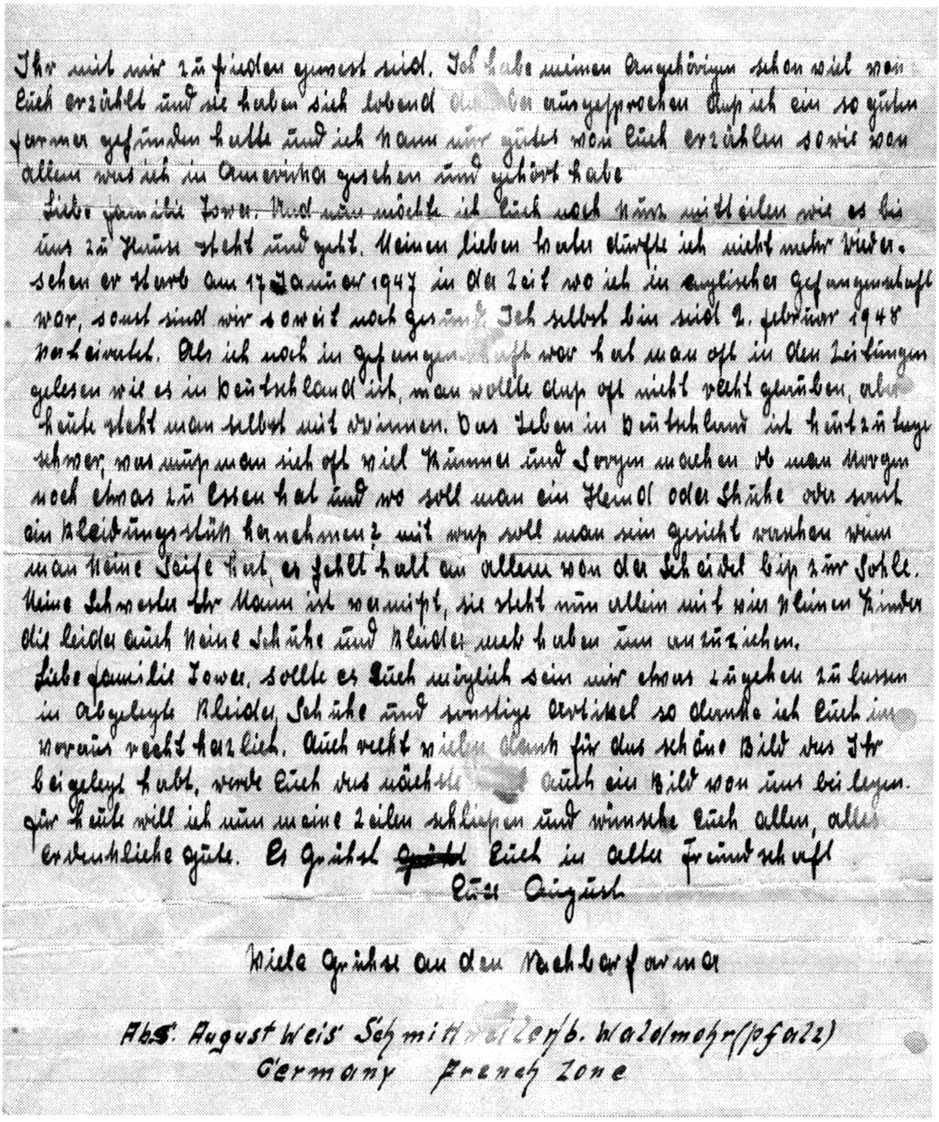

Ihr mit mir zufrieden gewesen seid. Ich habe meinen Angehörigen schon viel von
Euch erzählt und sie haben sich lobend darüber ausgesprochen daß ich ein so guten
farmer gefunden hatte und ich kann nur gutes von Euch erzählen sowie von
allem was ich in Amerika gesehen und gehört habe
Liebe familie Tower. Und nun möchte ich Euch noch kurz mitteilen wie es bei
uns zu Hause steht und geht. Meinen lieben Vater durfte ich nicht mehr wieder-
sehen er starb am 17 Januar 1947 in der Zeit wo ich in englischer Gefangenschaft
war, sonst sind wir soweit noch gesund. Ich selbst bin seit 2. Februar 1948
verheiratet. Als ich noch in Gefangenschaft war hat man oft in den Zeitungen
gelesen wie es in Deutschland ist, man wollte das oft nicht recht glauben, aber
heute steht man selbst mit drinnen. Das Leben in Deutschland ist heutzutage
schwer, was muß man sich oft viel Kummer und Sorgen machen ob man Morgen
noch etwas zu essen hat und wo soll man ein Hemd oder Schuhe oder sonst
ein Kleidungsstück hernehmen? mit was soll man sein Gesicht waschen wenn
man keine Seife hat, es fehlt halt an allem von der Scheitel bis zur Sohle.
Meine Schwester ihr Mann ist vermißt, sie steht nun allein mit vier kleinen Kinder
die leider auch keine Schuhe und Kleider mehr haben zum anzuziehen.
Liebe familie Tower, sollte es Euch möglich sein mir etwas zugehen zu lassen
in abgelegte Kleider, Schuhe und sonstige Artikel so danke ich Euch im
voraus recht herzlich. Auch recht vielen Dank für das schöne Bild das Ihr
beigelegt habt, werde Euch das nächste mal auch ein Bild von uns beilegen.
Für heute will ich nun meine Zeilen schließen und wünsche Euch allen, alles
erdenkliche Gute. Es grüßt ~~grüßt~~ Euch in alter Freundschaft
Euer August

Viele Grüße an den Nachbarfarmer

Abs: August Weis Schmittweiler b. Waldmohr (Pfalz)
Germany French Zone

Letter written by a former POW to the Tower family. (Courtesy Roderick Tower) *war in England. Otherwise we are doing well. I, myself, married on February 2, 1948. As I was a prisoner of war, I read quite often accounts in newspapers how it was in Germany at that time, which I had a hard time believing, but now I'm in the middle of it myself. Life in Germany is pretty difficult now a days and we have to struggle a lot and never know if we will have something to eat tomorrow or where we will get a shirt or shoes or other clothing. How shall you wash your face if you don't have any soap? We are missing everything from head to toe. My brother-in-law is still missing in action. My sister is all by herself with 4 little children who also have neither shoes nor clothing to wear.*

Dear Family Tower, in case it would be possible to send some second hand clothes, shoes and other articles, I would be greatly appreciated. I would like to thank you in advance for that. Many thanks for the nice photo you have included in your letter. Next time I will also try to send a photo of myself. For now, I would like to close and wish you all the best and old friendship.

Sincerely yours

Many greetings also to the farmers in your neighborhood.

"Two of the men were farmers in Germany and were very good workers on the farm," Rod said. "They trimmed trees, picked fruit, and did anything we needed. We couldn't speak German, but were able to communicate. The POWs were from Jack Hosmer's group. He took five; we had four; and one, Emil, helped build John Tower's chicken barn with Frank Jeffrey and his father. There was only one problem while they worked on the farm. We were supposed to get the POWs back to Fort Niagara, but couldn't find the guard. He was asleep under a fruit tree!"

There was only one atypical day while the prisoners worked on the farm. Rod heard the men yelling something in German, but he didn't understand. The prisoners pointed to the sky. It was a jet.

The last letter to the Tower family went unanswered. "When we found out about what the Germans did to the Jews in the camps, we stopped writing." As the years passed, "We learned more about what happened during the war once there was television" from the History Channel, Rod said.

SUPREME HEADQUARTERS ALLIED EXPEDITIONARY FORCE (SHAEF) was the headquarters of the Commander of Allied Forces in northwest Europe from late 1943 until the end of WWII. Gen. Dwight D. Eisenhower was in command of SHAEF during the war. Frank V. Nicolette, who grew up in the heart of the Italian section of the city of Niagara Falls near St. Joseph's Roman Catholic Church, became a part of SHAEF under Eisenhower.

Frank's parents lost their home during the depression and never owned an automobile. But Frank found enjoyment as he played sandlot football, softball, and basketball. He worked one summer as a pin-sticker at the bowling alley at the old Fort Niagara Beach, and in the city Frank held a job as a shoeshine boy on Pine Avenue. He carried his box from Nineteenth to Fourteenth Street, earning about ten cents a shine plus tips, sold newspapers on the busy intersection of Nineteenth Street and Pine Avenue, and worked for farmers at the City Market. While in high school, Frank worked part-time at Walter's Radio Shop on Nineteenth Street.[417]

He was born on June 21, 1922, in his grandparents' home on Twentieth Street in the city of Niagara Falls. His given name, Frank, was for his paternal grandfather, Francesco, and his middle name for the Italian statesman, Vittorio Orlando. Orlando was the prime minister of Italy during the later part of WWI. During the peace negotiations in Paris following the war, Orlando left the conference and resigned after failing to acquire expected territorial concessions, particularly the Town of Fiume, for Italy.[418]

Frank was a bank teller at Niagara County Savings Bank making $70.00 a month and working part-time at the Liberty Shoe Store, which was two stores north of Lincoln Place on the west side of Main Street. Frank and his high school sweetheart, Marie Marillo, married on April 14, 1942, at Sacred Heart Church, Niagara Falls, New York. Several months later, registration began for the draft and in October, Frank was drafted.

He received his uniform at Fort Niagara and resided in the temporary barracks on October 6, 1942, as he began active duty. From Fort Niagara to the railroad station in Niagara Falls, Frank's group left for Camp Crowder in Neosho, Missouri, about twenty miles from Joplin in the Ozark Mountain Region. "I was appointed the assistant group leader and was only twenty years old. It was an exciting time," Frank said.

At Crowder the training included picking up rocks from one side of the road and carrying them to the other side. Frank was hospitalized during the training while his group was sent to the Pacific. When he was discharged from the hospital Frank began his "career" of volunteering. "When the Camp Officers asked for volunteers to work in the office I raised my hand and became part of Cadre, assigned as an instructor, and taught typing. This was in the Signal Corps." One of the essential roles of the Signal Corps was the coordination and operation of communication systems. A friend from home, Vincent "Jim" Del Zoppo, ar-

TUESDAY, JUNE 6TH, 1944

SUPREME HEADQUARTERS
ALLIED EXPEDITIONARY FORCE

Soldiers, Sailors and Airmen of the Allied Expeditionary Force!

You are about to embark upon the Great Crusade, toward which we have striven these many months. The eyes of the world are upon you. The hopes and prayers of liberty-loving people everywhere march with you. In company with our brave Allies and brothers-in-arms on other Fronts, you will bring about the destruction of the German war machine, the elimination of Nazi tyranny over the oppressed peoples of Europe, and security for ourselves in a free world.

Your task will not be an easy one. Your enemy is well trained, well equipped and battle-hardened. He will fight savagely.

But this is the year 1944! Much has happened since the Nazi triumphs of 1940-41. The United Nations have inflicted upon the Germans great defeats, in open battle, man-to-man. Our air offensive has seriously reduced their strength in the air and their capacity to wage war on the ground. Our Home Fronts have given us an overwhelming superiority in weapons and munitions of war, and placed at our disposal great reserves of trained fighting men. The tide has turned! The free men of the world are marching together to Victory!

I have full confidence in your courage, devotion to duty and skill in battle. We will accept nothing less than full Victory!

Good Luck! And let us all beseech the blessing of Almighty God upon this great and noble undertaking.

Dwight Eisenhower

General Eisenhower's letter to the Allied troops just prior to the Normandy invasion. (Courtesy Frank Nicolette)

Frank Nicolette and his brother Louis reunited in Germany. (Courtesy Frank Nicolette)

rived at Crowder and became Frank's student. Other friends from the neighborhood also passed through the camp including Paul Colosi, Guido Gravino, Joe Basile, and Albert Proetti.

Orders came in January of 1944 for Frank to go to Camp Shenango in Greenville, Pennsylvania, to prepare for duty in England. From Pennsylvania, the troops went to Brooklyn, New York, to board a Liberty ship. Frank was "one year, four months, and one day" in the states before being shipped overseas on February 26, 1944. There was a strong north Atlantic storm and the ship was damaged. "We put in at Halifax, Nova Scotia, and were stuck there for a week or so. We were given ten hours off and I called my wife who was working at Wellesley's in Niagara Falls. Our call was cut off before I could tell her where we were," remembering that their telephone calls were monitored and their mail was censored.

A cargo ship carried the group of seventy-five enlisted men, fifteen officers, and the ship's crew across the Atlantic. The ship also transported military vehicles. "It was very rough on the ocean. You kept your life jacket on. The food was lousy, so I volunteered to work in the kitchen hoping to get something better to eat. We ate better than the captain," and he smiled remembering the first time he ate shrimp. When they arrived in England on March 30, 1944, Frank was assigned to the military government pool. Again he volunteered, and this time became part of the European Civil Affairs Division Headquarters in Manchester.

"My job as Personnel Technician was to keep track of officers' specialties. This was critical when assisting the occupied countries. For a time I was in London at the YMCA. The air-raid siren sounded and a loud explosion shook the building. London had just been hit by a buzz bomb."[419]

On D-Day the huge air armadas filled the sky as part of the invasion force headed towards Normandy. At the time Frank saw the bombers making their runs, he wondered what was happening. "About a month after D-Day we were in France keeping track of assignments and other records. We were initially quartered in tents and stationed in Troyes as part of the occupation.[420] In July I remember reading in the *Stars and Stripes* about the bomb assassination attempt on Hitler."

While in France, Frank prepared the assignments of officers for the occupation of various towns and villages, as they were recaptured from the Germans. During this time the Corazzi family befriended Frank. The Corazzis moved to France after the First World War and were excited because Frank could speak a little Italian.

Another relationship formed during the war was with the Foster family in Manchester, England. Mr. and Mrs. James Foster, and their twelve-year old daughter Patricia met Frank in church. He visited the family whenever he could and later returned on a furlough to England while stationed in France. The Foster family often wrote to Frank's wife, and after the war Frank and Marie's first child, was given the name Patricia in honor of the friendship with the Foster family.[421]

"After Christmas we went to Germany. It was the beginning of 1945 and the last big offensive. There was a lot of destruction in Aachen and many of the other German cities. I saw the people picking out food scraps and bones from our garbage. Our officer wouldn't let us give the Germans food. We did not know about what happened in the concentration camps at that time. While we were in Germany, I was able to access information to find out where my younger brother, Louis, was located. I surprised him and we met twice in

SHAEF headquarters in Frankfurt, Germany. (Courtesy Frank Nicolette)

Germany. When the war ended in May and our division broke up, I was reassigned to SHAEF in Eisenhower's headquarters in Frankfurt, Germany. I saw Eisenhower once, but only at a distance. After the war ended, I was offered a direct commission. When my commanding officer gave me a Bronze Star Medal, he asked why I didn't take the commission. I told him, I want to go home."

Frank served "one year, nine months, and fourteen days overseas" prior to arriving stateside on December 9, 1945. Five days later he separated from service at Fort Dix, New Jersey, and continued his education after the war through the G.I. Bill receiving his BBA Degree in Accounting in May of 1953 from Niagara University after seven years in night school.[422] He retired in 1984 as the Executive Vice-President and Secretary of the Niagara County Savings Bank.[423] He has taught Management, Money and Banking, and Mortgage courses part-time at Niagara University and Niagara Community College.

Frank proudly held his treasured citation for the Bonze Star Medal which he received for "meritorious service in connection with military operations as Chief Personnel Technician, G-1 Section, European Civil Affairs Division, from 22 September 1944 to 8 May 1945," as he began to speak about his military service. The citation noted his attention to duty and work beyond normal duty hours, and establishment of an exemplary accurate record system that was regularly referred to by higher headquarters in order to obtain current personnel statistics.

He examined his experiences and military service to pass on life lessons to the present generation. "Don't be naive, things are not always what they appear to be. Think things out and don't jump to conclusions. Be informed and do the best you can with what you have." He concluded that "the war and my military service made me a better person. I feel so grateful and proud."

THE MIRACULOUS MEDAL ~ Rick Penzotti graduated from Niagara Falls High School in June 1943 with a diploma in one hand and an induction notice in the other. His parents came to Niagara Falls in 1927 from Rossiter, Pennsylvania, looking for work.[424]

Rick's military history was part of the scenes from movies like *Saving Private Ryan* and *Band of Brothers*, but now his personal images and memories of death and pain are private. Before he left home, Rick's sister, Catherine, gave him a Miraculous Medal. The medal was the image of the Blessed Mother with her hands outstretched standing on the globe. On the reverse side there is an "M" on the Cross encircled by twelve stars with two hearts below representing the hearts of Jesus and Mary. Rick wore this medal throughout the war.

He was inducted at Fort Dix, New Jersey, and then sent to Fort Indiantown Gap outside Harrisburg, Pennsylvania. It was one of the largest regimental Army training camps in the country during the war. Seven Army divisions trained at Indiantown Gap en route to overseas service.[425] "It was mostly physical training. We were taught how to handle weapons and we also took classes on the history of war," Rick said.

About six months later Rick was sent to Boston where he boarded a Liberty ship with a couple hundred other soldiers. "It took ten days to reach England. It was rough because of the weather. I saw a couple of Liberty ships buckle and split in half. We didn't go in a straight line because the U-boats were very active. England was a good part of my life. We were billeted in public homes, and I became very friendly with the Colin White family. There were two of us that stayed there, just for sleeping quarters. We left early in the morning and went to a big field for training. When we returned Mrs. White served a cup of tea for us. I called her Mum White."

The White's had two young sons, Colin and Allen. Rick said that "sometimes two or three times a night we heard the siren signal for air-raids and went into the bomb shelter in the back yard with the Whites until the all-clear was sounded. This was in Bristol, England. After Bristol I went to Portsmouth and Southampton by the English Channel."

"The day before the invasion I saw Eisenhower speaking to the troops of the Eighty-Second Airborne Division. We knew it was big. We started to cross the Channel during the evening of the fifth, but were stopped because of the weather. We went in at 0630 on the sixth. I could see the gliders and parachute troops jumping behind the lines. Behind us the Battleship *Nevada* and another one, I think it was the *Arkansas*, were blasting away." The *Nevada* survived the bombings of Pearl Harbor on December 7, 1941.

"I was part of the First Engineer Special Brigade attached to the Fourth Infantry Division for the D-Day H-Hour invasion.[426] It was code-named 'Operation Overlord.'[427] We were the first Americans to go in on Utah Beach and Omaha Beach. The British were at Gold Beach and Sword, and the Canadians at Juno. There was less fighting at Utah than at Omaha Beach." Utah beach was the farthest west of the five landing beaches. The beaches are from west to east: Utah, Omaha, Gold, Juno, and Sword.

"One of the first churches I went to was Sainte Mère Église, which is shown in the movies about the invasion. This is where the 101st Airborne dropped. There was a chaplain for the whole regiment that said Mass out on the fields. Everyone prayed: Catholics, Protestants, Jews, and we all we went to Communion. It didn't matter what faith we were."

"We fought through to Belgium and took over Antwerp and were pushing through to the Ardennes Forest when we were transferred from the combat engineers to an infantry regiment. It was around Christmas. This was the Battle of the Bulge.[428] Our platoon became a family and we kept up our friendships after the war. I was lucky and got the most mail, ten to twelve letters. My sister, Catherine, wrote me a letter everyday."

The Battle of the Bulge was the largest land battle of WWII. Stormy winter weather kept Allied aircraft grounded in the first weeks and ground troops struggled in bitter sub-zero temperatures. It was the last German offensive. This epic battle cost more than 19,000 American lives. During the battle, near the Belgian Town of Malmedy, part of the First German Panzer Division massacred more than eighty American prisoners.

"We heard about the camps at Ohrdruf and Buchenwald and knew it was important to push on. We liberated the camps in Belgium. Then near the end of the war I remember when Roosevelt died, because it was on my birthday. On VE Day, I just thanked God that it was over. Because we were experienced troops (had combat experience), we were supposed to be on our way to Japan. I wondered why we couldn't go home. We were asked, 'Does anyone know how to type?' I took typing in high school and volunteered. I stayed in an old apartment building and worked at typing manifests. It was somewhere on the coast, either LeHavre or Cherbourg. Then I received my separation papers and returned to Fort Dix. From Jersey I took a train to the Buffalo railroad station where my sisters picked me up."

Rick was stationed overseas for almost two and a half years. His two younger twin brothers, John and Albert, were part of the occupation forces in Japan after the atomic bombs were dropped. Rick returned home with his Miraculous Medal. More than a century earlier in 1830, the Blessed Mother prophesied to Catherine Labouré in the Chapel of the Sisters of Charity in Rue du Bac, Paris. The Blessed Mother predicted dire times and misfortune for the French and the world, and much bloodshed. Mary also instructed Catherine to have a medal struck and promised that those who wear the medal would receive great graces. "They should wear it around the neck. Graces will abound for persons who wear it with confidence," and Rick did. Today, the body of St. Catherine lies uncorrupt in the chapel at Rue du Bac.

Shortly after the war, Rick went swimming with some buddies in Lake Ontario. He called it "Cows Road off Lake Road" by Hooker-on-the-Lake. Dietz Road was a dirt road in the 1940s.[429] "My medal came off and I dove down in the water several times trying to find it in the muddy bottom, but didn't. I asked my sister to give me another medal." Rick's wife Pearl thought that the devotion and wearing of the medal during combat had served its purpose.

Pearl Penzotti attended a Sodality breakfast at St. Joseph's Roman Catholic Church on Pine Avenue in Niagara Falls when Father Tom told the group about Pearl Harbor. Pearl added, "We were very shaken. A couple of my cousins were in the service and I wrote to them faithfully. I didn't know Rick then. My mother went to work at Bell Aircraft attaching wings to the airplanes. It was the first time she wore pants and worked outside the home. We were all stunned. My mother wore her one-piece jump suit and took the bus from Pine and Fourteenth Streets all the way to Bell at Wheatfield. She loved it and enjoyed the work. She bought a new kitchen table and chairs with her earnings."[430]

After the war Rick and Mrs. Ada White continued their friendship through correspondence. She wrote to Rick until her death and then her son, Colin, continued to write to the Penzotti family. Several years ago Colin and his wife Kate came to the United States to visit the Penzotti's at their home in Youngstown Estates.

Rick and Pearl have five daughters. Rick believes that military training teaches discipline and respect and that young people today could benefit from military service. He is concerned about the violence in our society and differentiated this from the necessary killing during the war for a just cause. The heart of his lesson about war that he taught his children is "When there is a war there is no victory. No one is a winner. Both sides lose and it is costly in lives. Most Americans do not know what war is like and the hardship that goes with the war."

Rick continues to wear a Miraculous Medal.

BELGIAN UNDERGROUND ~ On May 28, 1940, King Leopold III of Belgium surrendered to the Germans, but the Belgian military and the Underground continued to fight against Axis forces. Almost two years later in Colden, New York, a hilly rural town thousands of miles from Belgium, a young man working at the Donner-Hanna Coke Plant in Buffalo received a draft notice.[431]

"I was afraid that I was going to be picked to go into the infantry. At the time I just read some WWI books and thought, oh my God, I am never going to live through that in a trench. So when the opportunity arose to volunteer for Air Force Cadet training I jumped into it." Like many other young men Arnold Emil Frantz hoped to be a hotshot pilot, but didn't pass the vision tests. He was inducted at Fort Niagara in April 1942. "We were at Fort Niagara for several weeks. It was a nice place and I was with a good bunch of guys. We sympathized with each other wondering where we were going while we marched and drilled."

"I was sent to Sheppard Field, Wichita Falls, Texas, for Basic Training from July through September. It was a hellhole," Arnie said. "Everyone who was older than you thought they were a General and Texans didn't like us New Yorkers. We were all 'Yankees' to them so we were assigned unpleasant KP and guard duty." After a rushed basic training he was sent to the Cadet Center in San Antonio. "If you did not make the qualifying tests for pilot you could qualify for navigator, bombardier, or aerial gunner. I passed all the bombardier tests for vision and coordination. Pre-bombardier instruction at Ellington Field, south of Houston, Texas, and Big Springs took a few months. It was hotter than hell all summer. I was assigned to a pilot in a small two-engine plane for practice and instruction. After I passed and received my bombardier rating at Big Springs, I was sent to Wendover Field, Salt Lake City, Utah, from February to May, for 50-caliber machine gun training."

Arnie received his bombardier rating in Big Springs. In Pyote, Texas, "it was a flat desert and the prize of all places I went to," he said facetiously. "There we were formed into a crew and given instruction in combat flying. It was the first time you got to know all the guys you were going to fly with." His B-17 training group practiced flying night and day. "Night flying was very scary," Arnie said, remembering the constant presence of fear. "The pilot was in training only six months too and I thought does this guy know what he's doing? But he was a good pilot and serious." The crew went to Dalhart, Texas, for advanced training to practice maneuvers and flying with other groups, then to Keyster Field, Mississippi.

When the training was completed Arnie's group waited at Scott Field, Illinois, for three days before going overseas via Bangor, Maine and Goose Bay,

Labrador. "I asked Chesmore, the pilot, to pick a route over Western New York and to wave the wings when we were over the churches in Colden, and he did. Earlier, I wrote to my folks to look for the plane with the wings waving.[432] We landed in a blizzard in Bluey West One, Greenland, facing a white glacier mountain at the end of the runway." A winter storm delayed the next leg of the journey to Reykjavik, Iceland. Arnie and his buddies slept in their sheep lined flight suits in a cold barracks until they could take off for Prestwick, Scotland, to refuel, then onto Podington, England, where they were assigned to the Ninety-Second Bomb Group based a few miles northwest of London.

"Crossing the coast I thought, 'Are we going to make it?' We arrived in England during the first big disastrous raids on Germany. The main target was the Schweinfurt Ball Bearing Plant. The losses were terrific. German fighters shot down about fifty of our bombers the first day; that is five hundred men. The next day, the same thing happened, and we thought 'they are going to wipe us out!' After that an order was given that fighters escort bombers. The English flew at night and the Americans were flying during the daylight, but the Germans weren't going to have it. Every night, I looked around at the empty cots. It was a reminder of the guys that didn't make it that day and that maybe the next day it could be me. Our first mission was the shipyard in Bremen, Germany." Missions followed to Kiel, Wilhelmshaven, Emden, Ludwigshaven, Halberstadt, Frankfurt, and Bonn (Germany), Aalborg (Denmark), and La Rochelle, Chateaudun, and Pas-De-Calais (France). "Our first co-pilot, Bob Wolf, was awarded his own crew and on his first mission went down in the North Sea. It was a sad time."

Frankfurt was the target of the sixteenth mission on March 2, 1944. "On the way back, it seemed so strange, the group was spread out all over the sky. There were terrific headwinds over Belgium. It seemed like we weren't moving. All of a sudden there were black clouds and a thump. The tone of the engines changed. The gunners called out 'we are hit' and we started going down. The next thing I heard was 'abandon ship.' The escape hatch was right under the bombardier navigator's area and out the door we went. You always wondered what it was going to be like falling through the air since we never jumped before. My parachute opened and I saw our plane go down. Below were high-powered electric lines and I pulled on my chute lines to maneuver around the wires. I hit the ground with an awful whack and thought I was dead. All of the crew[433] made it, except for our pilot and co-pilot, Lt. Floyd Chesmore and Lieutenant Teachey; they went down with the ship."

"I hid my chute as kids and people gathered in the area which I thought would attract the German troops. A young boy told me to follow him. We were told to accept any help we could get. We went through the woods and he told me to get down in the canal. He told me 'help will come.' I lay in hiding for nearly five hours. At dark a man came on a bicycle, and said to follow him. He took me to an elderly lady who opened the door and welcomed me into her home. I stayed there for a few days. No one else was with me." During part of the time Arnie and Fred Greely, the navigator, traveled together on a southern escape route over the Pyrenees Mountains from France into Spain when an order came through the Underground shortly before D-Day to hold the escapees and they went back up to Belgium. Later, he discovered that the other crewmembers were captured and taken to POW camps.

The Underground moved Arnie a number of times to different safe houses including transporting him on a train with German troops. "On the train I was told to keep my mouth shut." One family's sacrifice made a life-long impression. "I stayed with an elderly couple that shared everything with me, and they had very little themselves. I stayed with Mr. and Mrs. Emile Bielande.[434] The Underground helped with foodstuffs for the families that hid me. We ate a lot of bread and what tasted like horsemeat. I don't know what kept us alive. One time while the Gestapo searched the area, I hid in an underground cavern under a trap door covered by bales of hay in their barn. I sat around most of the time, read books, and exercised. Occasionally, I went to the neighbor's house and listened to their hidden radio. There was news from the BBC that the invasion started. I hoped it was true. It was June 6, 1944, D-Day."

Arnie was touched by the goodness of the Belgian people, especially the Bielandes, who risked their lives and their families to hide him. He stood with the Bielandes' family and other town's people celebrating Belgium's liberation by the Allies in September 1944. Arnie rode with some of the troops back to Paris and then to England before being shipped to the states. He was missing-in-action for six months. A telegram from St. Amands, Belgium, dated December 26, 1944, arrived in Colden, New York, from Theodore Hooft to Arnie's parents "I sheltered your son when he bailed out of his plane." Arnie's love of children and his goodness impacted Hooft who named his daughter, Arnolde, for this American soldier.

Arnie was given thirty days leave at home then sent to Fort Logan Rehab Center near Denver in March 1945. "I saw German POWs held in the Denver area. They were treated very well. In May I was discharged. After the war I sent the Bielandes care packages and communicated with the man who saw our plane go down. I never stopped praying and always figured that God looked favorably on me."

B-29s IN THE PACIFIC ~ "I was seventeen years old shooting baskets at Kiski Prep School in Saltsburg when Roosevelt made the announcement about Pearl Harbor," he said. Richard "Dick" Kahl grew up in Vandergrift, north east of Pittsburgh.[435] "Everyone in town worked at the United States Steel Plant and Foundry except a few professional people. After I graduated from high school, I enrolled in a pre-med program at Allegheny College in Meadville, Pennsylvania, and soon enlisted. I met Beverley, my wife, while in college and we were married before I was sent overseas."[436]

"We were given all kinds of tests to qualify for pilot training. Following two months of pre-flight training at Maxwell Field, Alabama, I was sent to Lakeland, Florida, to complete primary. We were separated into pilots, bombardiers, and navigators." Dick graduated as a Second Lieutenant and was awarded "Outstanding Cadet" of his graduating class at Freeman Field, Indiana. He said that cadets were weeded out for qualification on single-engine or twin-engine aircraft. Dick received exportation orders to go to Europe, assigned to a B-24, but the orders were cancelled. Instead, he was sent to Nashville to train on B-29s.

Memories of humorous moments during Dick's pilot preparation started in a Piper Cub looking at the automobile traffic that was faster than his aircraft! He laughed remembering another incident when "I was practicing loops and spins in a Stearman bi-plane and the ratchet attached to the seat belt broke and about half my body was dangling out of the plane!"

Dick waited with his group for aircraft in Omaha. He was assigned to a B-29 bomber group based on Tinian Island, the central island in the Marianas group of islands about eighty miles north of Guam near Saipan. The control of Saipan and Tinian in the central Pacific was key to accommodating the B-29 bombers and became the staging bases for the incendiary bombing missions on Japanese cities. "My first mission took fourteen hours. I showed up dressed in my flak suit, uniform, and flight suit, which altogether weighed about two hundred pounds! We were waiting for the bombs to be loaded when a Russian instructor laughed at me and said if everyone else showed up with all their suits on we couldn't get the plane off the ground. I quickly stripped down to my flight suit and only a part of my uniform."

"A Japanese POW named Jimmy bartended in the officer's club. He told me 'you are going to bomb my hometown tomorrow.' I didn't believe he knew because we weren't told about the mission until the next morning. But Jimmy always knew where we were going. At the pilots' briefing, we were told to look to your left and look to your right and that chances are one of these guys is not going to return with you. I never thought it could be me. On one of our missions to Japan, after we dropped the bombs and turned around to return to Tinian, everyone fell asleep. The only land mass to identify our location was Iwo Jima and luckily, we picked up the radio signal from the island because we were low on fuel." Between missions Dick played bridge for one-tenth of a cent per point and enjoyed entertainer Charlie Ruggles at the USO Club where the servicemen received coffee and doughnuts.

Dick described the horror of incendiary bombing of Japan and the fighter escorts. "Sometimes when the fighters strafed they lost their compass. The pilot pulled up in front of us and pointed down indicating move to a lower altitude so he could get off oxygen. The orders were to jettison our bombs and escort the fighters when this happened."

"We heard that some kind of bomb was dropped on Hiroshima and a few days later we were part of a large massive air effort to provide a distraction for the detonation of the nuclear bomb over Nagasaki." It was August 9, 1945. "We weren't supposed to look and the heat was tremendous. But when we were over Mount Suribachi, we did look back. After that all the flights were grounded."

On September 2, 1945, in Tokyo Bay, "we flew a power mission with about three hundred other B-29s over the deck of the battleship *USS Missouri* at about 200 to 300 feet to make a display for the Japanese. The noise was incredible." On the battleship, the representatives of the Empire of Japan signed the Instrument of Surrender that ended WWII.

For the next several months Dick flew B-29s to be mothballed to Saipan, Tinian, and Guam then returned to the base via Navy ships. He was also given an assignment as a commissary officer to clean out the liquor locker at the Officer's Club. "A bottle of Imperial liquor sold for a dollar and a penny for a bottle of gin because no one wanted it without the fruit. Some Rangers took me for a ride on Tinian where we discovered some lemon and lime trees. We started to buy up the gin and went into the restaurant business," Dick chuckled.

The last flight home was on a war-weary B-29 that Dick flew from the Philippines. "One engineer flew with me. I lost one engine then climbed to 30,000 feet, then lost the second engine. We were gliding and I wanted to make a straight approach at Guam. I ran almost the entire ten thousand foot length of the runway when I pulled on the emergency brake. It was the best landing I ever made and with no brakes! I signed out with this B-29, and it took three days to turn it over to a General. I was worried someone was going to ask me for the aircraft when I got home! From Saipan, I boarded a hospital ship with seventeen feet of barnacles on it. At six miles per hour, it took almost two months for us to get from Saipan to San Francisco," Dick said.

"When the atomic bomb was dropped and the atom was split, everything I knew about chemistry changed, so I decided to enter the University of Buffalo for Law School after graduation from Alleghany." Dick practiced law serving the Lewiston-Porter community for more than half a century. He provided legal counsel as the Village of Youngstown Attorney for almost three decades and for the Lewiston-Porter School District for eighteen years. He was a very loved husband and father, and a well-respected attorney. Dick's home in Youngstown is a stone's throw from the south entrance to Fort Niagara State Park and the site of the German POW camp of Fort Niagara during the war. Dick's reflection on these pivotal moments was to remember that "No matter who our enemy is they should be treated as human beings."

Richard C. Kahl passed away at home on May 24, 2007.

PEACE DEMONSTRATIONS AT NIAGARA UNIVERSITY[437] ~ In November 1969 the American public began to learn from articles by journalist Seymour Hersh about the Army's investigation of charges against Lieutenant William Calley, Jr. and the 1968 My Lai massacre in Vietnam. Life seemed tumultuous. Racial riots in Niagara Falls brought a rush for gun permits. Ripples of the women's liberation movement began to impact society. College campus protests against the war in Vietnam broke out across the country and television news coverage brought the war to our homes and daily lives.

The following month on December 1, 1969, the first lottery drawing to institute the draft was held in Washington, DC. Capsules containing the 366 days of the year were drawn to assign order-of-call numbers by birth date for all males from the age of eighteen to twenty-six.[438] Anxiety swept the student center at Niagara University as the eligible males in the student body waited to learn their draft number. Girls waited too to learn the numbers for their boyfriends or brothers. The first date drawn was September 14; so all males born on that date between 1944 and 1950 were assigned the number one, the first to be called-up.

The Vietnam War entered our homes daily through the medium of television. Demonstrations were held across the country on college campuses and the shooting of four students at Kent State University in Kent, Ohio, at an anti-war rally on May 4, 1970, increased the division in the country about the war. Universities and colleges closed temporarily due to student strikes following the tragedy at Kent State.

John Victor Simon, Sue's father, was a WWII veteran. He drove his daughter to Niagara University on May 6, 1970, during a protest on campus and faced a barricade at the north entrance. John rolled his window down and told the students to get out of the way. They did not, and for a moment Sue could not breathe! Her father put the car in gear and drove forward as the students scurried. It was a time of questioning and searching for answers about the war and life, and a time of struggle trying to find her own identity from a father and a mother who were greatly respected.

Classes were disrupted and the main door to St. Vincent's building defaced with splashes of green paint. Father Slattery, the president of the university, stood on a table in the midst of a packed student body in the Gallagher Student Center and preached the merits of the war. "I can't believe it. He (Father Slattery) is a hawk," the coed told her father that evening. It jolted her understanding of clerics. She assumed priests to be pacifists. During the protests and Father's preaching, the student stood next to her friend, Bob Marinucci, who just returned from military service in the Navy aboard an aircraft carrier. Sue wondered how Bob and the other vets on campus felt about what was happening, but she didn't ask him. Father Slattery closed Niagara University for several days following the demonstration.

While Sue was growing up her father's favorite television shows were not old war movies, but Westerns. From time to time, she questioned John about the war, but he did not answer. She knew her father heard the question. It was as if his silence could keep the pain and atrocities of war, what he did, and what he saw, from ever harming others or himself again. She believed the path of war in her father's life was always very close to the surface, and the same strength it took to be a soldier and to wrestle with the necessity of violating the most ingrained moral code of "thou shall not kill" was the same strength it took to keep the pain and the memories of those times at bay.

In Sue's developing sense of independence to disagree with her father, they had a heated discussion about current events. John responded to his eldest daughter about Vietnam and the My Lai massacre and emphatically proclaimed, "You do not know what you are talking about! You do not understand what war was like. If an officer gave us an illegal or bad order during the war, we shot him rather than do something like Calley." He told Sue of the gruesome scenes of the atrocities of the Holocaust and the sight of two-story high piles of Jewish bodies exterminated by the Nazis and the photographs he took at the concentration camp. The stench of man's horrific cruelty, beyond comprehension, to other human beings remained with her father throughout his life.

Decades later and years after John passed away, Sue read *Good Soldiers* by Richard P. Matthews. It is the story of the history of the 353rd Infantry Regiment, part of the Eighty-ninth Infantry Division,[439] and the push into Germany. Sue discovered that one of the concentration camps her father witnessed was Ohrdruf, a sub-camp of Buchenwald. Eisenhower brought in the media to the camp to document the Holocaust because he was concerned that people would not believe what happened. He wanted all soldiers in the area to see what they were fighting for, and for the German people to know what happened in the camps.[440]

John was demoted a few times for instances when he disobeyed or participated in some other infraction. One of those moments began when he and another scout were sent ahead of their unit to check for the position of the German troops. A sniper killed the other soldier, so John returned to his unit, which was supposed to be a short distance behind them. He found them, not following, but back at camp imbibing. Outraged, he became involved in an altercation with the officer!

John grew up on the west side of the Niagara River in Niagara Falls, Ontario, Canada, and through a quirk of fate, John Victor Simon, known to family and friends as Donald, found himself a part of the United States Army. His eventual residence in the Town of Porter and military service evolved from an unusual story.

ESCAPING THE OTTOMANS ~ In the early 1900s, Afifa of Melhem arrived at Ellis Island on the immigrant ship *L'Aquitaine*, which sailed from Le Havre in France. Melhem was the given name of her father. Afifa (also spelled Afifi) was known by her father's first name, not by the family's surname of Milan. The ship manifest recorded Afifa Melhem as six years old, nationality Syrian, last residence as Beyrouth.[441] She was traveling with her mother, Fouz, and brothers, Milan and Said. They came to visit their father, Melhem Milan, who was trying to establish a business in Bridgeport, Ohio. One day he hoped to bring his family to settle in America and escape the harsh rule of the Ottoman Empire. Afifa returned to Lebanon with her siblings and several years later came to America as a teenager.

At that time the region of Lebanon was under the rule of Muhammed V also known as Mehmed V, Sultan of the Ottomans. Muhammed came to the throne after his brother Abd al-Hamid II was deposed during the Young Turk's revolution. During his reign most of the European possessions under the Ottomans were lost during the Balkan Wars (1912-1913). The empire, which was once at the doors of Vienna, was in decline, and during WWI Muhammed sided with the Central Powers.[442]

Affifa's brother, Peter Williams, served with the United States Army in WWI and on his Declaration for Citizenship renounced allegiance to "Mehemmed (sic) VI Emperor of the Ottomans." At that time the citizenship process was waived for those returning from military service. By 1924 the youngest brother, Thomas, would declare his intention to become a citizen and renounce allegiance to the "Republic of France" which now controlled Lebanon as a result of the Treaty of Versailles.

The Milans were Maronite Christians, an Eastern Rite of the Roman Catholic Church. After several years in the states, the patriarch of the Milan family became known as Thomas Williams, a successful merchant in Fredonia and Dunkirk, New York. The surname of Williams evolved from the rhythmic sound of Melhem in the Arabic language. Fouz, known as Rose, the wife of Melhem died in 1919. Melhem returned to Lebanon where he died in 1938. His children stayed in America; one of his daughters, Affifi, also known as Phoebe, spoke three languages, but could not read or write or drive an automobile. Phoebe and her sister Mary had arranged marriages to Lebanese brothers, Joseph and Aziz,[443] sons of Lebbus and Mary Simon.

Phoebe and Joseph Simon settled in Niagara Falls, Ontario, after their wedding on Thanksgiving Day in 1920. Three years later on Christmas morning, Phoebe's birthday, she was in labor with her third pregnancy and arrived at the Greater Niagara General Hospital to find "no room in the inn." She walked across the Rainbow Bridge connecting Niagara Falls, Ontario, to Niagara Falls, New York. A son, John Victor Simon, was born December 25, 1923. The unique circumstances of John's birth entitled him to dual citizenship. His chance birth in the United States proved to be a crossroads in his life when the Second World War broke out.

The family brick home is the first house on the east side of Cataract Avenue south of Bridge Street. Joseph established a restaurant known as *The Queens Restaurant* in Niagara Falls, Ontario, at the foot of Bridge Street near the Whirlpool Bridge.[444] During the lean years of the depression, John climbed up the hill behind the house to the railroad bridge with a bucket and picked up the coal that dropped off the rail cars. He was attending high school at Niagara Falls Collegiate in 1940 when the headlines of the *Niagara Review* were filled with news of the war. "Mass Raid by Nazis Repulsed" during heavy air attacks was reported from London, England. The Germans persisted on attacks directed chiefly at airdromes in southeastern England. An adjacent headline was entitled "RAF Bombers in Big Night Raids." Munich, known as the sacred city was bombed for the first time. The Royal Air Force bombers opened their second year of war striking heavily at the Boulogne region along the coast of German-held France.

On June 8, 1941, an Allied offensive in Vichy-French controlled Syria and Lebanon attempted to stop Germany from using the area as a road to attack Egypt. About two weeks later three million German and Axis troops opened a 1,000-mile front from the Baltic in the north to the Black Sea in the south, in a surprise attack on Russia.[445] During the fall, after Japan bombed Pearl Harbor, John crossed the border and signed up for the draft. He reported on January 30, 1943, in Buffalo and was inducted at Fort Niagara on February 6, 1943. Polk's *Buffalo City Directory of 1942* recorded the Army Recruiting and Induction Station at 243 Washington Street, Buffalo, New York, with Maj. W. V. Morrow in charge.

John wanted to be a pilot, but he didn't meet the requirements for the critical eye tests. The required immunizations for smallpox, typhoid, and tetanus in March 1944 left John with a life-long distaste for any injections. Later in life his wife, Salome, coaxed him to get the newly discovered polio vaccine.

"BROTHERS IN ALLIED FORCES" was the title of a *Niagara Review* newspaper clipping dated April 1, 1943, that Patrick, John's younger brother, saved for years. "Sons of Mr. and Mrs. Joseph Simon, Bridge Street, who are serving in the armed forces of Canada and the United States. Edward is a member of the Royal Canadian Artillery and Donald (John) is with the United States Engineers, and at present is stationed at Camp Swift, Texas" was the caption under the photograph. John told his daughter about attending Texas A & M University, while he was stateside, for Engineering Courses and of the impressive dining room. While at Camp Swift John, part of the Eighty-Second Engineers Co. C, purchased a War Savings Bond Series E.[446] His beneficiary was Mrs. Phoebe Simon, his mother, 120 Bridge Street, Niagara Falls, Ontario, Canada.[447]

Table 7.14
Plans of Class B Allotment War Savings Bonds

Plan 1	$2.75 Allotment	$25 Bond
Plan 2	$6.25 Allotment	$25 Bond
Plan 3	$18.75 Allotment	$25 Bond
Plan 4	$12.50 Allotment	$50 Bond
Plan 5	$37.50 Allotment	$50 Bond
Plan 6	$25.00 Allotment	$100 Bond
Plan 7	$75.00 Allotment	$100 Bond
Plan 8	$150.00 Allotment	Two $100 Bonds
Plan 9	$225.00 Allotment	Three $100 Bonds

Plan 10	$200.00 Allotment	Four $100 Bonds
Plan 11	$275.00 Allotment	$500 Bonds

Source: "Authorization of Class B Allotment for Purchase of War Savings Bonds," private collection, February 13, 1943.

On April 3, 1944, the Headquarters of the Sixty-Ninth Infantry Division at Camp Shelby, Mississippi, transferred Pvt. John V. Simon of Co. B 269th Engineer Battalion to the 655th Engineer Topographic Battalion Company at Fort McCoy, Wisconsin, by order of Colonel Maerdian. Wilbur D. Bickerstaff, WOJG USA, Pers O., 269th Engineer Combat Battalion certified that "Pvt. John V Simon will be last rationed to include supper 5 April 1944; will leave station at 1900 hours, 5 April 1944; mode of travel rail; monetary allowance in lieu of rations paid in advance." The finance office approved the monetary allowance for travel from April 6, 1944, to April 7, 1944, one and one-third days at three dollars per day. It was paid to John's younger brother, Patrick.[448]

John left for Europe on January 10, 1945, aboard a Liberty Ship, the *Marine Wolf.* English sailors staffed the ship and served boiled foods in the mess hall. Most of the soldiers couldn't eat because the voyage was rough and the stench made you sick if you weren't sick already. The bunks were four or five high. Enlisted men slept in canvas slings like hammocks. The ship docked at Le Havre in France January 22, 1945.[449] Back home in Canada the *Niagara Review*, undated article entitled "Now in France" reported that "Pvt. John Donald Simon of the United States Army, 353rd Infantry Unit, has arrived in France, according to official information, just received by his parents." The soldiers disembarked with only a duffel bag and waited for their armament and combat boots to arrive. Eventually, cattle trucks transported the troops to the tent city of Camp Lucky Strike. The weather was miserable and it was difficult to keep warm so the soldiers scrounged for wood.

353rd INFANTRY OF THE EIGHTY-NINTH DIVISION ~ The once secret "After Action Against Enemy Reports" from the Eighty-ninth United States Army Headquarters 353rd Infantry in the National Archives in Washington, DC, outlined the next several months of the movements of the 353rd and John's service in the European Theater in the first quarter of 1945. (Sue wondered where her father marched; now she knew.) The reports were sent by Robert M. Corl, Major Infantry S-3 for the Commanding Officer to the Commanding General of the European Theater Operations and gave an overview of John's days until Germany surrendered. The personal graphic images and anguish of those days are forever buried, but a few of the excerpts from the Reports identify several of the movements of the Division during the final push into Germany at the end of the war.

March 7, regiment concentrated in the vicinity of Mersh, Luxembourg.

March 8, prepared to move northeast towards Butzweiler, Germany.

March 13, the First and Third Battalions attacked at 0530...advanced in their zone...captured Hontheim, Wispelt, Holkembach, Kirnkhof and cleared the Kesselstetter (sic) forest.

March 14, Reconnoitered for crossing sites along the west bank of the Moselle River. Patrols crossed the river.

March 16, the Regiment made an assault crossing of the Moselle against light opposition...Grenerich, Bullay, and Zell were captured.

March 20, attacking at 0700 the Regiment crossed the Nahe River on bridges at Kirn and Martinstein. The Third Battalion advanced and cleared the town of Merxheim, Schihdekskopt, Limbacher-Höhe and occupied Meddersheim. Company K encountered strong enemy defensive positions at Limbacher-Höhe. The Second Battalion advanced and cleared Meckenbach, Kuppehem, Kirschroth...

March 25, continued Reconnaissance of the Rhine River between Kaub and Oberwesel...Casualties: four men killed, none wounded.

March 26, the 353rd Infantry with attachments made an assault crossing of the Rhine River at 0200... the First Battalion attacking east...captured Dorscheid, Dorscheid-Hohe and Weisel. The Third Battalion began the reduction of Kaub against very heavy opposition and at 1600 cleared the town and moved to the south and east to capture Wolfsbeck and Larchhausen. There was resistance and a great amount of artillery fire. Casualties: eight men killed and forty-four wounded...

From D-Day it took more than three months for American forces to reach the Siegfried Line, known as the West Wall, and almost five months to advance less than one hundred miles to the Rhine River in Germany. The Ninth Armored Division captured the Remagen Bridge south of Bonn, Germany, which enabled thousands of American troops to cross the Rhine River. Other troops crossed the river on pontoon bridges or boats at different points.

April 3, the battalions closed in at the Kirchheim concentration area at 1200. At 2330 they moved in line with the 90th Division east of Berka with the mission of attacking to the east and advancing as rapidly as practicable...

"Gord, Jim (Beck), John" in France at one of the cigarette camps that served as staging areas for the troops. (Courtesy Simon family)

April 5, the First Battalion remained north of Eisenach…Against moderate resistance the Second Battalion advanced to the west edge of Eisenach. The Third Battalion, against heavy resistance and over rough wooded terrain, assaulted Fortha, captured the town at nightfall. At 1600 the First Battalion sent a party into Eisenach demanding the surrender of the town, but the mission proved unsuccessful. Under cover of darkness the Second Battalion withdrew from the edge of Eisenach so that the city could be heavily shelled. There were twenty casualties.

April 10, the regiment remained in division reserve in the assembly areas. Security patrols were maintained and roadblocks constructed covering likely approaches. At 1530 the Regiment moved to the vicinity of Ohrdruf.

John photographed the atrocities at Ohrdruf. With horror and anger in his voice, he told his daughter about the "two-story high piled bodies" of Jews murdered in the camp.[450] The raw image of malevolent inhumanity pained him while he relived his witness to the unimaginable.

April 11, the Regiment remained in division reserve. At 1130 Co. B was detached to Arnstadt to guard Polish refugees. At 1630 the Regiment moved from the Ohrdruf concentration areas.

April 14, the Regiment made an assault crossing of the Salle River at 0800.

April 22, situation unchanged...Instructions were issued on the procedure for meeting Soviet troops. There were no casualties.

April 24-30, patrols continued to operate to the front and encountered scattered enemy resistance.

May 1,... the 353rd Infantry...maintained a defensive position...

May 8, the Regiment maintained its position and awaited the surrender of the German forces in its zone.[451]

The remainder of John's tour of duty overseas as part of the occupying forces was sketched in his photographs and the few words written on the back.

OCCUPATION ~ August 1945, John stood next to Mr. and Mrs. Massey, in front of their home at 196 Field Road, Bloxwich, Walsall Staffs, England, with another soldier Les. An unknown date in September was spent at the Rouen Carnival in France. November 12, 1945, John wrote, "Camp 20 Grand, Our Home, Herbert Hoover from Pennsylvania and Hugh Hays from Missouri."[452] On November 26 John was assigned duties as Assistant Company Clerk, Headquarters Company of the Eighty-third Division until March 1, 1946. December 16, 1945, was spent on leave in the Bavarian Alps.

January 16, 1946, John photographed "two Frauleins on the road to Gmunden" and in Bavaria Ebensee, a mountain lake at Berchtesgaden. The Ebensee Concentration Camp was a sub camp of the Mauthausen Camp. The labor from the Ebensee camp was used to build underground tunnels for research and eventual testing of intercontinental missiles.[453] Another day during January, John penned on the image of his buddies "Jim & Jack the two best Louie's in the Army." James D. "Don" Watson, from Blaney, South Carolina, was also with the 353rd Infantry, Eighty-ninth Division, and later the Eighty-third Division. After the war, Don spoke too about Berchtesgaden where they went on leave and being led by General Patton for whom he respected. He wanted to return to Austria in happier times, but like John was never able to make the trip.[454]

James D. Watson passed away January 22, 1995.

Liberation. The French people welcomed the Allied troops returning from the front after defeating Germany. (Courtesy Simon family)

On February 2, 1946 John, Eddie, and Little Joe enjoyed the Bavarian Alps at Berchtesgaden. John wrote, "The wolf pack from Linz Austria…Eddie from New Hampshire Joe's from Philly."

On another photo John wrote a buddy's address, "Joe Marnien 6443 Tulip Street, Philadelphia, 35, Pennsylvania." Joseph Luke Marnien's ancestors migrated to the Philly area from Canada sometime in the mid-nineteenth century. Born and raised in Philadelphia Joe graduated from Northeast Catholic High School and like many others who served did not talk about the war. But the night before he died, at the age of forty-three, Joe helped his thirteen-year old daughter who was working on a school report about the war. He told Mary

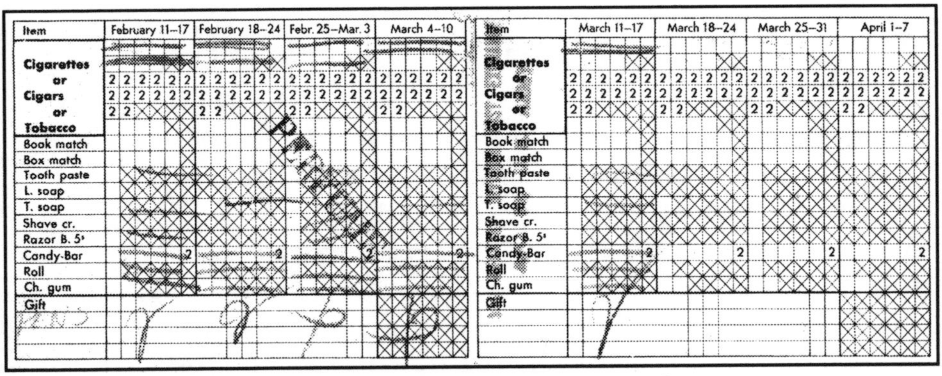

Item	February 11–17	February 18–24	Febr. 25–Mar. 3	March 4–10
Cigarettes or Cigars or Tobacco	2 2 2 2 2 2	2 2 2 2 2 2	2 2 2 2 2 2	2 2 2 2 2 2
	2 2 2 2 2 2	2 2 2 2 2 2	2 2 2 2 2 2	2 2 2 2 2 2
	2 2	2 2	2 2	2 2
Book match				
Box match				
Tooth paste				
L. soap				
T. soap				
Shave cr.				
Razor B. 5'				
Candy-Bar	2	2	2	2
Roll				
Ch. gum				
Gift				

Item	March 11–17	March 18–24	March 25–31	April 1–7
Cigarettes or Cigars or Tobacco	2 2 2 2 2 2	2 2 2 2 2 2	2 2 2 2 2 2	2 2 2 2 2 2
	2 2 2 2 2 2	2 2 2 2 2 2	2 2 2 2 2 2	2 2 2 2 2 2
	2 2	2 2	2 2	2 2
Book match				
Box match				
Tooth paste				
L. soap				
T. soap				
Shave cr.				
Razor B. 5'				
Candy-Bar	2	2	2	2
Roll				
Ch. gum				
Gift				

Above, John V. Simon's Army Exchange Ration card-European Theater. (Courtesy Marie Ann Simon Gwinn)

Below, Soldiers eager to return home wrote their accumulated points and names on the transport train "Widina, Albert V. 53 points Pittsburgh." (Courtesy Simon family)

Ellen about being the first ones to discover the concentration camps and helping to "clean things up for General Patton." Many years later Rita told her adult daughter more graphic information about the stench her father would never forget, and how he helped clean up the bodies. His wife, Rita, and their children: Joe, Gerard, Bill, Mary Ellen, and Daniel, survived him.[455]

Joseph Marnien passed away February 14, 1969.

March 18, 1946, John left for the states and arrived at the Fort Dix Separation Center, New Jersey, eight days later. John told his daughter that at one point he marched behind Patton, "a very colorful character." It was one of the rare times his eldest daughter saw her father smile. It sounded like he admired Patton. John was certainly a unique man himself, with his own special grit. One of the few stories John did tell was about meeting his oldest brother Edward in Europe. He was serving with the Royal Canadian Artillery.[456] The Canadian government did not have the same resources for their soldiers and entered the war earlier. Many suffered from lack of basic necessities during the fighting. John found his brother hungry from not eating for days and with no shoes. He gave Edward his boots, food, and other supplies.

John held a few warm memories of his military service. He loved Austria and her majestic mountains and spoke of returning someday to Berchtesgaden, his favorite place when he went on leave. But John kept the horrors of the war locked in his heart and mind. As with so many things about him, the war was one more venue for doing what was right, fighting when it was necessary, and having the strength and courage to do what was difficult.

John Victor Simon was discharged as a Technician Fifth Grade.[457] In his personal papers after his death, Sue saw for the first time the letter addressed to her father from the White House signed by President Harry Truman:

To you who answered the call of your country and served in its Armed Forces to bring about the total defeat of the enemy, I extend the heartfelt thanks of a grateful Nation. As one of the Nation's finest, you undertook the most severe task one can be called upon to perform. Because you demonstrated the fortitude, resourcefulness and calm judgment necessary to carry out that task, we now look to you for leadership and example in further exalting our country in peace.

John, like many others, took advantage of the G.I. Bill. He entered Niagara University and remained in the United States. He firmly declined participating in the traditional pledging rituals for entering freshman at the time, for the life and death experiences overseas forever changed him.

John and his wife and their children moved into the Johnson-Hunt house in January 1976. (See Chapter 1) Col. William and Edith Johnson Hunt lived in the house at 3735 Lower River Road, Youngstown, during the war. Their son Lt. Col. William H. Hunt was stationed at Niagara University as an assistant professor of military science and tactics in 1941 and 1942, served in England during the war, was assigned to the Adjutant General's Office in the Pentagon during 1945-46, and worked with the War Crimes Commission in Germany. Another son, Col. Richard J. Hunt, graduated from West Point Academy in 1932 and was assigned to the Twenty-ninth Infantry. He trained and commanded the 744th Light Tank Battalion for almost three and a half years during the war. William and Richard became good friends of John.

Col. William E. Hunt passed away December 23, 1946. He was a graduate of the infantry and cavalry school at Ft. Leavenworth, Kansas, the General Staff School at Washington, DC, and the Army War College.

Edith Johnson Hunt passed away at her home on February 1, 1964. Colonel and Mrs. Hunt and their son, Richard, were buried in Arlington National Cemetery, Section 11 Plot 311.

Col. Richard Johnson Hunt passed away April 3, 2001.[458]

Lt. Col. William Hugh Hunt passed away June 21, 1991.[459]

John Victor Simon, beloved husband and father, passed away December 14, 1998.

IN LOVE WITH A SOLDIER ~ John was the last soldier to ask Sally to marry him. It was their second year 1949-1950 at St. John's Law School in Jamaica, New York. They met during a class on marriage contracts while Sally was living in Brooklyn and working as a research clerk for Sullivan and Cromwell in New York City. Sally was hired because she was multilingual, and the firm was doing a lot of work overseas. John Foster Dulles was the senior partner of the firm. "We were in awe of him, the big boss at Sullivan and Cromwell! About fifteen top lawyers and about eighty other attorneys worked for the firm," Sally said.[460] President Truman sent Dulles to negotiate the peace treaty with Japan at the end of WWII. From 1953-1959 he served as Secretary of State under President Dwight Eisenhower.[461] Dulles enjoyed fishing and sailing, and attended regattas at the Youngstown Yacht Club while a guest at the home of his friend Charles Colbert at 3881 Lower River Road, Youngstown.[462]

John and Sally's first date was lengthy and as with most things about this young man who returned from the war, it was intense. They attended a double header of Niagara University and St. John's University basketball games at Madison Square Garden. During the second game John told Sally he was going to marry her. This was not the first time a soldier proposed, but he also took her college ring, which annoyed her immensely. They went to the Hotel Roosevelt for dinner and danced to Guy Lombardo, then attended Midnight Mass at St. Joseph's Cathedral in Brooklyn followed by a prolonged breakfast. "We talked about everything until dawn." After the first date John waited for Sally at the subway stop. Sally thought "how can I get rid of this guy…he's mental!" But his persistence won out. They made school history by being the first student couple to wed. Three of their classmates also made school history and became prominent New York government officials: Basil A. Patterson,[463] Secretary of State, and Hugh L. Carey and Mario M. Cuomo, Governors. Cuomo works for the firm of Willkie, Farr & Gallagher LLP. Wendell Willkie, one of the founders of the firm, ran unsuccessfully against FDR in his third bid for president.

Salome Marie Authier was born in 1925 in Springfield, Massachusetts. Sally was fifteen years old and attending Cathedral High School when the draft registration began. "It was scary. The guys were anxious about getting their number. Many were ready to join in defending the country, but a few tried to influence the draft board, enter the seminary, or tried to find a medical reason to be disqualified," Sally said.

Leo Millette was Sally's first boyfriend. She kept his Marine and Eagle Scout pins. He was one of the few at that moment who wanted to go to war. With memories of the First World War still fresh, the mood in the country was to avoid getting drawn into another world conflict. This changed after Pearl Harbor.

During the war Sally wrote to many of the soldiers overseas. Lists of names were posted at the USO. "I wrote to many boys, forty-five pen pals. That was what we all did. I told them about what was going on in my life and got lots of mail in return. Some of the letters were horrible. They (the soldiers) wrote back 'war is hell.' Some wrote poetry. All wrote about love. My cousin Charlie was a motorcycle courier. He wrote about the bombing of London. It was unnerving."

The USO dances were one of the ways Sally supported those who went off to war. Soldiers told her, "You are the one girl I am dreaming of all my life." There were a lot of proposals, and one night Sally came home with a ring. After a discussion with her father, the ring was returned.

About 1942 her aunt, Bertha Authier, encouraged Sally to join her cousins, Rita, Gabriel, and Jeannette Tetrault, and aunt as wardens. The volunteers studied First Aid and other training to obtain the necessary certificate to be a warden. "I minded the blackouts. When I became a warden we walked our assigned route in twos. I was scared walking in some of the neighborhoods. We carried a flashlight, but it could only be used sparingly."

WESTOVER AIR BASE ~ Springfield was near the Westover Air Base in Chicopee Falls, Massachusetts. Airplanes constantly flew overhead and large truck convoys rumbled through the streets. There was a lot of hype that their city could be bombed at any time. It was a time of uncertainty. The regularly timed sirens and the spontaneous sound of a siren heard when a plane was in distress or crashed were unnerving. The alarms seemed to be endless and were joined by the whine from the fire trucks as they prepared for a potential fire during a crash.

The reality of war became part of the neighborhood. The doctor who lived in the corner house near the Authier home was on the Bataan Death March. The boy next door returned shot and paralyzed; many never returned. Rationing and bartering were commonplace. Tire sales were discontinued on December 11, 1941, followed by automobile sales on the first of January 1942. In May of that year gasoline rationing began on the east coast and by August arrived in Western New York. In December there was nationwide gasoline rationing. Most cars were graded "A" as non-essential and received stamps for three gallons per week. A ban on pleasure driving followed. Sally's father, Emery Authier, operated a Chrysler car dealership on Front Street in Chicopee. He traded tires for shoes and butter. When car sales stopped, Emery and his wife, Juliette, opened a hot dog and ice cream stand. Sally's parents also worked the midnight shift at *Pratt and Whitney* in Connecticut. Juliette was a solderer at Sickles, a manufacturing plant, and became an accomplished welder during the war.

Sally never mentioned that Westover Air Force Base in Chicopee was a POW camp from October 6, 1944 to 1945. The camp was constructed in the mid-western part of the base surrounded by "chain link fences, and three by twelve foot steel runway mats…buried thirty inches deep to discourage tunneling" for initially 250 prisoners.[464] Eventually 523 POWs were at Westover and performed KP duties, worked on private labor projects, and harvested potatoes and tobacco from farms in Hatfield, North Amherst, and Hadley.[465]

Sally was a freshman at the University of Massachusetts when she and a friend Jean Crone tried to enter the Women Army Corps (WAC). In the exuberance of youth Sally thought that joining "the WACs would be a wonderful experience. It offered educational benefits and would be a good way to see Europe." It was not to be because of vision and other medical issues.

"I was terrified of the Nazis. I saw them as evil and I prayed. They were arrogant and their message horrible. How could the German people have elected Hitler," she wondered. Sally believed that dictators were always evil and would abuse power. Her feelings were the same for Mussolini.

Sally Simon photographed her classmates enjoying their interpretation of the sign for serviceman. (Courtesy Simon family)

On VE Day the area college students from Amherst, Smith, Mt. Holyoke, and University of Massachusetts came together and celebrated in the Town of Amherst. Church bells rang and the students drank!

In the 1950s Sally came face to face with the atrocities of the war when her husband showed the photographs he took at a concentration camp. She shook her head again at the memory of appalling images of the piles of bodies. The unfathomable reality of evil could not be denied. One of the few glimpses into what happened to her husband told the essence of John's war story. "He said, 'You couldn't think; it was horrible.' He had tears in his eyes as he showed me the pictures. The first time he killed someone it was up close. I can't remember if it was a knife or a rope. He was a scout then. He looked at him (the German soldier) and thought it could be someone he went to school with. He told me it was the hardest thing of his whole life. When he returned to the foxhole the

VE Day parade in Victoria Park, Niagara Falls, Ontario, on May 7, 1945, to celebrate Germany's surrender. The Joseph Simon family watched and joined in the festivities. (Courtesy Niagara Falls Ontario Public Library, Francis J. Petrie Collection)

VJ Day, the image of *Niagara Falls Gazette's* front-page news of the end of the war in the Pacific.

NEW YORK STATE'S TENTH CITY—POWER CITY OF THE WORLD

NIAGARA FALLS GAZETTE

PEACE!

JAPS SURRENDER UNCONDITIONALLY

Cabinet Quits On Mikado's Orders

The Key Men In The Drive To Victory

GEN. DOUGLAS MacARTHUR

ADM. CHESTER W. NIMITZ

Huge Allied War Machine Stilled

By JOHN M. HIGHTOWER

End Of War Brings Wild Celebration Here; All Business Suspended; Civic Program At Hyde Park Tonight; Two-Day Fete Proposed

soldier next to him had his brains blown out. He said he went crazy. 'You lost your conscience,' he told me."

Friends from law school and throughout life, Salem Joseph Simon and John, debated who was the best General during the war. Salem is the son of Yousef Simon and Nseem George, Lebanese immigrants. Salem, the name means "peace" in Arabic, served in the 286th Port Company of the Army. After basic training in Fort Laughton Seattle, WA, the unit was sent to Sitka in Alaska. They unloaded food, concrete, and other supplies that came into the port. After several months the company was shipped to Calcutta in India. Salem was a stevedore loading and unloading ships and managing warehouse supplies during the war. He expected to be part of the invasion of Japan. Salem and John talked about military strategy, not the atrocities, Sally said. Patton was the only good General as far as John was concerned. Salem argued for Montgomery and others. Sally heard John saying that if Patton had been in command in Africa it would have been better. While the men discussed generals, Sally and Regina, Salem's wife, shared about their children.

Salem Joseph Simon passed away May 15, 2006.

Regina M. Simon passed away November 20, 2002.

NAZI GENERAL WALTER DORNBERGER ~ After law school, John and Sally settled in Snyder, New York, in an apartment at Campus Manor.[466] There were two apartments on the first floor. The newlyweds lived in one apartment and the former Nazi Gen. Walter Dornberger and his wife, in the other. "Dad (speaking of her husband John) knew of him. I can remember Mrs. Dornberger saying 'I will send you to the moon dumpkopf.' Dad said that was appropriate!"

Dornberger was the engineer who directed construction of the German V-2 rocket developed by a group of scientists led by Dr. Wernher Von Braun whom Dornberger hired to help develop Germany's secret rocket program. The rocket was initially launched in 1942 and used against Paris on September 6, 1944.[467] Dornberger and Von Braun became part of America's space history. Dornberger immigrated to the United States after his release as a POW held by the British. He worked on guided missiles for the USAF and from 1950 to 1965 was a key consultant for Bell Aircraft on the development of rocket-powered aircraft. Von Braun worked for the National Aeronautics and Space Administration (NASA) to develop the Jupiter intermediate range ballistic missile and the Saturn V that helped propel the United States to the moon.[468]

There was a common laundry in the cellar at Campus Manor with coin-operated washing machines. "We hung out our clothes together and spoke about women's things. I didn't have much furniture. Mrs. Dornberger shared how it was when she got married and the struggles. She told me about the difficulties finding what she needed at the grocery store to cook what the General wanted. We both didn't drive and talked about what it meant. She had a heavy German accent and was a calming influence. She was a very lovely lady."

Bell Aircraft hired Dornberger at the time and coincidentally, John. He was working in J. Boardman Scovell's[469] law office in Lewiston for several years and didn't receive any compensation except for new clients that he personally retained. So, to provide for his wife and growing family, John worked the second shift at Bell until 1957.

Sally concluded, "There are some men who create wars. They are always soldiers and always those looking for a war. The war changed John forever."[470]

Salome Authier Simon, beloved wife and mother, passed away September 19, 2007, at her home in Youngstown, New York, on the fifteenth anniversary of the death of her brother, Emery Authier, Jr.

THE WHOLE WORLD IS KIN ~ During the War Between the States, the Civil War, brother fought brother and neighbor fought neighbor. In some ways during WWII the world was larger, but on close scrutiny some families in the Town of Porter and throughout the country discovered again that war pitted family members against each other. John and Sally's son-in-law, Raymond Dietz, was part of one of those families.

William Shakespeare wrote, "One Touch of Nature Makes the Whole World Kin," *Troilus and Cressida, Act III, Scene 3*. Centuries after the ink dried from Shakespeare's quill, Johann Friedrich Diez, the great-grandfather of Raymond, arrived in the Town of Porter c. 1867. His eldest brother, Johann Jakob Diez, remained in Germany. A search for Raymond's ancestors brought recently discovered German cousins to his front door on Lutts Road in 2002. Walter and Reinhold Diez stepped upon the dirt farmed by their common ancestor and embarked upon the truth of Shakespeare's insight into the psyche and behavior of humankind.

Walter and Reinhold's father, Jakob Diez, was thirty-one years old in 1939. He opposed the Nazi party's government and the war when he was drafted into the Wehrmacht. Jakob was at the front serving in Stalingrad on April 15, 1943, a fateful day when the British bombed the suburb of Stuttgart- Mühlhausen in error. The RAF attempted to target a factory that built engines for German aircraft. Johann Friedrich Diez and Marie Maier, Jacob's father and mother;

Anna Christina Hutlenlocher, his wife; Helga, Walter, and Gertrud, ages five, three and two, his children; and Hannelore Diez, age five, his nephew, were killed that day.

The Diez home in Mühlhausen and their church were also destroyed. The army let Jakob return home to bury his family only after someone agreed to take his place at the front. He remained in the Wehrmacht working in Stuttgart in a support and supply unit and became part of the resistance to Hitler and helping people in the camps. After the war Jakob married a widow, Hedwig Lindner Gabler.[471] Walter and Reinhold are the sons of Jakob and Hedwig. Jacob told his family that most Germans were not in support of Hitler, but that he and the military were very powerful.

Jakob Diez passed away in 1983.

Germany's neighbor, Poland, felt the torrent of Hitler's ambitions and military might. Surprisingly, Western New York and the Town of Porter held living evidence of the plight of the Polish people on September 1, 1939.

NOTES

[354] Abraham Lincoln, letter to George Opdyke and others, December 2, 1863.

[355] Joe Derhay, telephone interview by author, October 23, November 6, 2006, and letter to author, November 8, 2006.

[356] Margaret Johnnston Klomp Juergens, conversation with author, Youngstown, NY, 2007.

[357] Derhay, telephone interview, and "Came Home Via Thumb Route," *Jersey Journal*, May 3, 1946.

[358] James Holahan lived next door to the Slattery family and operated the Middleport Cold Storage with German POW workers from Fort Niagara.

[359] "Introduction," *The Army Nurse Corps*, http://history.amedd.army.mil/ANCWebsite/ANCWWIIbook/Introduction.htm [accessed April 25, 2007].

[360] Marguerite "Marge" Slattery Dyer, interview by author, Niagara Falls, NY, April 24, 2007.

[361] Mary Cavanero went overseas with Esther Slattery and later became a Brigadier General in the Nursing Corps.

[362] "Franklin D. Roosevelt State of the Union Address, July 6, 1945," *The* American Presidency Project, http://www.presidency.ucsb.edu/ws/print.php?pid=16595 [accessed April 25, 2007].

[363] Connie Vasilake was in basic training with Marge Dyer at Fort Niagara.

[364] Ernst Wille, a German POW, painted one of the murals in the Officer's Club.

[365] Y*e Olde Fort Inn* located at 110 Main Street in the Village of Youngstown near the south entrance of Fort Niagara State Park is presently known as the *Bistro at the Old Fort Inn. Ray-Ott* was a well-known supper club in the City of Niagara Falls, New York, on Falls Street. The club burned in the 1950s.

[366] "John W. Simpson, 1914-2007," *Institute of Electrical and Electronics Engineers History Center*, http://www.ieee.org/web/aboutus/history_center/biography/simpson.html [accessed March 5, 2008].

[367] Author, *Porter*, 86.

[368] Ruth Gates, telephone interview by author, July 26, 2006.

[369] The three-story brick mercantile store built in the nineteenth century by W. H. H. Ransom was located on the southwest side of the main intersection in Ransomville, NY. Clinton Burlingame was known as "Burly."

[370] Willard Ransom Harris and Ruth Harris Gates, *Willard Ransom Harris January 27, 1920 – June 22, 2001*, (Ransomville, NY: Ransomville Historical Room, 2001).

[371] Harris story, 2.

[372] "Camp Gordon Johnston," http://www.campgordonjohnston.com [accessed April 1, 2007]. Camp Gordon Johnston was originally named Camp Carrabelle.

[373] Harris and Gates, *Willard Ransom Harris,* 4.

[374] Most cars were graded A, non-essential. The owner received stamps for three gallons of gas per week. Grade B was for work use; grade C for essential personnel such as clerk, doctors, and civil defense; and grade T for long distance trucks. Source: The National World War II Museum, New Orleans, LA.

[375] Andrew Jackson Higgins designed and built mechanized landing crafts to ferry soldiers and equipment directly on the beaches. The LCVP (Landing Craft, Vehicle, Personnel) vehicles were the precursor to the LCMs (Landing Craft Mechanized) also built by Hig-

gins Industries in New Orleans. Source: The National World War II Museum, New Orleans, LA.

[376] Harris and Gates, *Willard Ransom Harris January 27, 1920 – June 22, 2001*, 7.

[377] LST – Landing Ship Tank known as "Large Slow Targets" by their crews.

[378] Pillboxes are small concrete structures built for defensive purposes, often camouflaged.

[379] The battle of the Hurtgen Forest from September 1944 to February 1945 was one of the worst battles ever experienced by the American Army.

[380] Harris and Gates, *Willard Ransom Harris January 27, 1920 – June 22, 2001*.

[381] Robert W. Jones, caretaker of the historical records for St. John's, served as an Aviation Electrician's Mate second class aboard the *USS Cumberland Sound* in the Pacific. The *Cumberland Sound* was in Tokyo Bay when Japan surrendered and participated in atomic bomb tests during the summer of 1946. Robert attended Whitney Avenue Aviation School, Niagara Falls, and then went to work at Bell Aircraft on the flight line until he entered the service. Theodore Jones Jr., Robert's older brother, served in the Aleutian Islands.

[382] Military archives files, Ransomville Historical Room.

[383] "In Solemn Memory" booklet, newspaper obituary, and Ellen Harpster, daughter of Eleanor Lare Plain Harpster, telephone conversation with author.

[384] Military archives files, Ransomville Historical Room, Ransomville, NY.

[385] Lt. Col. Peterson to Mrs. Jessie Canfield, October 28, 1944, Military archives files, Ransomville Historical Room, Ransomville, NY.

[386] "Falls Marine Prays During Lull in Iwo Battle," *Niagara Falls Gazette*, March 1, 1945. Edmund Fadel's son, Tom, saved the newspaper clipping. In 2007, Tom resides at the historic *Forty Acres* estate on Lower River Road, Youngstown.

[387] Grace Hays Reese telephone interview by author September 3, 2006. James Hays, telephone interview by author, September 11, 2006; Harry B. Hays, telephone interview by author, November 9, 2006; and Harriet Hays, *Memoirs*.

[388] Blairville was a hamlet adjacent to the Village of Youngstown, in the Town of Porter, NY. Church Street was also known as Four Mile Road on a map attached to the Title Search for the property.

[389] Local newspaper accounts note that Fillmore was a frequent visitor to the "Niagara Falls area." In the Niagara County Clerk's Office, Lockport, NY, in Liber 148 of Mortgages page 344, is a copy of Mortgage executed by Charles Wille and Jane, his wife, to Millard P. Fillmore as Executor and Caroline Fillmore, and also a Sheriff's Deed, in Liber 134 of Deeds page 209, referencing an action pending in Court between, Millard P. Fillmore as surviving Executor of the Last Will and Testament of Millard Fillmore, deceased, Plaintiff, against Charles Wille and Jane Will, his wife, Bradley D. Davis, Alfred Emerson, Lewis C. Beals, Feis Einstein and Henry S. Ware, Defendents. The Hays farm was part of Lot 31 described in the above Deed.

[390] Harry B. Hays said that David completed his flight training and was transitioning to combat aircraft when the medical condition was discovered. David re-enlisted as a glider pilot. Harry Hays, conversation with author, March 21, 2007.

[391] The Sanderson home and farm fronted on Youngstown-Wilson Road west of Cothran Road, adjacent to the Niagara Frontier Golf Course.

[392] Harry B. Hays said that his father and Ralph Sanderson were elders in the Youngstown Presbyterian Church.

[393] "World War II Listing," *American Battle Monuments Commission*, http://www.abmc.gov/search/wwii.php [accessed March 5, 2008].

[394] A1E was the Air Force official name for the Navy's Douglas built Skyraider, which the Navy gave the Air Force. It had been retired from the fleet, but was especially well suited to the situation in Vietnam.

[395] Harriet Hays, *Memoirs.*

[396] Harry Hays commented that the push across the Rhine was called the *Varsity Campaign* and the date was March 24, 1945.

[397] For heavy bombardment school, Harry added.

[398] Harry Hays explained that it was Fort Mead, MD, a European staging area.

[399] David was sent to Saipan and Iwo Jima; Harry clarified.

[400] Harriet Hays, *Memoirs.*

[401] Niagara Aerospace Museum located at 345 Third Street, Niagara Falls, NY, www.niagaramuseum.org.

[402] Patrick A. Geelan, interview by author, North Tonawanda, NY, June 16, 2006.

[403] John C. Nowak, *With the Eyes Of The Seventh Photo Group...Now It Can Be Told,!* June 16, 1945, 126.

[404] Nowak, 1-16, 126 and Geelan, interview.

[405] Richard Byron, interview by author, Niagara Aerospace Museum, Niagara Falls, NY, June 16, July 11, September 14, and November 1, 2006.

[406] Byron described this as what he called a "typical event" for the combat engineers.

[407] Byron described the difficulties of the Roer River crossing.

[408] "Roer Was an Engineer's Nightmare," *Stars and Stripes*, Liege Edition, March 3, 1945.

[409] Byron's account of the American air support and German resistance during the Roer operation.

[410] Lt. Col. Charles R. Keasey, Battalion Commander 171st Engineer Combat Battalion, "A Short History," June 25, 1945, 11.

[411] Byron's memory of the air support after the Rhine River crossing.

[412] Keasy, "A Short History," 11.

[413] Honshu is the largest island of Japan.

[414] "Jap Propaganda Plan Backfires, Soldier Writes," *The (St. Petersburg) Times*, January 16, 1944.

[415] Roderick Tower, interview by author (neighbor), Youngstown, NY, July 28, 2006.

[416] Lt. David Hays letter to Roderick Tower, postmarked December 25, 1944, as written.

[417] Frank V. Nicolette, interview by author, Youngstown, NY, October 4, 2006.

[418] "Who's Who: Vittorio Orlando," *First World War*, http://www.firstworldwar.com/bio/orlando.htm [accessed March 5,2008].

[419] Buzz bomb was the nickname for the Vergeltungswaffen because of it's sound.

[420] Troyes is near Paris.

[421] Patricia Nicolette Loncto can look out her window at the southeast grounds of Fort Niagara State Park that was part of the military complex when her father entered Fort Niagara during the war as the POW camp was being constructed.

[422] Frank Nicolette also earned his Master's Degree at Niagara University attending night school.

[423] Niagara County Savings Bank was taken over by the Bank of America.

[424] Rick Penzotti, interview by author, Youngstown, NY, November 10, 2006.

[425] "The Fort Indiantown Gap Story," *Fort Indiantown Gap Training Center*, http://www.dmva.state.pa.us/ftig/cwp/view.asp?A=3&Q=440835 [accessed March 18, 2007].

[426] D ~ the day of invasion, H ~ the hour.

[427] Eleven thousand aircraft; six thousand naval vessels; and two million soldiers, sailors, and airmen from fifteen countries took part in the D-Day invasion known as Operation Overlord that took two years of planning. Source The National WWII Museum, New Orleans, LA.

[428] The Battle of the Bulge was from December 16, 1944 until January 25, 1945. American troops suffered massive casualties. The German counter-offensive in the Ardennes pushed back allied lines creating what on a map looked like a bulge.

[429] Dietz Road is the east line of the original farm (now Four Mile State Park) owned by Johann Friedrich Dietz, great-grandfather of Raymond Dietz, author's husband. Friedrich owned five farms, which he eventually transferred to his five sons. Hooker-on-the-Lake has also been known as Oxy-on-the-Lake and in 2008 became a town park, Porter-on-the-Lake.

[430] Pearl Penzotti and Rick Penzotti, interview by author, Youngstown, NY, November 10, 2006.

[431] Arnold E. Frantz, interview by author, Colden, NY, June 18, 2007.

[432] Arnie's father and mother, Emil and Sarah, spoke German at home and operated a Red and White Grocery Store in Colden. Alsace-Lorraine, the birthplace of Arnie's father, was annexed by Germany in 1940.

[433] Crew Members: Navigator – Lt. Fred Greeley, Bombardier – Lt. Arnold E. Frantz, Engineer – Staff Sgt. Paul Mano, Radio Operator – Tech. Sgt. George Mazey, Ball turret – Staff Sgt. James Barnes, Waist Gunner – Staff Sgt. Ed Simulaki, Waist Gunner – Staff Sgt. Larry Brandon, Tail Gunner – Staff Sgt. Hugh Jack.

[434] Arnie did not know Mrs. Bielande's first name. He said, "I called her Madame."

[435] Richard C. Kahl, telephone interview by author, May 17, 2007.

[436] Beverley Rogers Kahl is from Niagara Falls, New York. Beverly and Dick married during his training in Alabama.

[437] Author's story about her father, John Victor Simon, and mother, Salome Authier Simon, was written in the third person.

[438] "The Vietnam Lotteries," *Selective Service System: History and Records*, http://www.sss.gov/lotter1.htm [accessed May 30, 2007].

[439] The Eighty-ninth Infantry Division participated in the Rhineland and Central Europe Campaigns. The Rhineland Campaign was the Allied advance from Paris to the Rhine. The Central Europe Campaign followed with the crossing of the Rhine River as the Allies advanced throughout western Germany.

[440] Richard P. Matthews, *Good Soldiers The History of the 353rd Infantry Regiment, 89th Infantry Division*, (USA: 2004), 365.

[441] Beyrouth – Beruit, Lebanon.

[442] MacMillan, *Paris 1919*, 267.

[443] Aziz was also known as Sam Simon and lived in Lackawanna, NY.

[444] The restaurant's name was changed to *Simon's Restaurant* and known as the oldest restau-

rant in the City of Niagara Falls, Ontario, presently operated by Patrick and Rosa Simon.

445 William L. Shirer, "The Germans Invade Russia," *Illustrated Story of WWII*, 264.

446 Second Lt. Robert V. Rhodes signed the authorization as the responsible officer.

447 Phoebe told her daughter-in-law, Sally, that during the war she regularly walked across the Whirlpool Rapids Bridge to Our Lady of Lebanon Church, 1120 Niagara St., Niagara Falls, NY, to pray a novena for the safety of her two sons, Edward and John.

448 Orders letter from Headquarters 69th Infantry Division, Camp Shelby, Mississippi, April 3, 1944.

449 Member of the 353rd Infantry Regiment's, requested his name be withheld, telephone interview by author.

450 See the 89th Infantry Division website http://www.89infdivww2.org/ohrdruf/index.htm for history of the camp and stories by some of the liberators and survivors.

451 "After Action Report 353rd Infantry," National Archives Building, Washington, DC. Some abbreviations were spelled out for readability.

452 The camps were named for popular cigarettes at the time such as Lucky Strike. Camp *Twenty Grand* was in Hénouville, a small village, in northern France between Le Havre and Rouen.

453 Museum of Modern History and Concentration Camp Memorial Ebensee, Zeitgeschichte Museum Ebensee, http://bob.swe.uni-linz.ac.at/Ebensee, [accessed April 18, 2008].

454 Jean Watson, wife of James Donald Watson, letter to author, July 27, 2005.

455 Gerard "Gerry" Marnien, telephone conversation and letter to author, September 5, 2006.

456 Edward Joseph Simon, Serial No. B44584, was inducted in Hamilton, Ontario, and served in the United Kingdom, Central Mediterranean Area, and Central Europe. He received the 1939-1945 Star, Italian Star, French and German Star, and CVSM (Canadian Volunteer Service Medal) & Clasp.

457 John V. Simon was awarded the Bronze Star Medal, Army Commendation Medal, Good Conduct Medal, American Campaign Medal, European-African-Middle Eastern Campaign Medal & Bronze Star Attachment (double), World War II Victory Medal, Combat Infantryman Badge 1st Award, and Honorable Service Lapel Button WWII.

458 "Col Richard J Hunt USA (Retired)," West-Point.org The West Point Connection, Deceased USMA Class of 1932, http://www.west-point.org/users/usma1932/9422/ [accessed April 19, 2008].

459 Social Security Death Index (SSDI), http://ssdi.rootsweb.ancestry.com/ [accessed May 24, 2008].

460 Salome "Sally" Authier Simon, interview by author (daughter), Youngstown, NY, June 13, July 11, and August 24, 2006.

461 Dulles provided legal counsel to President Woodrow Wilson at Versailles to negotiate peace at the end of WWI and argued against harsh economic reparations from Germany, which became one of the causes of WWII. Dulles purchased Duck Island on Lake Ontario for his private retreat. "John Foster Dulles, Secretary of State," http://www.arlingtoncemetery.net/jfdulles.htm [accessed April 10, 2008].

462 Charles Colbert's home is now *The Cameo Inn Bed and Breakfast.* http://www.cameoinn.com/index.html

463 Basil Patterson was the first African American Secretary of State for New York. He is the father of David Patterson, the fifty-fifth New York Governor, and first African American

Governor of New York. Both were minority leaders in the New York State Senate.

464 Frank Faulkner, *Westover Man, Base and Mission* (Springfield, 1990), 64.

465 Anne McCrory, "Prisoners at Westover helped local farmers," Republican, April 5, 2007.

466 Some of John and Sally Simon's personal papers identified the address as 230 Campus Manor, Snyder, NY.

467 "The V-2 Rocket," Inventors, http://inventors.about.com/library/inventors/blrocketv2.htm.

468 "Chrysler B-78 Jupiter," Fact Sheets, *National Museum of the USAF*, http://www.national-museum.af.mil/factsheets/factsheet.asp?id=2705 [accessed May 30, 2007].

469 Mr. Scovell was personally acquainted with every United States president from Groover Cleveland through Franklin Roosevelt, and a friend of Woodrow Wilson. Mr. Scovell sold his Lewiston Power Company in 1927 to Niagara Electric Share Co., the predecessor of Niagara Mohawk Power Corporation. Source: Muriel Scovell Ogden, *The Scovells*, Baldwinsville, NY: Ogden Energy, Inc., 48, 51.

470 John and Sally married September 7, 1950, and are the parents of Suzanne, Gerianne, Nannette, Juliette, John Jr., Jacqueline, Louise, Emery, Vivian, Marie, Richard (died August 30, 1963), Jeanne, and Yvonne.

471 Wilhelm Gabler died in 1943. Hedwig and Wilhelm's daughter, Christa, like many children born during the war, never knew her father.

CHAPTER 8

POLAND, SEPTEMBER 1, 1939

FOR MOST AMERICANS THE BEGINNING OF WWII stirred painful images of the casualties of the First World War, and evoked a strong sentiment to remain neutral and avoid being drawn into another war. But the people of Poland were unable to ignore the sudden and forceful attack by Germany in the early morning of September 1, 1939. Germany ignored Great Britain and France's ultimatum to withdraw from Poland and WWII began in Europe. Two young Polish men lived through those fateful events and began an arduous journey that eventually led them to Western New York.

STANLEY C. BLAKE[472] and his native Poland faced the German troops when they crossed the western border at four o'clock in the morning on September 1, 1939. He was seventeen and a member of Strzelec, a paramilitary organization. "We didn't shoot anybody. We would go to a shooting range and fire off five or ten rounds."[473]

Stanley was brought up in the city of Kielce, Poland. "It was poor condition, more than poor; I didn't have shoes. I lost my father in 1927. My mother went to Germany to work before Hitler came to power and (then) didn't allow foreign workers into Germany." Somehow, Stanley's mother continued to work while he stayed with his grandmother and his mother's sister. He loved to go to school, to read, and to learn from others. Stanley finished the traditional seven years of public school, but couldn't go on to the gymnasium (similar to high school). He sold newspapers to make a little money. "I liked to go to the movies. I loved American cowboy movies."

The commander of Strzelec found Stanley a job as a typist. When the war broke out his organization guarded empty buildings from looters. "People were stealing because they didn't even have shoes. I was coming home during an air bombardment when the Germans bombed the railroad station and I saw a guy being killed. When I came home, I said, 'Mama I can't do it. I saw a guy being completely taken apart.'" His mother told him that he must accept it as part of war. That evening there was a meeting as the course of Stanley's role in the war began to unfold.

He asked himself, "What are we going to do, where would I go? I can't go to my mother. She doesn't have a job. I don't have a job. (So with only a) French rifle and Polish ammunition our group went to stop the German tanks. The city of Kielce is at the cross points of railroad and regular roads. My Tech Sergeant in charge of our outfit said 'we are going to take a position on the rocks.' We knew Germans were coming, but we didn't have any ammunition or supplies left. (Before the Germans arrived and faced with the impossible task of defending themselves) the sergeant said 'go and hide yourself. Save yourself.' Two of us went to Holy Cross Mountains." Holy Cross Mountains are the central range in Poland.

"Then I joined the Polish military. We didn't have any front. The Germans were already here. We were near the Vistula River, which divides Poland east and west. Then, in that city, I forget the name; we were taken prisoner. We had summer uniforms, but we didn't have any dogtags because we were not regular soldiers and not under the Red Cross or the Geneva Convention. We were taken as a group by train to Czestochowa, the town of the shrine of the Black Madonna, to northwest Germany, Westphalia," Stanley said. After a few days, they were separated into smaller groups of twenty-five and assigned work details. "My friend, Stefan Grondziel, and I were told to go to a small village to work in the fields with German Jugens (youths). I speak German, Russian, and Polish. Stephan didn't. When I found out where we are, I get in contact with Stefan across the street. I tell him we are close to the French border. But we didn't know the area where we were was off limits, the Siegfried line. There were only old civilians, women, and kids. We escaped from that village with only the clothes we wore."

Stanley and Stefan traveled by night and were discovered one morning by a German man who saw them in his garden. He accused them of being Polish prisoners, took them to the village, and handed them over to the police. They were locked up and then taken to Mannheim, separated and interrogated. The police said "You are in an off limits area. You are a spy! I said no." For two or three months they were held in the Mannheim prison then sent to a town near the French border and questioned again. Stanley knew if he answered the questions he would be killed; so he said nothing hoping to stay alive. He was taken to a small concentration camp called Welzhen near Stuttgart, Germany. Stanley described his cell. "There were six bunks to one cell, so I go sleep on top because it is warmer. All the smell goes up but I say, the hell with it. I met people from Germany and the Ukraine coming from Romania through Hungary. The Germans put them in prison because they came from Russia. There was already snow. We had to clear the roads for the automobiles and farmers to go on the roads. It was the first time I noticed the Red Cross. I started waving to them to come over to us, but they just went by. Boy was I mad. I didn't know that since we were civilians we were not under Red Cross."

Germans needed people to work in the factory. When Stanley came to the concentration camp he was asked about his occupation. He replied, "I am a mechanic. They wanted mechanics so I tell Stefan to say he was a mechanic too. Somehow that saved my life. I was taken to a concentration camp outside Stuttgart. Each morning I checked in at the police station then went by streetcar to work. I met some Czech civilians and a German lady whose brother was also in a concentration camp. She brought me some bread because we got friendly and told me that Stefan was executed. I knew that I was next. I asked the Czech fellow a few questions about the area. One Saturday after work in the evening I packed my things and left from the window in the civilian house. It took me three weeks to reach the Polish border. Luckily, I found a family that kept me for two days and finally another family to help me get over the border; it was guarded. I went to Kielce and nobody was there, no family. (He could not find his mother.) I finally found a friend but he was in German uniform. I said to him what are you doing here? He was guarding a factory. I didn't trust him because of the uniform." The guard questioned Stanley asking where he came from. Stanley responded that he was visiting his girlfriend; then, he went to Stefan's family to tell them that their son had been executed.

Stanley found an acquaintance, a principal of a girls' college, and asked him for advice. "He told me to meet him at a particular time and place, and said 'Join us.' I asked him, what do you mean, join us? He says 'I tell you, but if I find out you are somebody else then you know what I am going to do; you know what will happen.' So two days later, I met him in the south of Kielce. We stayed in a hayloft for two weeks and wait for the rest of the unit to come. Then I became a member of the Polish Resistance in 1942. They asked me, 'can you shoot?' I was a sharp shooter when I was in school, but now we have only one rifle and no ammunition for about twenty-five of us."

The group waited for weapons and ammunition, but when the Germans bombed the area they left for Kraków. Stanley was sent to an area around Black Lake between the border of Poland and Czechoslovakia and stayed with some mountaineers. He didn't stay there long, and then returned to Kraków waiting for orders from the resistance headquarters in Warsaw. It was 1943. "We went to Auschwitz to try and get people out. Then, I went to Kraków and my commander told me that I was selected to be in intelligence. It was September or October of 1944. I was provided a place to live in the city of Vienna, a cross-point. We needed information. There were all kinds of people in Vienna: Greeks, Polish, French, many people. We did sabotage putting sand instead of oil in the engines at a factory. We did all kinds of things outside of Vienna too until the Americans bombed the hell out of the place."

In November 1944 three men approached Stanley and started to question him. "They asked me in German, 'what is your name?' I responded, 'what do you want?' They showed me their Gestapo badge." Stanley faced execution if his pistol hidden in the soffit was discovered. He was taken to the Fifth District Police Prison in Vienna until January and then moved to Mauthausen, a large concentration camp near Linz, Austria. Patton's troops liberated the camp in May. "The Americans took me to the base where they were stationed and a medic put cream on me. My body was wounds all over. We stayed with them from Austria to Bavaria. The captain told us the Americans had to go to California because of the war in Japan. I started to cry. They took one house and told us to stay there. They left so much food and uniforms for us. They said the war is over. When they left us I wondered what am I going to do and that one day if I ever have a chance to pay back the Americans I was going to."

After the war ended, Stanley worked in the coal mines in England for several years and in 1951 went to Detroit with some friends in the midst of wide scale unemployment. He responded to a recruitment sign for the Air Force and after completing basic training in San Antonio, Texas, Stanley served in Korea for four years. He kept his word and wrote his story, *"I kept my promise!"*

THE BOLSHEVIKS AND THE EASTERN FRONT ~ "My father, Tadeusz Lubicz-Sadowski, fought the Bolsheviks."[474] The Bolsheviks were a faction of the Marxist Russian Social-Democratic Labor Party (RSDLP) and eventually became the Communist Party of the Soviet Union, formed by Vladimir Lenin. They seized power in Russia during the Revolution in 1917, known as the *October Revolution,* and following the Russian Civil War, 1918-1921, founded the Soviet Union the first socialist state.[475]

"My father was born in Liepaja, Latvia, in 1898 and raised in Lithuania. I was born in Ostrów, Poland, on August 2, 1928." Kazimierz "Kasey" Sadowski's front door opens to a view of Fort Niagara State Park. Sixty-two years ago a barbed wire fence enclosed the present park grounds and the temporary barracks housing the German prisoners of war at Fort Niagara. But Kasey's story took place on the other side of the world.

The Sadowski family history was woven throughout the two world wars. "Lubicz" was the family coat of arms awarded to an ancestor by the King of Poland in 1199 for bravery in battle against the Prussians. The extensive chronology of the Sadowski family estate at Sugawdzie began in the mid-nineteenth century. Tadeusz's eldest brother, Ignacy, belonged to the illegal Polish Socialist Party in Warsaw and was involved with terrorism against Russian dignitaries and high-ranking officers. He was arrested for his activities, convicted, and sentenced to death by hanging when Tsar Nicholas II announced amnesty for all condemned political prisoners on the occasion of the birth of his first son, Tsarevitch Alexei on August 12, 1904. The sentence was commuted to a lifetime of hard labor in Siberia. Ignacy escaped to Kraków and continued to fight for freedom of his beloved Poland divided under German, Russian, and Austrian occupation.[47]

POLAND IN WWI ~ Tadeusz was with his mother in Liepaja, a port city close to the Lithuanian border, on July 31, 1914, as German Emperor Wilhelm II threatened war and ordered Russia to demobilize. Before nightfall that evening, Kasey's father saw the German ships move along the shore and heard the explosions. By the beginning of March, a transport of Russian soldiers arrived in Liepaja, and in May a decision was made to evacuate the schools. The soldiers started digging defensive trenches south and east of the city. Tadeusz wrote, "The morale among the soldier and civilian population was very low. Everyone lost faith in the strength of Russian armies, and no one believed any longer that the German invasion could be stopped…The Colonel, one of the Tsar's soldiers, told my mother they all surrendered."[477]

The Cossacks stationed in Sugawdzie, the family estate, retreated before the Germans arrived. In early March 1917 news came of the first Russian revolution and the violent strikes and demonstrations in the large cities. The parliament, the Duma, selected a committee, formed a new government, and Tsar Nicholas II abdicated the throne. The rule of the Romanovs ended and Russia became a republic. The unstable new Russian government led to a second revolution and on November 7, 1917, the Bolsheviks took control of the government. Fighting erupted all over the country and the Cossacks in the south were the last to surrender.[478]

Lithuania was in anarchy in 1918 and the Lithuanian Army ignored the Polish people. The Poles started to organize their own army and Tadeusz joined the ranks to fight the Bolsheviks. He was demobilized March 22, 1921, after more than two years of service in the Tenth Regiment of cavalry.[479] After the war, the land in Ostrów was subdivided into eleven parcels for the soldiers who fought for the freedom of Poland. It created much hatred and resentment by the local people towards the new settlers. The Belarusians lived in the surrounding villages for generations and believed the land belonged to them. "My father was called a 'sorcerer' for using fertilizers and being able to grow cabbage where it had not grown before," Kasey said.

The border of Poland after WWI was farther to the east from the border established after WWII. Vilnius, Pinsk, and L'viv were within the Polish border. Lithuania claimed Vilnius as its capital, Belarus claimed Pinsk, and Ukraine claimed L'viv. The eastern region was a mixture of Poles, Lithuanians in the north, Ukrainians in the south, Belarusians in the center, and Jews all over the region. (The Belarusians are the majority of the population in the Republic of Belarus and in the minority in Poland, Russia, Lithuania, and Ukraine.) Kasey said everyone claimed part of the country as their own.

SEPTEMBER 1, 1939 ~ Kasey's birthplace of Ostrów was a hamlet, an island in a swamp. There were only eleven Polish settlers living in Ostrów, each with about ten hectares of land. Just beyond the Zelwianka River to the east was the village of Zalaceeva. The population was Belarusian. In the south was the worst part of the swamp and the railroad station of Zelwa. Rogoznica and the church were northwest of the settlement.

"I was eleven years old when my father who was in the Reserves was mobilized the week before the war broke out on September 1, 1939. We had no paper and no radio. There were rumors about the threat of war before 1939. We were told in school that 'we have a great army and there is nothing to worry about.' But my father was a lieutenant in the Polish Army. He was nervous, but more afraid of the Bolsheviks than the Germans."[480] Kasey lived on a farm with his father, his mother Helena, and his brother Jan, who was two years older. A sister, Renia, died as a little girl from scarlet fever and was buried in Bialystok. The family had two horses, several cows, some pigs, turkeys, and chickens on their farm. Kasey's father was the bailiff (wójt) for the Township of Piaski, several surrounding villages, and some large estates. In 1932 Tadeusz resigned his position to spend more time working on his farm and his responsibilities as the elected Chairman of the Association of Military Settlers.[481]

Kasey and his brother were in a public school in the city of Vawkavysk about twenty-eight kilometers from their home. They lived in a private room with the Pawencki family under difficult conditions, and returned home only for Christ-

Sadowski family at Ostrów. Helena, Kazimierz, Jan, and Tadeusz Lubicz-Sadowski (Courtesy Kazimierz Sadowski)

mas and Easter. The war was coming closer to their homeland. German troops overran Sudetenland in October 1938. Sudetenland was the west part of Czechoslovakia occupied by many Sudenten Germans. Kasey's father said, "Hitler is not going to stop there!" In the summer of 1939 Kasey and Jan went to stay at their uncle's home in Góry until school started. The old house was surrounded by an orchard and overlooked the Pilica River. It was about seventy kilometers southwest of Warsaw and close to Germany's western border. "My father sent a telegram for us to come home. 'The war is imminent.' My uncle put us on a train and two weeks later, my father was mobilized on August 24, 1939."[482]

"My father started a nursery of fruit trees. Large numbers of trees were ready for market. This would be the first year of profit, but now everything was lost and twenty years of my father's work was for nothing. My mother was taking care of us since my father left for the army. The first day of the war, it was a beautiful sunny day, September 1, 1939. I heard the airplanes low humming sound then we heard the explosions. There was no other news. We realized the war was on and then we turned around and could see the German airplanes overhead. It was exciting for us. We could see the airplanes flying over the railroad station in Zelwa and climbed up on the roof of the stable to watch. We could see the airplanes flying very low and the bombs exploding. My mother yelled at us to get down," Kasey said. The family heard machine gun fire in the distance, but did not see any resistance by the Polish Air Force fighters from the base in Lida not far from Kasey's home. Later, there were rumors that at the end of August an order was given for concurrent general maintenance so the airplanes were easily destroyed on the ground.

That afternoon a Polish policeman came on a bicycle to the Sadowski home. He announced Martial Law and that all firearms and "white arms" (sabers or bayonets) must be turned in. The family had a .22 rifle, and two sabers. Kasey's father had one saber that was his officer's saber and the other was an old curved antique Cossack's saber. Jan and Kasey saddled a horse, then Jan with the rifle across his back and a saber strapped on each side of the saddle went to Kremienica, ten kilometers from Ostrów, to turn in the weapons to the police station.

SOVIET INVASION ~ Day to day nothing changed much until September 17, 1939, when the family heard airplanes again, but this time they were coming from the east. Bombers with a big Red Star flew very low and made quite a show. The earth rumbled from the approach of tanks from the south and the east. The Soviets invaded and crossed the eastern border of Poland to 'liberate' the oppressed population.

"Polish authority was disintegrating as local armed communists came to the surface and took control of this side of the country. Instantly, they declared themselves as the highest authority, and self-appointed prosecutors, judges, and executioners. The Polish settlers were the victims and many were murdered, some families completely wiped out. Not far from us at the settlement of Konna my father's friend, Ignatowski, and a few others were taken into the woods and executed. It was worse on the Ukrainian side," Kasey said. But the glory of the self-proclaimed authority did not last long and behind the Red Army came an army of politruks to take control of the 'liberated' country. They did not need the local communists' help. Some of the leaders were arrested and sent to Siberia, ahead of the Polish settlers.[483]

"There was a lot of propaganda. Russians showed movies in the market place in town and issued news reports. Some people had never seen a movie. The worst thing was the hatred between the Belarusians and the Polish. The Belarusians wore a red ribbon on their shoulder or chest. Armed men looking for our father stayed in our home, day and night, waiting for him to return home. There were rumors of him being on his way home, but this was not true," said Kasey. Instead Tadeusz, Kasey's father, was in command of 170 men, 100 wagons, 156 horses, a field kitchen, and shops for mobile blacksmiths, wheelwrights, a harness maker, a cobbler, and a tailor. They traveled at night and during the day tried to remain hidden from the Luftwaffe bomb attacks and machine gun fire. By September 20, 1939, Soviet aircraft approached flying low and sprayed machine gun fire that massacred the civilian refugees on the road. After bloody battles with German artillery and aircraft bombardment on the Polish Army's position, General Kleberg on October 6, 1939, issued his last order to lay down arms.[484]

Soldiers, from different parts of our country, I gathered you all here, under my command to fight together to the end. My main objective was to go with help to Warsaw. This became impossible (when) Warsaw capitulated to the overwhelming German forces. In spite of that defeat, you fought on. You did not lose hope. You showed the bravery and loyalty to your country.

Today we are surrounded by the enemy. Our food and ammunition are depleted. Further fighting does not give us any hope, only would spill more soldiers' blood, which still may be needed in the future. The privilege of a leader is to accept the responsibility on himself. Today I am taking this responsibility and ordering you to stop fighting and shedding more blood. I thank you all, for your bravery and discipline. I know, that you will stand up again, when the need comes.

Poland is not lost, and will live forever.

This order to be read in front of all the units. General Kleberg

This was the last battle of the September Campaign in which Tadeusz was personally involved.[485]

While Tadeusz began his time as a prisoner of war in Germany on October 8, 1939, he was worried about the fate of his family. Back at his home, refugees from the west arrived in the hamlet of Ostrów looking for shelter and food and bringing news of the war. Many Jews were running from the approaching Germans. The Aleksandrowicz family came from Warsaw and told of the terror bombing of the city, roads crowded with refugees, and German Luftwaffe spraying them with machine gun fire.[486]

There was a threat to the little settlement. "A Russian officer came to the hamlet and informed us of his authority. If any local, self-proclaimed commandants give us any problem we were to tell him. Later in the evening a young boy reported a story about a man who approached him while he was fishing on the river with a threat on (all) our lives. The man said that 'your blood will be flowing as the water in this river.' The news spread and we all gathered in one house. The men patrolled outside with axes. It was a terrible night. Women were praying the rosary. The whole settlement was Catholic, but there was friction between the Orthodox and Roman Catholics. Luckily nothing happened."

The Russians arrived at the settlement that night.

As winter approached, a cousin, Wieslaw Czarkowski, came to live with Kasey and his family. Wieslaw was a bachelor, in his twenties. He came to help on the farm. There had been no news from Kasey's father. He was taken prisoner by the Germans. While in prison Tadeusz met a man from Peski and gave him some money to get word to his family that he was alive. The winter of 1940 was very cold and people said that the Russians brought the cold weather from Siberia. The Sadowski family was living from day to day.

FORCED LABOR CAMP ~ It was very cold early in the morning of February 10, 1940; at dawn there was banging on the door of the Sadowski home. Russians with rifles and bayonets forced Kasey and his brother into one bed. His cousin was sitting on the floor. "They started searching my father's desk and taking documents. They went into the closets and through his books, everything. The front door was open as local people went by on their sleds. An officer came and read a notice that we would be deported to another state. One of the Russians held a bayonet to my mother, who fainted." Kasey choked back the emotion of a young boy watching terrified for his dear mother held at bay by a bayonet. After his mother was revived, the officer read the rest of the verdict. The family was given twenty minutes to take food for one month, warm clothing, and bedding.

Wieslaw took charge. He made a bundle with their bedding and filled it with bread and smoked hams. A bag of flour was placed on a sled. Soldiers armed with rifles and bayonets escorted all the families to a neighbor's house. "The next morning potatoes were boiled and eaten; then, we left and made our way on a horse drawn sled towards the railway station. We stopped at the local school for women to feed their babies. At the railyard we were put in boxcars. There were shelves in the cars that we used for sleeping. In the middle was a pot-bellied stove. One of the soldiers tried to help us start a fire. Our boxcar had a broken wheel. It was replaced on the train before we finally left. I couldn't see anything as I looked between the boards of the boxcar."

The train kept stopping as others passed on the adjacent tracks. "Back and forth people cried out to each other across the tracks and asked, 'Where are you from?' There were teachers, priests, doctors, and lawyers. All the educated people were put in jail or labor camps. Sometimes the train stopped for days before it moved again," Kasey said. It took about a month until they reached Chelyabinsk at the edge of the Ural Mountains in Siberia where they were transferred to a different railroad towards their final destination, a mining city, Karabash. Kasey and his family and other Poles arrived to work in the copper mines and factories for twelve hours a day. Others were taken to work in the forests.

Kasey's mother worked above ground firing boilers that produced the steam to run the machinery in the mines. Kasey and his brother spent much of their time standing in the endless line to get bread and searching for wood in the forest. The people were spread out in the beginning until some of the Polish men who were carpenters built new barracks. There were twenty-four rooms each twelve by sixteen feet. "Ours was No. 22," said Kasey. Each family lived in the one small room with a woodburning stove. A plank with two sawhorses was the bed for the three of them. There were some stools and a table of another board on sawhorses.

"Once when we needed firewood, two of us took sleds and went to the woods. The other boy had a light load and left me. The snow was getting deeper and the sled more difficult to pull. I sat down in the snow and was getting very weak. I took most of the load off and left just a few pieces. The snow was up to my knees and I started to fall asleep. A bell on a horse harness awakened me and luckily I made my way to the road. I yelled to the woman who brought me to the camp and crawled on my knees, so weak. The next day I found someone else took my wood."

Kasey continued to describe the harsh conditions and the long wait in lines. "When people heard that bread or other food was to be distributed, lines formed at night. People were hoping to be the first to get something, but instead at the opening you were called by name from the beginning of the alphabet from a list. They were the first to get bread. The next day it was distributed from the end. Those in the middle of the alphabet either got the bread every other day, or did not get it for days, depending on the delivery. There was never enough bread for everyone. What about us in the middle," Kasey exclaimed remembering the lines and the hunger. Farmers brought potatoes in horse drawn wagons and on sleds. Sometimes the children went to school. "Occasionally my mother's sister sent us buckwheat from Poland and other flours and barley. We received letters from our father through relatives in Poland. He was being held in an Oflag, a POW camp for officers. But when the Germans invaded Russia, we didn't know what happened to my father and lost contact with our relatives."

The Soviets signed a Non-Aggression Treaty with Germany on August 23, 1939, acknowledging their earlier Neutrality Agreement from 1926. Part of the secret negotiations included the question of boundaries in Eastern Europe. Poland was partitioned by the line of the rivers of Narew, Vistula, and San, which resulted in control by the Soviets generally on the east side of Poland and the west by the Germans.[487] The non-aggression pact lasted until June 22, 1941, when Germany invaded the Soviet Union.

On July 30, 1941, the exiled government of Poland, in London, made an agreement with Stalin. Kasey read from the *Agreement between Government of Polish Republic and Government of Soviet Union.* The first and second point acknowledged the recognition of the government of Poland and re-established diplomatic relations. Number three obligated both governments to help and support "in the present war against Hitler's Germany." The following article permitted the creation of the Polish Army on Soviet territory. The Agreement drawn in England was written in Polish and Russian, dated July 30, 1941, and resulted in amnesty for the deportees and the soldiers working in the forced labor camps.[488] "We got our freedom and documents to move around and could join the army. Units formed in Uzbekistan and Kazakhstan. We sold our few belongings and left Siberia in the fall of 1941. My mother thought we could be considered a military family so we went south on the railroad towards Tashkent in Uzbekistan. We were many weeks on the train and infected with lice. Once we left Karabash I did not have bath until I was admitted to the orphanage in Samarqand after Easter," Kasey said.

"We came as far as Tarab to the Amu Darya River.[489] Some organizers were directing traffic. Three barges were tied together and towed down the river. We were on the river for four days and nights. When we stopped at night, we cooked what little food we had. Then we came to the town of Turtkul in Karakalpakstan. They put us into collective farms to pick cotton and sorghum, and dig vegetables. It was one place that food was plentiful."

Kasey's family stayed there for about a month. There were rumors they were to go back to the railroad station. "It was good while we were there. The kitchens in the shed were used for cooking food for the workers. The soup was delightful – pots of carrots and white onions – so delicious, the best food I had in Russia." Then orders came and the group was placed on barges again with nothing to cook. They lived on bread and water while on the barge for five days. There was an outhouse hanging over the edge of the catwalk. The water drawn from the side of the barge was contaminated from the sewage.

Kasey's brother became very sick from the putrid water. There was no medical help and many people died. Some fell from the catwalk and drowned. In one incident two people fell over the edge of the boat. A rowboat was thrown over the side as someone tried to help the people in the water. Only one person was pulled to safety as the small boat filled with water struggling to to get to the shore. The other person drowned. "There was a lot of conflict. People argued that the Catholic was saved instead of the Jewish person who drowned. There were many Jews in our group on the barge."

The journey continued on the railroad north to Samarqand. Lice were a continuous problem. It was an almost comic scene when a local Uzbechian mother took off her child's dress and chopped the lice with her teeth along the seams of the clothing. At the station at Amin they were told to disembark and sent to different collective farms. There was almost nothing to eat. The ration of a little more than an once of barley per day per person was taken to the mill to grind for flour. "All we had was the flour. We made dough with water and cooked it. On a rare occasion we had sugar beets. This is how we survived the winter. We were living in a clay hut with other families and one single man. An Uzbecki neighbor had a little pet chicken. At Easter during the night, the other mother took the pet, wrung its neck, and cooked it for the seven of us. For two weeks the neighbor who owned the chicken called for her pet in the hills. After Easter we received news from Amin that a representative of the Polish government would come to take all the children to a shelter and we were put on a train to Samarqand and an orphanage. It was a church divided in thirds: one part for the railroad office, another for the kitchen and dining room, and the other third for us to sleep on the floor. My mother worked at a collective farm while we were in the orphanage." In the orphanage at Samarqand some normalcy began and the children were given food and a bath. Their hair was cut, boys and girls, and their clothing put in the oven to get rid of the lice.

THE POLISH ARMY ~ A train stopped in Samarqand and a friend of Kasey's mother came running into the orphanage and said to go quickly to the railroad station. The boys joined their mother and jumped on the train. She gave the conductor a few rubbles and they hid under a bench. At Kirmenay the Sadowskis were accepted as a military family. Boys were directed to the military school at Narpi. "My brother was sixteen now and I was fourteen. We lied and both said we were two years older so we could join the Polish Army. We were proud to be in the Army." In August 1942 the army was moving to Krasnovodsk on the east coast of the Caspian Sea.[490] They boarded a tanker. People squeezed on the deck and went without water for a whole day. The sun beat down; people fainted and one died. In the morning the dead man was thrown overboard.

The tanker docked in the port of Pahlevi (Anzali, on the Caspian shore of northern Iran). They called the camp as a joke "a dirty camp" because it was a

Left, Kazimierz Sadowski preparing to be a soldier.

Below, Young Polish soldiers, at the Roman ruins in Baalbeck (north-east of Beruit, Lebanon), preparing to serve as part of the Allied invasion of Italy.

(Both photos courtesy of Kazimierz Sadowski)

transit camp where they slept on straw mats. Eventually, they were moved to another camp and their infested clothing was removed. They went to the hot baths with a carbolic paste and were given tropical new uniforms. Everything that was brought from Russia was burned with gasoline. "My brother was in a different company. We were organized by our school grade then moved by trucks to Tehran and stayed there for a month. There were plenty of vegetables, all dehydrated and the women in the civilian camps cooked for us. The lamb, dehydrated too, was stamped '1918 New Zealand' and was wrapped in cheesecloth. We were in the desert in Iraq for several weeks living in tents. Sand was everywhere and in everything including our food."

Kasey's unit was transported to Palestine and received rifle training and regular schooling. "I started taking English language lessons, finished fifth and sixth grades in one year. The courses were accelerated to help us catch up to high school. I chose mechanical school for high school. In addition to the Polish instructors there were some Jewish instructors who spoke Russian. This education helped me to become a tool and die maker. I learned about lathes, welding, and blacksmith work." After the war ended in 1945, Kasey stayed in Palestine until 1947. He said, "There was fighting going on and the Jews told us to wear our Polish insignia so we couldn't be mistaken for the English and get killed. I was hitchhiking from Haifa to the camp. Just before the village a truck filled with English soldiers standing in the back passed us. Then a bus stopped and picked us up as the truck entered a traffic circle ahead. All of a sudden a roadside bomb exploded on the rear of the truck. English soldiers were lying all over!" Kasey relived the horror of the scene and his close encounter with death.

A bright spot during this time for Kasey was in the Cedar Reservation Rest Camp in Lebanon. He enjoyed the fresh fruits especially the bananas and apples grown in the region. While in the Middle East, news arrived about the Polish resistance. The English liberated Kasey's father, Tadeusz, who was running a farm after the war for the Red Cross. He wrote to the refugee camps looking for his family. Polish refugees were in India, East Africa, Uganda, Jerusalem, Turkey, and from Palestine to Cairo. "My brother was in Egypt in Air Force school training to be an engine mechanic. My mother was working in a hospital in Palestine. She joined the army earlier in Iran. Late in 1946 my mother went to Italy on leave to join my father and was demobilized. Then, she and my father went to England. My brother joined our parents, but I stayed on for another year and finished school. Our unit was moved from Palestine to England after the war in 1947, and then was demobilized. It was eight years since we had seen each other. My father was managing a surgeon's club for the Red Cross and my mother was working in a canteen in the same club. I had a mustache and long hair now when I saw my mother. She did not recognize me until I spoke to her then she said, go and meet your father."

STUTTGART POW CAMP ~ Tadeusz's journey from POW to the Red Cross in England began in 1939 at Fort Deblin where the Germans took control of the Army wagons and horses, and separated the officers from enlisted soldiers and non-commissioned officers after being searched. The POWs marched to Kielce and remained there for days. Then they were loaded on trucks and passed Czenstochowa and the sight of the church and monastery on top of the mountain. That evening, Tadeusz and the other officers said goodbye to their country. Insults and stones from the German people greeted their entry to Wroclaw. After a train ride and short stop at Frankfurt on the Oder River the train halted in Stuttgart and orders were shouted to disembark.[491]

Tadeusz' memories of Stuttgart were the worst. There was real hunger and no privacy. Latrines were deep trenches out in the open. Twice a day the Polish officers were required to stand in formation on the parade grounds.

"Achtung!" was shouted as an old General with a monocle in one eye gave a speech translated by an interpreter standing next to him. He began with the announcement that the war in Poland ended, and that Poland lost the war. Germans gave the prisoners propaganda to read. (It was several years until the spring in 1942 before a secret line of communication with the Allies was established providing reliable information.) In November, the train moved the group to Arnswalde and better conditions. A theater, a chorus, a camp press, and language courses gave the semblance of a thriving city rather than a POW camp. The Germans complied with the Geneva Convention and paid the officers half of their regular wages. After France capitulated in 1940 the conditions became crowded at the camp, but new prisoners brought fresh news of the war. [492]

The reality of rumors that Polish settlers and families of Polish officers were arrested and sent to Siberia by the Russians sent Tadeusz into a depression when he received a postcard from his family in Karabash in the Ural Mountains in March 1940. Overnight his hair turned white when he realized that his family was sent to Siberia. He received psychiatric treatment and eventually began focusing on serious studies of his pre-war interest of pomology to renew his spirit. All mail was stopped in 1941 as word came of the German invasion of the Soviet Union on June 22, 1941. People believed that Germany was overextending itself like Napoleon.

The prisoners were transferred again to Gross Born, Oflag II-D.[493] The camp was called the "Upper Camp" or "Dog's Hill." Nearby was the "Lower Camp" for the Russian prisoners of war where Tadeusz and his comrades witnessed some hideous scenes and evidence of extreme cruelty.[494] A corridor like fence connected the two camps.

The snow-covered highways became filled with horse drawn wagons and people on foot carrying bundles or dragging sleds heading west, evidence of the Germans retreating from the Russian front. At the end of January 1945, the sounds of artillery fire were heard by Tadeusz and the others from the camp as they marched through the snow and cold winds. Corpses were left by the side of the road as the march continued to Dramburg (now Drawskow), then on to Stargard, and the suburbs of Stettin, in Branderburg to the railroad station, and then to Hamburg and an air raid. There were casualties in all the boxcars. One loaf of bread was given for each group of ten men during a five-hour march to the next prison camp near Lüneburg. The conditions and the barracks were deplorable with bedbugs, lice, only cold water, and a diet of herb tea, thin turnip soup, and a shared loaf of bread for fourteen men. Again the POWs were moved, and rumors abounded that the SS was planning to drown the prisoners off the barges on the way to the sea. Eventually they made their way to Lübeck and freedom.[495] One week later Germany surrendered on May 7, 1945, and the war in Europe was over.

ENGLAND AFTER THE WAR ~ England needed workers after the war. His father found Kasey a job with the Red Cross in a canteen for soldiers at Shobdon. Twice a week Kasey skinned rabbits. He hated his job and quit after a year. He found work in an auto shop rebuilding old buses in Hereford. His father was transferred to Birmingham, and then Kasey went to work at British Industrial Plastic Tools, which he loved, since he could use his mechanical training. He was happy working there for four years gaining experience and making money. His father continued to run a Polish Home for the Red Cross. An older family friend shared a room with Kasey and read to him from a Polish newspaper about life in Canada. "People were doing well in Toronto. I was reading a book and my friend kept interrupting and dared me 'If it is so good, why don't we go?' I had a cousin living in Canada and applied to the Canadian Consul in London. My friend chickened out as the process continued, but I sold my motorbike, went to a travel agency, took a boat to Halifax, and then the train to Toronto." Kasey married Irene in St. Catharines and obtained a visa to come to the United States. Kasey worked at the Ford Stamping Plant in Hamburg,

The Sadowski family reunited in England in 1949. (Courtesy Kazimierz Sadowski)

then at Buffalo Tool and Die, and at Voss Manufacturing for more than twenty-five years.

Kazimierz Sadowski and his family endured terror, pain, losses, evils of war, and inhumane conditions. Yet he said, "People like Stalin who created these bad times are all dead, so it is no use of holding a grudge." Kasey spends his retirement years devoted to his family, reading, creating tables with tops of intricate and delicate design from small pieces of wood, and helping his neighbors. Over his computer is a small piece of paper with a quote by Henry Ford, "Anyone who stops learning is old." Kazimierz Sadowski is "young" and has worked through the darkness of suffering and evil to contribute beauty in the world through his industry and talent.

In November 2007, Lech Kaczynski, the President of the Republic of Poland, awarded Kazimierz Sadowski the "Cross of Siberian Deportees," via Krzysztof W. Kasprzyk, Consul General of the Republic of Poland in New York City, NY.

MEMORIAL AT KARABASH ~ More than one and a half million Poles were taken from their homes and deported by the Soviets to the camps in Siberia and other areas. Edward Kuczynski and Artur Wozniakowski, life-long friends of

Kasey, were at Karabash too with their families. Edward's father and many others died while working in the mines before "amnesty" was granted by the Soviets. Unable to find the graveyard in 2004, Edward Kuczynski established a monument in Karabash with the help of Irina Tumonova, a newspaper reporter from Karabash, to honor the memory of those who perished and all who were forced to work in the camps.[496] "Artur invited Irina and her husband to Poland. The Polish survivors' organization gave her a medal for her work and help to create the monument."[497]

The two-piece stone monument has three plaques on the top piece. The first is the image of the Polish Eagle. The other two plaques, one in Russian and one in Polish, read "1940-1942 To the memory of the Polish people to those buried here and to those who survived and gratitude/thanks to the citizens of Karabash for their help in difficult time."[498] At the base section there are five plaques with family names:

Family Name	
Sadowscy	Helena, Jan, Kazimierz
Kuczynscy	Agnieszka, Josef, Jozefa, Tadeusz, Edward
Wozniakowscy	Jadwiga, Mieczyslaw, Ryszard, Artur, Waclaw
Cybulski	Marian
Kacprzak	Helena, Jan, Jerzy, Janina, Jozef

"To my father Joseph I dedicate, E. Kuczynski, Detroit 2005."[499] Edward's father died in the labor camp. His older brother became part of the Polish Army that fought at Monte Cassino and was killed in action in Italy.[500]

While Kasey, Edward, and Artur were living out the history of the Soviet labor camps, the Germans were establishing extermination camps in Poland designed to kill all Jews from the countries occupied by the Germans. Rudolf Höss wrote in his autobiography *Death Dealer* that the Nazis also attempted to get Spain and other countries to send Jews to be killed.[501] The systematic effort of the Nazi regime to murder Jews is known as the Holocaust; six million Jews died in the concentration camps.[502] Germans established the first concentration camps of Dachau, Oranienburg, and others in 1933 to intern political prisoners who opposed the Nazis. About five million non-Jews also died in the camps including political dissidents, homosexuals, Jehovah Witnesses, Poles, Roma (gypsies), Soviets (especially prisoners of war), and others.

During the war, the residents of the Town of Porter were unaware of the Holocaust happening in Europe. Many Allied soldiers also did not know about the murder and killing of innocents in the concentration camps until the war was almost over. John Simon told his daughter what he saw at the camps at Ohrdruf and Buchenwald.

What happened in the concentration camps?

NOTES

[472] Stanley C. Blake was born Kazimierz Stanislaw Wojcik. On March 3, 1953, at Big Springs, TX, his name was legally changed. "Black Stanley" was the English translation of his name used in the Polish Underground. Stanley emphasized that when Germany invaded Poland there was no support from other countries.

[473] Stanley C. Blake, interview by author, Buffalo, NY, July 23, 2007.

[474] Kazimierz "Kasey" Sadowski, interview by author, Youngstown, NY, September 30, October 3, and October 31, 2006.

[475] The Russian Revolution of 1917 was a series of political events beginning with the riots and abdication of the Tsar, March 15, 1917. A provisional government was established and in October another revolution, known as the Bolshevik or October Revolution, led by Vladimir Lenin, overthrew the provisional government.

[476] Tadeusz Lubicz-Sadowski, *Memoirs*, translated to English from Polish by Kazimierz Sadowski, 3-4.

[477] Lubicz-Sadowski, 14.

[478] Lubicz-Sadowski, 18.

[479] Lubicz-Sadowski, *Memoirs*, Chapter 3, 1-2.

[480] Kasey Sadowski, interview by author, Youngstown, NY, September 30, October 3, and October 31, 2006.

[481] Kasey Sadowski, interview and Lubicz-Sadowski, *Memoirs*.

[482] Tadeusz Lubicz-Sadowski predicted the imminent German invasion.

[483] Kasey Sadowski described how the local communists took control of their settlement.

[484] Lubicz-Sadowski, *Memoirs*, 13-14.

[485] Lubicz-Sadowski wrote in his *Memoirs* the Order given by General Kleberg to the remaining units of Polish soldiers to surrender to the Germans.

[486] Kasey Sadowski, *Memoirs*, 7.

[487] Bradley Lightbody, "Invasion of Poland," Nazi-Soviet Pact WWII, *BBC*, "Text of the Nazi-Soviet Pact," The History Place WWII, http://www.bbc.co.uk/history/worldwars/wwtwo/invasion_poland_04.shtml [accessed March 5, 2008].

[488] Kasey Sadowski translated from Polish to English the Agreement between the government of the Polish Republic and the government of the Soviet Union, dated July 30, 1941, London.

[489] The Amu Darya River is also known as the Oxus River.

[490] Krasnovodsk became known as Turmenbashi, Turkmenistan.

[491] Lubicz-Sadowski, *Memoirs*, Chapter 4, 3.

[492] Lubicz-Sadowski, 7-8.

[493] Oflag was the name for a German POW camp for officers.

[494] Lubicz-Sadowski, *Memoirs*, Chapter 5, 15-16.

[495] Lubicz-Sadowski, Chapter 6, 1-14.

[496] "Return to Siberia," *The Polish Weekly*, December 2, 2004.

[497] Kasey Sadowski, interview by author, February 27, 2007.

[498] Translated from Russian and Polish to English by Kasey Sadowski, February 27, 2007.

[499] Names and inscription from the photograph of the Memorial monument at Karabash translated from Polish to English by Kasey Sadowski, February 27, 2007.

[500] Kasey Sadowski, interview.

[501] Rudolf Höss, *Death Dealer,* Memoirs of the SS Kommandant at Auschwitz translated by Andrew Pollinger and edited by Steven Paskuly, (New York: Prometheus Books, 1992), 47. Andrew Pollinger was a concentration camp survivor.

[502] "Frequently asked Questions," United States Holocaust Museum, http://www.ushmm.org/research/library/faq/#topic01 [accessed March 2, 2007].

CHAPTER 9

THE HOLOCAUST

IN 1944 THE GERMANS WERE RETREATING from the Russian front and the Allies were advancing. It appeared that the war was almost over and the Jews in Czechoslovakia were to be spared from the unbelievable horrors rumored about the concentration camps, but it was not to be so.

"It shall be a time unsurpassed in distress since nations began until that time."[503] The words were written to strengthen and comfort the Jewish people during their suffering from the persecution perpetrated by Antiochus IV Epiphanes. The apocalyptic writings in the Book of Daniel almost two millennium earlier were about to be revived.

In the lobby of the Jewish Community Center on North Forest Road in Amherst, New York, through the course of the morning, people called out a greeting or came to the table to pay their respects to Joseph Diamond, a survivor and living testament of the Holocaust "The Final Solution" by the Nazis to systematically exterminate an entire race.

The beauty of the beginning of this story beguiled the chapters that followed. It was a picturesque image of the Carpathian region in Czechoslovakia, a parliamentary democracy prior to the war.[504] Vineyards framed the little Village of Seredne nestled in the valley. Seredne translates as "middle." It was located between the two larger cities of Uzhhord and Munkachevo, a village of cultural diversity, which included Ruthenians, Hungarians, and Czechs.

"We were peasants. Many of the people were poor, but content. Conditions were primitive. Cows were stalled in the midst of houses." Joseph longed for the little village of his youth as he remembered those times. The stores, many owned by the Jews, were located on the one paved road, Main Street. This was a source of envy and anti-Semitism within the population of 1,600 residents.[505]

The days were long for young Joseph and other Jewish children. Religious school began at 7:00 a.m. with prayers and practice for the rote learning of the five Books of Moses, and then on to public school. At the end of the school

The Diamond family store in Seredne, Czechoslovakia. (Courtesy Joseph Diamond)

day, the Jewish children returned to religious school at 3:00 p.m. and continued until 7:00 p.m. This was their life, school and prayer, and no chance to play as most children.

RANTS OF HITLER ~ Rumors abounded about the possibility of another world war. Many were not surprised because it seemed to Joseph that "There were wars in Europe every two weeks." Newspapers were one-sided and filled with propaganda. The Diamond family listened to the rants of Adolph Hitler during the radio broadcasts. "Hitler always spoke about how Jews were responsible for the economic conditions. He said, Jews are the bankers. They are taking bread from the little boys and the farmers. If we don't do something they will wipe us out!" Stories came from Poland that people were being taken to camps. Bertha Siegel, Joseph's mother, was from Slovakia. "Her whole family was taken. People told me after the war that they were taken in trucks to Lublin. The trucks were so crowded that some people fell out and rolled down the hill. My mother used to get letters from Poland from her family about being there in the camp then suddenly the letters stopped, and afterwards they were taken, according to history, to extermination camps. They didn't know what was going to happen to them," he said.

Life remained somewhat normal for the Diamond family. But changes were about to occur as Edvard Beneš, the president, resigned and fled to London c. 1940. He became part of a government in exile while Hungary occupied Czechoslovakia. There were stories about what was happening in Poland and Denmark, but Joseph said, "You didn't believe it until it happens to you." The reality of the poison of Hitler and the Nazi party arrived in Seredne. "The Hungarians took over ownership of the stores and seventy percent of the profits. The remainder of thirty percent went to the Jewish owner." This impacted his family because they owned a clothing store. The Nuremberg Laws on Citizenship and Race, passed in Germany in 1935, stripped German Jews of their rights and became the basis for the harsh racial discrimination that found its way to Joseph's village. The state sponsored racism and violence preceded *The Final Solution* to exterminate the Jewish people.

Life began to change for the Jews in Seredne. "In 1939 we had to wear a yellow star, a symbol that we were Jewish. The Germans meant it as a symbol of ridicule, but I was proud of the ancient symbol of the Star of David. Kids couldn't use the pool at school. We couldn't walk on the sidewalks. It was considered a luxury to walk on the sidewalk. Children were bullied on their way to school and you had to be ready to fight," Joseph said. For a brief moment he returned to the present. "You can't blame Hitler for everything. People followed him. They were just as guilty. We (Americans) were guilty too. Roosevelt knew."

In January during the winter of 1944, German soldiers passed through the village returning from the Eastern front in Russia. The soldiers were gaunt and some looked like skeletons with depressed looks on many of their faces. "They couldn't handle the cold in Russia. Cities were being bombed. It looked like Germany was losing the war. We thought they would forget about us," but the Germans did not. *The Final Solution* created by the Nazis was going to rip apart the fabric of life of millions.

The newspapers on March 23, 1944, carried the startling notice to Jews to be packed and ready within twenty-four hours to help with the harvest. "Jews were considered a security risk. It was a real shock. Our family lived there for generations. We had vineyards and property." The next day the family packed their blankets, soap, towels, and other goods to be ready. "My mother dressed like she was going to a wedding. She was thirty-nine. I was about fifteen, my brother seven, and my father around forty-two years of age." Joseph shook his head remembering the irony of how his mother was nicely dressed on the way to an unimaginable journey in the days ahead.[506]

"Two Storm Troopers arrived at our home and asked: 'are you folks ready? We are going to take you to the school for processing. You will be checked for

The young Joseph Diamond was unaware of the historical events unfolding of an inconceivable genocide of the Jewish people. (Courtesy Joseph Diamond)

valuables.' It was a two and a half mile march to the school. As we walked towards the school the soldiers guarded in front and back as if we were criminals." All the Jewish neighbors were taken too. There was about one soldier for each person in the village. The soldiers were everywhere. They gathered up about six hundred people. Neighbors stood by and watched as Joseph and the other Jews were rounded up and marched out. Joseph tried again to understand a question he asked himself over and over. "How could our neighbors be bystanders? How could our own people in the United States not do anything, no protesting?"

The moment of facing the ugly reality of those who did nothing was amplified by the cruel shouts and apathetic looks. "The other people in the village didn't look upset. One guy yelled, 'Leave me your winter coat.' Another, 'It is about time to get rid of them.' I'll never forget that," Joseph said.

At the school everyone's luggage was checked for gold, jewelry, and other valuables. Sometimes people's fillings were extracted from their teeth. By midnight they were on a local train to a brick factory in the city of Uzhhord. The stop was going to be temporary, but days turned into weeks. There were no sanitary facilities in the expansive floor space of the factory. It was a time of uncertainty and fear of not knowing what was going to happen. Adding to the stress was that the Germans spoke nicely to the people. It was a tactic to keep people calm and easier to handle.

Three weeks later an announcement came over the public address system. People were told to line up in alphabetical order. Outside, trucks used to haul coal, waited to provide the degrading and inhospitable transport to the railroad station. Children were crying, lost in the confusion, and separated from their parents. Soldiers hit the children with rifle butts in an attempt to silence their cries. "When we arrived at the Bonhauf railroad station we noticed a lot of activity and railroad cattle cars lined up."[507]

Generally, the cattle cars held forty people, but about one hundred ten people were squeezed in like sardines, forced to stand and crushed against each other with only a tiny opening for air. People fainted after several hours and some young children died in the darkness under the oppressive conditions. It was midnight and all you could hear were people's cries for water. As the train finally came to a stop in Kraków, Poland, soldiers kicked out those who died. Mothers jumped off the train after their dead children. One light of kindness in this darkness of the night and inhumanity was a Polish woman approached the train with two buckets of water. "She was a human being," Joseph said. "But the SS kicked the buckets out from her," and the train moved on.

AUSCHWITZ ~ People did not know where they were as the cars halted at their final destination. The boxcar door opened to the greeting: welcome to Auschwitz and the sign over the gates "ARBEIT MACHT FREI" (work brings freedom). Auschwitz is located about 60 km, thirty-seven miles, west of Kraków. Auschwitz II or Birkenau was about three kilometers from the original camp of Auschwitz I, which was for prisoners of war. "We were told to start moving out fast because everyone was going to be interviewed. They told us to leave the luggage like we were going to a hotel. German soldiers starting pushing us out of the train with their bayonets fixed yelling 'raus' – move out! They told us to line up with our families so they can decide what work you were qualified for. There were about four thousand people waiting. The Germans were going to decide who would live or die, like they were gods."

At the front of the line there were two German soldiers and one officer. "The officer was Dr. Josef Mengele.[508] He spoke directly to my mother and asked her, 'How old is the young one?' She said, 'He is seven years old.' He told my mother that she and my brother were going to a resident labor camp and

The last Diamond family photo was sent to relatives in America. Left to right, Arie and Joseph are in front of their parents, Bertha and Maier Diamond. (Courtesy Joseph Diamond)

that my father and I were going to the work camp and that we would be able to visit them on weekends. We didn't have much time to say goodbye to each other. My mother and brother were put into trucks and taken away. We were told that 'soon you will have showers and water.' We were told to leave all our paperwork to be assessed for job assignments." It was a fateful moment and the last time Joseph saw his mother and brother.

"After being in Auschwitz for a week we found out that my mother and younger brother were immediately taken to the gas chambers." The elderly, the weak, and the handicapped were also taken directly to the chambers, anyone that was considered "useless." The four chimneys from the gas chambers were already going full blast. Joseph turned the pages of *The Auschwitz Album* by Peter Hellman to photographs that chronicled the horrific evil of genocide. In an abyss of anguish Joseph described the image of the last moments of life for his mother, Bertha, and his little brother, Arie. "The heavy metal doors swung open as they went into the gas chamber expecting showers. Several hundred people were forced into the small room. As the Cyclon B gas was released they struggled for air. People began to faint and became entwined with each other as they died. In about thirty minutes all were dead. It was mass production and the Germans were proud of this accomplishment as each day 1,500 to 2,000 people were killed. The extermination continued in the chambers; women carried their children hoping to somehow save them and were beaten on the way to the chambers or attacked by dogs. Some were shot outside because the furnaces were slow. I saw this."

Joseph and his father, Maier, were taken to the showers to be disinfected. They received their prison clothes and wooden shoes. "The camps and its chambers made all equal, the rich and the poor," Joseph said. When he looked at one man from their village, a millionaire in his prison attire, and with a teenage voice commented, "He looks ridiculous!"

The criminals in the camp wore the symbol of a green triangle. They were put in charge of the Jews at the camp. The man in charge of Joseph and his father's barracks had killed three wives. "The guard told us: I am in charge. There will be no question. Obey orders and you will be fine. Remember, you are three hundred feet from the gas chambers." The hushed and incredible rumors heard back in their village were true.

AGONY AND HUNGER ~ Joseph and his father became separated when some of the prisoners were moved to another camp. He questioned why his father had not argued to stay in the same camp with him. Joseph didn't know that his father was sent to Buchenwald. "I was alone. You had to get tough to survive." For a time their barrack was locked during a quarantine from scarlet fever. Joseph watched as other Jews prayed and then were sent to the gas chambers. He questioned how a God could let this happen. It appeared that all those who prayed died and that if there was a God, He had abandoned them.

The camp was crowded and the meals unpalatable. "There were about 3,500 guys in the barracks, from fourteen to seventeen years old. Three hundred people were in each barrack. The bunks for sleeping were three high. In the morning we were given a black coffee like drink and moldy bread. I couldn't eat it. Lunch was a soup of spoiled rotten vegetables and sawdust. I started eating to survive. At night it was a special meal, horse salami. There were no latrines in the barracks, but I was lucky to be chosen with another guy to go outside to take the human waste out. It was a horrible stench from the four chimneys that were going full blast. We were five hundred yards from the chambers. When we got back to the barracks I told the guys about the chambers."

There were twelve camp barracks. Joseph was with other Jews in *B Camp*. *E Camp* was for the gypsies that like the Jews were discriminated against, rounded up, and taken to the camps. July 22, 1944, was etched in Joseph's memory. "The men were removed from '*E*' for a work detail and then the camp was torched killing all the remaining women and children."

C Camp was to the right of *B Camp*. It was a women's camp separated by electric barbwire, Joseph said. "We could see them. Their hair was shorn off. They were wearing the horrible prison clothes. They looked confused. Some cried out to us. 'Have you seen my son? Where are my boys?' Guards whipped the women for not working fast enough." Some women in desperation grabbed the electric fence and committed suicide. It was a desperate image of suffering.

Every fifteen feet soldiers were stationed in guard posts. Frequent roll calls were held to count the prisoners. "The count was so important to the Germans. They had us carry bricks and blocks to a masonry area to build another chamber. You were beaten if you didn't move fast enough. We were weak and starving. It was not unusual to ask a German soldier for something to eat. Once when we had some free time and were standing outside, we yelled to the soldiers, 'Can you spare a piece of bread?' He threw a sandwich at us and a big group dived for it. It was survival of the fittest. To survive you would take the piece of bread a friend hid under his shirt. What kept you going was the image of seeing the face of the enemy at the end of the war and hopes of seeing my family again. But, when it became very cold people used corpses to keep warm. You started to forget about family, about everything."

As the days of agony and hunger continued "You dragged your feet and looked like you were fifty years old, but we were between the ages of fourteen and seventeen. Most of us looked like skeletons. We were starving and could not work. There were about thirty-five hundred people in the camp. One day an assembly was called in the main square of the camp. Dr. Mengele told us we were going to be sent to a brick laying school and become brick contractors. Instead eight hundred were sent to the gas chamber. I saw Dr. Mengele and he looked me over. I stood on bricks to look taller. He said, 'Stay here.' He did it in a nice way, a soft voice; he was a real bastard. I lost four of my buddies." Joseph reframed the moment to acknowledge the paradox that Mengele saved his life on that day.

Three weeks later there was another selection and Mengele appeared again.

"He appeared to enjoy the selection process and the power he held over who should die and who should live. But apparently I still looked strong enough and was spared a second time. The third selection came two weeks later and this time Mengele chose me. I didn't look so good. I was standing in line waiting to be interviewed and was shaken. I knew I was going to die. It was the one moment I did pray and ask for God to save me. Someone tapped me on the shoulder and said 'I will save you.' How, I asked? 'I don't know,' he said."

At midnight the man, a German criminal, who tapped Joseph on the shoulder, arrived with a rescue plan. "He told me to jump out through a window. I was hurt, but able to crawl on my stomach until I reached the outhouse. A Russian POW put me in the latrine and nailed the top down." Joseph worried as he spent the night in the nauseating sewage hoping the man would return to let him out and he did. "I mixed with this other group of prisoners when the guards did roll call. There was one man too much. But for some reason they forgot about me in the midst of these other prisoners."

LIBERATION ~ Soon, the sound of heavy artillery vibrated in the camp and the hope of liberation seemed to be within their grasp. But it wasn't. "The Germans decided to move everyone out of Auschwitz. We were taken by cattle train to near Berlin. The Allied bombing was getting closer. Then it was a death march for those of us who were still alive through the German cities. You were machine gunned down if you didn't keep moving."

The march through the cities stopped in Sachsenhausen, but the camp was filled. Germans forced the prisoners to stand at attention in sub-zero weather for eight hours and there was hardly any food as they waited. The remainder of the journey was by train to a camp called "Lieberose," dear rose. It was one of the many sub-camps of Sachsenhausen. Joseph and the others were to build barracks for German officers, as the Russians were getting closer.

The next stop was at Gunskirchen, one of the sub-camps of Mauthausen in Austria, as Joe detailed the last days before they were liberated. "All the stragglers were brought here. There were about fifteen thousand people. Rumors spread though the camp that the Germans were going to torch it before we could be liberated. Some of the guards used prisoners for target practice. They were bored. Finally, the Germans moved out and we moved out right after them; then the war was over. We walked for miles to find some food. After three miles I was on my own. I could see the trucks and jeeps coming towards me. It was the United States Forty-Seventh Infantry Division of the Third Army. They couldn't believe what we looked like and helped us. We were taken to hospitals. German civilians were brought in to help bury the dead. Bulldozers came and pushed the dirt over the remains."

Joe was taken to a hospital in Linz.[509] The doctors spoke German, which frightened him as he flashed back to the German soldiers' voices in the camps. So when he felt better Joe walked out without the required release paperwork thinking it was safer. "I tried to hitch hike my way home hoping to find my family. On the road away from the hospital some Russian soldiers in a truck stopped for me. I told them I want to find my family. 'It will take three weeks,' they told me. They were Mongolians and looked a little wild, but were human to me and asked if I was hungry." The soldiers gave Joseph a piece of Russian bread and put some sugar on it. They told him this was a "Russian cake."

Finally, Joseph arrived at his beloved Seredne. Only dirt roads remained and all the stores were closed. He returned to his home to find German civilians living in it. " The Russian authorities were occupying the area and I asked them to have my house back. They told me, 'We can have them out in ten minutes.' But I did not want to do that and replied, "Give them twenty-four hours." It was a bittersweet moment as he re-entered the home alone. Eventually his father returned to their home, but he did not immediately recognize his son. Maier was very ill. It took several weeks to re-gain his strength physically and mentally.

The people in town were not very helpful to the returning Jews; the war had not changed people's prejudice and lack of compassion. "Some of our neighbors asked me, 'How come you are alive? I thought they killed you all.' I knew then I did not want to stay there. We stayed in the house and my father opened a little grocery store in our home." But the memories of the earlier days were a weight of sadness and one day Maier told his son, "I am getting old and there is no future for you here, but I am going to stay." Joseph was angry and disappointed at what his father said then and again when he repeated his father's words.

"My father must have had his own plans," Joseph thought. But he didn't tell his son. So Joseph decided to leave his home, which came under Russian control. He was detained at the border because of his paperwork. One of the Czechoslovakian authorities examining Joseph's documents took them to the Russian official. "They don't look right," he said, as Joseph waited during that tense moment of decision that surrounded his future. The Russian waved off the authority's concern and said, "Let it go."

Joseph left and went west to what Germans called Sudetenland, the area bounded by the Sudeten Mountains on the north, and part of the disputed regions of Austria-Hungary after WWI. There was disagreement among the German-speaking people of Sudetenland at that time of being under the German umbrella or an alternate future under Czechoslovakia. In 1945 the Sudentenland region was restored to Czechoslovakia.[510]

In the village of Trutnov Joseph began his efforts to return to a normal life and to catch up with his schooling and desire to be a mechanical engineer. But there were only basic courses available. While in school another student said to him a phrase he had heard before, "I thought we got rid of Jews. I said to myself, there is no future here."

The war was starting in Palestine and there were underground movements to build a country, the future Israel. "I was approached to see if I wanted to enroll, receive training, and be sent to the Middle East." Joseph said yes and started his training in Northern Ireland in the town of Donaghadee on the east coast in County Down about eighteen miles from Belfast. He smiled as he recalled the help of the Protestant Orangemen and the Irish people. Joseph enjoyed the greeting "Top of the morning" and laughed remembering a Mr. Priestly who tried to get him to become a Protestant.

IMMIGRATION TO THE UNITED STATES ~ After spending two years in Ireland and England, Joseph decided to pursue immigration to the United States where he had relatives. His maternal uncles lived in Buffalo, New York. The airplane left from the airport in Shannon, Ireland, and stopped in Newfoundland. Joseph arrived in Buffalo in 1948, the same year the State of Israel was proclaimed. The immigration officers, who were Irish, greeted him with, "How are things in the old sod?" The accordion he purchased in England became a source of suspicion until Joseph picked it up and played "When Irish Eyes Are Smiling." There was not a dry eye on the face of the officials.

Joseph stayed with an uncle for a few days, then set off and hitchhiked towards New York City with only five dollars in his pocket. A bus stopped for him and took him to the city. He roomed at the YMCA and started looking for a job, which proved to be difficult. The GI's had returned from overseas, and work was scarce. So he registered with the unemployment office and took a job in a ladies dress factory. After three days he was fired because he was unable to keep up with the women assembling the dresses. As he pondered his future, the dreams of pursuing an education were unrealized again when he was drafted for the Korean War.

He arrived at Fort Dix, New Jersey, in 1950 for basic training. "I was proud to serve and to be an American. I was assigned to Korea, but at the last minute my orders were changed and I was shipped to Germany in Ludwigsburg." Ludwigsburg is about fifty miles southwest of Frankfurt. Joseph was in an anti-aircraft outfit assigned to Headquarters. He struggled with feelings of revenge. "When I arrived in Germany I thought about how I could get even about what happened. Then I saw the Germans in a different light. Children played and people doing the normal things people do in their life. I realized that I couldn't go around and kill them all, and must move on, but a lot of feelings stay with you."

After the Korean War Joseph returned to Western New York, became a builder and worked for Bennett Homes in North Tonawanda. In 1956, he married Annette Simon, of Russian ancestry, from the east side of Buffalo. Joseph did very well at Bennett and became their sales manager. But in 1964, the company went bankrupt; he went into business on his own and started working out of his cellar. He founded Diamond Kraft Homes and built homes for thirty-five years in the Western New York area.

For many years, Joseph thought people would not believe what happened and kept his story in the recesses of his mind and heart. Twenty-five years ago through the Holocaust Resource Center of Buffalo, Joseph Diamond began to repeat his story to schoolchildren. He tells them "don't be a bystander, help those who are in trouble, befriend those who are alone, educate yourself about government and those who govern, and don't let a Holocaust happen again."

Joseph Diamond lost forty-eight close family members in the concentration camps. His fortitude, courage, and message are part of what is needed to make the world a place where all can be at peace.

NOTES

[503] Daniel 12:1 [*New American Bible*]
[504] Czechoslovakia was divided in 1993 into the Czech Republic and Slovak Republic.
[505] Joseph Diamond, interview by author, Amherst, NY, September 29, 2006.
[506] Joseph Diamond held a 1944 *New York Times* article on page fourteen that reported how 400,000 Hungarian Jews were sent directly to the gas chambers at Birkenau.
[507] Joseph Diamond described the cruelty of the soldiers to children as they were moved into the rail cattle cars.
[508] Mengele was a physician and German SS Officer. He supervised the selection of arriving transports of prisoners determining who was to be sent to the gas chambers and who was to become a forced laborer. He performed gruesome experiments without anesthesia under the guise of research and was known as the *Angel of Death.*
[509] Hitler announced the Anschluss in the city of Linz.
[510] Sudetenland is now part of the Czech Republic.

EPILOGUE

"DO NOT BECOME THE EVIL THAT WAS DONE TO US" was a message proclaimed by a minister during the nationally televised memorial service after the attacks of September 11, 2001. The people in this story lost brothers and fathers, mothers and sisters, friends, and neighbors during the war. Others were persecuted and suffered unimaginable losses, but all responded in positive ways throughout their lives to make the world a better place. Two people that profoundly influenced my life in ways I am still discovering are my father, John Victor Simon, and my high school teacher, Miss Mary "Maria" Grotowska, a member of the faculty of Loretto Academy, Niagara Falls, Ontario.[511] Both were soldiers of war. My father wore an army uniform and Miss Grotowska, the uniform of disguise in the Underground Army of her beloved homeland of Poland.

Miss Grotowska was a very bright and demanding teacher, feared and yet most revered by me. When called on to answer we stood at our desk and were not allowed to respond "I do not know" or "Je ne sais pas" in Miss Grotowska's class! She stood in front of us in her own uniform of a plaid skirt, a plain blouse, with her arms often crossed, and a look of intensity through her glasses that kept you on the edge of your chair.

Her lessons went far beyond academics. She challenged us to think for ourselves, to pursue excellence, and the truth. She told us to "Always put your shoes under your bed. This will get you on your knees at night and again in the morning." Her students knew she was in the Underground, but little else and used to joke that "Miss Grotowska wore flat shoes so if the Gestapo came she could quickly escape and jump out the classroom window." Little did we know in the mid-1960s that our teacher was still wanted by the Soviet government!

Miss Grotowska taught history and French at Loretto from 1958 to 1968 and also taught college level studies at the neighboring Carmelite seminary overlooking the Horseshoe Falls. Miss Grotowska was the faculty advisor to the United Nations Club and Debate Team. One of the debate issues related to the defense of "just following orders" used during the Nuremberg trials prosecuting Nazi leaders for the Holocaust and war crimes. Whatever the argument, including the validity of capital punishment as an effective deterrent of crime, we debated both positions. I do not ever remember her telling us which position was the right one, including topics related to WWII.

I imagine Miss Grotowska knew about Father Maximilian Kolbe,[512] a Catholic priest from Poland, and read his article on the topic of truth in his last published issue of *Knight*. Father Kolbe challenged readers to examine their personal choices in the context of the war. "The real conflict is the inner conflict. Beyond armies of occupation and the hecatombs of extermination camps, there are two irreconcilable enemies in the depth of every soul: good and evil, sin and love. And what use are the victories on the battlefield if we ourselves are defeated in our innermost personal selves?"[513]

Miss Grotowska was born in 1916 in Jacmierz, Poland, in the Podkarpacie Region, between the towns of Krosno and Sanok, daughter of Wladyslawa Grotowski and Stanislawa Dydnska, a well-to-do family. Her only sibling, an older brother Franciszek, took over the farm after their father died. After graduating from high school in 1935, Miss Grotowska began her studies at the Jagiellonian University in Kraków, Poland, until her graduate work was interrupted when the Germans closed the colleges and universities shortly after invading Poland in September 1939.[514] In November 1939 Miss Grotowska applied to the Underground army organization to become part of the resistance. The regular Polish Army had been disbanded by the Germans, so civilians, especially young people in their twenties and thirties, took over the defense of their homeland in secret. Miss Grotowska was very active and brave in the resistance movement throughout the war. She was part of the Sanok County leadership and managed the women's section of the Underground Army (Armia Kraiowa, AK) in the county. Her pseudonym was Amazonka.[515]

Miss Grotowska dressed up as a young male, pretended to be illiterate, and risked her life many times smuggling arms and ammunition past German soldiers and transporting Underground newspapers and pamphlets from Krosno to Sanok. In 1945, when it was no longer safe for her in her own county, she moved to Kraków where she assisted with the clandestine transfer of wanted Underground army members from Poland to the West and the transfer from the West of radio communication equipment for a clandestine radio station back into Poland. It was very dangerous work, punishable by death.[516] A fellow countryman, Stefan Korbonski, instrumental in the founding of the Polish Underground State and Chief of Civil Resistance, wrote about the efforts to establish communications with the government in exile in England to report what was happening in Poland. *Fighting Warsaw The Story of the Polish Underground State 1939-*

1945 by Korbonski is a detailed and inspiring account of the Underground and the united efforts by the people of Poland against the German occupation.

Mary Piergies, a close family friend and goddaughter of Mary Grotowska, told the story of how Miss Grotowska took leave of her family home in Jacmierz towards the end of the war. She was walking home from Sanok one day when she saw several Gestapo cars parked in front of her family's house. Miss Grotowska turned around knowing that the Gestapo were looking for her, walked away, and went to a safe house in the area, then spent some months with other partisans living in the forest until she finally moved to Kraków. She never returned home, nor saw her mother or brother again. "When the Germans invaded, no one collaborated with them. Mary (Grotowska) told me (Mary Piergies) that close to ninety-nine percent of the Polish people were either actively involved in the resistance or supported it. You could knock on any door at any time of day or night and be let in and fed and housed. The nation was united against the German invaders and that is why the resistance movement in Poland was so successful. But when the Russians liberated and then took control of Poland after the war, people were divided about cooperating with them (Russians). Some Poles thought that now that the war was over, it was time to work on rebuilding Poland with the communists. Of course, other Poles including Mary (Grotowska) felt that they had not risked their lives fighting the Germans only to fall under Soviet rule and they continued the resistance even after the peace treaties were signed," said Mary Piergies.

Kazimierz Mirecki and Stanislawa Mirecka, neé Gliniak, met Miss Grotowska near the end of the war in Kraków. Kazimierz, born in 1910, was from Nisko. He was a provincial leader of the Underground Army in the province of Rzeszów during the war years, and Stanislawa, born in 1917, was from Jaroslaw. After Kazimierz was forced to flee Poland in 1946 because the communist security forces were looking for him, Mary Grotowska was assigned with Kazimierz's elder brother, Adam Mirecki, to get Stanislawa and her two-year old son, Tadzio, out of Poland. They bribed railroad personnel and were shot at by the secret police as they tried twice unsuccessfully to get out of the country. On the third attempt Miss Grotowska, Stanislaw, and Tadzio were able to leave on a train with a transport of French refugees. Adam Mirecki stayed behind to help with other clandestine activities and was captured by the security forces, imprisoned, tortured, and executed in 1956 after spending ten years in jail.[517]

Kazimierz lost his brother Adam to the Soviet-controlled security forces in 1956. Stanislawa lost her elder brother, Wladyslaw Gliniak, at the beginning of the war. The Gestapo arrested Wladyslaw for his activities in the Underground

Army, tortured, and killed him in Auschwitz as a political prisoner. He was thirty years old. His bride, Wiktoria, was also arrested and spent four years in Auschwitz. Wladyslaw and Wiktoria married ten days before being arrested.[518]

Mary Grotowska in 1962.
(Courtesy Mary Mirecki Pierges)

Six million Jews and about five million Christian Poles, gypsies, and political prisoners died or were killed in the concentration camps.

Mary Mirecki Piergies and her siblings were brought up under the valued tutelage of a beloved "Aunt Mary" with a few sketchy stories of their aunt carrying a machine gun, dressing as a young man, and hiding guns in coffins. Miss Grotowska was a member of the National Military Organization (NOW, Narodawa Organizacja Wojskowa) and the National Military Union (NZW, Narodowe Zjednoczenie Wojskowe), which operated from 1944 until 1956, and was also vice-chief of the Women's National Military Union (NZWK, Narodowe Zjednocznie Wojskowe Kobiet). Miss Grotowska distinguished herself against the Germans and later the Soviets, and she was on wanted lists by both. In December 1945 she was given a very important mission as a courier outside the country, but returned to Poland to fight for freedom against the Soviet occupiers and to help people who needed to leave the country for safety. Miss Grotowska left Poland with Stanislawa and Tadzio Mirecki in 1946 for Germany where they were reunited with Kazimierz. Eventually, they all moved to France and in 1951 immigrated to Canada.[519] Miss Grotowska resumed her studies and became a much-loved high school history and French teacher in Niagara Falls and Toronto. Miss Grotowska was awarded *The Cross of Merit* by the Polish Home Army world organization for her activities during the war.[520]

Mary Grotowska passed away on March 9, 1995.

My father fought the Germans too, but the nightmares of war and killing the enemy face to face haunted him. He struggled with the necessity of what he believed was malum in se, something that is intrinsically immoral, killing. Yet the truth was, is, and will continue to be, that my father witnessed the ultimate acts of man's inhumanity to man in the horrific sights at the concentration camps. What took place in the camps was evil and those images never left him. My father like Miss Grotowska was also someone who looked for the truth, in his law practice and in life.

There were times that I was convinced there was no arguing with my father. He was a very intelligent man, a slow and deliberate reader with a photographic memory. Dad's legal skills and philosophy background stymied most attempts by his offspring to sway his opinion in their discussions. But of more consequence in my father's life was his faith in God, strong ethical standards, and the life experience of being part of winning the war. It gave him a special wisdom and uncharacteristic foresight.

America was deeply divided in the late 1930s concerning the possibility of overseas involvement in the war. Fears of a repeat of WWI lingered across the country. It became the hot political issue of Franklin D. Roosevelt's pursuit of a third term in 1940. His opponent, Wendell Willkie, son of a German immigrant, was the dark horse candidate for the Republican Party. He was concerned about the United States being drawn into another war and preached isolationism. It was Willkie's first run for public office. He received 44.8% of the popular vote, but was buried in the Electoral College with 82 votes to Roosevelt's 449 votes. Within a short period of time Willkie became one of Roosevelt's unlikely allies.[521]

Willkie's story, *Unteilbare Welt*, of his fifty-one day journey around the world sponsored by Roosevelt, examined the governmental systems of other countries, their history, and their relationship with the United States. Willkie concluded that America as a world leader must follow a course to create equality of opportunity for every race and nation. Americans must also study the history and appreciate the culture of other countries. This was part of his plan to win and keep the peace.[522] POWs in camps across America including Fort Niagara read Willkie's book and other pieces of American literature as part of the secret re-education program designed to democratize the prisoners. The February 15, 1945, Red Cross inspection of the camp at Fort Niagara included complaints by the German POW spokesman about American propaganda. Apparently, the secret program was not so secret.

Both Willkie and Roosevelt died before the war ended. What would these two men with strong opposing opinions, yet eventually allies, think about how world events are unfolding, and what would Miss Grotowska and my father say to the question posed by German children to their parents in post-war Germany, "How did you let this happen?"

Will our children in the years ahead ask us the same question about the massacre of the Tutsis by the Hutus in Rwanda; about the government under Slobodan Milosevic and its attempt to wipe out Bosnian Muslims, Croats, and other non-Serbian civilians; about the killings in Darfur in the Sudan; and about other areas of the world where one group appears to want to wipe out another? Are we responsible for these genocides? How will we be judged in the next decades because of our government's actions or inactions?

The answer to our obligation in the world today lies in the response to the age-old question Cain posed to God after he killed Abel, "Am I my brother's keeper?" Can we allow the essential public debate of issues to continue to be reduced by the stifling inaction caused by partisanship? Can we make decisions based on fear, reduce civil liberties, and abhor those who have a different point of view and call them "un-American?" The foundations of a strong democracy are open to debate and liberty for all.

Part of the history of Germany and the rise of Hitler to power evolved out of fear. I believe we cannot address the evils of our world today without setting aside our fears, our prejudices, our partisanship, and our labels. We must take a consistent leadership role that respects the legacy of sacrifice and slaughter of innocents of WWII and proclaim "never again as at Auschwitz, Uganda, Yugoslavia, Darfur…"

Notes

[511] When the author entered Loretto Academy in 1963, it was an all girl's school.
[512] Father Kolbe died in the concentration camp at Auschwitz in 1941 after he took the place of Franciszek Gajowniczek who asked to be spared for the sake of his family.
[513] Mary Craig, "Blessed Maximilian Kolbe-Priest Hero of a Death Camp," EWTN, http://www.ewtn.com/library/MARY/KOLBE2.htm [accessed March 7, 2008].
[514] Mary Mirecki Piergies said that Napoleon was the subject of Mary Grotowska's Master's thesis.
[515] *Nasza Gmina*, Nr 3 (4) III kw. 2005 r., 15, translated by Anna Madra.
[516] Krzysztof Kaczmarski, *Podziemie Narodowe Na Rzeszowszcynie 1939-1944* (Institute of National Memory: 2003) and Mary Mirecki Piergies telephone conversations with author.
[517] Mary Mirecki Piergies, telephone interview by author, July 22, 2006. In the United States, Kazimierz and Stanislawa Mirecki were known as Casimir and Stella Mirecki.
[518] Piergies, telephone interview.
[519] Kaczmarski, *Podziemie*; Grotowska statement; and Piergies, telephone interview.
[520] "Death Announcement," *Niagara (Ontario) Review*, March 10, 1995.
[521] "Wendell L. Willkie Calls For An End to Isolationism," Video Gallery, The History Channel, http://www.history.com/media.do?id=0612&action=clip [accessed May 26, 2008].
[522] The English translation of *Unteilbare Welt* entitled *One World* was widely read.

ACKNOWLEDGEMENTS

How the people in this work became part of my life is another book. It has been my privilege to listen and to record for posterity their stories.

Thank you to my sisters, Nannette M. Simon and Yvonne S. Schiffer; Lt. Col. Nelson L. Beard, USAF Retired; Harry M. DeBan; Thomas Tower; Sister Mara Walton, OSF; and my husband who read the manuscript and made editing suggestions.

Thank you to Hugh Neeson for opening the hangar doors of Bell Aircraft, Robert Young for facilitating the work with the Allied POW group, Mary Pierges for the story of her godmother and my teacher, and Arnold Krammer for sharing his knowledge and expertise of German POWs in America and his efforts to uncover the history of Amazonka.

I am most grateful to my high school sweetheart and beloved husband, Raymond, for taking me to the prom at the Fort Niagara Officer's Club almost forty years ago, for his patience during this writing, and especially for holding my hand and heart as we walked through this global moment of history.

In deep appreciation to the following people for their contributions to this work, in alphabetical order:

Bernard J. Adamski; Dr. Mark Barner; Jack Beecher; Stanley Blake; Mary Ellen Blyzka; Dorothy Boyce; Jerome Brubaker, Curator of Old Fort Niagara Association; Richard Byron, Curator and Senior Historian Niagara Aerospace Museum; Col. Louis Ceechini, Retired; Tony Clark; Connecticut Valley Historical Museum, Springfield, MA; Violet Thurn Cowden; Harold Denny; Joe Derhay; Margaret Dineen; Kenneth W. Drehmer and Brian McCabe of Woodlawn National Cemetery, Elmira, NY; Joseph Diamond; Kenneth G. Diez; Neiland Diez; Richard Duerr; Melissa Dunlap, Executive Director of Niagara County Historical Society; Marguerite Slattery Dyer; Frances Serchia Esser; Tom Fadel; Maureen Fennie, Local History Department, Niagara Falls (New York) Public Library; Edward P. Feigenbaum I; Barbara Frantz; Arnold E. Frantz; Bud Gates; Ruth Harris Gates; Patrick A. Geelan;

Bob Gibson; Frank Gilson; Jim Gilson; Mariano Giuga; Don Gray; John D. Griffin; Edwin Grzywa; Annette T. Harris, Joan Carney Gray Holland; Ellen Harpster; Gary Harris; Gail Hays; Harry Hays; Lt. Col. James O. Hays, USAF Retired; Roberta Henderson; Janet Jachlewski, Village of Youngstown Historian; Millie Hillman, Curator Ransomville Historical Room; Mervin Hurtgam; Beverly Bills Jeffrey; John Jircitano; Julie Jircitano; Loretta Joseph; Margaret Johnston Juergens; Beverley Kahl; Richard Kahl; Benedict L. Klinshaw; John Kohl; Paul Lehmann, Cornell Cooperative Extension of Niagara County; Michael Locurcio; Patricia Nicolette Loncto; Joel MacDonald; Tracey MacGowan and Dawn Letson of the Texas Woman's University, Blagg-Huey Library, Woman's Collection, Denton, TX; Robert E. MacPherson; Anna Madra; A. Joseph Marchese; Metro Marchyn; Robert Marinucci; Gerry Marnien; John Maroon; James McCann; Kathleen McMurray; Donald Meckle; Barbara Mirecki; Jeffrey Morrow; Richard H. Morse; Gertie Myers; Robert Myers; National Archives and Records Administration Staff at College Park, MD; Hugh Neeson, Development Director of the Niagara Aerospace Museum; Burt Erickson Nelson; Etta Myers Davis Newman; Frank V. Nicolette; Stanley Nowak; Dr. Arnold Krammer; Lake Ontario VFW Post 313; Sister Isabelle O'Reilly, OSF; Eugene Pacia; Elwyn F. Palmerton; Pearl Penzotti; Rick Penzotti; Patricia Hutchison Phillips; Mary Piergies; Dominick Poliseno, Andrew Porteus Niagara Falls (Ontario) Reference Librarian; POW Support Group of Buffalo; Ronald Quiett; Grace Hays Reese; Jane Richardson; John Richardson; Major Claude W. Rockabrand, Retired; Steve C. Rockabrand; John Rolfe; Irene Sadowski; Kazimierz Sadowski; Yvonne S. Schiffer; Audrey Schillo; Sylvia Schwartz of The Holocaust Resource Center of Buffalo; Maureen Schug; Mickey Schultz; Christine Serchia; Jennifer Serchia; Frank Serchia; Mariam Simon Shannon; Peggy Tower Shear; Renata Holody Sikoski; Lt. Col. James Simon, USAF Retired; Nannette M. Simon; Salome Authier Simon; Dr. C. Stolinski, Chairman, Polish Underground Movement (1939-1945) Study Trust, London, England; Margery Stratton, President Porter Historical Society; Douglas Tower; Richard Tower; Roderick Tower; William Tower; Ellen Graves Truesdell; Lt. Col. Marjorie Clark Varuska, USAF Retired; William J. Veronica; Freida Wangelin; Jean Watson; Olga Strassburg Wermuth; Mary Hodge Wieland; Lt. Col. Betty Jane Williams, USAF Retired; Joan Wolfgang; Robert Young, POW coordinator, VA Crisis Services; and John S. Zale.

APPENDICES

APPENDIX A

Prisoners of War held at Fort Niagara served in these Divisions

	Herman Goering (Göring)	115th	Infantry Division
		115th	Infantry Division
1st	Fallscherm-Division	148th	Infantry Division
2nd	Fallscherm-Division	15th	Infantry Division
3rd	Fallscherm-Division	162nd	Infantry Division
4th	Fallscherm-Division	164th	Infantry Division
5th	Fallscherm-Division	16th	Infantry Division
6th	Fallscherm-Division	171st	Infantry Division
13th	Flak-Division	20th	Infantry Division
143rd	Flak-Division	211th	Infantry Division
154th	Flak-Division	227th	Infantry Division
16th	Flak-Division	242nd	Infantry Division
19th	Flak-Division	243rd	Infantry Division
1st	Flak-Division	251st	Infantry Division
20th	Flak-Division	265th	Infantry Division
20th	Flak-Division	266th	Infantry Division
9th	Flak-Division	26th	Infantry Division
1st	Flieger-Division	270th	Infantry Division
2nd	Flieger-Division	275th	Infantry Division
5th	Flieger-Division	326th	Infantry Division
103rd	Infantry Division	334th	Infantry Division
108th	Infantry Division	344th	Infantry Division
110th	Infantry Division	344th	Infantry Division
111th	Infantry Division	347th	Infantry Division
112th	Infantry Division	352nd	Infantry Division
114th	Infantry Division	353rd	Infantry Division

354th	Infantry Division	9th	Light Africa Division
362nd	Infantry Division	18th	Luftwaffen-Felddivision
389th	Infantry Division	19th	Luftwaffen-Felddivision
416th	Infantry Division		Miscellaneous Units
44th	Infantry Division	2nd	Mountain Division
463rd	Infantry Division		Organisation Todt
57th	Infantry Division	116th	Panzer
708th	Infantry Division	26th	Panzer
709th	Infantry Division	10th	Panzer Division
716th	Infantry Division	15th	Panzer Division
719th	Infantry Division	16th	Panzer Division
71st	Infantry Division	1st	Panzer Division
726th	Infantry Division	21st	Panzer Division
72nd	Infantry Division	2nd	Panzer Division
73rd	Infantry Division	9th	Panzer Division
756th	Infantry Division	29th	Panzer Grenadier Division
77th	Infantry Division		
84th	Infantry Division	3rd	Panzer Grenadier Division
90th	Infantry Division		
91st	Infantry Division		Panzer Lehr Division
94th	Infantry Division		Polizei
959th	Infantry Division		Reichsarbeitsdienst
19th	Infantry Division (VG)	2nd	SS Panzer Division
212th	Infantry Division (VG)	17th	SS Panzer Grenadier Division
349th	Infantry Division (VG)		
36th	Infantry Division (VG)	6th	SS-Gebirgs-Division Nord
47th	Infantry Division (VG)		
62nd	Infantry Division (VG)		Unknown Units
9th	Infantry Division (VG)		Volkstrum
	Kriegsmarine-Weiften		Zollgrzenzschutz

Source: Detention Rosters, College Park, MD.

Appendix B
Instructions for Persons Using Prisoner of War Labor

1. Do not try to gain information from POW.
2. Do not believe a POW likes you. He does not.
3. Do not attempt to fraternize with POW.
4. Do not think a POW works for you because he likes you. He does not. He works because he is ordered to work.
5. Do not think a POW will not escape if he can. He will.
6. Do not take any written letters, slips of paper or packages from a POW.
7. Do not give them anything. If you want to give them anything, go through the POW Commander.
8. Do not talk to POW except in the line of duty.
9. Do not employ POW on any work directly connected with the war effort, such as handling ammunition, supplies destined for overseas, construction of target ranges or other combat training aids.
10. Do not employ POW on unhealthful or dangerous work.
11. POW are accustomed to orders so give your orders to the German leader in charge of the detail.
12. Do not try to discipline POW on the job. That is the Camp Commander's right.
13. Report any violation of above orders at once to the camp commander.
14. You are as responsible for security of POW as the armed guards.

Source: Farm Labor Association Organization Records, Notebook II, 2006.1.62, Town Hall, Town of Porter, Youngstown, NY.

Appendix C
Instructions to the Contractor for Prisoner of War Labor

The treatment and employment of prisoners of war are governed by an international treaty, called the Geneva Convention. The United States Government is bound to follow the terms of this treaty. It is important to do so and to treat enemy prisoners fairly in order to avoid reprisals against Americans held as prisoners by enemy countries. You have agreed to comply with War Department directions relative to the employment of prisoners of war and the following instructions are for your guidance:

1. In the event of an escape or unwarranted conduct on the part of any prisoner of war, you should inform the guard in charge of the prisoners, who is responsible for their conduct. You should make your telephone available to the guard in order that he may telephone the camp commander at any time.

2. You should cooperate fully with the military authorities and guards to assist them in avoiding escapes of prisoners.

3. The clothing of prisoners of war has been marked to identify them as prisoners of war. Under no circumstances will you give them any clothing, money, or other unauthorized articles.

4. All prisoner of war mail, even to persons in the United States, must be mailed in the camp so that it may be censored. It is very important that you cooperate fully with the guard in preventing any prisoner from mailing letters, cards, or packages from your premises. You must prevent persons who might smuggle mail from mixing with the prisoners. Prisoners must not make telephone calls or send cables or telegrams. You should report to the guard any prisoner who violates or attempts to violate this rule.

5. Requests of newspaper reporters, news photographers, newsreel cameramen, or others to secure information or to photograph the prisoner of war camp must be referred to the camp commander. You must not give out any publicity regarding the prisoners of war.

6. You should not fraternize with prisoners of war or allow any other persons

to do so. Only such conversation as is necessary to supervise the prisoners in the performance of their work should be allowed.

7. If you fraternize with prisoners of war, or permit others to do so unnecessarily, give them clothing or other articles, accept or deliver mail for them, and there is an escape, your action might tend to make it appear that you had aided in the escape. Aiding a prisoner of war to escape may result in serious criminal consequences.

8. Your civilian employees and others who may come in contact with the prisoners of war in the performance of the contract shall be informed of these instructions and should be enjoined to carry them out.

9. You should occupy fully the prisoners' time. If, for any reason, they cannot work, notify the guard so the prisoners can be returned to camp instead of being idle around your premises.

10. In order to insure efficient use of prisoner of war labor supplied under your contract:

a. You should give at least 12 hours notice to the camp commanding officer, if it is necessary for you to cancel the employment of prisoners of war temporarily for any reason.

b. You should plan the work carefully to avoid inactivity of the prisoners of war due to improper or insufficient supervision, tools, or materials.

c. You are responsible for the work supervision and training of the prisoners of war. Always be sure that they understand what you want done and how you want them to do it. Do not argue with the prisoners. If they do not do as they are told, report them, and action will be taken by the responsible officers.

11. The War Department expects your cooperation in these matters so that the prisoner of war labor program will be successful. Failure on your part to follow these instructions, and other instructions given you by the military authorities, may result in cancellation of the contract and refusal of the War Department to furnish prisoner of war labor to you in the future. The Government reserves the right to supplement or change these instructions.

12. These instructions do not in any way limit your obligation under the contract.

Source: Farm Labor Association Organization Records, Notebook II, 2006.1.129a-b, Town Hall, Town of Porter, Youngstown, NY.

Appendix D

Major Prisoner of War Camps in United States

Alabama	Camp Aliceville
Alabama	Camp Opelika
Alabama	Camp Sibert
Alabama	Fort McClellan
Alabama	Camp Rucker
Arizona	Camp Florence
Arizona	Camp Papago Park
Arizona	Camp Pima
Arkansas	Camp Chaffee
Arkansas	Camp Dermott
Arkansas	Camp Jerome
Arkansas	Camp Monticello
Arkansas	Camp Jos. T. Robinson
Arkansas	Pine Bluff Arsenal
California	Camp Angel Island
California	Camp Beale
California	Camp Cooke
California	Camp Stockton
California	Ford Ord
Colorado	Camp Carson
Colorado	Camp Hale
Colorado	Camp Trinidad
Colorado	Fort Greely
Delaware	Fort DuPont
Florida	Camp Blanding
Florida	Camp Gordon Johnston
Florida	Eglin Army Air Field
Georgia	Camp Stewart
Georgia	Camp Wheeler
Georgia	Fort Benning
Georgia	Fort Gordon
Georgia	Fort Oglethorpe
Idaho	Camp Algoma
Idaho	Camp Farragut
Idaho	Camp Rupert
Illinois	Camp Ellis
Illinois	Camp Grant
Illinois	Fort Sheridan
Indiana	Camp Atterbury
Indiana	Fort Benjamin Harrison
Iowa	Camp Clarinda
Kansas	Camp Concordia
Kansas	Camp Phillips
Kansas	Fort Leavenworth
Kansas	Fort Henry
Kentucky	Camp Breckinridge
Kentucky	Camp Campbell
Kentucky	Fort Knox
Louisiana	Camp Claiborne
Louisiana	Camp Polk
Louisiana	Camp Ruston
Louisiana	New Orleans Port of Embarkation
Louisiana	Camp Livingston
Maine	Camp Houlton
Maryland	Camp David
Maryland	Camp Somerset
Maryland	Fort Meade
Maryland	Edgewood Arsenal
Maryland	Holabird Signal Depot
Massachusetts	Camp Edwards
Massachusetts	Fort Devens
Massachusetts	Westover Field
Michigan	Camp Evelyn
Michigan	Fort Custer
Mississippi	Camp Como

Mississippi	Camp McCain
Mississippi	Camp Shelby
Mississippi	Camp Van Dorn
Missouri	Camp Clark
Missouri	Camp Crowder
Missouri	Fort Leonard Wood
Nebraska	Camp Atlanta
Nebraska	Camp Indianola
Nebraska	Camp Scottsbluff
Nebraska	Fort Robinson
New Jersey	Fort Dix
New Mexico	Camp Lourdsburg
New Mexico	Camp Roswell
New York	Camp Popolopen
New York	Fort Niagara
New York	Halloran General Hospital
North Carolina	Camp Butner
North Carolina	Camp Mackall
North Carolina	Camp Sutton
North Carolina	Fort Bragg
Ohio	Camp Perry
Oklahoma	Camp Tonkawa
Oklahoma	Fort Reno
Oklahoma	Camp Alva
Oklahoma	Camp Gruber
Oklahoma	Camp McAlester
Oklahoma	Camp Pryor
Oklahoma	Fort Sill
Oklahoma	Glennan General Hospital
Oregon	Camp White
Pennsylvania	Camp New Cumberland
Pennsylvania	Camp Reynolds
Pennsylvania	Indiantown Gap Military
Pennsylvania	Olmsted Field
Pennsylvania	Tobyhanna Military Reservation
Rhode Island	Fort Kearny
South Carolina	Camp Croft
South Carolina	Fort Jackson
Tennessee	Camp Crossville
Tennessee	Camp Forrest
Tennessee	Memphis General Depot
Texas	Camp Barkeley
Texas	Camp Bowie
Texas	Camp Brady
Texas	Camp Fannin
Texas	Camp Hearne
Texas	Camp Hood
Texas	Camp Howze
Texas	Camp Hulen
Texas	Camp Huntsville
Texas	Camp McLean
Texas	Camp Maxey
Texas	Camp Mexia
Texas	Camp Swift
Texas	Camp Wallace
Texas	Camp Wolters
Texas	Fort Bliss
Texas	Fort Crockett
Texas	Fort D.W. Russell
Texas	Fort Sam Houston
Texas	McCloskey General Hospital
Utah	Camp Ogden
Virginia	Camp Ashby
Virginia	Camp Lee
Virginia	Camp Peary
Virginia	Camp Pickett
Virginia	Fort Curtis
Virginia	Fort Eustis
Virginia	Fort Patrick Henry

Virginia	Hampton Roads Port of Embarkation	West Virginia	Camp Ashford
Virginia	Richmond ASF Depot	Wisconsin	Camp McCoy
Washington	Fort Lewis	Wyoming	Camp Douglas
		Wyoming	Fort F. E. Warren

Source: Adapted from Arnold Krammer, *Nazi Prisoners of War*, 268, with permission.

Appendix E
Fort Niagara Modern Post Cemetery

Name	Date of Death	Military Information
Adams, Pvt. James C.	06/02/1924	Infantry
Andrews, Pvt. Eugene S.	02/28/1900	Co. E 16 Infantry
Andrus, Maj. Frank B., Ret.	09/22/1924	U.S. Army
Andrus, Hermione (wife of Maj. Frank Burton Andrus)	06/04/1926	Ret. USA
Barley, Sgt. Toney M.	03/20/1942	Co. D 28th U.S. Infantry
Bauer, Sgt. Charles A.	03/20/1923	Co. C 28th U.S. Infantry also 10th Rec. Co. C.S.I.
Boran, Pvt. Jan	10/06/1918	Bn. U.S. Guards
Brennan, Artificer John	06/19/1896	13 U.S. Infantry
Buckner, Musician John	12/23/1899	Co. E 13th Regt
Busse, Sgt. Hugh H.	06/01/1913	Co. B 29th U.S. Infantry
Carey, Pvt. John J.	06/21/1945	U.S.Army PW Camp 1206th SCU
Carson, Sgt. William J.	01/27/1912	Co. K 8th U.S. Infantry
Colby, Civilian George W.	02/28/1920	
Cousins, Elaine Shirley (infant daughter of Sgt. Frederick L. Cousins)	07/16/1942	Co. D 1213th R. Center
Cox, Cook Edward	02/05/1917	9th U.S. Infantry Retired
Cramer, Pvt. Dorothy C.	05/25/1945	WAC Sq C 4000 AAF Base Unit Wright Field, Dayton, OH.
Crouch, Cpl. Clarence L.	03/23/1936	Co. H 28th U.S. Infantry
Downer, Pvt. Simeon	11/02/1899	Co. M 42nd U.S. Vol. Infantry
Duncombe, Pvt. Allan	11/10/1930	Medical Dept.
Dunham, Sgt. William B.	07/25/1926	14th U.S. Infantry
Elwood, Pvt. William J.	07/18/1905	Co. L 8th U.S. Infantry
Ferguson, Capt. George W.	07/16/1934	U.S. Army Retired
Freudenstein, Karl	08/23/1945	German POW

Gardepe, John Stanley (son of Sgt. S.J. Gardepe)	07/01/1928	USA
Garrison, Capt. Herbert W.	05/18/1931	Infantry
Gerdes, Erhard	07/18/1945	Civilian German POW
Gilbert, — (son of Pvt. Leone E. Gilbert)	10/21/1941	Co. D 1213th RC
Gilson, Pvt. Edward	05/24/1906	Co. B 9th U.S. Infantry
Glaser, GM3c Henry	12/25/1943	USNR
Gross, Pfc. Earl G.	10/14/1918	Co. I 22nd U.S. Infantry
Hackett, Artificer Edward P.	10/20/1900	Co. H 21st U.S. Infantry
Hancock, Pvt. George W.	05/24/1906	Co. H 12th Infantry
Hathaway, Pvt. Edward	01/29/1901	Co. H 15th U.S. Infantry
Hines, Sgt. George James	10/07/1937	Co. H 28th Infantry
Huntington, Mary E. (wife of Sgt. Roscow W. Huntington)	05/12/1944	Hq & Hq Co. 1206th SCU
Jordan, Leroy (son of Cpl. Roy Jordan)	01/13/1937	Ser Co. 28th Infantry
Kelly, Pvt. Dennis	07/23/1911	Co. G 29th U.S. Infantry
Kelly, Mary Bigham (wife of 1st Lt. Verner B. Kelly)	12/01/1944	ORD Third Echelon Shop, Buffalo, NY
Kenny, Pfc. Joseph A.	10/07/1929	Det Q. M. Corps.
Leacock, Pfc. James L.	06/14/1923	Hq 16th U.S. Infantry
Liskowski, Pvt. Radian	04/28/1917	74th NY Infantry N.G.
Lutze, Ellen (wife of Sgt. Frederick Lutze)	06/06/1926	Co. A 12th U.S. Infantry
Lutze, Sgt. Frederick D.	08/12/1912	Co. A 12th U.S. Infantry
Manning, John Wesley (son of Pvt. Roy C. Manning)	02/04/1941	Co. D 1213th RC
Mansfield, Pvt. George D.	03/03/1902	Co. H 13th Infantry
Maron, Johannes	09/06/1945	German POW
Milot, Pvt. Joshua J.	10/22/1908	Co. A 12th U.S. Infantry
Moran, Sgt. Dennis	01/21/1928	U.S. Army
Moskal, Walter, Jr. (son of Pfc. Walter F. Moskal)	02/06/1938	Ser Co. 28th Infantry
Murphy, Pvt. James A.	03/09/1915	Co. C 29th U.S. Infantry 17 Div.

Nash, Pfc. John	08/18/1908	Co. E U.S. Engrs 2 Bn
Owens, — (son of Sgt. Robert Arthur Owens)	08/22/1913	Co. C 28th U.S. Infantry
Owens, Cpl. Robert A.	07/03/1924	Co. C 28th U.S. Infantry
Peak, Laura Edith (daughter of Pvt. Willard S. Peak)	09/27/1934	USA
Pendergraft, Pvt. Elmer M.	12/04/1903	Co. K 1st U.S. Infantry
Persson, Chief Musician Ludwig	06/26/1924	13 U.S. Infantry
Peverill, Mildred E. (daughter of Pvt. Peverill, G.D.)	09/01/1914	USA
Phillips, Ralph Don (son of Sgt. Gordon M. Phillips)	10/16/1931	USA
Pinsadino, Pvt. Carl	05/04/1940	Co. G 28th U.S. Infantry
Prpich, Pvt. John	04/03/1919	152 Depot Brigade
Robbins, Pvt. Albert	06/03/1903	Co. C 11th Infantry
Robbins, Harriett (wife of Pvt. Albert Robbins)	06/09/1921	11th U.S. Infantry
Rucks, Cook Albert J.	01/11/1908	Co. C 12th U.S. Infantry
Sadler, Pvt. Al	04/08/1929	Co. K 28th U.S. Infantry
Sanford, 1st Lt. George E.	03/29/1945	USA Retired (Retirement 01/31/1944)
Schreier, Hugo	08/29/1945	Civilian German POW
Sheehan, Pvt. Daniel	09/24/1912	Co. L 23rd U.S. Infantry
St. Laurent, Evelyn Reuben (wife of Sgt. Peter J. St. Laurent)	01/30/1942	Co. A 1213 R.C.
Stover, Helen Irene (daughter of Capt. Charles V. Stover)	07/03/1945	712th MP Bn
Svenson, Pfc. Vincent	12/13/1927	Band 28th U.S. Infantry
Tavalieri, Sgt. David John (son of Tavalieri, A.)[523]	06/24/1937[524]	Band 28th U.S. Infantry

Vowell, Sgt. Dan	05/26/1939	Co. C 28th U.S. Infantry
Whitson, Pvt. Larry	03/25/1909	Co. M 12th U.S. Infantry
Williams, Pvt. Arthur	07/05/1909	Co. I
Winieski, Theodore	10/15/1918	Draft Deserter
McIntyre,[525] Pvt. Henry D.	07/08/1927	remains received by Bell Funeral Service Inc.
Wheeler, 1st Sgt. Elisha	01/16/1939	remains received by Elizabeth B. Wheeler, wife
Horner, Peter A.	03/21/1945	remains received by Mary B. Horner, wife

Source: Physical survey by author and spouse on June 29, 2006, of monuments and re-interment burial forms at Woodlawn National Cemetery, Elmira, NY. Re-interments occurred from April 30, 1949 to May 9, 1949.

NOTES

[523] Spelled Tavolieri in Modern Post Cemetery folder, Old Fort Niagara, Archaeology Building, Youngstown, NY.

[524] Modern Post Cemetery folder lists the date of death as June 25, 1937.

[525] Spelled MacIntyre in Modern Post Cemetery folder.

Appendix F ~ Youngstown Town of Porter Veterans Monument Service in World War II

Adamski, Bernard J.
Adamson, Robert Jr.
Albright, Arthur
Allen, Herbert James
Ames, William T.
Andrews, James Douglas
Ankenbauer, Harold B.
Arcuri, Patsy
Arnold, Elwin E.
Atherton, George T. Jr.
Atkin, Richard Jacko
Austin, Harold L.
Austin William L.
Axtell, Richard L.
Bak, John C.
Baker, Arthur F.
Baldassaro, James
Bale, Ray L.
Bale, Richard S.
Barnes, Maurice W.
Bars, Harrison W.
Bauer, Albert
Baumhofer, Melvin
Bayne, Justin A.
Behrens, Robert C.
Betts, Chester, Jr.
Beutel, Frederick H.
Blackwell, Alex
Blackwell, L. D.
Bliss, H. Donald
Boardman, James H.
Bodkin, Edward John
Bohnstadt, Richard L.
Bonnett, Daniel H.
Bonnett, Melvin
Bosso, John A.
Bowen, Albert C.
Bowen, Richard L.
Bradley, Russell
Brainard, Jay B. Sr.
Breckon, Haldred Charles
Britt, Jack
Broeker, Donald
Brown, Alton Wayne
Brown, Edison
Brown, Edward L.
Brown, George W.
Brown, Gilbert M.
Brown, James R.
Buchner, Lester W.
Buerster, Raymond William
Burlingame, William
Burns, John E., Jr.
Bush, Arthur Joseph
Caldwell, Willard J.
Campbell, James
Campbell, Roy L.
Canfield, Lewis
Canfield, Rex H.
Caraglin, James
Carew, Jack W.
Carew, Richard
Carey, Robert R.
Carlo, Anthony Louis
Carpenter, Clinton W.
Carroll, V. Sumner
Carter, Kenneth M.
Carter, Stewart Howard
Cary, Richard, Jr.
Chestnut, James

Chestnut, John
Chestnut, William
Clapsaddle, Clive P. Sr.
Clark, Charles M.
Clark, George J.
Clark, Lela
Clark, Lynford Irish
Clark, Robert
Clark, Robert F.
Clark, Thomas Aaron
Clark, Wilson G.
Coleman, Robert M.
Coleman, Ronald G.
Collins, John F.
Collins, Raymond F.
Colliver, Ray L.
Comerford, Kenneth K.
Connor, Clifford
Cook, Merrill S.
Cornell, Raymond C.
Cornell, Roy Douglas
Cothran, Arthur H. Sr.
Courtney, Ralph Frederick
Coykendall, Robert
Cummings, Albert J.
Curtis, Howard
Cutler, Charles R.
Cutler, Charles Rodney
Cutler, George John
D'Anna, Russell N.
Davis, Howard F.
DeGolier, John Frederick
Deitschel, Robert
Demin, Elton
Dent, Calvin W.
DePetris, Steve
Derner, Edward A.
Dewey, Albert
Dibble, William Cyrenus
Diem, Henry J.
Dieter, Robert G.
Dieter, Robert George
Dietz, Gordon E. Sr.
Dlugosz, Edward
D'Luhy, Emil A.
Doty, Carl M. Sr.
Doty, Harold Jr.
Dowey, Albert
Drinkwater, James
Drinkwater, Robert
Drinkwater, Victor
Dritschel, Robert
Duerr, Richard D.
Duke, Don Barton
Dumond, Sinai
Duret, Arthur Jerry
Durfy, James R.
Edwards, Harold James
Edwards, Kenneth R.
Edwards, William F.
Eodice, S. John
Everts, William C.
Falkner, William J.
Farquharson, George
Feigenbaum, Edward P. I
Fellows, Marshall G.
Ferrara, Louis J.
Fickett, Russell F.
Figura, Bruno
Figura, Henry
Figura, Paul
Finkle, Donald B. Sr.
Flay, David M.
Fraize, William G.
Fredericks, Clarence
French, Rev. Albert C.

Frey, Floyd
Frost, George Watson
Furman, Clarence
Furman, Gerald
Geartz, Roger
Gentle, A. Spencer
Giuga, Mariano T.
Glenn, Benny
Glover, Homer G.
Golding, John H.
Gooch, Frank C.
Goodman, Janet
Goodman, Lyle S.
Goodman, Malcom
Goodman, Norvel
Graham, Norman C.
Gratz, Walter E.
Green, Robert Gordon
Griffin, J. Donald
Griffin, John Donald
Grzybowski, Edward
Grzywa, Edwin F.
Gunzelman, George Jr.
Hann, Albert B.
Hardison, Gerald A.
Hardy, Leroy Martin
Harmon, Eugene W.
Harris, Willard R.
Haskell, Leo N.
Haussener, Whitney D.
Hays, David S.
Hays, Harry B.
Hays, Paul N.
Hays, Sidney
Healy, Daniel J.
Heinrich, Christian Charles
Hellman, Richard E.
Helsel, Walter R.
Helwig, Erwin Jr.
Henry, Mortimer L.
Henschel, Paul
Hildebrandt, Phillip E.
Hillman, Eugene H.
Hindersinn, Raymond R.
Hochadel, Leonard
Hoffman, Quentin J. Jr.
Holland, Donald H.
Holman, Eugene
Hooks, Arvel L.
Hoover, Samuel H.
Houser, George H.
Huckins, Stanley H.
Hughes, James S.
Hurlbut, Paul W.
Hutchison, Harold Hutch
Hutchison, Robert W.
Ingraham, James
Ingraham, Max
Ingraham, Richard
Jablonski, Stanley A.
Jachlewski, Richard H.
Jackson, Clarence R.
Jarrett, Jack
Jeffery, Arthur M.
Jeffords, Elton V.
Jenosheck, William Clarence
Jindra, E. V.
Jircitano, John Mark
Johnson, Clifford E.
Johnson, Eugene
Johnson, Jack C.
Johnson, John N. III
Johnson, Roy Stanley
Johnston, John R.
Johnston, William Russell
Jones, Robert Willliam

Kagel, Kenneth
Kahl, Richard C.
Kania, Raymond J.
Kathan, George L
Kathan, Richard Webster
Kay, James Richard
Kendall, Douglas H.
Kennedy, John Earl
Kiely, Virginia G.
Kile, Mary Jane
King, George R.
King, Robert J.
King, William E.
Klaffka, Arthur
Klingler, Arthur O.
Klinshaw, Benedict L.
Knapp, Glenn L.
Knapp, Richard A.
Knarr, Carl
Kneeple, Charles
Koepke, Frederick W.
Kolloff, Clyde L.
Kowalski, William
Kraatz, Gerald Walter
Krzyscin, Stanley F.
Kulak, Henry W.
Labushesky, Leonard Arthur
LaFrance, John Joseph
Lagace, Edwin R.
LaGasse, Joseph
Lammerts, Henry Parkinson
Lane, Robert T., Sr.
Lang, Mary Elizabeth
Langdon, Lawrence
Lanphear, Erwin Daniel
Larson, John I.
LaRue, Joseph William
Lauer, Lewis F.
LaVelle, Eugene T.
Lawson, William George
Lederhouse, Albert J.
Lederhouse, Chester A. Sr.
Lederhouse, John
LeGasse, Joseph L.
Lindsay, Warren
Lisman, Francis
Litchard, Edward B. Jr.
Litchard, Ernest
Littke, Albert Wilfred
Lloyd, John Arthur
Lloyd, Russell B.
Lochren, George H.
Lovell, Walter G.
Lubas, Frank R. Sr.
Ludwig, August H.
Ludwig, Ernest K.
Ludwig, Herman Otto
Ludwig, John A.
Lyndhurst, Harold
Maacks, Loren F.
Maacks, Ralph
Mac Pherson, Robert E.
Mann, Arthur
Mann, John A.
Mann, Reginald
Manning, Donald S.
Marchyn, Metro Jim
Markel, Franklin
Maroon, John J.
Martin, Harold C.
Martin, John
Martin, Robert E.
Martino, John
Masiello, Ralph John
Masters, Kenneth
Masters, Leslie

Masters, Robert
Mateer, Clair E.
Matthews, Charles Duane
Matthews, Charles Frederick
Matthews, Duane
Mattice, Donald L.
Mattison, Burton Whitney
Maulis, Eman
Mays, Harry L.
Mazur, Sigmund J.
McClure, Walter
McCormick, Charles J. Sr.
McGrath, James
McKeever, Daniel J.
McKie, Donald
McLaughlin, William J.
McMahon, Harry Mortimer
Meckle, Donald
Meteer, Clair E.
Metzler, Daniel A.
Mies, Frances Furman
Miller, Louis M.
Mitchell, Millard G.
Mitchell, Robert F.
Moag, John Edward
Mocniak, Walter George
Molyneaux, Garrett
Molyneaux, R. L.
Monnen, Charles F.
Monnen, Millard C.
Monteleone, Ernest F.
Moore, Charles
Moore, E. Keith
Moore, Willis
Moose, Raymond
Morse, James G.
Morse, Richard
Moss, Kenneth
Moxham, Howard
Mundy, Joseph Francis
Murphy, William J.
Murray, Neil W.
Myers, Douglas
Myers, Eric
Myers, Guy Erman
Myers, Henry
Myers, Irving
Myers, R. E.
Myers, William E.
Nagy, Frank
Nelson, William
Neubauer, Albert W.
Neumann, Laurence W.
Newson, Lincoln B.
Nichols, Henry W.
Nichols, Merwin L.
Nixon, Donald O.
Noble, Roy L.
Nortz, Edward Ralph
Ogden, William E.
O'Neil, Joseph R.
Orr, George Allman Jr.
Ortt, Gordon
Ortt, Milfort
Owler, William G.
Palmatier, Curtis W. Jr.
Palmerton, Elwyn F.
Parker, Milford
Parker, Stephen G.
Patterson, James
Pawlicki, Milton J.
Pedley, Lamont C.
Penders, Carl D.
Penzotti, Rick R.
Petit, Jarvis
Piazza, Dr. Salvatore J.

Pirinelli, Sam L.
Plain, Gardner
Plain, Roger
Pless, James
Poler, Donal S.
Poliseno, Dominick F.
Pollock, John
Pollow, John
Porter, Bernard C.
Powell, Robert Edgar
Profeta, Samuel
Pronobus, Rev. Andrew
Quirk, William T.
Rayl, Stephen E.
Reece, Wallace R.
Reese, Andrew F.
Reese, Wilbur
Reichert, John W.
Reid, Daniel E.
Reubens, Harold E.
Rice, Donald Munson
Ridosh, Steve
Riordan, Emerson R.
Rix, William A.
Robertson, Carlleen
Robinson, Raymond Louis
Rose, Ralph W.
Rudy, Oliver Sr.
Ryan, Leland
Rye, John J.
Sakach, Nick
Sargeant, Thomas Don
Schisler, Eugene J.
Schrader, Albert
Schultz, Calvin C.
Schultz, Harold S.
Schultz, John
Schumacker, Charles Steele
Seefeldt, Bernard S.
Seefeldt, Howard
Seefeldt, Ralph
Serba, Chester P.
Serba, Edward J.
Sharp, Richard G.
Sherrow, Warren D. Sr.
Shultz, Howard
Shultz, John
Shultz, Norman
Shultz, Robert
Sider, Frank
Sievert, Donald
Sikowski, John
Simon, John Victor
Sion, William G.
Sirianni, Edward J.
Skurski, Benny
Smith, James L.
Smithson, Donald
Smithson, Jack T.
Smithson, Raymond D.
Smithson, Richard Jr.
Snyder, Elmer H.
Socie, Frank O.
Spry, William J.
Stacey, William J.
Stahlman, Mahlon C.
Staie, Paul L.
Steiner, Earl K.
Stepien, John J.
Stesiak, Chester
Stevens, Alfred
Stevens, Norman G.
Stivers, Roy
Stratton, Wendell DeWitt
Suraniak, George
Sutherland, Donald R.

Sutherland, Kenneth
Sutherland, Ronald
Sweatman, Jack T.
Szupello, Edwin H.
Thaler, Robert E. Sr.
Theis, Archie
Theis, William
Thielman, Francis
Thomas, Albert J.
Thompson, Richard H.
Toner, John J.
Tooke, Edward A.
Torba, Edwin P.
Tower, Everett
Tower, Gerald V.
Tower, Jean Elizabeth
Tower, Richard Pierce
Truesdell, Donald
Truesdell, Merton A.
Truesdell, Neil Elwood
Ueltz, Herbert F. G.
Upper, Alvin Franklin
Vas, Frank P.
Velsy, Gordon
Veronica, William J.
VeRost, Martin A.
Vickers, William H.
Vince, M. P. Jr.
Walker, Gottfried Heinz
Warren, Gertrude
Wasmund, Norman E.
Weiss, Andrew Francis
White, Charles W. Sr.
Whitt, Richard
Whittaker, Don James
Whittaker, Merrill
Whyte, George
Wieland, Nelson Herbert
Wiepert, Gerald Carl
Wiepert, Louis
Wilkesmore, Kenneth William
Wills, John
Wise, William H.
Withey, Richard A.
Woolson, Nathan
Wysocki, Edward
Zale, John Stanley
Zastrow, Glenwood

Source: Veterans Of The Ages Monument, Village of Youngstown Veterans' Park kiosk and *Veterans' Books*, Porter Town Hall, Youngstown, NY. A duplicate set of books is displayed in the Porter Historical Museum, Youngstown, NY, with additional military information submitted by veterans or family members.

All veterans or their families are encouraged to contact the Town of Porter Historical Society to include a name and service record. The previous Town Historian Vee Housman, a veteran of the United States Navy, began the veterans project. Vee operated the link trainer at the Oakland Naval Air Station, California, simulating flight for pilot trainees during the Vietnam War.

Vee Housman passed away October 1, 2005.

APPENDIX G

POWs at Niagara Fruit Industries, Inc.

Bauer, Kurt
Beyer, Heinz
Bischhorn, Engelburt
Bleier, Josef
Boehles, Karl
Borchardt, Kurt
Bracht, Erich
Bratfisch, Heino
Broschinski, Georg
Burkard, Theodor
Dattner, Herbert
Dropsch, Helmut
Engel, Siegfried
Faist, Wilhelm
Fritzsche, Kurt
Freudenstein, Karl
Gaertner, Andreas
Goeke, Albert
Gross, Wilfried
Hammermueller, W.
Hermann, Gerhard
Herrmann, Josef
Holste, Friedrich
Horejsi, Eduard
Kammerer, Hans
Kaufmann, Albert
Herbert, Robert
Kineinker, Leonhard
Klein, Hans
Klostermeier, Thomas
Koch, Rudolph
Koechling, Heinrich
Koelbel, Alfred
Kortenbeck, Michael
Knappe, Hans
Kratschmann, Franz
Krenz, Walter
Leunemann, Johann
Luther, Karl
Malling, Otto
Matt, Ernst
Meier, Josef
Moebius, Erich
Muehlig, Paul
Nass, Paul
Neumann, Helmut
Neurohr, Willi
Niedermeyer, Karl
Oehme, Klaus
Oehmler, Karl
Ohr, Johannes
Paessler, Bruno
Peters, Johann
Platte, Karl
Protzer, Ernst
Reichardt, Alfred
Reim, Willi
Reisenbichler, Friedrich
Rosenthal, Alfred
Sauer, Josef
Schaeffner, Helmut
Schauerte, Josef
Scheer, Georg
Schmidt, Wilhelm
Schon, Jakob
Schulz, Paul

Schwarzkopf, Horst
Selltischek, Albert
Sick, Walter
Spagenberg, Gerhard
Steudtner, Oskr
Stoecker, Rudolf
Widi, Johann
Wissgott, Rudolf
Wuerfel, Reinhard
Zedler, Max
Zewe, Alfred
Zewingel, Fritz
Ziegler, Willi

Source: Distribution of POW Labor Niagara Fruit Industries, Book II, 2006.1.69a, 2006.1.69b, 2006.1.70a, 2006.1.70b, 2006.1.71a, 2006,1.71b, 2006.1.82, Town Hall, Youngstown, NY. POW Labor for the weeks of January 8-13, January 15-20, January 22-27, and February 23-24, 1945. The POWs worked as few as one or two days, and others worked as many as six and a half days. Kineinker is also spelled Kieninker in the records.

Wages Rates

Strappers	$5.76 per 8 hour day
Flippers	$4.96 per 8 hour day
Pushers	$4.96 per 8 hour day
Folders	$4.96 per 8 hour day
Gluer	$4.96 per 8 hour day
Stitchers	$5.76 per 8 hour day
Loaders	$6.16 per 8 hour day

Source: Distribution of POW Labor Niagara Fruit Industries, Book II, Youngstown, NY.

APPENDIX H
In Service from Dickersonville

Albright, Donald
Albright, Gordon
Albright, Arthur
Bickford, Franklin
Bonnett, Charles
Bonnett, Daniel
Bowen, Richard
Britt, Jack
Campbell, James
Davis, Arthur*
Davis, Robert
Drinkwater, Perry
Eaton, William*
Eaton, Reginald*
Flood, Franes
Goodman, Malcolm
Goodman, Norval
Goodman, Lyle
Helmich, Jerry
Holz, Clifford
Kneeple, Charles
Leggett, Robert
Leggett, Dorothy
Leggett, Doris
Moss, Kenneth
Nichols, A. Jack
Nichols, Mervin
Olver, Charles
Pedley, Lamont
Pedley, Richard
Scarupa, Henry
Schultz, Robert
Schultz, Russel
Sutherland, Ronald
Sutherland, Kenneth
Velzy, Gordon
White, George
Williams, Jack
Woolson, Ira Nathan

Source: Plaque, Ransomville Historial Room, Ransomville, NY; was originally displayed at the former Dickersonville Methodist Church.

APPENDIX I
Ransomville Roll of Honor

Ames, William
Arnold, Elwin
Austin, Harold L.
Austin, William L.
Baker, Arthur
Bale, R. Spencer
Bale, Ray L.
Bauer, Albert C.
Blackwell, Loren
Blackwell, Alex L.
Bohnstadt, Ronald
Bonnett, Daniel
Bonnett, Melvin
Bowen, Richard I.
Bowman, Harold
Bradley, Russell
Bradley, Grant
Britt, Jack
Burlingame, William R.
Burlingame, John S.
Burmaster, W. Jenning
Campbell, Roy
Campbell, James H.
Canfield, Lewis
Canfield, Rex H.
Carew, Gordon R.
Carew, Jack W.
Carraglin, James
Carter, Kenneth
Chestnut, William H.
Chestnut, John A.
Chestnut, James
Clark, Robert N.
Clarke, Robert R.
Clement, Robert
Collins, Raymond
Colliver, Ray
Colliver, Calvin
Connor, Clifford T.
Cornell, Raymond
Cornell, Douglas
Curtiss, Howard
Demmin, Elton
Demmin, Carson
Dent, Calvin W.
Drinkwalter, Victor
Drinkwalter, Robert
Drinkwalter, James
Durfy, James R.
Eaton, Reginald
Edwards, William
Einstein, Paul H.
Etherton, George N.
Farquarson, John
Farquharson, George
Faust, Leonard
Figura, Bruno
Figura, Henry
Flood, Frances
Foster, Marvin
Fredricks, Clarence
Frey, Floyd
Furman, Clarence
Furman, Gerald
Geartz, Roger
Gentle, A. Spencer
Golding, John
Goodman, Lyle
Goodman, Janet A.
Goodman, Norval

Goodman, Malcolm E.
Gratz, Walter
Grzybowski, Edward
Hardison, Gerald
Harris, Willard
Helwig Jr., Ervin M.
Henschel, Paul
Hesher, Ervin
Hillman, Eugene
Hochadel, Leonard
Holman, Eugene
Ingraham, Maton
Ingraham, Richard
Jarrett, Jack
Jindra, Eugene V.
Johnson, Jack
Johnson, Gene
Johnston, Clifford
Keaty, John
Knapp, Glenn
Knapp, Darwin
Kneeppel, Charles T.
Kraatz, Gerald
Kunz, Roger
Langdon, Lawrence
Lederhouse, John
Lederhouse, Albert
Lederhouse, Chester
Lederhouse, Stanley C.
Leggett, Robert L.
Lindhurst, Harold
Lindsay, Warren
Lisman, Francis
Maacks, Loren
Maacks, Ralph
Maacks Jr., Alvin
Mahar, Ronald
Mann, Reginald
Mann, J. Arthur
Manning, Donald S.
Markell, Franklin O.
Martin, Arthur
Masters, Robert
Masters, Leslie
Masters, Kenneth
Mathews, Duane
McClelland Jr., Frank
McClure, Walter
McGrath, James
McKee, Donald
Molyneux, Robert L.
Molyneux, Garrett
Moore, Charles A.
Moose, Raymond
Moss, Kenneth
Moxham, Howard
Myers, William
Myers, H. Elric
Myers, Irvine R.
Myers, Richard E.
Myers, Howard R.
Neumann, Lawrence
Neumann, William
Ortt, Gordon C.
Ortt, Milford
Parker, W. Milford
Patterson, James
Payne, William
Pedley, Richard
Peley, LamMont
Perry, Clinton C.
Plain, Gardner
Plain, Roger
Pless, James
Pollow, John J.
Pollow, Frederick

Reese, Wilbur R.
Reese, Andrew F.
Rose, Ralph W.
Ryon, Leland W.
Schultz, Norman
Schultz, Robert H.
Seefeldt, Howard
Shaver, Harold C.
Shaver, Norman G.
Shirley, Lewis
Sievert, Ronald
Smithson, Raymond
Smithson, Donald R.
Smithson, Richard
Smithson, Jack T.
Stacey, William
Stevens, Alfred E.
Stevens, Clifford F.
Talerico, Orlando
Thielman, Frances
Thies, William
Thies, Archie
Tower, Gerald
Tower, Everett
Truesdell, Merton A.
Truesdell, Donald W.
Upper, Alvin
Vince, Martin
Warren, Gertrude
Wasmund, Norman
Whitt, Richard
Whitt, Cheter
Whyte, George W.
Wiepert, Louis
Wiepert, Gerald C.
Williamson, Harold
Zimmerman, Junior E.

Source: Names from the photograph of the "Ransomville Roll of Honor" in front of the Masonic Building, Ransomville, NY. The original Roll of Honor display is missing. Photo at Ransomville Historical Room.

BIBLIOGRAPHY

BOOKS

Ambrose, Stephen E. *The Wild Blue: The Men and Boys Who Flew the B-24s Over Germany*. New York: Simon & Schuster, 2001.

Author. *Lewiston*. Charleston, SC: Arcadia Publishing Co., 2006.

___. *Porter*. London, England: Arcadia Publishing Co., 2005.

Bell Aircraft Corporation. *An Aviation Story The History of Bell Aircraft Corp., Tenth Anniversary Edition*. Buffalo, NY: Bell Aircraft Corporation, July 1945.

Bischof, Gunter and Stephen E. Ambrose, ed. *Eisenhower and the German POWs*. Baton Rouge: Louisiana University Press, 1992.

Casaldi, Silvano. *Gli Uomini Dello Sbarco Anzio/Nettuno 1944 The Men of the Landing*. Roma: Herold Editore, 2006.

Gansberg, Judith M. *Stalag: U.S.A*. New York: Thomas Y. Crowell Company, 1997.

Gaertner, Georg with Arnold Krammer. *Hitler's Last Soldier in America*. New York: Stein and Day Publishers, 1985.

Harris, Annette T. *WWII Prisoner of War Camps in Wayne County, New York and Their Prisoners*. Clyde, NY: Pine Hollow, 2004.

Hartzell, Karl Drew, Ph.D. *The Empire State at War WWII*. The State of New York, 1949.

Höss, Rudolph. *Death Dealer*. ed. Steven Paskuly translated Andrew Pollinger. Buffalo, NY: Prometheus Books. 1992.

Johnsen, Frederick A. *Bell P-39/P63*. North Branch, MN: Specialty Press Publishers and Wholesalers, 1998.

Korbonski, Stefan. *Fighting Warsaw The Story of the Polish Underground State 1939-1945*. New York Hippocrene Books, Inc., 2004.

Krammer, Arnold. *Nazi Prisoners of War in America*. New York: Stein and Day

Publishers, 1979.
MacMillan, Margaret. *Paris 1919*. New York: Random House Inc., 2003.
Matthews, Birch. *Cobra! Bell Aircraft Corporation 1934-46*. Atglen, PA: Schiffer-Publishing Ltd., 1996.
Matthews, Richard P. *Good Soldiers The History of the 353rd Infantry Regiment, 89th Infantry Division 1942-1945*. United States, 2004.
Neary, Bob, *Stalag Luft III Sagan…Nuernberg…Moosburg*, North Wales, PA, 1946.
Ogden, Muriel Scovell. *The Scovells*. Baldwinsville, NY: Ogden Energy Inc., (1990s).
Return of the Brave. New York: Medallion Publishing Co., 2002.
Schule, Professor Albert. *Heimatbuch Der Gemeinde Dettingen Unter Teck*. Dettingen unter Teck, Deutschland: Herausgegeben von der Gemeinde, 1981.
Stanton, Shelby L. *WWII Order Of Battle*. New York: Galahad Books, 1991.
Toliver, Raymond F. *The Interrogator: The Story of Hans Joachim Scharff Master Interrogator of the Luftwaffe*. Atglen, PA: Schiffer Publishing Ltd., 1997.
Truman, Harry S. *Memoirs 1945 Year of Decisions*. Garden City, NY: Doubleday & Co., Inc., 1955.
Young, Peter, Collins, James L. Jr., Barnett, Correlli and Innex, Brian. *Illustrated WWII Encyclopedia*. United States: H. S. Stuttman Inc., 1978.
Willkie, Wendell L. *Unteilbare Welt*, New York, Simon and Schuster, 1943.

PERIODICALS AND JOURNALS

Byrnes, Thomas E. *Chemung County 1890-1975*. Elmira, NY: Chemung County Historical Society, Inc., 1976.
Der Volksfreund/People's Friend. "Noted German artist, former POW, returns to camp." V, No. 4, July/August 1998: 1, 9.
Dickinson, David L. "Kriegsgefangenschaft bei Fort Niagara: Fort Niagara's World War II Prisoners-of-War." *Fortress Niagara*, Vol. II No. 2 December 2000.
"Die PW Woche," *YANK The Army Weekly*, December 31, 1943.
Hilbert, Alfred G. "Van Etten CCC Camp Housed Nazi POWs." *The Chemung Historical Journal*. Elmira, NY. 22 No. 4 June, 1977: 2709-2710.
"History of New Fort Niagara," *Youngstown Centennial Magazine*, 1954: 37, 39,

41.

Keesler Field Mississippi, San Antonio, TX: Universal Press, July 1942.

Mayer, S. L., ed. *Signal: Hitler's Wartime Picture Magazine*. Englewood Cliffs, NJ: Prentice Hall, Inc. 1976.

Mazuzan, George T. and Nancy Walker, "Restricted Areas: German Prisoner-of-War Camps in Western New York, 1944-1945," *New York History*, V, LVIX, No. 1, January 1978.

Niagara Falls Women's Air Raid Wardens' Service Force, *The Blackout*, Vol. 1, No. 4, March 20, 1942.

Roetter, Joseph. *Der Volksfreund/People's Friend*, "Consul General Awards Medal to Area Historian," Vol. XI, No. 3, May/June 2004, 1.

Scarisbrick, Sean. *Artvoice*. "A Christmas Spent as a Prisoner of the Third Reich," December 21-27, 2000, V11 N51.

Student Handbook, T. L. 282, Radio Operator Mechanic Training, Scott Field, Illinois.

Tyndall Field Flexible Gunnery Class 43-5, Houston, TX, E.M. Berry, 1943.

Worthington Buffalo Works News, Vol. 2, No. 2 June 1944 and No. 8 December 1944, Vol. 3 No. 1 May 1945.

REPORT DOCUMENTS

Cornell University Cooperative Extension archival records prepared by Christine Derby-Cuadrado, Project Archivist under direction of Paul Westfall, Executive Director of the Cornell Cooperative Extension, Box #13, 15-3, Folders 1-6; Cooperative Extension, Lockport, NY.

Enemy POW Information Services, Report Branch, Subject File 1942-46; Camp Labor Report – Second Service Company, Delaware to NY; Record Group 389, Entry 461; Niagara, Fort Folder; National Archives Building, College Park, MD.

"Camp – Memphis ASF Depot to Pine," Enemy POW Info. Bureau Rep.; Branch Subject File 1942-46; Record Group 389, Entry 461; National Archives Building, College Park, MD.

"Other Inspection Reports," Fort Niagara, NY Folder, Provost Marshal General Enemy POW Info. Bureau, Reporting Branch, Subject File 1942-46; Record Group 389, Entry 461; October 9, 1944, February 15, 1945, March 8, 1945, and August 27, 1945; National Archives Building,

College Park, MD.

"PMG Inspection Reports," Niagara, NY Folder; Record Group No. 389, Entry 461; National Archives Building, College Park, MD.

Semi-monthly Reports on WWII Prisoners of War, Headquarters Army Service Forces, Office of the Provost Marshall General, Washington 25, DC; 1944-45; Record NWCTM Ref. Collection; Record Group No. 389, Entry 461; National Archives Building, College Park, MD.

INTERNET ADDRESSES

BBC- History. http://www.bbc.co.uk/history/worldwars/

Miraculous Medal. http://www.ladyofallnations.org/rudubac.htm

Moosburg Online: Kriegsgefangenenlager (Liste). http://www.moosburg.org/info/stalag/laglist.html

National Archives and Records Administration http://www.archives.gov/index.html Archival Databases: "World War II Army Enlistment Records" and "Records of World War II Prisoners of War"

National Museum of United States Air Force. http://www.nationalmuseum.af.mil

Sisters of St. Francis of Penance and Christian Charity. http://www.franciscans-stella-niagara.org

The History Channel. http://www.history.com

The Holocaust Resource Center of Buffalo. http://www.holocaustcenterbuff.com

The Jewish Virtual Library. http://www.jewishvirtuallibrary.org/index

U.S. Army Corps of Engineers Buffalo District. http://www.lrb.usace.army.mil/

ORAL HISTORY

Adamski, Bernard J. Interview by author, Buffalo, NY, July 23, 2007.

Blake, Stanley C. Interview by author, Buffalo, NY, July 23, 2007.

Byron, Richard. Interview by author, Niagara Aerospace Museum, June 16, July 11, September 14, and November 1, 2006.

Clark, Tony. Interview by author, Youngstown, NY, May 30, 2006.

Cowden, Violet Thurn. Telephone interview by author, October 27, 2006.

Denny Harold. Telephone interview by author, May 16, 2006.

Derhay, Joe. Telephone interview by author, October 23, and November 5, November 7, and November 11, 2006.

Diamond, Joseph: Auschwitz Survivor. Interview by author, Buffalo, NY, September 29 and November 17, 2006.

Diez, Kenneth. Interview by author (daughter-in-law), Youngstown, NY, April 26, 2006.

Dineen, Margaret "Peggy." Telephone interview by author, February 9 and November 26, 2006.

Duerr, Richard. Interview by author, Buffalo, NY, May 8, 2006.

Dyer, Marguerite Slattery. Interview by author, Niagara Falls, NY April 24, 2007.

Esser, Frances Serchia. Telephone interview by author, July 11 and July 19, 2006.

Fadel, Tom. Interview by author, Youngstown, NY, August 25, 2006.

Feigenbaum I, Edward. Interview by author, Wilson, NY, March 12, 2007.

Frantz, Arnold E. Interview by author, Colden, NY, June 18, 2007.

Gates, Ruth Harris and Bud. Telephone interview by author, July 26 and July 27, 2006.

Geelan, Patrick A. Interview by author, North Tonawanda, NY, June 15, 2006, and Niagara Aerospace Museum, June 24, 2006.

Gilson, Jim. Telephone interview by author, December 4, 2006.

Gilson, Frank. Interview by author, Youngstown, NY, December 12, 2006, and telephone interview by author, February 20, 2007.

Giuga, Mariano. Interview by author, Buffalo, NY, July 23, 2007.

Griffin, J. Donald. Interview by author, Buffalo, NY, July 3, 2007.

Grzywa, Edwin. Interview by author, Buffalo, NY, July 13, 2007.

Hardison, Denton. Telephone interview by author, June 6, 2006.

Hays, Harry B. Telephone interview by author, October 7, November 9, 2006.

Hays, James O. Lt. Col. Retired. Email to author September to October 2006.

Henderson, Roberta. Interview by author, Buffalo, NY, August 15, 2006.

Holland, Joan Carney Gray. Interview by author, Youngstown, NY, February 21, 2007.

Hurtgam, Mervin. Interview by author, Ransomville Historical Room, May 27, 2006.

Jircitano, John. Interview by author, Youngstown, NY, January 26, March 24, and April 9, 2006.

Joseph, Loretta Connors. Telephone interview by author July 25, 2006.

Juergens, Margaret Johnston Klomp. Interview by author, Youngstown, NY, October 31, 2006.

Kahl, Richard C. Telephone interview by author, May 17, 2007.

Klinshaw, Benedict L. Interview by author, Buffalo, NY, July 13, 2007.

Kohl, John. Interview by author, Lewiston, NY, July 2006.

Locurcio, Michael. Interview by author, Buffalo, NY, August 15, 2006.

MacDonald, Joel. Telephone interview by author, November 1, 2006.

MacPherson, Robert E. Interview by author, Buffalo, NY, July 12, 2007.

Marchese, A. Joseph. Interview by author, Buffalo, NY, August 15, 2006.

Marchyn, Metro "Jim." Interview by author, Buffalo, NY, October 25, 2007.

Maroon, John. Interview by author (cousin), Buffalo, NY, February 22, 2007.

McCann, James. Telephone interview by author, August 27, 2006.

Meckle, Donald. Interview by author, Buffalo, NY, January 24, 2008.

Morse, Richard H. Interview by author, Buffalo, NY, November 14, 2007.

Myers, Gertie and Robert. Interview by author, Ransomville, NY, July 10, August 8, 2006.

Neeson, Hugh M. Interview by author, Lewiston, NY, August 12, August 15, August 23, and September 4, 2006.

Newman, Etta Myers Davis. Telephone interview by author, June 6 and June 22, 2006.

Nicolette, Frank V. Interview by author, Youngstown, NY, October 4 and November 4, 2006.

O'Reilly, Sister Isabelle. Interview by author, Stella Niagara, NY, March 6, 2006.

Pacia, Eugene. Interview by author, Youngstown, NY, May 24 and August 21, 2006.

Palmerton, Elwyn F. Interview by author, Town of Lewiston, NY, June 27, 2007.

Penzotti, Rick and Pearl. Interview by author, Youngstown, NY, November 10, 2006.

Phillips, Pat Hutchison. Interview by author, Youngstown, NY, July 31, 2006.

Piergies, Mary Mirecki, Telephone interview by author, October 23, 2006.

Poliseno, Dominic. Interview by author, Buffalo, NY, June 12, 2007.

POW Support Group meetings, Buffalo, NY, various dates 2007.

Quiett, Ronald. Interview by author, Youngstown, NY, June 6, 2006.

Palmerton, Elwyn F. Interview by author, Town of Lewiston, NY, June 27, 2007.

Reese, Grace Hays. Telephone interview by author, September 3, 2006.

Richardson, Jane. Interview by author, Youngstown, NY, July 6, August 10, and September 1, 2006.

Richardson, John. Interview by author, Youngstown, NY, 10 August 10, September 1, 2006.

Rockabrand, Maj. Claude W., Retired. Telephone interview by author, April 26, 2006.

Rolfe, John. Interview by author, Youngstown, NY, May 26, September 15, 2006.

Sadowski, Kazimierz. Interview by author, Youngstown, NY, September 30, October 3, and October 31, 2006.

Schillo, Audrey. Interview by author, Youngstown, NY, August 23, 2006.

Schultz, Mickey. Interview by author, Youngstown, NY, January 10, May 16, 2006.

Serchia, Frank. Interview by author (sister-in-law), Youngstown, NY, July 11, 2006.

Sikoski, Renata Holody. Interview by author, Youngstown, NY, May 24 and June 8, 2006.

Simon, Salome Authier. Interview by author (daughter), Youngstown, NY, June 13, July 11, and August 24, 2006.

Tower, Douglas. Interview by author, North Collins, NY, July 10, 2006; Youngstown, NY, August 3, 2006.

Tower, Roderick. Interview by author (neighbor), July 28, 2006.

Truesdell, Ellen Graves. Interview by author, Ransomville, NY, March 21, 2007.

Veronica, William J. Interview by author, Buffalo, NY, July 3, 2007.

Wermuth, Olga Strassburg. Interview by author, Youngstown, NY, July 18, 2006.

Wieland, Mary Hodge. Interview by author, Youngstown, NY, June 25, 2006.

Williams, Lt. Col. Betty J., USAF Retired. Telephone interview by author, September 1 and October 16, 2006.

Zale, John (ne Zubrzycki). Interview by author, Buffalo, NY, July 23, 2007.

MISCELLANEOUS SOURCES

Abels, Margaret. *Western New York Women in Defense Industries*, WWII, Canisius College, WNY Heritage Program Occasional Papers, Dr. David Valaik, December 6, 1989.

Aero Club of Buffalo and Bell News Association. *First Supersonic Flight: Western New York's Salute to the Bell Aircraft X-1 50th Anniversary 1947-1997 Breaking the Sound Barrier.* Cheektowaga, NY, 1997.

Barner, Mark. *Production Soldiers: WNY's Working Women of WWII.* Video: 2004.

Dickinson, David L., Dr. Peter K. Gessner and Lt. Col. Robert C. Bienvenue, "Four Grand Murals and the Artists of The Officers Club & Bachelor Quarters Building," Youngstown, NY, Officers Club Museum Coalition, 1999.

Esser, Frances Serchia. Speeches given at The Palm Springs Air Museum, May 3, 2003, May 7, 2005.

Faneuf, Leston. "Lawrence D. Bell A Man and His Company," Speech delivered at the "1958 Niagara Dinner" of The Newcomen Society in North America, Buffalo Club, NY, May 15, 1958.

Frigidaire Division General Motors Corporation. "GM Frigidaire at War." Dayton, OH: Frigidaire Division General Motors Corp., 1944.

Harris, Willard Ransom and Gates, Ruth Harris. *Willard Ransom Harris January 27, 1920 – June 22, 2001*, Ransomville, NY: Ransomville Historical Room, 2001.

Hays, Harriet. *Memoirs.*

Hostess Reception and Closing Program of USO Second Street, Youngstown, NY, December 14, 1945, Youngstown, NY, Porter Historical Museum.

Keasey, Lt. Col. Charles R., Battalion Commander 171st Combat Engineers. "A Short History," June 25, 1945.

Lubicz-Sadowski, Tadeusz. *My Remembrance*, translated from Polish by Kazimierz Sadowski, 2001.

Nowak, John C. *With the Eyes Of The Seventh Photo Group... Now It Can Be Told!* June 16, 1945.

Rockabrand, Maj. Claude W., Retired. *A Test Pilot's Tale.* Thousand Oaks, CA, DVD, June 16, 2006.

Sadowski, Kazimierz. Personal notes.

Stidham Jr., Clayton Randall. "Grandparent Essay: Etta Davis," April 28, 1992.

Williams, Lt. Col. Betty J., USAF Retired. "Women Air Force Service Pilots World War II – 1942-1944," July 1991.

NEWSPAPERS

Air Force Print News (Nashville, TN).

Buffalo Evening News aka *Buffalo News* (Buffalo, NY).

Courier Express aka *Buffalo Courier Express* (Buffalo, NY).

Desert Sun (Palm Springs, CA).

Jersey Journal (NJ).

Los Angeles Times (Los Angeles, CA).

Niagara Falls Gazette aka *Niagara Gazette* (Niagara Falls, NY).

Niagara Review (Niagara Falls, ON).

Polish Weekly (Detroit, MI).

Reno Gazette (Reno, NV).

Stars and Stripes (Liege Edition).

The Times (St. Petersburg, FL).

Union-Sun & Journal (Lockport, NY).

Associated Press. "Army Changes Prisoner Fare," *Union-Sun & Journal*, April 24, 1945.

Balme, Bob. "Fort Niagara, Deactivated by Army, to Become Park," *Buffalo Evening News*, January 11, 1962.

Barker, Robert. "Recalling the WASPs WWII Woman Pilot Keeps Memories of Unit Alive," *Los Angeles Times*. February 12, 1993.

Brydges, Jerauld. "German recalls Fort Niagara POW Camp," *Niagara*

Gazette, July 29, 1984.
Buffalo Evening News. "Air Plants Fueled War Effort," August 28, 1989.
___. "Marching into War," Special Section, August 31, 1989.
___. "USO to Get Half Money Raised in National War Fund 1943 Appeal," November 1943.
___. "Victory in Europe – When Fort Niagara was a Prison," May 7,1995.
___. "Save Historic Officers Club," April 12, 1998.
___. "WWII: Beginning," August 27, 1989.
___. "WWII: The Home Front," August 29, 1989.
Courier Express. "New Chapel to be Dedicated," August 3, 1941.
___. "Army to Transfer 75 Bodies," April 17, 1949.
___. "German Prisoners See 'Bomb Damage' at Falls," Buffalo, NY, June 13, 1944.
___. "Sightseers to Take Over Historic Battlements," November 18, 1945.
___. "To Remove Dead From Cemeteries," January 19, 1947.
Clark, Stephen. "89-Year-Old Takes a Fall and Is Up For Another," *Los Angeles Times*. April 10, 2006.
Crawford, Annette, "Three Air Force trailblazers among Hall of Fame inductees," *Air Force Print News,* March 27, 2006.
Dickinson, David. "County's 'German Invasion' Detailed." *Union Sun & Journal*, September 7, 1996.
Elia, Joseph C., Capt. "Ageless China Retains Ancient Customs in Midst of Modern War and Sees Glorious Future Ahead," *Niagara Gazette*, 1940s.
"Final Retreat on Monday to End 219-Year Military History of Fort Niagara," unidentified newspaper clipping, December 29, 1945.
"Flier Killed Over Germany," Ransomville Historical Room, Ransomville, NY, military archives.
Foltz, John. "Fort Niagara Site of German POW Camp," *Union Sun & Journal*, 1940s.
Fraser, Joan, "Falls Celebrated Win in Gay Style," NF Local History Library archives of WWII.
Jersey Journal, "Came Home Via Thumb Route," May 3, 1946.
McBride, Ann. "Women Vital to War Effort," *Niagara Gazette*, September 5, 1999.
Newsday The Long Island Newspaper, "Salute to War's Female Pilots," March 30,

2001.
Niagara Falls Gazette, "A Peep into the Past," April 4, 1959.
___. "A Peep into the Past," July 18, 1959.
___. "Army Point System for Discharge of Men is Announced," May 10, 1945.
___. "Attention! AWVS Canteen USO," 1940s.
___. "Attractive Show at AWVS Canteen," 1940s.
___. "AWVS Canteen Show at Youngstown," 1940s.
___. "AWVS Party," (1940s)
___. "Ball to Feature USO Performers," 1940s.
___. "Citizens Gave Greatly of Time, Efforts for Civilian Defense Work," May 7, 1945.
___. "Civilian Forces Join Military In Protection Plan," December 8, 1941.
___. "Falls Airport Brought War Plane Plant Here," May 7, 1945.
___. "Falls Marine Prays During Lull in Iwo Battle," March 1, 1945.
___. "Falls Men Meet in China," January 12, 1944.
___. "Falls Physician With Chennault on Secret Mission – Dr. Joseph C. Elia Flies with Famous Air General; Forced Down in India," June 23, 1943.
___. "Fire Auxiliary of Youngstown Meets Tonight," April 1, 1943.
___. "First Lieutenant," 1940s.
___. "Flying Physician Wins Citations," 1940s.
___. "400 Nazi War Prisoners Arrive at Fort Niagara for Work in Farm Areas," June 13, 1944.
___. "Germany Surrenders," May 7, 1945.
___. "Hero of Iwo Jima Battle Dies at 44," September 26, 1969.
___. "Hold Conference, War Council and Red Cross Groups, Meet at Youngstown," October 26, 1942.
___. "Hopes of Early Surrender Fade," May 2, 1945.
___. "Junior Hostesses Plan Card Party," 1940s.
___. "Local AWVS Canteen USO Presents Novel Program at Rochester USO," 1940s.
___. "Many Services Offered at AWVS," 1940s.
___. "Nazi Prisoner Dies at Work," *Niagara Falls Gazette*, September 7, 1945.
___. "Nazi Prisoners to Leave Fort," November 26, 1945.
___. "Need helpers to Make Dressings," 1944.

___. "Over 450 Enroll for Civil Defence in First District, Town of Porter, January 12, 1942.

___. "Prisoners of War to be Housed at Fort Niagara while working on Farms," June 2, 1944.

___. "Prisoners Worked," February 26, 1945.

___. "Proud Record Compiled by Niagara Falls AWVS," May 7, 1945.

___. "Rationing Program Gives Falls Folks Equal Shares," May 7, 1945.

___. "712th Battalion Holds Blind Date Show," 1940s.

___. "Service Men Guests, AWVS Motor Corps to Give Halloween Party for Service Men," 1940s.

___. "Seventeen Given Diplomas at 14th Commencement at Youngstown High," June 26, 1940.

___. "Soldiers at Fort Niagara Hosts to Belles Tomorrow," 1940s.

___. "Successful Quiz Party at AWVS," August 1944.

___. Supplement on WWII, May 30, 1976.

___. "Tells How China Celebrates her Fourth of July," 1943.

___. "To Give Formal Ball at AWVS," September 1944.

___. "Unique Program at AWVS Canteen," September 1944.

___. "USO Services Brought to Close at Youngstown; Certificates and Pins Presented for Long Service," December 17, 1945.

___. "Veterans Are Welcomed Home at Dinner Here," 1940s.

___. "Witches Frolic Given at AWVS," 1940s.

___. "Women's Volunteer Services – at Youngstown PTA Meeting," February 6, 1942.

___. "Youngstown Red Cross Aid Needed," October 1944.

___. "Youngstown Red Cross Has Produced 105,202 Dressings Since Inception," November 20, 1946.

___. "Women Vital to War Effort," September 5, 1999.

___. "Workers Help Cheer Soldiers at A.W.V.S.," September 23, 1944.

Niagara Review. "Brothers in Allied Forces", April 1, 1943.

___. "Death Announcement Mary Grotowska," March 19, 1995.

Otey, Robert. "5 Germans Hanged for Killing Companion," Fort Leavenworth, KS, (AP), July 10, 1945.

The Polish Weekly, "Return to Siberia," December 2, 2004.

"Ransomville Man Among 17 Killed in Plane Crash," Ransomville Historical

Room, Ransomville, NY, military collection, 1940s.

"Ransomville Man Killed in Action," Ransomville Historical Room, Ransomville, NY, military collection, 1940s.

Reno Gazette, "Doctor 'Joe' dies at 93," November 27, 2003.

Skimin, Frank. *Niagara Falls Gazette*, "No Coddling of War Prisoners, Visit to Fort Niagara Shows," September 9, 1944.

Stars and Stripes. Liege Edition, "Roer Was an Engineer's Nightmare," March 3, 1945.

Swartz, Jr., James, "7 More Germans Die for Traitor Slaying," Fort Leavenworth, KS, (AP), August 25, 1945.

The Desert Sun. "Air museum honors servicewomen," May 8, 2005.

___. "Public Invited to look at A-4, listen to women's war stories," May 3, 2003.

___. "Women warriors of WWII," May 7, 2005.

The (St. Petersburg) *Times*. "Jap Propaganda Plan Backfires, Soldier Writes," January 16, 1944.

Union-Sun & Journal. "Captive Nazi Listed as Driver in Accident," July 3, 1945.

___. "Cigarettes Not Sold to Nazis, Army Man Says," March 16, 1945.

___. "German Prisoners Allowed Dogs," June 16, 1945.

___. "More Prisoners Arrive at Fort," July 15, 1944.

___. "Nazi Prisoners Refuse Sweet Corn," September 9, 1944.

___. "Niagara Historical Society Accepts Sachs Sketch Donation," October 16, 1997.

___. "Prisoner Care Follows Treaty," February 26, 1945.

___. "Soldier Help Eases Crisis In Orchards," September 6, 1941.

Vogel, Mike. *Buffalo News*, "German POWs ended war at Fort Niagara," May 7, 1995.

___. "State experts to get glimpse of historic Fort murals," September 21, 1997.

"William Myers Killed in Action," Ransomville Historical Room, Ransomville, NY, military archives, 1940s.

INDEX

C

G

H

M

N